Using HOMEWORK Assignments in COGNITIVE BEHAVIOR THERAPY

Laurence Bristow
Cognitive Therapist
MHR PCT

Using HOMEWORK Assignments in COGNITIVE BEHAVIOR THERAPY

Edited by
Nikolaos Kazantzis, Frank P. Deane
Kevin R. Ronan, Luciano L'Abate

Routledge
Taylor & Francis Group

NEW YORK   LONDON

Published in 2005 by
Routledge
Taylor & Francis Group
270 Madison Avenue
New York, NY 10016

Published in Great Britain by
Routledge
Taylor & Francis Group
2 Park Square
Milton Park, Abingdon
Oxon OX14 4RN

© 2005 by Taylor & Francis Group, LLC
Routledge is an imprint of Taylor & Francis Group

Printed in the United States of America on acid-free paper
10 9 8 7 6 5 4 3 2 1

International Standard Book Number-10: 0-415-94773-1 (Hardcover)
International Standard Book Number-13: 978-0-415-94773-2 (Hardcover)
Library of Congress Card Number 2005001385

Library of Congress Cataloging-in-Publication Data

Using homework assignments in cognitive behavior therapy / Nikolaos Kazantzis ... [et al.], editors.
    p. cm.
  Includes bibliographical references and index.
  ISBN 0-415-94773-1 (hardback)
  1. Cognitive therapy. 2. Homework. I. Kazantzis, Nikolaos, 1973-

RC489.C63U85 2005
616.89'142--dc22   2005001385

Taylor & Francis Group
is the Academic Division of T&F Informa plc.

Visit the Taylor & Francis Web site at
http://www.taylorandfrancis.com

and the Routledge Web site at
http://www.routledge-ny.com

Contents

About the Editors

Nikolaos Kazantzis, Ph.D., is Associate Professor (Senior Lecturer equivalent) at the School of Psychology, Massey University, New Zealand. He has published widely on the topic of homework assignments in psychotherapy, including serving as a Guest Editor for special issues on this topic in the *Journal of Clinical Psychology* (2002) and the *Journal of Psychotherapy Integration* (2005). He has coauthored more than 40 articles and book Chapters and has participated in national and international conferences related to his research interests. He is also a recipient of the Royal Society of New Zealand Science and Technology Award for Beginning Scientists, and Australian Association for Cognitive Behaviour Therapy (AACBT) Tracy Goodall Early Career Award. Dr. Kazantzis is a licensed (registered) clinical psychologist and maintains a part-time practice in Auckland, New Zealand.

Frank P. Deane, Ph.D., is Professor at the Department of Psychology, and Director of the Illawarra Institute for Mental Health, University of Wollongong, Australia. He completed clinical training at Massey University, New Zealand, and spent his internship year at Lake Alice Hospital. He has worked as a clinical psychologist in corrections and community mental health centers in North Carolina for six years before returning to New Zealand to complete his Ph.D. He is currently co–chief investigator on an National Health and Medical Research Council (NHMRC)-funded project assessing the effects of a recovery-oriented model of care for people with chronic and recurring mental illness.

Kevin R. Ronan, Ph.D., is a Professor of Psychology (Clinical) and planned Director of a new clinical psychology training program at the School of Psychology and Sociology at Central Queensland University, Australia. In addition to an ongoing interest in homework in therapy, he has published widely in areas of clinical psychology such as disaster psychology (including a book in press with Springer on increasing community resilience), treatment outcome with youth and families (e.g., anxiety, conduct-disorder), schizophrenia, and other areas. He maintains an active clinical practice and advocates—both in his practice and a Director of Clinical Training—for the clinician as "local scientist" (e.g., engaging in pragmatic evaluation of practice, use of the evidence in day-to-day practice, and increasing accountability for producing outcomes).

Luciano L'Abate, Ph.D., is Professor Emeritus of Psychology, Georgia State University, Atlanta, Georgia, USA where he was Director of the Family Psychology Training Program and the Family Study Center. He completed his Ph.D. at Duke University, with post-doctoral specialization at Michael Reese Hospital in Chicago. He worked in the Psychiatry Departments of the Schools of Medicine of Washington University (St. Louis) and Emory University (Atlanta) before moving to Georgia State University, where he spent his entire academic career. He was in part-time private and consulting and clinical practice for 42 years. He published (authored, coauthored, edited, and coedited) 35 books, 3 of which are in press, as well as over 250 papers in scientific and professional journals.

Contributors

David W. Coon, Ph.D., is a licensed psychologist and Associate Professor at the Department of Social and Behavioral Sciences at Arizona State University. He was previously Research Scientist and Project Director at the Institute on Aging Research Center and Associate Director of the Older Adult and Family Center, Stanford University School of Medicine, and the VA Palo Alto Health Care System.

Frank M. Dattilio, Ph.D., ABPP, maintains a dual faculty appointment in the Department of Psychiatry at Harvard Medical School and the University of Pennsylvania School of Medicine. Dr. Dattilio is the Clinical Director of the Center for Integrative Psychotherapy in Allentown, Pennsylvania, and is a licensed psychologist in the states of Pennsylvania, New Jersey, New York, and Delaware. He is board certified in both behavioral psychology and clinical psychology through the American Board of Professional Psychology (ABPP).

Martin E. Franklin, Ph.D., is an Assistant Professor of Clinical Psychology in Psychiatry and Clinical Director of the Center for the Treatment and Study of Anxiety at the University of Pennsylvania School of Medicine.

Arthur Freeman, Ed.D., ABPP, is a Professor of Psychology at the University of St. Francis in Fort Wayne Indiana. Prior to his move to Indiana, he was Professor and Chair of the Department of Psychology at the Philadelphia College of Osteopathic Medicine (PCOM). He is board certified in clinical psychology and behavioral psychology by the American Board of Professional Psychology.

Robert D. Friedberg, Ph.D., is an Associate Professor in the Department of Psychiatry in the Penn State Milton Hershey Medical Center, Penn State College of Medicine.

Gina M. Fusco, M.A., is Clinical Director for Alternative Behavioral Services and Adjunct Professor of Psychology at Philadelphia College of Osteopathic Medicine.

Dolores Gallagher-Thompson, Ph.D., ABPP, is Professor of Research in the Department of Psychiatry and Behavioral Sciences at Stanford University School of Medicine and is the Director of the Older Adult and Family Center, Stanford University School of Medicine and the VA Palo Alto Health Care System.

Anne Garland is a Nurse Consultant in Psychological Therapies at the Nottingham Psychotherapy Unit, Nottingham, England. She was Assistant Course Director of the Newcastle Cognitive Therapy Course and was also cofounder of the Salford Cognitive Therapy Course. She is coauthor of the 2003 book *Cognitive Therapy for Chronic and Persistent Depression*, published by John Wiley and Sons, and is currently President-Elect of the British Association of Behavioral and Cognitive Psychotherapies (BABCP).

Jennifer L. Hudson, Ph.D., received her Ph.D. in clinical psychology from Macquarie University and completed a 2-year postdoctoral fellowship at the Child and Adolescent Anxiety Disorders Clinic, Temple University, Philadelphia. Dr. Hudson is currently a Millennium Research Fellow in the Department of Psychology, Macquarie University, Sydney, Australia.

Jonathan D. Huppert, Ph.D., is an Assistant Professor of Clinical Psychology in Psychiatry at the University of Pennsylvania.

Philip C. Kendall, Ph.D., ABPP, is Laura H. Carnell Professor of Psychology and Director of the Child and Adolescent Anxiety Disorders Clinic at Temple University. Dr. Kendall is currently the Editor of *Clinical Psychology: Science and Practice.*

Georgios K. Lampropoulos is a doctoral student in counseling psychology at Ball State University, Muncie, Indiana, and an intern at the Centre for Addiction and Mental Health, Mood and Anxiety Program, Toronto, Canada.

Robert L. Leahy, Ph.D., is Founder and Director of the American Institute for Cognitive Therapy, New York City. Currently, Dr. Leahy is Professor of Psychology in Psychiatry at Cornell University Medical School, Associate Editor of the *Journal of Cognitive Psychotherapy*, and serves on the executive committee of the International Association of Cognitive Psychotherapy as well as on the Executive Board of the Academy of Cognitive Therapy. Dr. Leahy is a Founding Fellow of the Academy of Cognitive Therapy.

Jamie Mac Ewan was a masters student in psychology at Massey University, Auckland, New Zealand. He is currently a therapist at Addictions Resource Center, Taupo, New Zealand.

Jessica M. McClure, Psy.D., is a faculty member at the Children's Hospital of Cincinnati-Mason.

Hamish J. McLeod, Ph.D., is a Lecturer at the Department of Psychology, University of Wollongong, and an affiliated researcher with the Illawarra Institute for Mental Health, Wollongong, Australia.

Lisa M. Najavits, Ph.D., is Associate Professor in Psychiatry, Harvard Medical School, Boston, and Director of the Trauma Research Program in the Alcohol and Drug Abuse Treatment Center of McLean Hospital, Belmont, Massachusetts.

Hazel E. Nelson is a Consultant Clinical Psychologist in private practice in London.

Nancy A. Pachana, Ph.D., is a Senior Lecturer and Deputy Head of School at the School of Psychology at the University of Queensland, Australia. She currently serves as Editor of the journal *Clinical Psychologist*, the official journal of the Australian Psychological Society College of Clinical Psychologists.

Yaron G. Rabinowitz, M.A., M.S., is a doctoral candidate at Pacific Graduate School of Psychology, Palo Alto, California.

Deborah A. Roth-Ledley, Ph.D., is a Professor of Clinical Psychology in Psychiatry at the University of Pennsylvania and Director of the Center for the Treatment and Study of Anxiety.

Jan Scott, M.D., is Professor of Psychological Treatments Research, Department of Psychological Medicine, Institute of Psychiatry, London. Dr. Scott is an internationally renowned researcher, practitioner, and trainer in cognitive therapy for chronic and severe affective disorders and Distinguished Founding Fellow of the Academy for Cognitive Therapy.

Kate Sofronoff, Ph.D., is a Lecturer at the School of Psychology at the University of Queensland, Australia.

Larry W. Thompson, Ph.D., is Professor Emeritus, Stanford University School of Medicine, and currently is the Goldman Family Professor of Psychology at Pacific Graduate School of Psychology, Palo Alto, California.

Acknowledgments

It has been a wonderful learning experience to produce this book. When we first considered the idea of working on a book on the use of homework assignments in cognitive behavioral therapy, we had no idea that so many experienced and knowledgeable individuals would participate. Our contributors are skilled practitioners and researchers. Needless to say, the book would not exist without their work, and we are fortunate to present their teaching on using homework assignments as represented in this book.

Just as important as our contributors are our clients, who engaged in the homework assignments and contributed to our understanding of this core process in cognitive behavioral therapy. Our interests in this topic would not have existed without their courage, strength, ingenuity, and perseverance.

We wish to extend our thanks to our research collaborators on our *Cognitive Behavior Therapy Homework Project* for their interest, encouragement, and inspiration. We are privileged to have the opportunity to work with individuals who have already contributed extensively to the empirical and practice literature in cognitive behavioral therapy. We thank (in alphabetical order) Frank M. Dattilio, Keith S. Dobson, Ian M. Evans, Lydia Fehm, Malcolm Johnson, Georgios K. Lampropoulos, Paul L. Merrick, Robert A. Neimeyer, Frederick L. Newman, Nancy A. Pachana, Michael J. Scheel, Jan Scott, and Michael A. Tompkins. We also express our appreciation to the students in our research laboratory—their intelligence, enthusiasm, and hard work are the driving force to our efforts.

We thank Linda Kemp and Kathryn Lee at the School of Psychology at Massey University for secretarial support for this book. We also thank Margo Munro for producing the subject index and Yolanda Duncan for editorial feed back on page proofs. We are also grateful for the editorial and production staff at Routledge, in particular, George Zimmar, Publishing Director, Dana Bliss, Associate Editor, and Glenon Butler, Project Editor, for guiding the project through to completion.

Finally, we thank our partners, spouses, families, and friends for their support and encouragement while we were working on this project.

CHAPTER 1

Introduction and Overview

NIKOLAOS KAZANTZIS

This book is designed for both beginning and more experienced practitioners of cognitive behavioral therapy. It assumes a basic knowledge of cognitive and behavioral theory, research, and practice as well as the ability to conduct an assessment, construct an individualized cognitive conceptualization, and deliver cognitive behavioral therapy. This book presents focused teaching on the use of homework assignments in the therapy, explaining in detail how the practitioner can design, assign, and review therapeutic homework activities. This teaching is based primarily on the work of A. T. Beck's (1976) cognitive theory and system of psychotherapy.

Treatments identified as cognitive or cognitive behavioral therapy comprise a number of approaches. Cognitive behavioral therapies share the proposition that cognition is linked with behavior, cognition can be assessed and modified, and behavioral change can occur through cognitive change (Dobson, 2001). The model of therapy developed by Aaron T. Beck for the treatment of depression (A. T. Beck, Rush, Shaw, & Emery, 1979; J. Beck, 1995) has been subject to extensive empirical study since its inception (e.g., DeRubeis, Beck, & Tang, 2001; Dobson, 1989), and is regarded as the "standard form" of cognitive behavioral therapy (Clark, 1995).

Homework assignments are a core feature of the cognitive behavioral therapy process. In pragmatic terms, they represent the opportunity for clients to transfer the skills and ideas from therapy to the everyday situations in which their problems actually occur. To our knowledge, there is no generally agreed upon definition for therapeutic homework assignments in the literature. This conceptual variation is illustrated by the broad range in terminology that has been used to describe homework assignments in published articles, such as "extratherapy assignments" (Kornblith, Rehm, O'Hara, & Lamparski, 1983), "extratreatment practice assignments" (Kazdin & Mascitelli, 1982), "in vivo behavioral practice assignments" (Ingram & Salzberg, 1990), "self-help assignments" (Burns, 1989; Burns, Adams, & Anastopoulos, 1985), "show that I can tasks" (Hudson & Kendall, 2002; Kendall et al., 1997), and "home practice activities" (Blanchard, Nicholson, Radnitz, et al., 1991; Blanchard, Nicholson, Taylor, et al., 1991). However, it is likely that the variation in terminology reflects the negative associations with the term *homework* that are often held by clients and practitioners (Fehm & Kazantzis, 2004). Drawing on the work of Judith Beck (1995), we have operationalized homework assignments as follows:

> Homework assignments are planned therapeutic activities undertaken by clients between therapy sessions. Their content is derived primarily from the empirically supported cognitive behavioral therapy model for the particular presenting problem but is tailored for the client based on an individualized conceptualization. Designed collaboratively, homework assignments are focused on the client's goals for therapy. Homework assignments represent the main process by which clients experience behavioral and cognitive therapeutic change, practice and maintain new skills and techniques, and experiment with new behaviors. Homework assignments also provide an opportunity for clients to collect information regarding their thoughts, moods, physiology, and behaviors in different situations and to read information related to therapy and their presenting problems.

Reflecting their core and crucial role, homework assignments have received more empirical attention than any other single aspect of cognitive behavioral therapy process (Persons, Davidson, & Tompkins, 2001). Studies of psychotherapy process and outcome have produced evidence demonstrating that cognitive behavioral therapy involving homework assignments produces significantly better outcomes than those from therapy consisting entirely of in-session work (Beutler et al., 2004; Kazantzis, Deane, & Ronan, 2000). This research has also shown that treatment outcome is significantly enhanced when clients complete their homework assignments, and this link continues to be replicated in a variety of applications of cognitive behavioral therapy (Abramowitz, Franklin, Zoellner, & DiBernardo, 2002;

Burns & Spangler, 2000; Coon & Thompson, 2003; Neimeyer, Kazantzis, & Kassler, 2005; Schmidt & Woolaway-Bickel, 2000; see also Kazantzis, Ronan, & Deane, 2001).

Practitioners report using homework assignments in their clinical work (Kazantzis & Deane, 1999; Kazantzis, Lampropoulos, & Deane, in press) and consider them important for a wide variety of clinical populations. At the same time, however, survey research has shown that there is a distance between practitioners' self-reports of homework use and what is described in treatment manuals (Kazantzis, Busch, Ronan, & Merrick, 2005; Kazantzis & Deane, 1999). There are also data to suggest that practitioners hold a range of attitudes regarding homework's effects on the process and outcome of therapy (Fehm & Kazantzis, 2004; Kazantzis et al., in press).

While there is evidence to support the overall effects of homework assignments in ensuring the outcomes of cognitive behavioral therapy, there are relatively few data to clarify the underlying mechanism for these effects. We know that homework assignments produce an effect in therapy that is distinctive, measurable, and leads to improved outcomes. We also know that clients who complete homework assignments are more likely to experience therapeutic benefits. However, there is very little theoretical or empirical work designed to clarify the factors that lead to client engagement in homework assignments and the extent to which their in-session review and design with the therapist impacts client adherence.

In order to contribute to the existing literature, a team research project was initiated at the School of Psychology, Massey University, New Zealand called the Cognitive Behavior Therapy Homework Project. The core research team comprises Nikolaos Kazantzis (PI) at Massey University, Kevin Ronan now at Central Queensland University, and Frank Deane, now at the University of Wollongong, Australia; it also benefits from the contributions of Luciano L'Abate (Georgia State University) and other international collaborators. This team research project is committed to developing an understanding of the mechanism by which homework produces its effects in cognitive behavioral therapy. Specifically, the project has been designed to address several broad objectives: (a) to conduct conventional and statistical reviews of the empirical literature in order to clarify the current knowledge regarding "homework effects" in therapy, (b) to survey psychologists' use of homework assignments in clinical practice as a means of determining the necessity and utility of further research, (c) to design a theoretical model and associated treatment manual for the use of homework assignments in therapy, (d) to design conceptually based driven methods of assessing homework completion and therapist competence in using homework and to evaluate their psychometric properties, and (e) to conduct prospective process and treatment outcome research to evaluate the utility of the theoretical model and associated treatment manual. At the time of this writing, our team had achieved the first four objectives for the research program, and it was decided that a resource that outlined the theoretical foundations, reviewed the current empirical evidence, and described the process of integrating homework assignments in cognitive behavioral therapy would be helpful for practitioners.

The resulting volume comprises three distinct parts. Part I consists of three chapters that distill the existing theoretical and empirical work and highlight the methodological issues related to the study of homework assignments. Chapter 2 presents a summary of the theoretical foundations for the use of homework assignments. Chapter 3 focuses on the empirical basis for the use of homework assignments in therapy and discusses research on therapy process and outcome, as well as the findings and implications from surveys of clinical practice. Drawing on the theoretical foundations in Chapter 2 and limitations of prior research discussed in Chapter 3, the measurement of client adherence to homework assignments is discussed in Chapter 4. This includes the description of a new measure designed for use in clinical training, practice, and supervision.

Part II of the book consists of twelve chapters that describe the process of using homework assignments for a range of clinical populations and problems (Chapters 5 to 16). The first five chapters describe the use of homework for different clinical populations, namely children, adolescents, older adults, couples, and families. The remaining seven chapters describe the use of homework assignments for different presenting problems, namely panic and generalized anxiety, depression, substance abuse, delusions and hallucinations, obsessions and compulsions, sexual problems, and borderline personality traits.

As we were proposing a book on cognitive behavioral therapy covering a range of different clinical groups, we decided not to constrain our contributors by asking them to look only at a particular aspect of the process or to be prescriptive in terms of what types of difficulties to discuss or what type of detailed case example(s) to include. Our instructions to authors encouraged them to broadly consider the process of using homework for their particular clinical population, so that an integrated guiding model for practice could be presented in a later section. Thus, we invited primarily clinical chapters including the following:

1. Overview of common barriers to the successful use of homework assignments
2. Strategies for the effective use of homework

3. A brief outline of the types of homework activities within the empirically supported cognitive behavioral therapy model(s)
4. Relevant case studies of cognitive behavioral practice

The final part of the book consists of two chapters designed to summarize and synthesize the two preceding sections. Chapter 17 summarizes the clinical recommendations from previous chapters in the service of presenting a generic "guiding model" for the integration of homework into therapy. Chapter 18 also offers general recommendations for furthering the understanding of the process by which homework produces its effects.

As the reader will note, the field is left with many as yet unanswered questions about the role of homework assignments in cognitive behavioral therapy. In the interest of progressing towards our final research objective, our intention is to utilize the resulting guiding model as the basis for a treatment manual in prospective treatment outcome research.

This book aims to provide readers with focused teaching on how to effectively use homework assignments in cognitive behavioral therapy for different clinical groups. It is also our hope that this book will encourage further conceptual and empirical work on this central aspect of therapy process. We are optimistic that the extension of this knowledge in future research will advance our understanding of the therapist, client, and relationship factors that facilitate client learning through the completion of homework assignments.

References

Abramowitz, J. S., Franklin, M. E., Zoellner, L. A., & DiBernardo, C. L. (2002). Treatment compliance and outcome in obsessive-compulsive disorder. *Behavior Modification, 26,* 447–463.

Beck, A. T. (1976). *Cognitive therapy and the emotional disorders.* New York: International Universities Press.

Beck, A. T., Rush, J. A., Shaw, B. F., & Emery, G. (1979). *Cognitive therapy of depression.* New York: Guilford.

Beck, J. (1995). *Cognitive therapy: Basics and beyond.* New York: Guilford Press.

Beutler, L. E., Malik, M., Alimohamed, S., Harwood, T. M., Talebi, H., Noble, S., & Wong, E. (2004). Therapist variables. In M. J. Lambert (Ed.), *Bergin and Garfield's Handbook of psychotherapy and behavior change* (5th ed., pp. 227–306). New York: Wiley.

Blanchard, E. B., Nicholson, N. L., Radnitz, C. L., Steffek, B. D., Appelbaum, K. A., & Dentinger, M. P. (1991). The role of home practice in thermal biofeedback. *Journal of Consulting and Clinical Psychology, 59,* 507–512.

Blanchard, E. B., Nicholson, N. L., Taylor, A. E., Steffek, B. D., Radnitz, C. L., & Appelbaum, K. A. (1991). The role of regular home practice in the relaxation treatment of tension headache. *Journal of Consulting and Clinical Psychology, 59,* 467–470.

Burns, D. D. (1989). *The feeling good handbook.* New York: William Morrow.

Burns, D. D., Adams, R. L., & Anastopoulos, A. D. (1985). The role of self-help assignments in the treatment of depression. In E. E. Berckham & W. R. Leber (Eds.), *Handbook of depression: Treatment, assessment, and research* (pp. 635–668). Homewood, IL: Dorsey Press.

Burns, D. D., & Spangler, D. (2000). Does psychotherapy homework lead to changes in depression in cognitive behavioral therapy? Or does clinical improvement lead to homework compliance? *Journal of Consulting and Clinical Psychology, 68,* 46–56.

Clark, D. A. (1995). Perceived limitations of standard cognitive therapy: A consideration of efforts to revise Beck's theory and therapy. *Journal of Cognitive Psychotherapy, 9,* 153–172

Coon, D. W., & Thompson, L. W. (2003). The relationship between homework compliance and treatment outcomes among older adult outpatients with mild-to-moderate depression. *American Journal of Psychiatry, 11,* 53–61.

DeRubeis, R. J., Beck, A. T., & Tang, T. Z. (2001). Cognitive therapy. In K. Dobson (Ed.), *Handbook of cognitive-behavioral therapies* (2nd ed., pp. 349–392). New York: Guilford.

Dobson, K. (1989). A meta-analysis of the efficacy of cognitive therapy for depression. *Journal of Consulting and Clinical Psychology, 57,* 414–419.

Dobson, K. (2001). *Handbook of cognitive-behavioral therapies* (2nd ed.). New York: Guilford Press.

Fehm, L., & Kazantzis, N. (2004). Attitudes and use of homework assignments in therapy: A survey of German psychotherapists. *Clinical Psychology & Psychotherapy, 11,* 332–343.

Hollon, S. D. (2003). Does cognitive therapy have an enduring effect? *Cognitive Therapy & Research, 27,* 71–75.

Hudson, J. L., & Kendall, P. C. (2002). Showing you can do it: Homework in therapy for children and adolescents with anxiety disorders. *Journal of Clinical Psychology, 58,* 525–534.

Ingram, J. A., & Salzberg, H. C. (1990). Effects of *in vivo* behavioral rehearsal on the learning of assertive behaviors with a substance abusing population. *Addictive Behaviors, 15,* 189–194.

Kazantzis, N., Busch, R., Ronan, K. R., & Merrick, P. L. (2005). *Mental health practitioners' use and perceived importance of homework assignments in psychotherapy.* Manuscript submitted for publication.

Kazantzis, N., & Deane, F. P. (1999). Psychologists' use of homework assignments in clinical practice. *Professional Psychology: Research and Practice, 30,* 581–585.

Kazantzis, N., Deane, F. P., & Ronan, K. R. (2000). Homework assignments in cognitive and behavioral therapy: A meta-analysis. *Clinical Psychology: Science and Practice, 7,* 189–202.

Kazantzis, N., Lampropoulos, G. L., & Deane, F. P. (in press). A national survey of practicing psychologists' use and attitudes towards homework in psychotherapy. *Journal of Consulting and Clinical Psychology.*

Kazantzis, N., Ronan, K. R., & Deane, F. P. (2001). Concluding causation from correlation: Comment on Burns and Spangler (2000). *Journal of Consulting and Clinical Psychology, 69,* 1079–1083.

Kazdin, A. E., & Mascitelli, S. (1982). Covert and overt rehearsal and homework practice in developing assertiveness. *Journal of Consulting and Clinical Psychology, 50,* 250–258.

Kendall, P. C., Flannery-Schroeder, E., Panichelli-Mindel, S., Southam-Gerow, M., Henin, A., & Warman, M. (1997). Therapy for youth with anxiety disorders: A second randomized clinical trial. *Journal of Consulting & Clinical Psychology, 65,* 366–380.

Kornblith, S. J., Rehm, L. P., O'Hara, M. W., & Lamparski, D. M. (1983). The contribution of self-reinforcement training and behavioral assignments to the efficacy of self-control therapy for depression. *Cognitive Therapy and Research, 7,* 499–528.

Neimeyer, R., Kazantzis, N., & Kessler, D. (2005). *Homework compliance and skill acquisition as predictors of outcome in cognitive-behavioral group therapy for depression.* Manuscript submitted for publication.

Persons, J. B., Davidson, J., & Tompkins, M. A. (2001). *Essential components of cognitive-behavior therapy for depression.* Washington, DC: American Psychological Association.

Schmidt, N. B., & Woolaway-Bickel, K. (2000). The effects of treatment compliance on outcome in cognitive-behavioral therapy for panic disorder: Quality versus quantity. *Journal of Consulting and Clinical Psychology, 68,* 13–18.

PART I

Theoretical and Empirical Foundations

CHAPTER 2

Theoretical Foundations

NIKOLAOS KAZANTZIS and LUCIANO L'ABATE

Homework assignments are a core and crucial feature of cognitive behavioral therapy. They are widely used by practitioners; yet to be effective, they require a sound therapist understanding of how they work. It is surprising that there is very little written on the theoretical foundations for the role of homework assignments in cognitive behavioral therapy and why they are included as part of the approach.

The purpose of this Chapter is to provide a discussion of key behavioral and cognitive theories that underpin the use of homework assignments in cognitive behavioral therapy (A. T. Beck, 1964; A. T. Beck, Rush, Shaw, & Emery, 1979). This Chapter is divided into three sections. The first provides a discussion of key behavioral theories. It describes how principles of classical and operant conditioning form the basic justification for the use of between-session homework assignments. The second section describes cognitive theory or "social learning/cognitive" foundations and broadens the range of factors that determine clients' completion of homework assignments. The final section in this Chapter provides a brief summary and synthesis of the behavioral and cognitive underpinnings.

Our aim is to provide the reader with a firm grounding in the theoretical basis for the use of homework in cognitive behavioral therapy. In particular, we aim to answer the questions "*Why does cognitive behavioral therapy include homework assignments?*" and "*What are the determinants of a client's decision to complete homework?*" rather than "*How can the process of integrating homework assignments be more effective for clients?"* even though the former have implications for the latter. Brief clinical examples are provided to illustrate the behavioral and cognitive theories. These theoretical underpinnings are further exemplified in Parts II and III, in the Chapters describing the use of homework in cognitive behavioral therapy for a range of clinical presentations.[1] We then, in Part IV, synthesize these theoretical foundations with the clinical recommendations to provide a guiding "model for practice" for the use of homework assignments.

The Role of Homework in Therapy

Effective treatment is determined by the extent to which clients can apply ideas or techniques to the everyday situations in which their problems actually occur. Changes to the way in which clients perceive, experience, and behave in their environment may be influenced by therapeutic work occurring in therapy sessions, and/or through clients choosing to transfer skills on their own accord (cf. Kornblith, Rehm, O'Hara, & Lamparski 1983). However, transfer of skills outside the session, the maintenance of skills, and the overall effectiveness of therapy are likely to be enhanced with the use of specific assignments discussed with the therapist.

Although not conceptualized as "homework," several writers have discussed the regular use of between-session activities as a means of increasing the effectiveness of therapy in different theoretical approaches (e.g., Carr, 1997; Greenberg, Watson, & Goldman, 1988; Nelson, 1994). Homework is embedded in behavioral (Kanfer, 1970; Shelton & Ackerman, 1974), client-centered (Brodley, in press), emotion-focused experiential (Greenberg, Watson, & Goldman, 1988), interpersonal (Klerman, Weissman, Rounsaville, & Chevron, 1984), integrative (Allen, in press), personal construct (Kelly, 1955), rational-emotive (Ellis, 1962, 1988; Maultsby, 1971), systemic (Dattilio, 2002; Hansen & MacMillan, 1990; Nelson, 1994; O'Connell & Gomez, 1995), short-term dynamic (Carich, 1990; Halligan, 1995; Stricker, in press; Stricker & Gold, 1996), solution-focused (Beyebach, Morejon, Palenzuela, & Rodriguez-Arias, 1996), and other therapies (see Kazantzis & Ronan, in press). Furthermore, several practitioner surveys have produced data to support the assertion that this representation of homework assignments in a range of psychotherapies has been transferred to practice. For example, a recent survey by Kazantzis, Lampropoulos, and Deane (in press) found that 68% of a broad sample ($N = 827$) of American Psychological Association members reported using homework

---

[1]This Chapter does not aim to provide a comprehensive discussion of the process of change in cognitive behavioral therapy, as this is presented elsewhere (i.e., Clark, A. T. Beck, & Alford, 1999).

assignments as a routine feature of their clinical work. This finding was independent of theoretical orientation. (In reviewing the empirical foundations, Chapter 3 presents a review of the practitioner survey research on the use of homework in psychotherapy.)

Homework assignments are not merely an "add-on" or adjunctive procedure in cognitive behavioral therapy (A. T. Beck et al., 1979). Some writers consider the systematic use of homework assignments to be a defining feature of the therapeutic approach, suggesting that a therapy without homework cannot be considered cognitive behavioral (Thase & Callan, in press). The importance of homework is reflected in the fact that clients are encouraged to carry out specific activities for homework after *every* therapy session. The typical structure of a therapy session involves the review of homework at the outset of the session and a summary of the homework and discussion of its specific details toward the end of the session (J. Beck, 1995).

As a practical basis for using homework assignments, applying skills to salient situations enables clients to take responsibility and ownership for their improvement in therapy. Learning through homework completion is an opportunity to read information relevant to therapy, collect data, test out beliefs, and to experiment and monitor the utility of new skills and behaviors in preparation for the time when therapy ends (A. T. Beck & Weishaar, 1989). Clients apply skills they have learned to new everyday situations without the therapist's guidance and take the opportunity to modify and adapt them as best suits their needs. Client experiences through engagement in homework assignments provide important information for the conceptualization and, when completed, provide an indication of involvement, learning, and outcome in therapy (Kazantzis, Deane, & Ronan, 2000). It is this processes of generalization and maintenance of behavioral and cognitive skills that are attributed to the long-term benefits of the approach (A. T. Beck, 1976).

Behavioral Theory Foundations

The use of homework assignments in therapy rests on the foundation of behavioral and cognitive theories. Though implied in many guides for practice and empirical studies of homework in cognitive behavioral therapy, a detailed explication of its theoretical foundations is difficult to find in the literature. Behavioral theory and its focus on empirically supported applications in therapy has provided several important contributions to our understanding of learning in therapy.

Classical Conditioning Theory

Classical conditioning refers to relationship between two stimuli, such as the occurrence of a second (unconditioned stimulus) is contingent upon the occurrence of the first (conditioned stimulus). As shown in Figure 2.1, this contingency results in a behavior being evoked by the first conditioned stimulus (i.e., conditioned response), where it was previously only evoked by the second (i.e., unconditioned response). Operating on the principle that the conditioned behaviors extinguish when they are no longer reinforced, classical conditioning has been extended to a number of behavioral therapy interventions (e.g., systematic desensitization, flooding and implosion, and aversion therapy). These techniques rely repeated exposure to a feared stimulus and the absence of the degree of original distress in the presence of that stimulus (see also Levis & Malloy, 1982).

Extensions of classical conditioning have highlighted the importance of the predictive link between the conditioned stimulus and the unconditioned response, and the ability for a stimulus to serve as a "safety signal" by predicting when an aversive event will not occur (Rescorla, 1988). Behavioral theorists note that all "stimuli" in everyday life comprise elements that have a particular significance to an individual, based on their previous experiences, and that these experiences may interfere with conditioning to novel elements in the environment (Bouton, 1988). Further to the classical conditioning standpoint, words and images are conceptualized as conditioned stimuli that carry with them the experiences of prior learning. The way in which words are evaluated derives from the same associative processes as classical conditioning, as do general preferences and attitudes (Staats, 1996).

Classical conditioning processes are evident in behavioral homework assignments used in the treatment of anxiety disorders, particularly where the aim is to "expose" and "desensitize" an object or situation that provokes an anxiety response. Exposure often entails confrontation of external situations, places, or activities that trigger fear and anxiety symptoms, with homework involving the same (or similar) exposures that were conducted in session or variations of them (Huppert, Roth, & Foa, in press). Using a systematic desensitization process involves presenting the stimulus so faintly at first that the client does not experience the same anxiety response, then increasing the intensity of the stimulus so gradually that the client continues not to experience intense anxiety. Systematic desensitization procedures are often aided by the use of relaxation practice, which enables the client to effectively replace a previously conditioned response. The important feature of this latter counterconditioning procedure is that

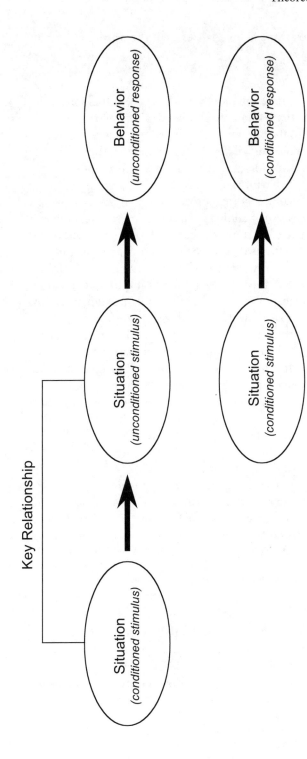

Fig. 2.1 Summary of classical conditioning principles.

the new response (relaxation) is inconsistent with the previous conditioned response (anxiety).

Operant Conditioning Theory

In order to understand the function of a client's behavior, a therapist needs to analyze the variables that, when manipulated, alter its frequency. In basic terms, "Instrumental or operant conditioning" theory states that contingencies that are positive will increase a behavior, those that are negative will decrease a behavior, and those that are neither positive nor negative will extinguish a behavior (see Figure 2.2).

The critical issue for recommending homework assignments is that any behavior conceptualized as a maintaining factor to the presenting problems usually has a wide variety of functions for the client. In operant terms, the client has developed expectations that this behavior provides some benefit or reward. Consequently, a key feature of integrating homework into therapy is to hypothesize, and then test what the possible unique functions are those that maintain behaviors such as subtle avoidance in panic, withdrawal in depression, or reassurance seeking in generalized anxiety. Thus, it is helpful for therapists to consider reinforcement and punishment contingencies (i.e., costs and benefits) as motivational variables that encourage a client to dedicate time and energy on homework assignments that clearly produce adaptive outcomes. The process of learning is cumulative and hierarchical, and differences in client experiences, even with the most straightforward homework assignments, highlight that there are considerable individual variations in response to what is ostensibly the application of the same assignment.

The central thesis from the behaviorist standpoint is that contiguity between stimulus and response determines the likelihood for learning. As illustrated in Figure 2.2, the key relationship is between behavior and its consequences, occurring in the context of situational antecedents. This early learning theory stressed the transfer of learning or of training, that preceded the later construct of generalization (Tharp & Wetzel, 1969).

Principle of Generality or "Generalization"

Of particular relevance to homework in psychotherapy are core elements of generalization, where there is transfer of trained skills (or behaviors) to a new setting or the development of skills that were not specifically trained. If generalization were not possible, a client would need to learn a new skill for every newly problematic situation. This theoretical observation was initially made within the context of generalizing conditioned responses to similar yet different stimuli in the classical or Pavlovian context.

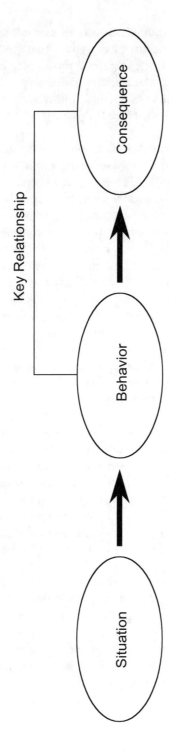

Fig. 2.2 Summary of operant conditioning principles.

As therapists, we often introduce new activities or techniques to clients for practice in their naturally occurring everyday situations. The process of generalization is assumed by many therapy approaches to occur naturally, as a by-product of whatever is taking place in the therapy session. Without the specific use of homework assignments, however, therapists may not have the opportunity to explicitly test out this assumption, which in most cases is kept tacit.

It would be difficult to provide data to evaluate the generalization of adaptive skills if psychotherapy was based solely on in-session discussion with the therapist (L'Abate, 1999). For example, a client may have noticed that practicing a progressive muscle relaxation exercise in the therapist's office significantly reduces the physiological symptoms of anxiety. It is only when the client is able to use relaxation to relieve these symptoms as they occur during the rest of the week that we can say the behavior of relaxation has been generalized to new stimuli or situations. Further to this idea, the client would ideally be generalizing the use of relaxation to the wide range of naturally occurring anxiety-provoking situations (e.g., difficulty getting to sleep, frequently waking through the night, difficulty getting back to sleep after waking up). Similarly, it is only when a client is able to apply behavioral and cognitive techniques to effectively curtail the onset of a naturally occurring panic attack to the same extent as in response to physiological symptoms induced in the therapy session that we can say generalization has occurred.

In general, we are also interested in the client being able to use the particular skills or techniques that are going to be helpful for the particular situation. Our client in the above example noticed the benefits of a full progressive muscle relaxation procedure but decided to use a brief version of the procedure to relieve naturally occurring physiological symptoms in other situations. Another client, having acquired some similar relaxation skills, instead decided to use a version focusing specifically on the controlled breathing component to relieve intense anxiety symptoms. In both instances, these clients exhibited generalization to other responses or new skills.

One of the first therapy approaches to emphasize the role of learning and the process of generalization was couples sex therapy (e.g., Maddock, 1975), where generalization would ensue if there were sufficient repetition and rehearsal to achieve the desired criterion of mastery. Thus, to be effective, a therapeutic intervention must show generalization from the consultation setting to the client's natural environment and should sometimes show generalization to new responses or skills.

Principles of Maintenance and Shaping

It is one thing for a client to practice a particular therapeutic skill between sessions; it is something else for that skill to last. Skinner suggested that all behaviors are controlled by their environmental contingencies, and that emphasis should be placed on how a behavior should be controlled (Lieberman, 1993; Skinner, 1971). Thus, according to behavioral theory, maintenance depends on whether a behavior will continue to be reinforced in the new environment or setting.

Operant theory outlines a detailed process involving reinforcement as a means of *shaping* and *maintaining* desired behaviors (Mahoney, Kazdin, & Lesswing, 1974; Skinner, 1971). For a "reinforcer" to be effective, it needs to be something that is desirable, ideally immediate, and conditional upon the behavior. Applied to the present context, we may conceptualize rein-forcers as rewards or incentives that may have an impact on a client's phys-ical sensations (e.g., reduced anxiety symptoms through coping strategies) and emotions (e.g., reduced distress through thought record completion) and that may be determined extrinsically (e.g., receiving praise and encouragement from therapist), and intrinsically (e.g., experiencing a sense of progress or achievement toward reduction of presenting problems and toward goals for therapy). One important implication from these principles is that behaviors need to be practiced for the maintenance of therapeutic gains (L'Abate, 1984, 1986, 1994, 1997). A second important implication from this is that although the therapist's praise, encourage-ment, and other extrinsic rewards may help clients engage in homework activities, such external reinforcement may not be reliable for sustained long-term change. Clients are likely to benefit more from activities that have clear intrinsic rewards, in terms of their reduced experience of dis-tress, and increased experience of positive affect.

Behavioral theory also proposes that different *schedules of reinforcement* produce different degrees of *maintained* behavior. After observing the limited utility of continuous reinforcement, Skinner proposed that inter-mittent schedules requiring differing quantities of the desired behavior, expressed in differing time periods, are most likely to make the new behavior persistent (Skinner, 1971). The implication is that the learning a new, complex pattern of behavior, such as improving mood through the schedule of pleasure and mastery tasks, is maintained through various conse-quences. Scheduling of a particular activity may not always produce an improvement in mood to the same extent; in some situations it may result in an improvement in physiology or require different quantity of the behavior to produce the effect. For instance, taking a walk or some other form of exercise may not always produce an improvement or the same degree of improvement in mood.

Extending these principles of behavior modification would suggest that a complex-pattern behavior, such as documenting a week's worth of mood fluctuations on an activity schedule for homework, can be "shaped" or learned by first breaking it down into smaller segments. In this example, smaller segments would involve devising a tailored rating scale, learning how to use the rating scale, rating mood before and after a session, before and after a recent distressing event, during a particular in-session activity, and then rating a series of activities in the schedule. Behaviors that are steps toward a final goal need to be reinforced and established first, with rewards given for partial accomplishment if necessary. Thus, sequences of behaviors that accomplish a goal can be considered to be "chains" of operants, with each step serving a discriminative antecedent function for the next response. In our example, gaining an understanding of how moods fluctuate based on activity might lead to increased sense of mastery or progress toward therapeutic goals, and serve as a naturally occurring reinforcement. One complication of this process is that new skills must replace or compete with former coping strategies that often provide their own benefits (e.g., social withdrawal), habitual behaviors (e.g., spending long periods of time watching television), or behaviors cued by the environment (e.g., partner has a controlling interpersonal style that makes assertiveness challenging).

Figure 2.3 presents an illustrative summary of the behavioral foundations for homework assignments in cognitive behavioral therapy. In the main, both classical and operant conditioning processes are involved and can be used to explain the process by which homework is helpful for clients. As illustrated, there are usually particular situations or aspects of a situation in the client's natural environment that indicate to a client that the application of a particular intervention would be beneficial. The intervention may be shaped through a process of successive approximations toward a complex task (or chaining of successive operants). In behavioral terms, the repeated intrinsic rewards of the intervention are considered to control its maintenance.

Bridge to Cognitive Theory Foundations

Although these behavioral foundations have some utility, the stimulus-response pathway to learning has been a point of debate among writers. This debate concerns whether there is some mediating factor between stimulus and response that regulates behavior. Positions on this have been divided over whether behavior is governed primarily as a consequence of rewards or punishments or through prior feedback. Various mediating

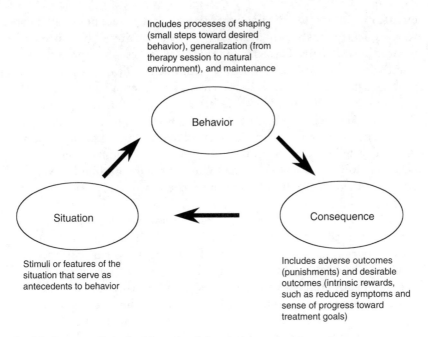

Fig. 2.3 Summary of behavioral theory foundations for homework assignments.

variables have been proposed, including the idea of forming habits, the role of instinctive drives, and cognitions in determining behavior. This debate has continued, with the emphasis on the importance of a client's perception and attitude toward the environment as an influence on behavior (Bergin, 1971). In addition, the view that clients' thoughts, feelings, and behaviors are connected to their environment culminated in a number of theories emphasizing cognition within the process of learning. These cognitive theories have been designed to complement behavioral theoretical foundations, not replace them, and have direct relevance to homework assignments in cognitive behavioral therapy (Mahoney et al., 1974).

Cognitive Theory Foundations

Cognitive theories propose that behavioral change is influenced by the environment, personal factors, and perceived aspects of the behavior itself. While there are several versions to theories emphasizing the role of cognition in learning, otherwise known as "social learning" theories (Crosbie-Brunett & Lewis, 1993), they share three basic tenets: (a) response consequences influence the likelihood that a person will perform a particular behavior again in a particular situation; (b) people can learn by observing others, in addition to learning by participating in an act personally; and (c) people are most likely to model behavior exhibited by those with whom they identify. These three tenets are represented throughout a number of theoretical developments, including the ideas of learning from generalized expectancies of reinforcement and internal/external locus of control (i.e., self-initiated change versus change influenced by others). Rotter (1954) suggested that health outcomes could be improved by the development of a sense of personal control over a client's life; this view has been subjected to research on the notion of control and its application to behavior (Rotter, 1990, 1992). The following section outlines the various cognitive mediating variables that have been proposed in determining behavior.

One theory to emerge from the social learning movement was the "theory of reasoned action" (Ajzen & Fishbein, 1977). According to it, the most important determinant of a client's engaging in a particular activity is intent. The client's intention to engage in an activity is a combination of her attitude toward performing the activity and her corresponding perception of subjective norms about the behavior. According to this theory, if a client perceives that an exposure assignment is useful, the he will have a positive attitude and intent to engage in the activity. Similarly, if significant others see engaging in the assignment as positive and the individual is motivated to meet the expectations of relevant others, then the theory would predict that she would also hold a positive subjective norm for the assignment. The opposite can also be stated if the exposure assignment is thought to be highly distressing and unhelpful by the individual or others.

This theory was revised as the "theory of planned behavior" (Ajzen, 1985, 1988) and included a third determinant of behavioral intention: perceived behavioral control (see Table 2.1). In the context of using homework in cognitive behavioral therapy, this theory would predict that a client's motivation is influenced by how difficult the activity seems, as well as how much he can gain from engaging in the activity. According to this theory, if a client has a view that his assigned homework activity is practically possible, has considered the various practical obstacles to the activity, and the activity itself is within a manageable level of difficulty, he will have high perceived control over what is involved in the homework activity. On the other hand, a client will have a low perceived control or confidence in her ability to engage in the homework activity if she expects that the activity will be overwhelming or simply too difficult or demanding. To facilitate this process, A. T. Beck et al. (1979) outlined recommendations for integrating homework assignments into therapy, where the therapist is encouraged to provide a detailed rationale for the task, problem solve with clients the

TABLE 2.1 Summary of "Mediating" Variables from Cognitive Theories

Model	Variables
Health belief model	Susceptibility, severity, benefits, barriers, self-efficacy, cues to action, "other variables" (e.g., demographic characteristics)
Theory of planned behavior	Beliefs, attitude, subjective norm, perceived control, intentions
Protection motivation theory	Environmental and interpersonal sources of information, intrinsic/extrinsic rewards, severity/vulnerability, threat appraisal, response/self-efficacy, response costs
Self-regulation theory of illness cognition	Vulnerability, response efficacy, self-efficacy, fear
Cognitive response theory	Listener involvement, message strength, heuristic cues (e.g., source credibility; emotional potential of message)

practical obstacles to carrying out the task, consider the client's ability and the difficulty of the task, and talk with the client about his or her attitudes and beliefs about carrying out the task.

Perceived behavioral control is also an underlying theoretical determinant in paradoxical intention, which involves the deliberate practice and exaggeration of an unhelpful behavior or habit in an effort to learn a degree of control or mastery. Predominantly associated with Adlerian and family systems therapies (e.g., Weeks & L'Abate, 1982), paradoxical techniques have some experimental and clinical support (Ascher & Efrem 1978; Hunsley, 1993). L'Abate (1984) has since extended this seemingly circular concept of assigning the unhelpful behavior to a linear exercise focused on learning through the completion of specific between-session activities (e.g., "Spend 20 minutes writing down what happened on Mondays, Wednesdays, and Fridays at 8 p.m. and make sure you learn what went on during those times, days, and durations").

Bridge to Social Cognition Theories

As summarized in Figure 2.4, social learning theories suggest that a client's intention (or motivation) to engage in a particular homework assignment is determined by a balance between the costs and benefits of the activity. The cost is the perceived difficulty and/or distress caused by engaging in the activity (e.g., *"Attempting this exposure exercise will produce some anxiety for me, but I have strategies to cope"*), the benefit being the perceived

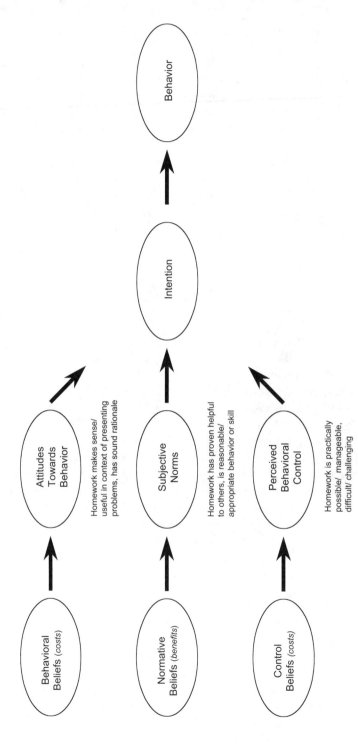

Fig. 2.4 Summary of theory of planned behavior as applied to using homework assignments.

gain of understanding or skill acquisition in the therapeutic skill (e.g., "*I have been able to approach less distressing situations on my hierarchy and have seen that my anxiety lessened after I was in the situation for some time*"). Social learning theory also incorporates the understanding that clients will have highly *individualized* beliefs tied to the costs and benefits of engaging in a particular homework activity based on the meaning they apply to it (see Kelly, 1955; Neimeyer, 1985). These foundations have been further developed with Albert Bandura's work in producing a social cognition theory.

Bandura's Social Cognition Theory. Bandura's (1977) application of social learning theory places a heavy emphasis on cognitive concepts and focuses on how individuals perceive their social experiences and how these cognitions then influence behavior and development. Bandura's theory was the first to incorporate the notion of modeling, or vicarious learning, as a form of social learning. In addition, Bandura also introduced several other important concepts, including reciprocal determinism, self-efficacy, and the idea that there can be a significant temporal variation in time lapse between cause and effect. Bandura renamed his social learning theory "social cognitive theory," seeing this as a better description of what he had been advocating since the 1960s (Bandura, 1986).

Social cognition theory stems from the behaviorist notion that response consequences mediate behavior, but it posits that behavior is largely regulated through cognitive processes (Miller & Dollard, 1941). Within this framework, response consequences of a behavior are used to form expectations of behavioral outcomes. It is the ability to form these expectations that gives individuals the ability to predict the outcomes of their behavior before the behavior is performed.

Social cognition theory conceptualizes an individual's behavior as being uniquely determined by personal, behavioral, and environmental factors (Bandura, 1986). Bandura's theory recognizes that some sources of influence are stronger than others and that they do not all occur simultaneously. In fact, the interaction between the three factors will differ based on the individual, the particular behavior being examined, and the specific situation in which the behavior occurs (Bandura, 1989). Thus, Bandura's work emphasized a bidirectional link between cognitive, emotional, physiological, and behavioral aspects of a person's experience. Furthermore, the theory highlights the bidirectional relationship between the different aspects of a person's experience and the environment (Bandura, 1977, 1986, 1989). Bandura's social cognitive perspective also emphasized an individual's ability to symbolize, plan alternative strategies (i.e., forethought), learn through vicarious experience, self-regulate, and self-reflect.

Bandura's work has been extended into many variations and applications, but common to the various social cognition models is the assumption that motivation to engage and maintain behavior arises from beliefs that influence the interpretation of experiences, and beliefs that guide behavior (see Conner & Haywood-Everett, 1998). In particular, Bandura (1989) proposed that people have "self-efficacy beliefs," or a degree of confidence that they can perform or endure the actions necessary to obtain a goal (see Figure 2.5).

In the present context, self-efficacy beliefs have relevance to a client's decision to engage in a homework activity. According to the theory, clients are likely to engage in tasks and activities in which they feel competent and confident and to avoid those in which they do not. Unless clients believe that their efforts toward a homework activity will have the desired outcome, they are likely to have little incentive to engage in the activity. Self-efficacy beliefs also have relevance for determining how much effort clients will expend on a homework activity, how long they will persevere when they confront obstacles, and how resilient they will be in the face of adverse situations.

Past Experience. The most influential source in determining self-efficacy beliefs is the interpreted result of previous performance, or mastery experience. A general process involves a client engaging in a homework task, an interpretation of the results of his efforts, the development of beliefs about his capability to engage in subsequent homework tasks or activities, and a degree of willingness to engage in future tasks. Outcomes interpreted as "successful" typically increase self-efficacy, and those interpreted as "unsuccessful" lower it. Of course, mastery represents only one influence in how clients synthesize their experiences and their learning outcomes from having engaged in homework.

Observing Other People's Examples (or Modeling). In addition to interpreting the results of their actions, people form self-efficacy beliefs through the experience of observing others perform tasks. The process of observational (or vicarious) learning occurs through observing the consequences of someone else's actions (Mischel, 1968, 1973, 1979). As long as the person engaging in the homework activity is similar in some way to the client (e.g., has similar presenting problems), has seen to benefit from the activity (e.g., improvement in mood through having completed a thought record), and has some long-term benefit (e.g., increased sense of coping), then learning through observation is likely to occur. This may take the form of completing examples of desired skills, such as completed thought record examples, or through therapist modeling of the particular response, as is often utilized in assertiveness and other interpersonal skills training.

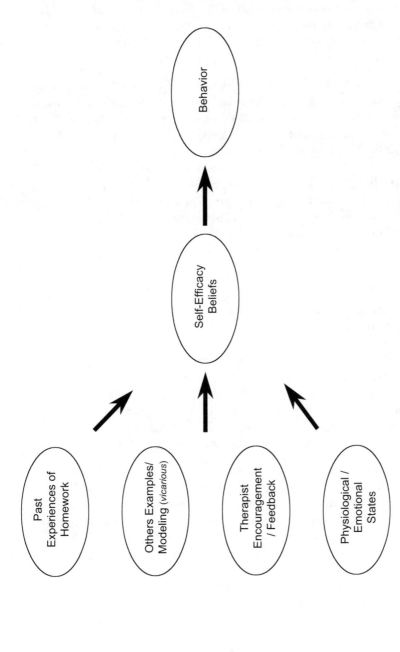

Fig. 2.5 Summary of Albert Bandura's social cognitive theory as applied to using homework assignments.

Learning through modeling can be particularly relevant in the context of using homework assignments, especially when a client has little prior experience with what is required for the task. Indeed, key recommendations for integrating homework into therapy by A. T Beck et al. (1979) included a rationale for the homework based on its benefits for other clients, and modeling the homework assignment for the client where appropriate.

Encouragement and Feedback. Individuals also create and develop self-efficacy beliefs as a result of the social persuasions they receive from others. In the present context, the therapist has the role of "persuading," or more appropriately, encouraging the client to have a degree of confidence in her ability to complete the homework assignment (i.e., self-efficacy belief) while at the same time ensuring that the envisioned activity is attainable. In A. T. Beck's (1979) recommendations for practice, individually tailoring homework assignments for clients' presenting problems and particular skill levels is also part of encouraging the client to complete an activity. However, this "encouragement" role could also be extended to partners and family members to increase the social influence for the particular homework activity.

Physiological and Emotional Triggers. Somatic and emotional states such as anxiety, stress, arousal, and mood states also provide information about efficacy beliefs. According to the theory, clients are likely to gauge their degree of confidence by the emotional state they experience as they contemplate a homework activity. A therapist might ask the client to use guided imagery to explore whether she has strong emotional, physiological, and cognitive reactions (J. Beck, 1995), which may provide cues about the anticipated cost and benefit for the activity. A client's sense of self-efficacy that is linked to somatic symptoms and emotional distress may occur disproportionately to the particular homework assignment.

Self-Regulatory Processes. An important final aspect of Bandura's social cognition theory is that a specific behavior, besides merely producing an external outcome, also leads to some form of self-evaluative reflection or synthesis. Translated to the present context, clients reflect on the utility of the homework task and then form conclusions and beliefs on the basis of their degree of engagement and learning from having completed it. Therefore Bandura suggests that contingencies to behavior are both external and internal (or self-evaluative). This suggests that external reinforcement certainly works, but it will be most effective when it is consistent with a positive conclusion or synthesis from the client's own learning experience.

Specific Social Cognition Models

Stemming from social cognition theory, a number of specific models have been formulated as a means of explaining health behaviors. The "health belief model" was one of the first formal models that purported to explain health behaviors (Rosenstock, 1960). It is one of several models generally based on the assertion that behaviors are determined by the value of a particular outcome (e.g., reduction in panic attacks) and the expectation that a behavior (e.g., graded exposure homework) will contribute to, or allow, the avoidance of that outcome (Weinstein, 1993). Table 2.1 presents a summary of the cognitive mediators proposed within the health belief model.

Over time, however, additional variables have been added to the model, making it more comprehensive but also less clear about causal relationships among model elements (Strecher, Champion, & Rosenstock, 1997). As applied to the present context, the model lists five belief domains: beliefs about (a) whether one is susceptible to symptom distress and impairment in functioning, (b) how severe or serious the distress and impairment might be in terms of their consequences, (c) the perceived benefits of engaging in a activity, (d) barriers or the negative aspects associated with a homework activity, and (e) whether one is able to competently perform the homework assignment (self-efficacy). Thus, one prominent feature of the model is that a client's beliefs about a particular situation will determine whether the particular intervention is applied (e.g., use of a thought record).

Rogers introduced his "protection motivation theory" to improve understanding of the effects of threatening information on attitude and behavior change (Rippetoe & Rogers, 1987; Rogers & Prentice-Dunn, 1997). This theory is similar to the health belief model in its comprehensive list of variables, including historical factors (e.g., observational learning, prior experience, personality). The theory focuses on a few cognitive mediating processes and, when applied to the present context, proposes a list of mediating factors that enable the therapist to predict whether a client will engage in homework assignment (see Table 2.1). For example, the theory would suggest that a client with depression would consider whether to carry out scheduled activation activities as a means of improving low mood and fatigue (i.e., severity/ vulnerability) but consider the benefits in light of his degree of symptom distress and impairment in functioning (i.e., threat appraisal).[2]

---

[2]For example, the issue of favoring the short-term benefits of avoiding homework assignments has been discussed in the context of resistance and the process of change in psychotherapy by Alford and Lantka (2000).

More recently, theorists have suggested that clients making a decisions about whether to adopt a "health-protective behavior" often move through a series of qualitatively distinct stages. The "transtheoretical model" (DiClemente et al., 1991; Prochaska & DiClemente, 1982) attempts to conceptualize how behavior change occurs by proposing a framework in which individuals are at various stages of readiness to change (see Table 2.1). As applied to the context of engaging in homework assignments, the transtheoretical model suggests that clients can be at a *precontemplative stage* about engaging in a task (i.e., not thinking about engaging in a homework activity), *contemplative stage* (i.e., actively thinking about engaging in the activity in the near future), *decision stage* (i.e., making a plan to engage in the activity), *action stage* (i.e., implementing the plan to change behavior), and *maintenance stage* (i.e., sustained practice of the activity). This theoretical conception for using homework in cognitive behavioral therapy can provide a helpful framework for therapists in talking with clients about the perceived benefits and costs of engaging in a homework assignment. That is, considering a given homework assignment in these terms enables the therapist to determine whether a client is ready to consider alternative and more adaptive strategies to deal with her distress. For example, receiving benefit from scheduling a series of pleasurable activities may encourage a client to move from being contemplative about alternatives to alcohol and drug use, to making an explicit abstinence and treatment plan. (Other stage models, such as Schwarzer, 1992, differentiate between planning and behavior stages, which are less helpful in determining why clients progress to the stage where they engage in a homework activity.)

Leventhal's "self-regulation theory of illness cognition" is particularly noteworthy among the social cognition theories in that it explicitly addresses the role of emotion as a predictor of health-protective behavior (Cameron, 1997; Leventhal, 1970). Leventhal proposes that a threat prompts parallel motives to cope with the health threat and the emotional arousal caused by the threat (see Table 2.1). Thus, emotional distress is a motivating factor toward behavior in this model. The extent to which a therapist can suggest a homework activity that will assist in the treatment of that condition and relieve emotional distress will determine the likelihood that a client will engage in that activity (Leventhal, Nerenz, & Steele, 1984).

The final social cognition model of relevance to the use of homework assignments in cognitive behavioral therapy is Petty and Cacioppo's (1981) "elaboration likelihood model." Petty and Cacioppo propose that attitudes can be formed via different routes, and when clients are motivated to process thoughtfully, their cognitive responses to the message content become important (see also A. T. Beck, 1974). The implication here is that when clients agree with the "persuasive" message from the therapist regarding the homework activity, this may be sufficient to encourage the client to adopt a different attitude in favor of engaging in the activity (see Table 2.1).

Cognitive-Behavioral Foundations: Summary and Synthesis

This Chapter has discussed the theoretical foundations for the specific process of using homework assignments in cognitive behavioral therapy. In discussing the foundations of behavioral theory, we have described how classical and operant conditioning principles underlie the mechanism by which homework produces its effects. In describing the foundations of cognitive theory, we have described the host of cognitive mediating factors that are involved in this learning process, both in making sense of learning from homework completion and in determining whether a homework assignment will be carried out.

As a means of synthesizing this theory, we present a "cognitive behavioral theoretical foundations model" in Figure 2.6. Because the integration of homework assignments into therapy involves a collaborative discussion with the client to design and assign homework, the client carrying out or doing the homework activity, and a review of the homework at the following session (A. T. Beck et al., 1979; Kazantzis & Lampropoulos, 2002), we use this framework to synthesize the theoretical recommendations in this Chapter (see also Kolb, 1984).

Starting with homework design and assign, there are usually emotional, physiological, cognitive, or situational triggers, or antecedents, to indicate whether the application (or generalization) of a particular intervention or adaptive skill would be helpful. However, the extent to which a client will feel confident (or "intend") to apply the intervention or skill will depend on practical *obstacles* and his or her beliefs about the homework. Before engaging in the homework activity, beliefs based on prior in-session or homework experience of the particular task, the relevance of the homework to therapy goals, and information that has benefited others in a similar situation (*rationale*), determine whether the homework will be carried out. Beliefs also include understanding of what is involved in terms of emotional and other costs (*comprehension*), specificity in designing the task (*specificity*), and the extent to which the therapist can involve the client in tailoring and encouraging completion (*collaboration*).

Assuming the client has a reasonable degree of belief in the activity as well as its relevance and benefits and has the ability to carry it out, the likelihood is that it will be carried out. Engaging in the homework task

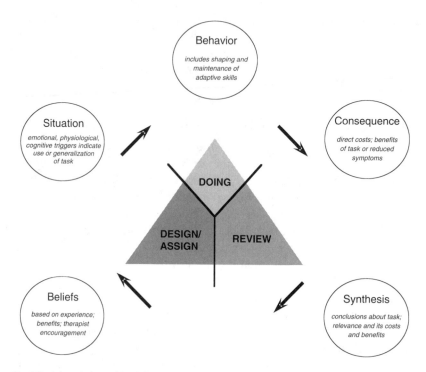

Fig. 2.6 Integrated cognitive behavioral theoretical foundations.

(*quantity and quality of completion*) is usually facilitated by asking the client to try small achievable portions of the final behavior or skill and, through a process of successive approximations, to gain the ability to complete the entire task. The intrinsic benefits of engaging in the activity, such as reduced cognitive, affective, physiological symptoms, and/or sense of progress toward goals will determine the extent to which the behavior or skill is maintained.

A final stage involves the client reflecting on his or her experience of the homework assignment. This provides the opportunity for the client to synthesize and form conclusions about the particular activity, namely its relevance (*match with therapy goals*), benefits (*pleasure, mastery, progress*), and the client's ability to carry it out (*difficulty*). The broad practical implication of this theoretical discussion is that therapists should work to evaluate the client's beliefs about the process and specific content of homework activities.

In writing this Chapter, our aim was to provide the reader with a firm grounding in the theoretical basis for the use of homework in cognitive behavioral therapy. The specific purpose was to answer the question

"Why does cognitive behavioral therapy include homework assignments?" and *"What are the determinants of a client's decision to complete homework?"* These theoretical underpinnings for using homework are further exemplified in the Chapters describing the use of homework in cognitive behavioral therapy for a range of clinical presentation in Part II of this book. In the interim, we review the existing empirical support for using homework in cognitive behavioral therapy in Chapter 3 and apply these theoretical foundations to the measurement of adherence with homework assignments in Chapter 4.

References

Ajzen, I. (1985). From intentions to actions: A theory of planned behavior. In J. Kuhl & J. Beckman (Eds.), *Action-control: From cognition to behavior* (pp. 11–39). Heidelberg: Springer.

Ajzen, I. (1988). *Attitudes, personality, and behavior.* Chicago, IL: Dorsey.

Ajzen, I., & Fishbein, M. (1977). Attitude-behavior relations: A theoretical analysis and review of empirical research. *Psychological Bulletin, 84,* 888–914.

Alford, B. A., & Lantka, A. L. (2000). Processes of clinical change and resistance. *Behaviour Modification, 24,* 566–579.

Allen, D. M. (in press). Use of between-session homework in systems-oriented individual psychotherapy. *Journal of Psychotherapy Integration.*

Ascher, L., & Efrem, J. (1978). Use of paradoxical intention in a behavioral program for sleep onset insomnia. *Journal of Consulting and Clinical Psychology, 46,* 547–550.

Bandura, A. (1977). Self-efficacy: Toward a unifying theory of behavioral change. *Psychological Review, 84,* 191–215.

Bandura, A. (1986). *Social foundations of thought and action: A social cognitive theory.* Englewood Cliffs, NJ: Prentice Hall.

Bandura, A. (1989). Human agency in social cognitive theory. *American Psychologist, 44,* 1175–1184.

Bandura, A. (1991). Social cognitive theory of self-regulation. *Organizational Behavior and Human Decision Processes, 50,* 248–287.

Beck, A. T. (1964). Thinking and depression: Theory and therapy. *Archives of General Psychiatry, 10,* 561–571.

Beck, A. T. (1974). The development of depression: A cognitive model. In R. Friedman & M. Katz (Eds.), *Psychology of depression: Contemporary theory and research* (pp. 3–27). Wasington, DC: Winston-Wiley.

Beck, A. T. (1976). *Cognitive therapy and the emotional disorders.* New York: International Universities Press.

Beck, A. T., Rush, J. A., Shaw, B. F., & Emery, G. (1979). *Cognitive therapy of depression.* New York: Guilford Press.

Beck, A. T. & Weishaar, M. E. (1989). Cognitive therapy. In D. Wedding & R. Corsini (Eds.), *Current psychotherapies,* (4th ed.). Ithaca, IL: Peacock.

Beck, J. (1995). *Cognitive therapy: Basics and beyond.* New York: Guilford Press.

Bergin, A. E. (1971). The evaluation of therapeutic outcomes. In A. E. Bergin & S. L. Garfield (Eds.), *Handbook of psychotherapy and behavior change* (pp. 217–270). New York: Wiley.

Beyebach, M., Morejon, A. R., Palenzvela, D. L., & Rodriguez-Arias, J. L. (1996). Research on the process of solution-focused therapy. In S. D. Miller, M. A. Hubble, & B. L. Duncan (Eds.), *Handbook of solution-focused brief therapy* (pp. 299–334). San Francisco: Jossey-Bass.

Bouton, M. E. (1988). Context and ambiguity in the extinction of emotional learning: Implications for exposure therapy. *Behaviour Research & Therapy, 26,* 137–149.

Brodley, B. T. (in press). Client-initiated homework in client-centered therapy. *Journal of Psychotherapy Integration.*

Cameron, L. D. (1997). Screening for cancer: Illness perceptions and illness worry. In K. J. Petrie and J. A. Weinman (Eds.), *Perceptions of health and illness: Current research and applications* (pp. 291–322). Amsterdam: Harwood.

Carich, M. S. (1990). Utilizing task assignments within Adlerian therapy. *Individual Psychology, 46,* 217–224.

Carr, A. (1997). Positive practice in family therapy. *Journal of Marital and Family Therapy, 23,* 271–293.

Clark, D. A., Beck, A. T., & Alford, B. A. (1999). *Scientific foundations of cognitive theory and therapy of depression.* New York: Wiley.

Conner, M., & Heywood-Everett, S. (1998). Addressing mental health problems with the theory of planned behaviour. *Psychology, Health & Medicine, 3,* 87–96.

Crosbie-Burnett, M., & Lewis, E. A. (1993). Theoretical contributions from social and cognitive-behavioral psychology. In P. G. Boss & W. J. Doherty (Eds.), *Sourcebook of family theories and methods: A contextual approach* (pp. 531–561). New York: Plenum Press.

Dattilio, F. M. (2002). Homework assignments in couple and family therapy. *Journal of Clinical Psychology, 58,* 535–549.

DiClemente, C. C., Prochaska, J. O., Fairhurst, S. K., Velicer, W. F., Velasquez, M. M., & Rossi, J. S. (1991). The process of smoking cessation: An analysis of precontemplation, contemplation, and preparation stages of change. *Journal of Consulting and Clinical Psychology, 59,* 295–304.

Ellis, A. (1962). *Reason and emotion in psychotherapy.* Secaucus, NJ: Lyle Stuart.

Ellis, A. (1988). Can we legitimately evaluate ourselves? A reply to Robert C. Roberts. *Psychotherapy, 25,* 314–316.

Greenberg, L. S., Watson, J. C., & Goldman, R. (Eds.). (1988). *Process-experiential therapy of depression: Handbook of experiential psychotherapy* (pp. 227–248). New York: Guilford Press.

Halligan, F. R. (1995). The challenge: Short-term dynamic psychotherapy for college counseling centers. *Psychotherapy, 32,* 113–121.

Hansen, D. J., & MacMillan, V. M. (1990). Behavioral assessment of child-abusive and neglectful families: Recent developments and current issues. *Behavior Modification, 14,* 255–278.

Hunsley, J. (1993). Treatment acceptability of symptom prescription techniques. *Journal of Counseling Psychology, 40,* 139–143.

Huppert, J. D., Roth, D. A., & Foa, E. B. (in press). The use of homework in behavior therapy for anxiety disorders. *Journal of Psychotherapy Integration.*

Kanfer, F. H. (1970). Self-monitoring, methodological limitations, and clinical applications. *Journal of Consulting and Clinical Psychology, 35,* 148–152.

Kazantzis, N., Deane, F. P., & Ronan, K. R. (2000). Homework assignments in cognitive and behavioral therapy: A meta-analysis. *Clinical Psychology: Science and Practice, 7,* 189–202.

Kazantzis, N., & Lampropoulos, G. L. (2002). Reflecting on homework in psychotherapy: What can we conclude from research and experience? *Journal of Clinical Psychology, 58,* 577–585.

Kazantzis, N., Lampropoulos, G. L., & Deane, F. P. (in press). A national survey of psychologists attitudes towards homework assignments. *Journal of Consulting and Clinical Psychology.*

Kazantzis, N., & Ronan, K. R. (Eds.). (in press). The use of between-session (homework) activities in different psychotherapy approaches [Special Issue]. *Journal of Psychotherapy Integration.*

Klerman, G. L., Weissman, M. M., Rounsaville, B. J., & Chevron, E. (1984). *Interpersonal psychotherapy of depression.* New York: Basic Books.

Kolb, D. (1984). *Experiential learning: Experience as the source of learning and development.* Englewood Cliffs, NJ: Prentice Hall.

Kornblith, S. J., Rehm, L. P., O'Hara, M. W., & Lamparski, D. M. (1983). The contribution of self-reinforcement training and behavioral assignments to the efficacy of self-control therapy for depression. *Cognitive Therapy and Research, 7,* 499–528.

Kelly, G. A. (1955). *The psychology of personal constructs.* New York: Norton.

L'Abate, L. (1984). Beyond paradox: Issues of control. *American Journal of Family Therapy, 12,* 12–20.

L'Abate, L. (1994). *A theory of personality development.* New York: Wiley.

L'Abate, L. (1997). *The self in the family: A classification of personality, criminality, and psychopathology.* New York: Wiley.

L'Abate, L. (1999). Taking the bull by the horns: Beyond talking psychological interventions. *The Family Journal: Therapy and Counseling for Couples and Families, 7,* 206–220.

Leventhal, H. (1970). Findings and theory in the study of fear communications. In L. Berkowitz (Ed.), *Advances in experimental social psychology* (Vol. 3, pp. 119–186). New York: Academic Press.

Leventhal, H., Nerenz, D. R., & Steele, D. J. (1984). Illness representations and coping with health threats. In A. Baum, S. E. Taylor, & J. E. Singer (Eds.), *Handbook of psychology and health* (Vol. 4). Hillsdale, NJ: Erlbaum.

Levis, D. J., & Malloy, P. F. (1982). Research in infrahuman and human conditioning. In G. T. Wilson & C. M. Franks (Eds.), *Contemporary behavior therapy: Conceptual and empirical foundations* (pp. 65–118). New York: Guilford Press.

Lieberman, P. A. (1993). *Learning: Behavior and cognition.* Pacific Grove, CA: Brooks/ Cole.

Maddock, J. W. (1975). Initiation problems and time structuring in brief sex therapy. *Journal of Sex & Marital Therapy, 1,* 190–197.

Mahoney, M. J., Kazdin, A. E., & Lesswing, N. J. (1974). Behavior modification: Delusion or deliverance? In C. M. Franks & G. T. Wilson (Eds.). *Annual review of behavior therapy and practice* (Vol. 2; pp. 169–193). New York: Brunner/ Mazel.

Maultsby, M. C. (1971). *Handbook of rational self-counseling.* Lexington, KY: University of Kentucky Press.

Miller, N. E., & Dollard, J. (1941). *Social learning and imitation.* New Haven, CT: Yale University Press.

Mischel, W. (1968). *Personality and assessment.* New York: John Wiley & Sons.

Mischel, W. (1973). Facing the issues. *Journal of Abnormal Psychology, 82,* 541–542.

Mischel, W. (1979). On the interface of cognition and personality: Beyond the person-situation debate. American Psychologist, 34, 740–754.

Neimeyer, R. A. (1985). *The development of personal construct psychology.* Lincoln, NE: University of Nebraska Press.

Nelson, T. S. (1994). Do-overs. *Journal of Family Psychotherapy, 5,* 71–74.

O'Connell, W. E., & Gomez, E. A. (1995). Marital and family therapy as an empowering of cooperation-as-equals. *Individual Psychology: Journal of Adlerian Theory, Research & Practice, 51,* 37–45.

Petty, R. E., & Cacioppo, J. T. (1981). *Attitudes and persuasion: Classic and contemporary approaches.* Dubuque, IA: Brown.

Prochaska, J. O., & DiClemente, C. C. (1982). Transtheoretical therapy: Toward a more integrative model of change. *Psychotherapy: Theory, Research and Practice, 19,* 276–288.

Rescorla, R. A., (1988). Pavlovian conditioning: It's not what you think it is. *American Psychologist, 43,* 151–160.

Rippetoe, P. A., & Rogers, R. W. (1987). Effects of components of protection-motivation theory on adaptive and maladaptive coping with a health threat. *Journal of Personality and Social Psychology, 52,* 596–604.

Rogers, R. W., & Prentice-Dunn, S. (1997). Protection motivation theory. In David S. Gochman (Ed.), *Handbook of health behavior research* (Vol.1, pp. 113–132). New York: Plenum Press.

Rosenstock, I. M. (1960). What research in motivation suggests for public health. *American Journal of Public Health, 50,* 295–301.

Rotter, J. B. (1954). *Social learning and clinical psychology.* Oxford, UK: Prentice Hall.

Rotter, J. B. (1990). Internal versus external control of reinforcement: A case history of a variable. *American Psychologist, 45,* 489–493.

Rotter, J. B. (1992). Cognates of personal control: Locus of control, self-efficacy, and explanatory style [Comment]. *Applied & Preventive Psychology, 1,* 127–129.

Schwarzer, R. (1992). Self-efficacy: *Thought control of action.* Washington, DC: Hemisphere Publishing.

Shelton, J. L., & Ackerman, J. M. (1974). *Homework in counseling and psychotherapy: Examples of systematic assignments for therapeutic use by mental health professionals.* Springfield, IL: Thomas.

Skinner, B. F. (1971). *Beyond freedom and dignity.* New York: Knopf.

Staats, A. W. (1996). *Behavior and personality: Psychological behaviorism.* New York: Springer.

Strecher, V. J., Champion, V. L., & Rosenstock, I. W. (1997). In D. S. Gochman (Ed.), *Handbook of health behavior research I: Personal and social determinants* (pp. 71–91). New York: Plenum Press.

Stricker, G. (in press). Using homework in psychodynamic psychotherapy. *Journal of Psychotherapy Integration*.

Stricker, G., & Gold, J. R. (1996). Psychotherapy integration: An assimilative, psychodynamic approach. *Clinical Psychology: Science and Practice, 3,* 47–58.

Tharp, R. G., & Wetzel, R. J. (1969). *Behavior modification in the natural environment.* New York: Academic Press.

Thase, M. E., & Callan, J. A. (in press). The role of homework in cognitive behavior therapy of depression. *Journal of Psychotherapy Integration*.

Weeks, G., & L'Abate, L. (1982). *Paradoxical psychotherapy: Theory and practice with individuals, couples, and families.* New York: Brunner/Mazel.

Weinstein, N. D. (1993). Testing four competing theories of health-protective behavior. *Health Psychology, 12,* 324–333.

CHAPTER 3

Empirical Foundations

NIKOLAOS KAZANTZIS, FRANK P. DEANE, KEVIN R. RONAN,
and GEORGIOS K. LAMPROPOULOS

One of the things that practitioners observe in their everyday clinical work is that clients are more likely to benefit from cognitive behavioral therapy if they apply adaptive skills and techniques between sessions. Homework assignments are the vehicle by which these skills and techniques are transferred to the client's natural environment, thereby facilitating the "outwards focus" of the therapeutic approach (Beck, 1976; Blackburn & Twaddle, 1996). In the same way that we encourage our clients to collect empirical data to test out ideas or beliefs, researchers have sought to collect empirical data to test out the theoretical foundations upon which homework is based.

The aim of this Chapter is to provide an overview of the empirical data that form the foundation for the use of homework assignments in cognitive behavioral therapy. In order to achieve this aim, we have divided the material into four sections that each reflect different sets of research questions examined in the literature. The first section provides a brief overview of the research examining the relationship between homework assignments and treatment outcome in behavioral and cognitive therapies. The second section provides a review of the research examining the extent to which homework assignments are transferred into clinical practice. The third section provides a review of the client and therapist correlates of homework assignments in therapy. The fourth section provides a review of key research examining the role of homework assignments in the treatment of the range of clinical populations and problems covered in Parts II and III of this book (Chapters 5 to 16). To preface our conclusions concerning the empirical foundations, the evidence reviewed in this Chapter converges to form a strong basis to justify the use of homework assignments in cognitive behavioral therapy.

The Relationship Between Homework and Treatment Outcome

The role of homework assignments in psychotherapy has received increased research attention over the past few decades. A recent Delphi poll (Norcross, Hedges, & Prochaska, 2002) ranked homework assignments first among the 38 interventions likely to increase in the field in the next 10 years. Research has focused on either (a) direct contrast of therapy with and without homework assignments to examine homework's specific effects on treatment outcome or (b) the association between client compliance with homework and treatment outcome in a single group of clients. Even though these different methodologies address two very different research questions, they have often been discussed as a single group of studies. In this section, we review these two set of studies separately and discuss the limitations of the existing literature as an impetus for new avenues of research.

Does Homework Enhance Treatment Outcome?

Studies contrasting therapies with and without homework assignments to examine homework's specific effects have produced inconsistent results. Some have found that homework assignments produce statistically significant effects on treatment outcome compared to conditions without homework (e.g., Kazdin & Mascitelli, 1982; Marks et al. 1988), but others have not been able to detect effects. Interestingly, a few researchers observed effects to be clinically meaningful but not statistically significant (e.g., Blanchard et al., 1991), whereas others have only detected effects on a selection of treatment outcome measures (e.g., Neimeyer & Feixas, 1990).

With the apparent inconsistency in the experimental/quasi-experimental literature, we decided to undertake a statistical power survey and meta-analysis of this literature as the initial step of our *Cognitive Behavior Therapy Homework Project* (outlined in Chapter 1). Statistical power refers to a study's probability of detecting an effect, given that one exists. When statistical power is low, the likelihood of obtaining a null result increases, and the interpretation of results is problematic (Cohen, 1988). The power survey (Kazantzis, 2000) found that studies attempting to demonstrate homework effects had, on average, a 58% chance of detecting a *large* effect size (based on Cohen's conventional value for a large effect size, with alpha set at 0.05). These studies had even less probability of detecting medium (32%) or small effect (9%) sizes. In other words, studies seeking to examine homework effects had a 42% chance of *not detecting large* effect sizes, assuming that they existed.

In order to bypass the limitations of low statistical power, we also conducted a meta-analysis to aggregate the findings from the studies designed to examine homework effects (Kazantzis, Deane, & Ronan, 2000). The meta-analysis included 27 studies, representing the data from 1702 clients receiving behavioral and cognitive-behavioral therapies. The meta-analysis results indicated that homework assignments produce a distinct effect size in the medium range ($r = .36$). In practice, this effect size suggests that 68% of clients would be likely to improve in therapy involving homework, in contrast to a rate of 32% in therapy consisting entirely of in-session work.

Does Homework Compliance Correlate with Treatment Outcome?

Studies examining the association between client compliance with homework and treatment outcome in a single group of clients have produced consistent results. Studies of cognitive behavioral therapy for mood (Addis & Jacobson, 2000; Burns & Spangler, 2000; Bryant, Simons, & Thase, 1999) and anxiety disorders (Leung & Heimberg, 1996) have shown a positive correlation between levels of client homework completion and reduced symptom severity assessment at termination. The relationship between homework compliance and treatment outcome has not been universally demonstrated in the context of anxiety disorders, and so we included the research examining the homework compliance-outcome relationship as a second part of our meta-analysis (Kazantzis et al., 2000). Across client characteristics and types of homework assignments, the meta-analysis produced a homogeneous effect size linking homework compliance and therapy outcome ($r = .22$).

In summary, there have been a number of studies designed to examine the relationship between homework and treatment outcome. Research has demonstrated that therapy involving homework assignments produces a greater effect than therapy without homework. Research has also shown that the extent to which clients engage in homework activities is associated with their degree of improvement. Therefore we conclude that there are firm empirical grounds to involve clients in homework assignments, and those clients who actively engage in homework assignments, are more likely to benefit from therapy.

The Use of Homework Assignments

It is one thing to measure the effects or correlates of homework assignments in research studies; it is something altogether different to ascertain *how* homework assignments are transferred to clinical practice. Interestingly, very little has been published on the extent to which homework assignments are actually used by cognitive behavioral therapy practitioners. In this section, we provide a review of the published surveys of homework use in psychotherapy research and practice. Because researchers have sought to survey the use of homework in published treatment outcome studies, we discuss this literature before moving to practitioner surveys.

Surveys of the Literature

In an effort to examine the hypothesis that homework compliance was not being measured in outcome studies, Shelton and Levy (1981a) published a survey of the use of homework in published treatment outcome research. Their review was comprehensive in that it spanned eight scholarly journals from 1973 to 1980. Shelton and Levy reported that 68% of the articles described the use of homework assignments to promote treatment gains and illustrated that homework was most commonly assigned for social skills training (80%), obsessive-compulsive symptoms (79%), and sexual dysfunction (79%). On the basis of their findings and best practice guidelines for enhancing medication compliance at that time, Shelton and Levy published a book that included a "model for practice" for using homework assignments in psychotherapy (Shelton & Levy, 1981b). Using their model as a criterion for "systematic administration," Shelton and Levy reported that only a small proportion of studies (2%) outlined when, where, how often, and how long the homework assignments should take to be practical. Although it is unlikely that the summary data from research can be directly applied to use of homework in clinical practice, the Shelton and Levy survey has been influential and often cited where researchers are interested in underscoring the frequency with which homework is used in manualized behavioral and cognitive behavioral therapies.

A second survey of published research, by Mahrer, Nordin, and Miller (1995), demonstrates that homework assignments have continued to be incorporated as components of manualized treatment protocols across most problem areas. Mahrer et al. corroborated Shelton and Levy's (1981a) main finding regarding the use of homework in published research and attempted to link the use of homework with particular clinical presentations in order to derive implications for clinical practice.

Surveys of Clinical Practice

Turning now to surveys of clinical practice, Warren and McLellarn (1987) surveyed the use of homework among 144 qualified rational-emotive therapists. The study showed that a wide variety of bibliotherapy, writing, and activity assignments were generally used among their practitioner sample. However, the survey was not designed to provide an overall estimate of the frequency with which homework assignments were used in practice, and its results have questionable external validity, given the small sample size and specific therapeutic orientation of the therapists.

Kemmler, Borgart, and Gärke (1992) surveyed a German psychologist sample on their use and perceived importance of homework assignments ($N = 61$). The sample described using a range of theoretical backgrounds, including psychodynamic and cognitive behavioral, but the vast majority (87%) of the sample still rated homework as either important or extremely important for their practice of therapy. This study was limited in its significance because of the small sample, but it provided beginning evidence to suggest that practitioners do not use a predetermined list of homework assignments. That is, only 25% of the sample sometimes designed homework assignments before the therapy session, with the majority indicating that they linked the assignment to the content of the session.

A naturalistic study of 109 counseling sessions from the practice of 27 senior staff psychologists, interns, and practicum students found that 9 out of 10 sessions involved an assignment of therapeutic homework. However, once again the sample size and setting of the study limits the external validity of the findings (Scheel, Seaman, Roach, Mulin, & Blackwell-Mahoney, 1999).

As there was a dearth of information on clinical practice at the time, we decided to embark on a series of surveys to examine use of homework assignments in clinical practice. We considered practitioner surveys essential for determining the future direction for our *Cognitive Behavior Therapy Homework Project.* We conducted our first survey among New Zealand practicing psychologists, and of the 358 registered with "clinical" as their primary work activity, we obtained a good response, with 221 deciding to participate (Kazantzis & Deane, 1999). The data showed that homework assignments were frequently assigned by the majority of our sample (98% reported homework use), but there was some variation among practitioners of different theoretical orientations. That is, those reporting a cognitive-behavioral orientation tended to assign homework activities that involved a specific recording component and tended to follow Shelton and Levy's (1981b) recommendations for assigning homework more consistently than their counterparts.

Encouraged by the results of our first survey among psychologists, we conducted our second survey with a broader sample of mental health professionals (Kazantzis, Busch, Ronan, & Merrick, 2005). Our study included medical professionals (7% psychiatrist or physician), nurses (5%), social workers (12%), psychologists (29%), and counselors (52%). The nonrandomized and modest sample ($N = 330$) represent limitations to this study, but it was noteworthy that 83% reported the use of between-session homework assignments in their practice of psychotherapy. It was also interesting that regardless of professional training and background, those who were cognitive-behavioral in theoretical approach used homework more often and more "systematically" according to Shelton and Levy's criteria. As we outlined in the report (Kazantzis et al., 2004), Shelton and Levy's model is primarily concerned with attaining a degree of behavioral specificity in assigning homework and misses important aspects of the process of integrating homework into therapy. In addition to the modest sample sizes, these two preliminary surveys also had limited generalizability, because New Zealand's university-based training programs and practitioners generally adopt a cognitive behavioral approach to research and practice (see Kazantzis & Deane, 1998).

Emerging data suggest that practitioner beliefs are linked with particular aspects of clinical practice (e.g., Addis & Krasnow, 2000), and there is greater awareness of the influence of therapist attitudes in training and supervision in cognitive behavioral therapy (e.g., J. Beck, 1995; Padesky, 1999). Therefore we decided to expand on these earlier contributions to the literature by surveying therapist attitudes to homework assignments in Germany and North America.

Our third survey obtained data on psychologists' attitudes to homework assignments in Germany ($N = 140$), with a particular focus on attitudes to homework's impact on therapy process and outcome (Fehm & Kazantzis, 2004). In terms of attitudes on therapy process, cognitive behavioral practitioners rated greater agreement with the suggestion that therapists and clients should design homework together and that therapists should take some of the responsibility to encourage clients to do homework. Conversely, psychoanalytic practitioners considered the process of using homework as requiring more creativity than did cognitive behavioral practitioners. In terms of attitudes on therapy outcome, psychoanalytic practitioners were more likely to agree that there is a lack of empirical support for homework and that assignments are not necessary for every patient. On the other hand, cognitive behavioral practitioners were significantly more likely to agree with the assertions that homework is indispensable, enhances outcomes, is related to practitioners' success, and facilitates behavioral change. In the main, practitioners employed in university settings considered homework to be indispensable, related to therapists' success, and necessary for behavioral change.

Consistent with our previous findings, the Fehm and Kazantzis (2004) survey found that the majority of German practitioners surveyed used homework with at least half of their clients. A sizable minority (37%) reported using homework for all their clients, 26% reported use for two thirds, and 13% reported use for half their clients. The study also found that psychoanalytic practitioners generally used less homework and assigned a more restricted range of homework activities than cognitive behavioral practitioners.

Our fourth survey was a randomized survey of 3,000 American Psychological Association (APA) members' attitudes toward homework assignments (Kazantzis, Lampropoulos, & Deane, in press). The 28% response rate was similar to prior studies (i.e., Addis & Krasnow, 2000) and yielded a sample of 827 that was highly consistent in demographic characteristics to the overall APA membership. The data showed that most practicing psychologists use between-session homework assignments in their practice of therapy, with 77% indicating that they assigned one between-session assignment per therapy session, and 68% reporting that they "often" or "almost always" use between-session assignments. In this sample, psychologists identifying themselves as cognitive behavioral in orientation reported using more homework assignments, being more committed, and giving more thought to the therapeutic use of time between sessions compared to practitioners from other orientations.

In terms of attitudes to homework assignments, we constructed a questionnaire that asked psychologists to rate their degree of agreement to a series of 17 statements, such as *"Between-session activities enhance therapy by facilitating the acquisition of clients' adaptive skills in everyday situations," "Between-session activities reinforce the notion that clients are responsible for their own progress in psychotherapy," "Regardless of their utility, between-session activities place unrealistic expectations on clients,"* and *"Using between-session activities overemphasizes a therapist-prescriptive and directive approach to therapy."* Findings indicated that practicing psychologists have a range of attitudes regarding the use of homework assignments in psychotherapy that reflect beliefs centering on the themes regarding the influence on therapy process (i.e., *"Homework assignments have a negative impact on therapy process"*), and effects on therapy outcome (i.e., *"Homework assignments enhance therapy outcome"*). Consistent with our prior research, we found that cognitive behavioral practitioners reported more positive attitudes. Psychodynamic/analytic practitioners reported fewer positive attitudes to the effects of homework assignments on process and outcome, with mean scores on these factors close to the "neutral" option on the response scale.

In summary, there have been a number of practitioner surveys in several countries to support the assertion that homework assignments are often used in clinical practice. As might be expected, one consistent finding has been that cognitive behavioral therapists use homework assignments more frequently and assign more specific homework activities. Cognitive behavioral therapists also report more positive attitudes to homework in its role in therapy process and its subsequent effects on treatment outcome.

The Process of Integrating Homework Into Therapy

We have illustrated that there are strong links between homework assignments and treatment outcome, and that homework assignments are frequently used among cognitive behavioral therapy practitioners. In this section, we provide an overview of research studies designed to examine aspects of therapy process in the prediction of homework compliance. We do not aim to provide a comprehensive review of all published research in this section and have chosen to focus on key articles appearing after the publication of Beck, Rush, Shaw, and Emery's (1979) seminal text *Cognitive Therapy for Depression*.

Client, Therapist, and Other Factors

A relatively small collection of studies have attempted to link client factors to homework compliance. It is possible that clients who are more distressed have a greater need to gain control over the problems in their lives and therefore are more willing to engage in homework assignments that promise clear benefits. Consequently, some studies have sought to examine the link between client symptom severity and compliance with homework activities. For example, client symptom severity was linked with compliance in the cognitive behavioral therapy for 56 clients with social phobia (Edelman & Chambless, 1993), but this association was not replicated in a study involving 52 clients with agoraphobia (Edelman & Chambless, 1995). In a study of cognitive behavioral therapy for depression, Burns and Spangler (2000) were also unable to substantiate a link between symptom severity and client compliance with homework ($N = 521$). Thus, there is an inconsistency in the findings concerning the role of symptom severity.

Separate from symptom severity, a range of other client factors have been explored as possible correlates of compliance with homework assignments.

For instance, one study explored pretreatment expectations among 307 clients receiving private practice cognitive behavioral therapy, but it was unable to demonstrate an association with homework compliance (Burns & Nolen-Hoeksema, 1991). A second study showed a link between early compliance with homework and later homework compliance in the treatment of social phobia (Leung & Heimberg, 1996, $N = 104$). Early and midtreatment compliance with homework assignments has also been shown to be associated with acceptance of the treatment rationale (Addis & Jacobson, 2000, $N = 150$; Fennell & Teasdale, 1987, $N = 34$). Older clients who were unemployed exhibited greater learning and "quality" of homework compliance (Schmidt & Woolaway-Bickel, 2000, $N = 48$), but much like the other studies in this section, the research was conducted in an exploratory fashion and many of the findings have yet to be replicated.

As discussed in Chapter 2, a client's decision to apply a homework assignment is based on the perceived benefits of the task for the presenting problem as well as her beliefs about the task and her ability to undertake the activity. Situational factors such as emotional, physiological, and cognitive symptoms may serve as triggers for clients, persuading them that the application of a particular activity or skill will be helpful. Taken together, we suggest that a direct correlation between client factors such as symptom severity, either assessed at intake or throughout therapy, is likely to be missing a range of important underlying theoretical factors that determine whether a client is likely to engage in a homework assignment.

In an attempt to pursue conceptually driven research, three psychotherapy process studies have examined aspects of the process of *designing* and *assigning* between-session homework activities. Conoley, Padula, Payton, and Daniels (1994) evaluated the process of assigning homework through an analysis of videotaped counseling sessions. Conoley et al. were particularly interested in the extent to which clients found the homework assignments to be acceptable. Together with a follow-up study (Scheel, Hoggan, Willie, McDonald, & Tonin, 1998), these findings suggested that client beliefs about (a) the benefits of the assignment and client's presenting problems, (b) the difficulty and costs of the activity (i.e., time, effort, complexity), (c) building on client's existing skills (i.e., shape, generalize, or maintain behavior), and (d) the degree of social influence or "encouragement" from the therapist all influenced acceptability.

A similar study surveyed 31 session transcripts to examine the therapist behaviors associated with client commitment to carry out between-session homework activities (Mahrer, Gagnon, Fiarweather, Boulet, & Herring, 1994). Although there was a high degree of diversity in the therapeutic approaches adopted by therapists, the results revealed that several aspects of therapy process were associated with client commitment: (a) therapist follow-up of a client-initiated idea, (b) discussion of the client's willingness and readiness to carry out a task, (c) defining the task in a specific and concrete manner, (d) therapist encouragement, (e) in-session practice of activity, and (f) seeking a "contractual" commitment from the client. Although conducted within a broad theoretical context, the Mahrer et al. and previous studies (Conoley et al. 1994; Scheel et al., 1998) offer preliminary support for the underlying theoretical foundations in designing and assigning homework outlined in Chapter 2.

A limited number of studies have sought to examine the interaction between client and therapist factors as predictors of client homework compliance. Worthington (1986) conducted an exploratory study of 61 clients of a career counseling service in the interests of identifying predictors of compliance with homework assignments. Involving clients in homework assignments early in therapy, some prior history of homework compliance, and whether the therapist checked the client's attitude to homework were the only predictors of compliance.

Startup and Edmonds (1994) aimed to identify a number of therapist behaviors in predicting homework compliance among 25 clients over 235 sessions of cognitive behavioral therapy for depression. Although there was a link between compliance and outcome, contrary to expectation, collaboration, clarity of explanation, and the use of a cogent rationale did not emerge as predictors of homework compliance.

Some studies have focused more exclusively on therapist behaviors. Bryant, Simons, and Thase (1999) utilized the archived videotaped dataset from the National Institute of Mental Health Treatment of Depression Collaborative Project (Elkin, Parloff, Hadley, & Autry, 1985) to examine the therapist behaviors that predict compliance with homework in cognitive behavioral therapy for depression ($N = 26$). Bryant et al. revised the ratings of therapist competence in administrating homework assignments on the Cognitive Therapy Scale (Young & Beck, 1980) and used independent observers' ratings to show that therapist review of homework assignments was positively related to homework compliance.

Cox, Tisdelle, and Culbert (1988) conducted a randomized trial contrasting written versus verbally administered homework assignments for 30 clients at a behavioral medicine clinic. The study demonstrated significantly improved rates of client compliance among those receiving written copies of the assigned homework activity.

In summary, there have been a handful of psychotherapy process studies evaluating the factors associated with client compliance with homework assignments. Many of the studies have been exploratory and not designed to examine the underlying theoretical foundations for homework. Most were conducted within a particular approach to psychotherapy or have yet to be replicated with larger samples. However, the studies do provide useful preliminary information about the process factors associated with compliance, and it is noteworthy that findings to date are largely supportive of the theoretical foundations outlined in Chapter 2.

Three of the studies illustrated that early client compliance with homework is associated with later compliance and acceptance of the treatment rationale in cognitive therapy. A series of studies from the counseling literature have supported several of the theoretical foundations for the use of homework in therapy, including ensuring that the client's beliefs (i.e., benefits of task, difficulty, costs of the activity) are discussed as part of *designing* and *assigning* homework. Therapist encouragement, checking the client's attitude, enabling in-session practice, recommending homework assignments that build on client strengths and existing skills, seeking a contractual agreement, and providing specific, concrete, written summaries of the homework task have all shown promise in enhancing client compliance. In terms of *reviewing* homework, therapists' competence in reviewing homework assignments has emerged as a predictor of compliance.

We suggest that future research attempting to unravel the mechanism by which homework produces its effects could pursue research questions that are more theoretically driven. The existing research has been conducted in a piecemeal fashion, and with the exception of the studies from counseling psychology, most studies have examined one or two isolated factors in an attempt to predict homework compliance. It is also interesting that no research has sought to examine more specifically the interaction between client and therapist factors in the prediction of homework compliance, the therapeutic relationship, or extent to which the process of integrating homework can be adjusted based on the cognitive conceptualization for the client. We hope that the theoretical foundations outlined in Chapter 2 will serve as a useful starting point for more conceptually driven research efforts.

Empirical Foundations for Specific Populations and Problems

The previous sections of this Chapter have discussed the links between homework assignments and treatment outcome, reviewed the literature on the use of homework in clinical practice, and considered the correlates of homework compliance. In this section, we provide a brief overview of the empirical research on the specific populations and problems discussed in Parts II and III of this book. In some instances, we have selected four or five examples of empirical articles for each clinical population. In instances where less research has been conducted, we were able to review all the research that was available at the time of writing this Chapter.

Children

We were unable to locate any empirical studies that offer direct support for the use of homework assignments in cognitive behavioral therapy for children. However, therapy for children often involves reading self-help information relevant to therapy, and therefore represents a specific type of homework or "bibliotherapy" assignment.

One recent study compared the effectiveness of group-administered cognitive behavioral therapy with a self-help intervention for pediatric headache (Kroener-Herwig & Denecke, 2002). This study randomly assigned 77 youth aged 10 to 14 years to treatment conditions and a waiting list control. The cognitive behavioral therapy intervention consisted of 8 sessions of 90 minutes each, and self-help was administered via manualized procedures that consisted of giving instructions on how to carry out tasks at home. Both interventions produced significant change compared to the waiting list, but results did not differ between the two treatment conditions. In addition, from posttreatment to follow-up, continuing changes occurred, with around 70% reporting clinically significant change in headaches. These positive results are consistent with the assertion that homework alone can be sufficient to bring about meaningful changes in symptoms, but the support for homework is still indirect in these studies (see also Ackerson, Scogin, McKendree-Smith, & Lyman, 1998; Rapee, Abbott, & Gaston, 2001).

In Chapter 5, Jennifer Hudson and Philip Kendall extend these indirect research findings by discussing the role of self-help and other homework assignments in cognitive behavioral therapy for children.

We were also unable to locate empirical studies of therapy process for adolescents and clients with borderline personality disorder. In Chapter 6, Robert Friedberg and Jessica McClure share their clinical experience in a discussion of the use of homework assignments in cognitive behavioral therapy for adolescents.

Older Adults

There has been a surge of research directed toward the formulation and evaluation of cognitive behavioral therapies for older adults. This evidence has emerged in the treatment of anxiety and depression among older adults (e.g., Gallagher-Thompson & Steffen, 1994; Wetherell, Gatz, & Craske, 2003), as well as in the treatment of family caregiver distress (e.g., Coon, Gallagher-Thompson, & Thompson, 2003). As with many of the other clinical populations discussed in this section, there is only beginning evidence to link homework with treatment outcome for older adults.

Two studies by the research team including Dolores Gallagher-Thompson, Larry Thompson, and David Coon have demonstrated that the association between homework compliance and treatment holds for depressed older adults. These studies have demonstrated that older adults' ratings of the utility of homework were related to the extent to which they benefited from therapy (Thompson & Gallagher-Thompson, 1984), and that those older adults who completed more homework assignments received more benefits from therapy (Coon & Thompson, 2003). In Chapter 7, this research team shares their clinical experiences in discussing the role of homework assignments in cognitive behavioral therapy for older adults.

Couples

Cognitive behavioral therapy for couples is well established (Dattilio & Bevilacqua, 2000; Dattilio & Padesky, 1990), but there is little empirical work on how homework assignments may contribute to its effectiveness. Aside from the work with substance abuse populations outlined earlier in this Chapter, there is very little empirical work linking homework with treatment outcome.

Holtzworth-Munroe, Jacobson, DeKlyen, and Whisman (1989) examined the predictors of treatment outcome among 32 couples receiving behavioral marital therapy. After controlling for pretreatment symptom severity, therapist ratings of homework compliance predicted therapeutic improvement assessed posttreatment. The data showed that client ratings corroborated the homework compliance–outcome link in this study, as those who described having experienced more gains were also more compliant with homework.

Davidson and Horvath (1997) developed a homework rating scale to gather information on 32 couples' completion of homework assignments in brief couples therapy. The results showed that 73% of couples complied with the homework between the first and second sessions, but this rate declined to 35% compliance between the second and third sessions. While the overall rate of homework compliance was quite similar for those couples who benefited from therapy and those who did not benefit, homework compliance was a significant predictor of treatment outcome after pretherapy variables had been controlled.

In Chapter 8, Frank Dattilio describes his approach to using homework assignments in cognitive behavioral therapy for couples and presents several detailed case studies.

Families

While family therapy is able to draw on empirically supported models and therapies for the treatment of family members, we could not find specific empirical support for the use of homework. This subsection provides an example of the preliminary research in the context of multiple family group therapy.

Multiple family groups draw heavily from the family treatment approaches of Anderson, Hogarty, and Reiss (1980) and Falloon (1988), and usually involve six to eight families engaged in biweekly meetings focusing on formal problem solving. Multiple family groups also involve families in the completion of graded homework assignments (McFarlane, Gingerich, Deakins, Dunne, Horen, & Newmark, 2002).

A recent study of the role of homework in multiple family group therapy for people with schizophrenia obtained data to suggest that there was little agreement between family and therapist ratings of homework compliance (Talyekhan, Deane, Lambert & Pickard, 2003). There was also considerable variation in homework ratings among family members, though family compliance ratings were correlated with perceived *mastery* (i.e., how much the homework helped them gain control over their problems) and ratings of *progress* from having completed the assignment (i.e., how much the homework helped them progress in therapy). In contrast, clinician ratings of *compliance* were associated only with family ratings of *obstacles* to homework completion.

Talyekhan et al. (2003) concluded that individuals within a family may have quite different views on how much and how well homework was completed. At a minimum, the results underscore the value in providing each family member the opportunity to comment on how well the homework was completed and any ensuing problems with carrying it out.

The question of whether the findings of Talyekhan et al. (2003) can be translated into cognitive behavioral family therapy remains an empirical one. However, it is interesting that their study showed homework compliance to be positively correlated with ratings of mastery and progress. This link between compliance and client reflection of the consequence of engaging in the homework activity supports the theoretical proposition that clients synthesize their homework experiences and form beliefs about the task and progress (see Chapter 2).

In Chapter 9, Frank Dattilio discusses the use of homework assignments in cognitive behavioral family therapy with Luciano L'Abate, and Frank Deane. The detailed case study provides the beginning step in the process toward conducting empirical work on homework assignments for this population.

In summary, there is beginning research to demonstrate the link between homework and treatment outcome in cognitive behavioral therapy for a range of clinical problems and populations. However, research here is in its infancy. We suggest that it would be useful to have further research to examine the extent to which the use of homework assignments, and choice of different homework activities, are effective for particular client problems and populations. We also suggest that it would be helpful to identify further therapist behaviors that enhance homework effects.

Panic, Agoraphobia, and Generalized Anxiety

Five recent studies have examined the role of homework in the treatment of panic disorder (i.e., Lampropoulos & Rector, 2004; Park et al., 2001; Schmidt & Woolaway-Bickel, 2000; Westling & Ost, 1999; Woods, Chambless, & Steketee, 2002), but we were able to locate only one recent study that assessed the role of homework assignments in the treatment of generalized anxiety disorder (i.e., Wetherell, 2002).

Lampropoulos and Rector (2004) assessed the relationship between *quantity* (i.e., time spent on homework) and *quality* (i.e., degree of learning) with outcome in 22 patients who received cognitive behavioral therapy for panic disorder (with or without agoraphobia), and 30 patients with social phobia. After controlling for pretreatment severity, the study was unable to demonstrate that therapist ratings of quantity and quality of homework completion predicted treatment outcome. In addition, pretreatment severity and patient demographic characteristics (i.e., age, gender, diagnosis) were not associated with homework compliance. As the authors point out, the small sample size and high levels of patient compliance were likely limitations to the study.

Similarly, Schmidt and Woolaway-Bickel (2000) assessed the relationship between *quantity* and *quality* of homework compliance and treatment outcome in 48 patients who participated in a 12-session cognitive behavioral therapy protocol for panic disorder. In terms of homework quantity, they found that clinician ratings of homework compliance were predictive of outcome in four of nine measures (i.e., medium-sized relationships, with standardized beta weights ranging from 0.30 to 0.50). However, client ratings of homework quantity were generally not predictive of outcome. In terms of homework quality, therapist ratings were predictive of outcome in seven of nine measures (medium-sized relationships, with standardized beta weights between 0.31 and 0.51) after controlling for pretreatment severity and other demographic variables. Therapist ratings of homework quality were better predictors of outcome than therapist ratings of homework quantity.

Woods et al. (2002) assessed the relationship of homework compliance to the outcome of behavioral therapy (in vivo exposure) for 35 outpatients with panic disorder with agoraphobia and 47 patients with obsessive-compulsive disorder. Quantity ratings of homework compliance (total number of assignments completed and time spent on homework) did not predict outcome. Quality ratings of homework compliance (average change in client distress per homework exposure assignment) had only one small but negative effect ($\beta = -.25$) on one of two outcome measures (residual change target symptom ratings). This result was surprising insofar as it suggested higher quality of homework is a negative predictor of outcome in behavioral therapy. Overall, the results of this study indicated that the quality and quantity of homework were not predictive of treatment outcome.

The two remaining studies examined the role of homework in treatment outcome either as a secondary research question (Park et al., 2001) or indirectly (Westling & Ost, 1999). Park et al. (2001) studied the effect of self-exposure homework compliance to the outcome of exposure therapy for a mixed sample of 16 clients with agoraphobia, 22 clients with social phobia, and 30 clients with specific phobias. Patients were categorized as either compliant (defined as completing more than 85% of homework exposures assigned during the first eight weeks of treatment) or as noncompliant (defined as completing less than 50% of assigned exposures). They found that the 15 homework-compliant patients had a significantly larger improvement on fear and avoidance compared to the 12 noncompliant patients at both 26-week and 2-year posttreatment follow-ups.

Westling and Ost (1999) conducted a pilot study of a shortened version of cognitive behavioral therapy for ten patients with panic disorder (with or without mild agoraphobia). The study found that a four-session therapy format with significantly more homework compared to the regular treatment was effective in treating panic disorder across all outcome measures posttreatment and at a 6-month follow-up. Although Westling and Ost did not directly test homework effects, their findings provided some indirect support for the importance of homework on the outcome of cognitive behavioral therapy for panic disorder.

The only recent empirical findings on homework in cognitive behavioral therapy for generalized anxiety has come from a randomized controlled trial contrasting cognitive behavioral therapy and other treatments for older adults (Wetherell, 2002). Homework use was examined only as a secondary question in this study, which found that treatment responders in the cognitive behavioral therapy condition completed more homework than nonresponders.

In Chapter 10, Robert Leahy outlines his approach to the use of homework assignments in cognitive behavioral therapy for panic disorder, agoraphobia, and generalized anxiety. As with all the Chapters in Parts II and III of this book, the clinical recommendations for using homework with anxiety are illustrated with detailed case studies.

Obsessions and Compulsions

Only three recent studies (i.e., Abramowitz, Franklin, Zoellner, & DiBernardo, 2002; De Araujo, Ito, & Marks, 1995; Woods et al., 2002) have examined the role of homework in therapy for obsessions and compulsions. Of these, the findings of the study by Woods et al. (2002) of a mixed sample of obsessions and compulsions and panic disorder have been described earlier in this Chapter. It should also be noted that our analysis of the data for obsessions and compulsions has been conducted in the context of behaviorally focused therapy.

De Araujo et al. (1995) examined the predictors of treatment outcome for 46 clients with obsessive-compulsive disorder. Consistent with research with other clinical populations, they found that the best predictor of outcome was therapist-rated compliance with homework exposure (percentage of completed homework) in the first week of treatment. These findings were found on two of three outcome measures at posttreatment and at a follow-up. Lower symptom severity, less rigidity in beliefs, and a younger age predicted homework compliance at the first week of treatment.

Abramowitz et al. (2002) studied the effects of homework compliance on the outcome of exposure and ritual prevention for 28 clients with obsessive-compulsive disorder. Within the context of several measures of treatment compliance (i.e., understanding of the treatment rationale and compliance with in-session exposure), therapists rated clients' homework compliance (i.e., compliance with between-session exposure and compliance self-monitoring of rituals). Controlling for pretreatment severity, compliance with homework exposure (but not with self-monitoring of rituals) was strongly correlated with treatment outcome. However, these findings may have been confounded by the retrospective nature of homework compliance ratings. It is also worth noting that pretreatment severity, comorbidity, frequency of sessions, and medication use did not predict homework compliance.

In Chapter 11, the team from the University of Pennsylvania School of Medicine discusses the use of homework assignments in cognitive behavioral therapy for anxiety. Martin Franklin, Jonathan Huppert, and Deborah Roth extend their research contributions in discussing the process of integrating homework for this population.

Depression

There has been more research on the role of homework assignments in cognitive behavioral therapy for depression than for any other clinical problem. At least three studies have sought to examine whether homework can enhance treatment outcome in behavioral and cognitive behavioral therapy. Harmon, Nelson, and Hayes (1980) contrasted therapy with and without homework for a small group of clients ($N = 8$) and illustrated a clinically significant homework enhancement effect. Conversely, Kornblith, Rehm, O'Hara, and Lamparski (1983) assigned 49 depressed clients to four therapy conditions and showed no advantage for those conditions involving between-session homework assignments. However, Kornblith et al. found that clients in the no-homework conditions decided to practice therapeutic activities of their own accord, and it is likely that this client-initiated between-session activity confounded the study. Zettle and Haynes (1987) assigned a small sample ($N = 12$) to a therapy condition involving behavioral homework and a therapy condition involving no-homework, but they were unable to detect any effects. At face value, these studies do not provide clear support for the additional benefits of using homework assignments in the treatment of depression. However, as previously discussed, these studies were conducted with very small sample sizes and low statistical power (or design sensitivity) to detect homework effects.

Several studies have demonstrated the link between homework compliance and treatment outcome in cognitive behavioral therapies for depression. This relationship was demonstrated in both group (Neimeyer & Feixas, 1990, $N = 63$) and individual therapy formats (Addis & Jacobson, 2000, $N = 48$; Burns & Nolen-Hoeksema, 1991, 1992, $N = 125$ and 185; Persons, Burns, & Perloff, 1988, $N = 70$; Startup & Edmonds, 1994, $N = 25$). In extending and reanalyzing an existing private practice dataset, Burns and Spangler (2000) used structural equation modeling to demonstrate that the relationship between compliance and outcome was consistent with the hypothesis that homework compliance leads to improved outcomes in cognitive behavioral therapy for depression (see also Kazantzis, Ronan, & Deane, 2001).

In Chapter 12, Jan Scott and Anne Garland present an overview of the process in using homework assignments in cognitive behavioral therapy for depression. In doing so, they extend beyond the empirical foundations outlined in this Chapter.

Substance Abuse

Although homework is a core component of most treatments for substance abuse disorders, there are relatively few studies that have specifically investigated the role of homework on treatment outcomes. Instead, homework has been generally considered a part of the overall treatment package. Consistent with other aspects of the literature in this section, our selected review provides examples of the work that has been conducted and highlights the need for further research.

McCrady et al., (1986) randomly assigned 53 clients with alcohol-related disorders (and their spouses) to one of three outpatient behavioral treatments. Homework assignments were assigned for the clients and their spouse on a weekly basis. Although there were differences in homework compliance between treatment conditions, this was not explored further in the study.

Epstein et al. (1994) examined attrition in 90 couples in the marital treatment of alcohol-related disorders. Therapists recorded homework compliance, and the percentage of completed homework was calculated for the first four sessions attended (some couples attended fewer than four sessions). There were significant differences in the percentage of home-work assignments completed between (a) early treatment dropouts (30%), (b) partial completers (71%), and (c) completers (77%). Stepwise discrim-inant analysis further revealed that percentage of homework completed was the most influential variable ($R^2 = .30$), followed by clinical experience ($R^2 = .07$) in predicting attrition (i.e., lower homework completion leading to increased attrition). A subsequent analysis of the Epstein et al. (1994) study focused on 68 couples who completed five or more treatment sessions (McCrady et al., 1996). Although there were no significant differ-ences in the percentage homework completed in the conditions of the study (66% versus 77%), spouses involved in conditions that had unique homework elements completed significantly more homework (81%) than those in other conditions (60% and 70%), and were more likely to complete homework assignments as part of relapse prevention (68%) as compared to others (37%).

This series of studies is helpful in understanding the role of homework in the treatment of substance abuse problems. Taken together, they suggest that clients, spouses of clients, and married couples are likely to demon-strate variable homework compliance, and low compliance with home-work in early treatment may predict attrition and other indicators of commitment to therapy. However, these studies have been limited by their focus on a small number of clients with alcohol-related disorders and a restricted emphasis on homework *compliance* rather than the learning of adaptive skills. Moreover, the studies sought to examine the correlation between homework compliance and treatment outcome and did not examine other factors that are conceptually important in this process.

In Chapter 13, Lisa Najavits describes the use of homework assignments in cognitive behavioral therapy for substance abuse. The clinical illustrations of substance abuse are effective in extending the empirical foundations outlined in this Chapter.

Delusions and Hallucinations

There has been considerable interest in applications of cognitive behavioral therapy for delusions and hallucinations (e.g., Beck & Rector, 2002; Byrne, Trower, Birchwood, Meaden, & Nelson, 2003). Although the use of homework assignments rests on firm theoretical foundations, there is only emerging empirical support for the overall approach for psychotic populations and few data on the role of homework assignments (Glaser, Kazantzis, Deane, & Oades, 2000).

Bailer, Takats, and Schmitt (2002) examined the predictors of outcome for 39 outpatients who received 24 sessions of cognitive behavioral therapy in addition to the their routine treatment. Bailer et al. reported that the strongest predictor of treatment response was consistent homework compliance throughout the course of treatment.

Dunn, Morrison, and Bentall (2002) presented a qualitative study of clients' experience of homework assignments in cognitive behavioral therapy for psychotic symptoms. The study was not designed to examine the relationship between homework compliance and treatment outcome, but clients who had completed more homework assignments were found to demonstrate greater understanding of the application of adaptive skills.

In Chapter 14, Hamish McLeod and Hazel Nelson describe their approach to using homework assignments in cognitive behavioral therapy for delusions and hallucinations. They draw on the existing literature and their experiences in practice to present a cogent account of the process of homework for this population.

Sexual Problems

Homework assignments have historically been the main feature in the treatment of sexual dysfunction for individual and couple therapy formats. Descriptions of the role of between-session activities for sexual dysfunction continue to be published (e.g., Charlton & Yalom, 1997; Whitman & Boyd, 2003) and explained in case studies in the literature (e.g., J. G. Beck, 1995).

However, despite its use in practice, there is relatively little empirical support for the use of homework assignments in the treatment of sexual problems. Hawton and Catalan (1990) showed that early compliance with homework assignments (by the time of the third treatment session) was an important predictor of outcome in 30 couples' sex therapy. The researchers replicated this finding in showing that early homework compliance was one of the predictors of outcome for 36 couples' sex therapy prompted by the male partner's erectile dysfunction. These findings are promising, but it would be helpful to gather data to extend these findings for other sexual problems.

In Chapter 15, Nancy Pachana and Kate Sofronoff discuss the clinical application of homework assignments in cognitive behavioral therapy for sexual dysfunction. They utilize examples from their experience in working with couples and older adults to illustrate their recommendations.

In Chapter 16, Arthur Freeman and Gina Fusco present a compelling case for the use of homework assignments in cognitive behavioral therapy for borderline personality disorder.

Synthesis and Summary

Our aim in writing this Chapter was to provide the reader with an overview of the empirical foundations for using homework assignments in cognitive behavioral therapy. We first discussed the research designed to link homework to treatment outcome and concluded that there is now sufficient evidence to suggest that homework assignments produce a distinct and measurable effect in cognitive behavioral therapy.

In the second section, we reviewed the literature aiming to determine the use of homework assignments. Surveys of published treatment outcome studies have shown that homework assignments are frequently incorporated into treatment protocols. Studies that surveyed clinical practice have consistently demonstrated that the use of homework assignments is high among practitioners of cognitive behavioral therapy, and that they show a greater commitment, a greater degree of specificity in assigning homework, and more positive attitudes in comparison to practitioners from other therapeutic orientatons.

In the third section, we reviewed the correlates of homework compliance in therapy. There is emerging support for the role of client factors (i.e., clients' beliefs about benefits of task, difficulty, costs of the activity) and therapist factors in *designing* and *assigning* homework (i.e., degree of encouragement, check of client attitude, facilitation of in-session practice, ability to build on client strengths, and specific, concrete, and written summaries) as well as in reviewing homework (i.e., therapists' competence in reviewing homework). Although the existing data provide some preliminary support, further research is required to examine whether the theoretical foundations for homework can be extended to the context of cognitive behavioral therapy. We also concluded that there is now a need for more conceptually driven research that extends beyond correlational relationships between homework compliance and singular aspects of therapy process. Such research is necessary for the evaluation of the theoretical foundations that underpin homework's role in therapy.

In the fourth section, we provided examples of the existing research on homework assignments within the range of clinical populations discussed in detail in Parts II and III of this book. Although the existing data are generally supportive of homework's utility in the treatment of the range of clinical presentations and populations, the fact remains that it would be helpful to have empirical support to guide the process by which it can be integrated into therapy. In the interests of contributing to this literature, the next step in our own *Cognitive Behavior Therapy Homework Project* will be to conduct process outcome research to examine the theoretical foundations that determine client completion and learning through homework assignments.

To date, the majority of the research examining homework assignments in therapy has focused on client "compliance" with homework assignments. We suggest that compliance may not be the most useful operationalization of client learning and acquisition of adaptive skills in cognitive behavioral therapy. In Chapter 4, we present an alternative conception of client completion of homework assignments, drawing on the theoretical foundations outlined in Chapter 2.

References

Abramowitz, J. S., Franklin, M. E., Zoellner, L. A., & DiBernardo, C. L. (2002). Treatment compliance and outcome in obsessive-compulsive disorder. *Behavior Modification, 26*, 447–463.

Ackerson, J., Scogin, F., McKendree-Smith, N., & Lyman, R. D. (1998). Cognitive bibliotherapy for mild and moderate adolescent depressive symptomatology. *Journal of Consulting and Clinical Psychology, 66*, 685–690.

Addis, M. E., & Jacobson, N. S. (2000). A closer look at the treatment rationale and homework compliance in cognitive behavioral therapy for depression. *Cognitive Therapy and Research, 24*, 313–326.

Addis, M. E., & Krasnow, A. D. (2000). A national survey of practicing psychologists' attitude towards psychotherapy treatment manuals. *Journal of Consulting and Clinical Psychology, 68*, 331–339.

Anderson, C. M., Hogarty, G., & Reiss, D. J. (1980). Family treatment of adult schizophrenic patients: A psychoeducational approach. *Schizophrenia Bulletin, 6*, 490–505.

Bailer, J., Takats, I., & Schmitt, A. (2002). Individualized cognitive-behavioral therapy for schizophrenic patients with negative symptoms and social disabilities: II. Responder analysis and predictors of treatment response. *Verhaltenstherapie, 12*, 192–203.

Beck, A. T. (1976). *Cognitive therapy and the emotional disorders.* New York: International Universities Press.

Beck, A. T., & Rector, N. A. (2002). Delusions: A cognitive perspective. *Journal of Cognitive Psychotherapy: An International Quarterly, 16*, 455–468.

Beck, A. T., Rush, J. A., Shaw, B. F., & Emery, G. (1979). *Cognitive therapy of depression.* New York: Guilford Press.

Beck, J. (1995). *Cognitive therapy: Basics and beyond.* New York: Guilford Press.

Beck, J. G. (1995). What's love got to do with it?: The interplay between low and excessive desire disorders. In R. C. Rosen & S. R. Leiblum (Eds.), *Case studies in sex therapy* (pp. 46–64). New York: Guilford Press.

Blackburn, I. M., & Twaddle, V. (1996). *Cognitive therapy in action: A practitioner's casebook.* London: Souvenir.

Blanchard, E. B., Nicholson, N. L., Taylor, A. E., Steffek, B. D., Radnitz, C. L., & Appelbaum, K. A. (1991). The role of regular home practice in the relaxation treatment of tension headache. *Journal of Consulting and Clinical Psychology, 59,* 467–470.

Bryant, M. J., Simons, A. D., & Thase, M. E. (1999). Therapist skill and patient variables in home-work compliance: Controlling a uncontrolled variable in cognitive therapy outcome research. *Cognitive Therapy and Research, 23,* 381–399.

Burns, D. D., & Nolen-Hoeksema, S. (1991). Coping styles, homework compliance, and the effectiveness of cognitive behavioral therapy. *Journal of Consulting and Clinical Psychology, 59,* 305–311.

Burns, D. D., & Spangler, D. (2000). Does psychotherapy homework lead to changes in depression in cognitive behavioral therapy? Or does clinical improvement lead to homework compliance? *Journal of Consulting and Clinical Psychology, 68,* 46–56.

Byrne, S., Trower, P., Birchwood, M., Meaden, A., & Nelson, A. (2003). Command hallucinations: Cognitive theory, therapy, and research. *Journal of Cognitive Psychotherapy: An International Quarterly, 17,* 67–84.

Charlton, R. S., & Yalom, I. D. (1997). Couple therapy of sexual disorders. In S. Borrelli-Kerner & B. Bernell (Eds.), *Treating sexual disorders* (pp. 165–199). San Francisco, CA: Jossey-Bass.

Cohen, J. (1988). *Statistical power analysis for the behavioral sciences* (2nd ed.). Hillsdale, NJ: Erlbaum.

Conoley, C. W., Padula, M. A., Payton, D. S., & Daniels, J. A. (1994). Predictors of client implementation of counselor recommendations: Match with problem, difficulty level, and building on client strengths. *Journal of Counseling Psychology, 41,* 3–7.

Coon, D. W., Gallagher-Thompson, D., & Thompson, L. (Eds.). (2003). *Innovative interventions to reduce dementia caregiver distress: A clinical guide.* New York: Springer.

Coon, D. W. & Thompson, L. W. (2003). Association between homework compliance and treatment outcome among older adult outpatients with depression. *American Journal of Geriatric Psychiatry, 11,* 53–61.

Coon, D. W., Thompson, L. W., Steffen. A., Sorocco, K., & Gallagher-Thompson, D. (2003). Anger and depression management: Psychoeducational skill training interventions for women caregivers of a relative with dementia. *The Gerontologist, 43,* 678–689.

Cox, D. J., Tisdelle, D. A., & Culbert, J. P. (1988). Increasing adherence to behavioral homework assignments. *Journal of Behavioral Medicine, 11,* 519–522.

Dattilio, F. M., & Bevilacqua, L. J. (Eds.). (2000). *Comparative treatments for relationship dysfunction.* London: Free Association Books.

Dattilio, F. M., & Padesky, C. A. (1990). *Cognitive therapy with couples.* Sarasota, FL: Professional Resource Exchange.

Davidson, G. N. S., & Horvath, A. O. (1997). Three sessions of brief couples therapy: A clinical trial. *Journal of Family Psychology, 11,* 422–435.

De Araujo, L. A., Ito, L. M., Marks, I. M., & Deale, A. (1995). Does imagined exposure to the consequences of not ritualising enhance live exposure for OCD? A controlled study I. Main outcome. *British Journal of Psychiatry, 167,* 65–70.

Dunn, H., Morrison, A. P., & Bentall, R. P. (2002). Patients' experiences of homework tasks in cognitive behavioral therapy for psychosis: A qualitative analysis. *Clinical Psychology and Psychotherapy, 9,* 361–369.

Edelman, R. E., & Chambless, D. L. (1993). Compliance during sessions and homework in exposure-based treatment of agoraphobia. *Behaviour Research and Therapy, 31,* 767–773.

Edelman, R. E., & Chambless, D. L. (1995). Adherence during sessions and homework in cognitive-behavioral group treatment of social phobia. *Behaviour Research and Therapy, 33,* 573–577.

Elkin, I., Parloff, M. B., Hadley, S. W., & Autry, J. H. (1985). NIMH treatment of Depression Collaborative Research Program: Background and research plan. *Archives of General Psychiatry, 42,* 305–316.

Epstein, E. E., McCrady, B. S., Miller, K. J., & Steinberg, M. (1994). Attrition from conjoint alcoholism treatment: Do dropouts differ from completers? *Journal of Substance Abuse, 6,* 249–265.

Falloon, I. R. H. (Ed.). (1988). *The handbook of behavioral family therapy.* New York: Guilford.

Fehm, L., & Kazantzis, N. (2004). Attitudes and use of homework assignments in therapy: A survey of German psychotherapists. *Clinical Psychology & Psychotherapy, 11,* 332–343.

Fennell, M. J. V., & Teasdale, J. D. (1987). Cognitive therapy for depression: Individual differences and the process of change. *Cognitive Therapy and Research, 11,* 253–271.

Gallagher-Thompson, D., & Steffen, A. M. (1994). Comparative effects of cognitive behavioral and brief psychodynamic psychotherapies for depressed family caregivers. *Journal of Consulting and Clinical Psychology, 62,* 543–549.

Glaser, N. M., Kazantzis, N., Deane, F. P., & Oades, L. G. (2000). Critical issues in using homework assignments within cognitive-behavioral therapy for schizophrenia. *Journal of Rational-Emotive and Cognitive-Behavior Therapy, 18,* 247–261.

Harmon, T. M., Nelson, R. O., & Hayes, S. C. (1980). Self-monitoring of mood versus activity by depressed clients. *Journal of Counseling and Clinical Psychology, 48,* 30–38.

Hawton, K., & Catalan, J. (1990). Sex therapy for vaginismus: Characteristics of couples and treatment outcome. *Sexual and Marital Therapy, 5,* 39–48.

Holtzworth-Munroe, A., Jacobson, N. S., DeKlyen, M., & Whisman, M. A. (1989). Relationship between behavioral marital therapy outcome and process variables. *Journal of Consulting and Clinical Psychology, 57,* 658–662.

Kazantzis, N. (2000). Power to detect homework effects in psychotherapy outcome research. *Journal of Consulting and Clinical Psychology, 68,* 166–170.

Kazantzis, N., Busch, R., Ronan, K. R., & Merrick, P. L. (2005). Mental health practitioners' use and perceived importance of homework assignments in psychotherapy. Manuscript submitted for publication.

Kazantzis, N., & Deane, F. P. (1998). Theoretical orientations of New Zealand psychologists: An international comparison. *Journal of Psychotherapy Integration, 8,* 97–113.

Kazantzis, N., & Deane, F. P. (1999). Psychologists' use of homework assignments in clinical practice. *Professional Psychology: Research and Practice, 30,* 581–585.

Kazantzis, N., Deane, F. P., & Ronan, K. R. (2000). Homework assignments in cognitive and behavioral therapy: A meta-analysis. *Clinical Psychology: Science and Practice, 7,* 189–202.

Kazantzis, N., Lampropoulos, G. L., & Deane, F. P. (in press). A national survey of practicing psychologists' use and attitudes towards homework in psychotherapy. *Journal of Consulting and Clinical Psychology.*

Kazantzis, N., Ronan, K. R., & Deane, F. P. (2001). Concluding causation from correlation: Comment on Burns and Spangler (2000). *Journal of Consulting and Clinical Psychology, 69,* 1079–1083.

Kazdin, A. E., & Mascitelli, S. (1982). Covert and overt rehearsal and homework practice in developing assertiveness. *Journal of Consulting and Clinical Psychology, 50,* 250–258.

Kemmler, L., Borgart, E.-J., & Gärke, R. (1992). Der Einsatz von Hausaufgaben in der Psychotherapie. Eine Praktikerbefragung. *Report Psychologie, 9–18.*

Kornblith, S. J., Rehm, L. P., O'Hara, M. W., & Lamparski, D. M. (1983). The contribution of self-reinforcement training and behavioral assignments to the efficacy of self-control therapy for depression. *Cognitive Therapy and Research, 7,* 499–528.

Kroener-Herwig, B. & Denecke, H. (2002). Cognitive-behavioral therapy of pediatric headache: Are there differences in efficacy between a therapist-administered group training and a self-help format? *Journal of Psychosomatic Research, 53,* 1107–1114.

Lampropoulos, G. K., & Rector, N. A. (2004, June). Homework compliance in cognitive behavior therapy for anxiety disorders: Predictors of outcome. Poster presented at the 30th Annual Harvey Stancer Research Day, Department of Psychiatry, University of Toronto, Toronto.

Leung, A. W., & Heimberg, R. G. (1996). Homework compliance, perceptions of control, and outcome of cognitive-behavioral treatment of social phobia. *Behaviour Research and Therapy, 34,* 423–432.

Mahrer, A. R., Gagnon, R., Fiarweather, D. R., Boulet, D. B., & Herring, C. B. (1994). Client commitment and resolve to carry out postsession behaviors. *Journal of Counseling Psychology, 41,* 407–414.

Mahrer, A. R., Nordin, S., & Miller, L. S. (1995). If a client has this kind of problem, prescribe that kind of post-session behavior. *Psychotherapy, 32,* 194–203.

Marks, I. M., Lelliott, P., Basoglu, M., Noshirvani, H., Monteiro, W., Cohen, D., & Kasvikis, Y. (1988). Clomipramine, self-exposure, and therapist-aided exposure for obsessive-compulsive rituals. *British Journal of Psychiatry, 152,* 522–534.

McCrady, B. S., Noel, N. E., Abrams, D. B., Stout, R. L., Nelson, H. F., & Hay, W. M. (1986). Comparative effectiveness of three types of spouse involvement in outpatient behavioral alcoholism treatment. *Journal of Studies on Alcohol, 47,* 459–467.

McFarlane, W. R., Gingerich, S., Deakins, S. M., Dunne, E., Horen, B. T., & Newmark, M. (2002). Problem solving in multifamily groups. In W. R. McFarlane (Ed.). *Multifamily groups in the treatment of severe psychiatric disorders* (pp. 142–171). New York: Guilford Press.

Neimeyer, R. A., & Feixas, G. (1990). The role of homework and skill acquisition in the outcome of group cognitive therapy for depression. *Behavior Therapy, 21,* 281–292.

Norcross, J. C., Hedges, M., & Prochaska, J. O. (2002). The face of 2010: A Delphi poll on the future of psychotherapy. *Professional Psychology: Research and Practice, 33,* 316–322.

Padesky, C. A. (1999). *Therapist beliefs: Protocols, personalities, and guided exercises* (Cassette Recording No. TB1). Huntington Beach, CA: Center for Cognitive Therapy.

Park, J. M., Mataix-Cols, D., Marks, I. M., Ngamthipwatthana, T., Marks, M., Araya, R., Al-Kubaisy, T. (2001). Two-year follow-up after a randomized controlled trial of self- and clinician-accompanied exposure for phobia/panic disorders. *British Journal of Psychiatry, 178,* 543–548.

Persons, J. B., Burns, D. D., & Perloff, J. M. (1988). Predictors of dropout and outcome in cognitive therapy for depression in a private practice setting. *Cognitive Therapy and Research, 12,* 557–575.

Rapee, R. M., Abbott, M., & Gaston, J. (2001, July). Bibliotherapy in the treatment of children with anxiety disorders. Paper presented at the triannual meeting of the World Congress of Behavioral and Cognitive Therapies, Vancouver, Canada.

Scheel, M. J., Hoggan, K., Willie, D., McDonald, K., & Tonin, S. (1998). Client understanding of homework determined through therapist delivery. Poster presented at the 106th Annual Convention of the American Psychological Association, San Francisco.

Scheel, M. J., Seaman, S., Roach, K., Mullin, T., & Mahoney, K. B. (1999). Client implementation of therapist recommendations predicted by client perception of fit, difficulty of implementation, and therapist influence. *Journal of Counseling Psychology, 46,* 308–316.

Schmidt, N. B., & Woolaway-Bickel, K. (2000). The effects of treatment compliance on outcome in cognitive-behavioral therapy for panic disorder: Quality versus quantity. *Journal of Consulting and Clinical Psychology, 68,* 13–18.

Shelton, J. L., & Levy, R. L. (1981a). A survey of the reported use of assigned homework activities in contemporary behavior therapy literature. *The Behavior Therapist, 4,* 13–14.

Shelton, J. L., & Levy, R. L. (1981b). *Behavioral assignments and treatment compliance: A handbook of clinical strategies.* Champaign, IL: Research Press.

Startup, M., & Edmonds, J. (1994). Compliance with homework assignments in cognitive-behavioral psychotherapy for depression: Relation to outcome and methods of enhancement. *Cognitive Therapy and Research, 18,* 567–579.

Talyarkhan, A., Deane, F. P., Lambert, G., & Pickard, J. (2003). Homework adherence in multiple family therapy for schizophrenia. Manuscript in preparation.

Thompson, L. W., & Gallagher, D. (1984). Efficacy of psychotherapy in the treatment of late-life depression. *Advances in Behaviour Research and Therapy, 6,* 127–139.

Warren, R., & McLellarn, R. W. (1987). What do RET therapists think they are doing? An international survey. *Journal of Rational Emotive Therapy, 5,* 71–91.

Westling, B. E., & Ost, L. G. (1999). Brief cognitive behaviour therapy of panic disorder. *Scandinavian Journal of Behaviour Therapy, 28,* 49–57.

Wetherell, J. L. (2002). Treatment of generalized anxiety disorder in older adults. *Dissertation Abstracts International, 63*(5-B), 2613.

Wetherell, J. L., Gatz, M., & Craske, M. G. (2003). Treatment of generalized anxiety disorder in older adults. Journal of *Consulting & Clinical Psychology, 71,* 31–40.

Whitman, J. S., & Boyd, C. J. (2003). *Therapist's notebook for lesbian, gay, and bisexual clients: Homework, handouts, and activities for use in psychotherapy.* New York: Haworth Clinical Practice Press.

Woods, C. M., Chambless, D. L., & Steketee, G. (2002). Homework compliance and behavior therapy outcome for panic with agoraphobia and obsessive compulsive disorder. *Cognitive Behaviour Therapy, 31,* 88–95.

Worthington, E. L., Jr. (1986). Client compliance with homework directives during counseling. *Journal of Counseling Psychology, 33,* 124–130.

Young, J., & Beck, A. T. (1980). Cognitive therapy scale: Rating manual. (Available from the Beck Institute for Cognitive Therapy and Research, GSB Building, One Belmont Avenue, Suite 700, Bala Cynwyd, PA 19004–1610).

Zettle, R. D., & Hayes, S. C. (1987). Component and process analysis of cognitive therapy. *Psychological Reports, 61,* 939–953.

CHAPTER 4

Assessment of Homework Completion

NIKOLAOS KAZANTZIS, FRANK P. DEANE, and KEVIN R. RONAN

The process of learning through completion of homework assignments can serve several functions. Homework enables the collection of data to evaluate thoughts and beliefs, provides an opportunity for the learning and maintenance of adaptive skills, and shifts the focus of therapy to the more objective and concrete (Beck, Rush, Shaw, & Emery, 1979). In many ways then, a client's completion of homework assignments is important in ensuring the short- and long-term benefits of therapy.

As outlined in Chapter 3, studies examining homework compliance have repeatedly documented its association with treatment outcome. Studies have also provided emerging data to suggest that the extent of homework compliance is related to improvement for a range of clinical presentations. More specifically, recent studies have demonstrated this relationship for clients presenting with depression (Burns & Spangler, 2000), obsessions and compulsions (Abramowitz, Franklin, Zoellner, & DiBernardo, 2002), panic disorder (Westling & Ost, 1999), social phobia (Leung & Heimberg, 1996), and substance abuse (McCrady, Epstein, & Hirsch, 1996). The implication from these studies is that clients who do not complete their homework assignments may not receive full or long-lasting benefits from therapy.

It is usually of clinical and conceptual interest when clients do not undertake homework activities, are able to undertake only part of the homework activity, or decide to engage in activities different from those discussed in their therapy sessions. However, homework *noncompliance* also has a role to play in therapy. At the very least, noncompliance provides the opportunity to obtain further information for the cognitive conceptualization and to review treatment goals—both of which are likely to improve treatment outcome. Since homework assignments were originally conceived as an opportunity for gathering information and learning, we propose that "compliance" is an imprecise construct for measuring a client's engagement with homework activities.

The aim of this Chapter is to discuss the issues in assessing homework completion in cognitive behavioral therapy. We begin by discussing the definition of homework completion, review existing measures available in the literature, and propose a new measure of homework completion drawing on the theoretical basis for homework outlined in Chapter 2.

Defining Homework Completion

Homework "compliance" or "adherence" may be broadly defined as the degree to which a client's between-session behaviors follow the discussed homework assignment from the previous session. Despite the fact that researchers often measure compliance, such adherence may be measuring only a portion of the process. There can be no universal metric for what defines rates of "low," "medium," or "high" compliance because of the wide variety of homework assignments and the ways in which they are individually tailored for clients. Variation in homework activities also means that there can be no universal criteria for what constitutes "poor," "satisfactory," or "excellent" compliance. Indeed, there are situations in which clients could carry out too much homework or take a reasonable expectation to a unreasonable end (e.g., aiming to reach a "perfect" standard). In these situations, reliance on "compliance" or the "quantity" of homework completion is likely to be counterproductive. Consequently, the assessment of client completion of homework presents a range of challenges for practitioners and researchers.

In the first instance, it is clear that appropriate completion of homework assignments must be individually defined for each client and for that person's particular set of homework activities. How a practitioner determines what is useful homework completion is integrally related to the aims of the particular homework activity. A flexible criterion of appropriate, acceptable, or reasonable homework completion may not need precise measurement methodology. However, defining what is meant by *appropriate* and monitoring patterns of homework completion is important in determining the client's response to therapy. It is likely to be more clinically useful to focus on *appropriate homework completion*—that is, completion that produces some increase in understanding or skill acquisition.

We also suggest that it is likely to be more clinically useful to focus on *noncompletion*—where a client is unable to complete an assigned homework activity. Although noncompletion of homework may raise concerns about the extent to which a client is engaging or benefiting from therapy, such examination often proves instructive and useful. For example, a discussion about noncompletion may indicate that the client and therapist have not effectively linked the homework assignment to treatment goals or adequately contextualized the homework within the conceptualization for the client. That is, partial or noncompletion of homework can prompt the therapist to refine the conceptualization for the client or lead to a reconsideration of therapy goals. In other instances, noncompletion may reveal that the task was too challenging or difficult or that it was nonspecific, poorly planned, or misunderstood. Even in the case of outright refusal at an initial session, discussions are necessary to understand and explore the reasons for the client's unwillingness to complete homework activities, which in itself is likely to provide important information for the conceptualization.

Therefore we suggest that a focus on simple compliance with homework assignments is less representative of the factors that therapists consider in reviewing homework assignments. Our argument is that *compliance is a necessary but not sufficient criterion for determining whether clients are benefiting from homework assignments.* We suggest that it would be helpful to focus on a broader set of factors that might better be referred to as *homework completion.* In dealing with these issues, the first question is: How can such a broader range of factors be measured?

Measuring Homework Completion

In everyday clinical work, cognitive behavioral therapists form impressions of the extent to which their clients engage in homework activities. These impressions both influence and are influenced by the therapeutic relationship, the client's goals for therapy, and conceptualization of the client's problems. One main source of data on which therapists form their impressions is a client's self-report of homework completion.

As part of our *Cognitive Behavior Therapy Homework Project,* we conducted a systematic review of the methods of homework compliance assessment in the empirical research (i.e., Kazantzis, Deane, & Ronan, 2004). That review illustrated that client self-report was indeed the most common source of homework compliance data, with 28% of 32 studies using client data as either the primary or secondary source.

A few studies have examined the accuracy of self-report data on homework compliance. Three studies have compared self-report with an objective measure of homework completion in listening to relaxation audiotapes in the treatment of anxiety and hypertension (Hoelscher, Lichstein, & Rosenthal, 1984, 1986; Taylor, Agras, Schneider, & Allen, 1983). Overall, these studies suggest that clients may exaggerate their self-reports of homework compliance. In addition, the particular context of these studies raised the distinct possibility that clients suspected the equipment incorporated a hidden measurement device and simply left the audiotape player running. Thus it is unclear to what extent these results can be generalized, particularly to the context of other homework activities for other clinical problems.

Client self-report of homework completion has been obtained through in-session discussion or interview (e.g., Kazdin & Mascitelli, 1982), client records or diaries (e.g., Fennell & Teasdale, 1987; Harmon, Nelson, & Hayes, 1980), and questionnaires (e.g., Burns & Nolen-Hoeksema, 1991, 1992; Burns & Spangler, 2000). In fact, our review (Kazantzis et al., 2004) showed that only four studies used the same self-report measure of homework compliance (i.e., Abramowitz et al., 2002; Bryant, Simons, & Thase, 1999; Leung & Heimberg, 1996; Woody & Adessky, 2002). These investigations used a single-item rating originally proposed in a review by Primakoff et al. (1986), which used a six-point scale ranging from 1 (*the patient did not attempt the assigned homework*) to 6 (*the patient did more of assigned homework than was requested*). More generally, single-item global ratings of homework compliance were the most consistently used format for homework compliance assessment ($n = 12$; 38% of all studies).

Four studies have attempted to examine the reliability between client and therapist ratings of compliance. One study did not find high consistency between therapist and client ratings (i.e., Kazdin & Mascitelli, 1982), whereas the other three reported a significant correlation between the two (Burns & Nolen-Hoeksema, 1991, 1992; Holtzworth-Munroe, Jacobson, DeKlyen, & Whisman, 1989). In addition to the inconsistency in the results, the range of assessment instruments used in these studies makes it difficult to draw any firm conclusions regarding these comparisons. Here, once again, single-item measures of homework compliance were predominant.

With few exceptions (i.e., Neimeyer & Feixas, 1990; Schmidt & Woolaway-Bickel, 2000), the majority of prior research has focused on the global assessment of quantity of homework compliance rather than the "quality" or extent of learning through the completion of homework assignments. Reliance on single-item global measures and the confounded constructs of quantity and quality suggest that there is a need for a new measure that takes account of these limitations. Therefore, as the next step in our *Cognitive Behavior Therapy Homework Project*, we designed a conceptually and empirically driven method for assessing homework completion in cognitive behavioral therapy. The next section provides a rationale and description of this new measure.

Homework Rating Scale II

As the first step towards the development of more reliable and valid measure of homework completion, we constructed a homework rating scale (HRS) as a tool for clinical practice (Kazantzis et al., 2004). The HRS is a 12-item client self-report measure designed to measure a range of aspects in the process of designing homework, engaging in homework, and reviewing the experience of have engaged in the homework. Clients are asked to provide their responses on a five-point Likert scale.

When adherence or compliance behavior is monitored by methods that are known by both client and therapist, there is a possibility that the client's response will be subject to demand characteristics of the monitoring situation. That is, clients' responses on the original HRS may be subject to a degree of reactivity simply because they are being asked to report on their homework completion. The tendency for clients to give their clinicians positive answers or to respond in a socially desirable fashion is well known in the medication compliance literature (cf. Morisky, Green, & Levine, 1986). Together with the data suggesting that clients may exaggerate their degree of compliance with homework assignments, we revised the original HRS and present the HRS II in this Chapter. The HRS II reverses the wording of items about the way that client might experience non- or part-completion of homework assignments (see also Foddy, 1993; Horne, 1997, 2000; Sudman & Bradburn, 1982). Thus, rather than attempting to overcome the possibility of social-desirability bias, the HRS II aims to use that bias to obtain information about difficulties in the completing homework assignments. For instance, the instructions on the questionnaire now take into account that there may be differences between the way in which homework was discussed in the therapy session and that there may have been obstacles and other difficulties with the homework assignment (Figure 4.1).

The construction of HRS and HRS II was based on the theoretical and empirical foundations for homework assignments in cognitive behavioral therapy. The direction of item content was chosen based on the nature of what was being asked: negative items were chosen for negative experiences (i.e., "difficulty" and "obstacles"), and positive items were chosen for positive experiences from homework completion (e.g., "pleasure," "mastery," "progress"). (See review in Barnette, 2000.) Since the Kazantzis et al. (2004) article summarized the empirical basis for HRS item content, here we will outline the integrated cognitive and behavioral theoretical

HRS II

Instructions: Many people find ways to engage in activities between therapy sessions in a way that suits them. This may differ from the way in which the activity was discussed with their therapist. This questionnaire asks about your activities from last session. Below are some ways in which people have said that they have engaged and learned from their activities. Please read each question carefully, and for each of the statements, circle the **one response** that best applies to you.

1. Quantity
I was able to do the activity

- 0   not at all
- 1   a little
- 2   some
- 3   a lot
- 4   completely

2. Quality
I was able to do the activity well

- 0   not at all
- 1   somewhat
- 2   moderately
- 3   very
- 4   extremely

3. Difficulty
The activity was difficult for me

- 0   not at all
- 1   somewhat
- 2   moderately
- 3   very
- 4   extremely

4. Obstacles
I experienced obstacles in doing the activity

- 0   not at all
- 1   a little
- 2   some
- 3   a lot
- 4   extensive

5. Comprehension
I understood what to do for the activity

- 0   not at all
- 1   a little
- 2   somewhat
- 3   a lot
- 4   completely

6. Rationale
The reason for doing the activity was clear to me

- 0   not at all
- 1   somewhat
- 2   moderately
- 3   very
- 4   completely

7. Collaboration
I had an active role in planning the activity

- 0   not at all
- 1   a little
- 2   some
- 3   a lot
- 4   extensive

8. Specificity
The guidelines for how to carry out the activity were specific

- 0   not at all
- 1   somewhat
- 2   moderately
- 3   very
- 4   extremely

9. Match with Therapy Goals
The activity matched with my goals for therapy

- 0   not at all
- 1   a little
- 2   somewhat
- 3   a lot
- 4   completely

10. Pleasure
I enjoyed the activity

- 0   not at all
- 1   a little
- 2   somewhat
- 3   a lot
- 4   extremely

11. Mastery
I gained a sense of control over my problems

- 0   not at all
- 1   a little
- 2   somewhat
- 3   a lot
- 4   extensively

12. Progress
The activity helped with my progress in therapy

- 0   not at all
- 1   a little
- 2   somewhat
- 3   a lot
- 4   extremely

Fig. 4.1   Homework Rating Scale—II (client version). Copyright 2005 by Nikolaos Kazantzis, Frank Deane, and Kevin Ronan. From the book *Using Homework Assignments in Cognitive Behavior Therapy*, by N. Kazantzis, F. P. Deane, K. R. Ronan, & L. L'Abate (2005). New York: Routledge.

foundations of homework assignments, as outlined in Chapter 2 and as extended in Figure 4.2, for convenience. In the next sections in this Chapter, we discuss these theoretical foundations as they relate to the assessment of homework completion and as justification for items on the HRS II. Although the focus of this Chapter is to discuss assessment, it is important to note that some components may appear in more than one part of the process of integrating homework into therapy (i.e., "design, assign, and review"). For instance, considering whether the homework assignment matches with therapy goals may play a role in both the review and the design of homework.

Although the HRS II may later demonstrate utility as a process measure in cognitive behavioral therapy research, we did not have psychometric information on the measure at the time this Chapter was written. We have found it useful to ask clients to complete the HRS II on a semiregular basis in the waiting room before a therapy session, to be discussed as part of reviewing homework. Aside from saving time, clients' responses on these items often function as a way of prioritizing the barriers to the effective use of homework.

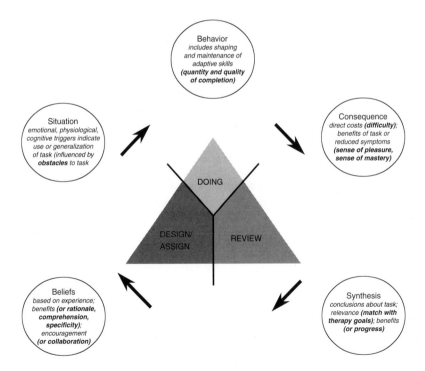

Fig. 4.2 Integrated cognitive behavioral theoretical foundations.

Rationale, Comprehension, Specificity, Collaboration

The contributions of cognitive theory to these foundations have underscored the value of exploring client beliefs about the homework assignment being considered. The client may have attitudes, rules, or beliefs about the homework activity or her ability to complete it. According to the theory, these beliefs are usually based on the client's own experiences and the experiences of other people (i.e., normative beliefs). If sufficiently explored, the client's beliefs about engaging in a homework task are likely to be consistent with his presentation and conceptualization. For example, an anxious client with a belief system that is characterized by a sense of vulnerability, involving beliefs about herself as helpless, others as strong, and the world as demanding may underestimate her own ability to carry out a particular homework activity. This conceptual information would be helpful to the therapist in linking the homework task with some aspect of the client's past experience in order to make the assignment more achievable. Seeing the homework task as achievable requires an understanding of what is involved, why the particular assignment is being discussed, sufficient detail on what and how the assignment is be carried out, and a degree of encouragement and active involvement on the client's part in designing and assigning the activity. The HRS II has four items designed to examine client beliefs regarding the homework activity and the process of designing and assigning it during the previous session. Specifically, the HRS II asks clients to rate the extent to which they understood what to do for the activity (*comprehension*), understood the reason for doing the activity (*rationale*), had an active role in planning the activity (*collaboration*), and found the guidelines for how to carry out the activity to be specific (*specificity*).

Obstacles

Even when homework assignments are designed to the extent that the client has clear understanding and involvement in setting the activity, there may still be several reasons why the assignment is not carried out. As shown in Figure 4.2, theory suggests that emotional, physiological, or cognitive triggers determine whether a homework activity will be carried out or not. Situational triggers (or antecedents) cue clients that the particular application (or generalization) of an intervention would be helpful. A client's emotional response to a situation often serves as one such trigger. For example, assertiveness or controlled breathing would be beneficial in reducing intense physiological arousal during an interpersonal interaction where a client's tendency to put the needs of others first was being activated. Thus, a client's ability to identify and express emotions, monitor his physiological sensations, be awarene of his cognitions, and have insight into his compensatory strategies can determine whether a homework assignment will be carried out. In other words, one possible explanation for noncompletion may be that the homework activity is more difficult than the client and therapist anticipated and extends beyond the client's current level of ability or skill (Beck et al., 1979).

Of course, there may be practical obstacles in the client's environment that can interfere with homework completion, despite attempts to identify them during the therapy session (Shelton & Levy, 1981; Beck et al., 1979). Consequently, the HRS II asks clients to rate the extent to which they experienced obstacles in completing the activity (*obstacles*).

Quantity, Quality

When clients are able to carry out homework assignments, they do so to varying degrees. For some clients, completing a three-column thought record on four occasions during a given week may be sufficient practice to allow them to be comfortable in attempting a five- or seven-column thought record as part of their next in-session activity. For other clients, it may take many more three-column thought record assignments before they are ready to pursue the next approximation of a complex skill. In either case, it is clinically useful to know how much of the homework activity the client has carried out. To this end, the HRS II asks clients to rate the amount of the homework activity completed (*quantity*) and the degree to which they were able to learn through doing the homework well (*quality*).

Difficulty, Pleasure, Mastery

As depicted in Chapter 2, behavioral theories make compelling arguments for the links between behavior and its consequences. On carrying out the homework activity or some portion of it, there are immediate consequences to the client's behavior. These consequences may be environmental, as with the client who has generalized in-session assertiveness practice to a naturalistic interpersonal interaction. They may also be internal, as with the client who reflects on her efforts in completing three-column thought records and experiences reduced sadness and an increased sense of mastery in completing the task. Since focusing on the negative emotion and negative automatic thoughts generally increases the intensity of those emotions, other clients may not experience a degree of mastery or pleasure until they have progressed through the entire thought record and reached a more balanced alternative. Consistent with these examples, cognitive theories suggest that intrinsic consequences for behavior are crucial for determining a client's evaluation of the costs and benefits of a given homework assignment.

The HRS II has three items designed to examine client interpretation of the consequences of having carried out the homework assignment. Specifically, the HRS II asks clients to rate the extent to which they found the assignment difficult (*difficulty*), enjoyed doing the activity (*pleasure*), and had a sense of control over their problems as a consequence of carrying out the task (*mastery*).

Match With Therapy Goals, Progress

The following therapy session presents the opportunity for the client and therapist to discuss the homework assignment. As Beck et al. (1979) outline it in discussing the process of integrating homework assignments in therapy, the review of homework assignments is part of the process of *systematically* incorporating homework into therapy. Reviewing homework at the following session also enables clients to synthesize their experience and form conclusions based on their learning. Cognitive theories suggest that clients engage in a synthesizing process after engaging in an activity. Thus, it makes good sense that a therapist is able to work with the client to facilitate this process.

As shown in the behavioral and cognitive foundations for homework in Figure 4.2, the basic rationale for any assignment is that it promotes learning. Part of this learning process involves the client's reflection and synthesis of the homework activity, and in particular, considering whether it was helpful in enabling them to progress toward their therapy goals.

The HRS II has two items designed to examine clients' synthesis of their experience in carrying out the homework activity. Specifically, the HRS II asks clients to rate the extent to which they found that the activity matched their goals for therapy (*match with therapy goals*) and found the activity helpful to their progress in therapy (*progress*).

Recommendations for Using the HRS II in Therapy

As we hope will be clear from the description in this Chapter, the HRS II is not a measure of homework compliance; it is a measure of homework *completion*. Consistent with this broad description, the HRS II is not intended to be the primary means by which the therapist determines the extent of homework completion or to what extent the client experienced learning or skill acquisition. Rather, we encourage the use of the HRS II within a collaborative therapeutic relationship that encourages openness, curiosity, and experimentation with ideas. The therapist should explain that the HRS II provides a means of efficiently collecting information about the homework and an opportunity for the client and therapist to reflect on the client's experience in homework completion. The HRS II allows for constructive problem solving around homework and provides a useful opportunity to gather information for the cognitive conceptualization. No two clients will have the same experience of homework in cognitive behavioral therapy; some find particular activities more helpful or more challenging than others, and they often adapt and modify the activity to best suit their particular situation. The HRS II provides an efficient means of addressing aspects of the process theorized to be important in determining homework completion.

Although we use HRS II in our clinical work, we have not yet gathered sufficient data for pilot testing and psychometric analysis. We have two research studies under way designed to examine the psychometric properties of the HRS II. The intention here will be to conduct a direct comparison between client and therapist versions of the HRS II (see Appendix).

Summary and Concluding Comments

The aim of this Chapter was to discuss a new measure for assessing homework completion in cognitive behavioral therapy. We began by discussing the definition of homework completion, discussed existing measures available in the literature identified in Chapter 3, and proposed the HRS II as a more comprehensive measure of homework completion. In this Chapter, we showed how the questionnaire items were drawn from the theoretical foundations for homework outlined in Chapter 2.

The issue of how best to assess homework completion remains an empirical one. Taking into account the theoretical and empirical evidence to date, we have constructed a new measure for the assessment of homework completion that clinicians can use in their everyday practice. The HRS II is more extensive than existing measures, both in terms of the number of items and the measurement of several theoretically based dimensions of the process of designing, assigning, carrying out, and reviewing homework assignments. The measure itself is currently undergoing evaluation in our *Cognitive Behavior Therapy Homework Project* as well as being used in our own clinical practices.

References

Abramowitz, J. S., Franklin, M. E., Zoellner, L. A., & DiBernardo, C. L. (2002). Treatment compliance and outcome in obsessive-compulsive disorder. *Behavior Modification, 26*, 447–463.

Barnette, J. J. (2000). Effects of stem and Likert response option reversals on survey internal consistency: If you feel the need, there is a better alternative to using those negatively worded stems. *Educational and Psychological Measurement, 60*, 361–370.

Beck, A. T., Rush, J. A., Shaw, B. F., & Emery, G. (1979). *Cognitive therapy of depression*. New York: Guilford.

Bryant, M. J., Simons, A. D., & Thase, M. E. (1999). Therapist skill and patient variables in homework compliance: Controlling a uncontrolled variable in cognitive therapy outcome research. *Cognitive Therapy and Research, 23*, 381–399.

Burns, D. D., & Nolen-Hoeksema, S. (1991). Coping styles, homework compliance, and the effectiveness of cognitive behavioral therapy. *Journal of Consulting and Clinical Psychology, 59,* 305–311.

Burns, D. D., & Nolen-Hoeksema, S. (1992). Therapist empathy and recovery from depression in cognitive behavioral therapy: A structural equation model. *Journal of Consulting and Clinical Psychology, 60,* 441–449.

Burns, D. D., & Spangler, D. (2000). Does psychotherapy homework lead to changes in depression in cognitive behavioral therapy? Or does clinical improvement lead to homework compliance? *Journal of Consulting and Clinical Psychology, 68,* 46–56.

Fennell, M. J. V., & Teasdale, J. D. (1987). Cognitive therapy for depression: Individual differences and the process of change. *Cognitive Therapy and Research, 11,* 253–271.

Foddy, W. (1993). *Constructing questions for interviews and questionnaires: Theory and practice in social research.* Melbourne: Cambridge University Press.

Harmon, T. M., Nelson, R. O., & Hayes, S. C. (1980). Self-monitoring of mood versus activity by depressed clients. *Journal of Counseling and Clinical Psychology, 48,* 30–38.

Hoelscher, T. J., Lichstein, K. L., & Rosenthal, T. L. (1984). Objective vs. subjective assessment of relaxation compliance among anxious individuals. *Behaviour Research and Therapy, 22,* 187–193.

Hoelscher, T. J., Lichstein, K. L., & Rosenthal, T. L. (1986). Home relaxation practice in hypertension treatment: Objective assessment and compliance induction. *Journal of Consulting and Clinical Psychology, 54,* 217–221.

Holtzworth-Munroe, A., Jacobson, N. S., DeKlyen, M., & Whisman, M. A. (1989). Relationship between behavioral marital therapy outcome and process variables. *Journal of Consulting and Clinical Psychology, 57,* 658–662.

Horne, R. (1997) Representations of medication and treatment: advances in theory and measurement. In Petrie, K. J. and Weinman, J., (Eds.), *Perceptions of health and illness: Current research and applications* (pp. 155–187). London: Harwood Academic.

Horne, R. (2000). Assessing perceptions of medication: Psychological perspectives. In Drug Utilization Research Group "Handbook of drug research methodology." Unpublished manuscript.

Kazantzis, N., Deane, F. P., & Ronan, K. R. (2004). Assessing compliance with homework assignments: Review and recommendations for clinical practice. *Journal of Clinical Psychology, 60,* 627–641.

Kazdin, A. E., & Mascitelli, S. (1982). Covert and overt rehearsal and homework practice in developing assertiveness. *Journal of Consulting and Clinical Psychology, 50,* 250–258.

Leung, A. W., & Heimberg, R. G. (1996). Homework compliance, perceptions of control, and outcome of cognitive-behavioral treatment of social phobia. *Behaviour Research and Therapy, 34,* 423–432.

McCrady, B. S., Epstein, E. E., & Hirsch, L. S. (1996). Issues in the implementation of a randomized clinical trial that includes Alcoholics Anonymous: Studying AA-related behaviors during treatment. *Journal of Studies on Alcohol, 57,* 604–612.

Morisky, D. E., Green, L. W., & Levine, D. M. (1986). Concurrent and predictive validity of a self-report measure of medication adherence. *Medical Care, 24,* 67–74.

Neimeyer, R. A., & Feixas, G. (1990). The role of homework and skill acquisition in the outcome of group cognitive therapy for depression. *Behavior Therapy, 21,* 281–292.

Primakoff, L., Epstein, N., & Covi, L. (1986). Homework compliance: An uncontrolled variable in cognitive therapy outcome research. *Behavior Therapy, 17,* 433–446.

Schmidt, N. B., & Woolaway-Bickel, K. (2000). The effects of treatment compliance on outcome in cognitive-behavioral therapy for panic disorder: Quality versus quantity. *Journal of Consulting and Clinical Psychology, 68,* 13–18.

Shelton, J. L., & Levy, R. L. (1981). *Behavioral assignments and treatment compliance: A handbook of clinical strategies.* Champaign, IL: Research Press.

Sudman, S., & Bradburn, N. M. (1982). *Asking questions.* San Francisco: Jossey-Bass.

Taylor, L. B., Agras, W. S., Schneider, J. A., & Allen, R. A. (1983). Adherence to instructions to practice relaxation exercises. *Journal of Consulting and Clinical Psychology, 51,* 952–953.

Westling, B.E., & Ost, L. G. (1999). Brief cognitive behaviour therapy of panic disorder. *Scandinavian Journal of Behaviour Therapy, 28,* 49–57.

Woody, S. R., & Adessky, R. S. (2002). Therapeutic alliance, group cohesion, and homework compliance during cognitive-behavioral group treatment of social phobia. *Behavior Therapy, 33,* 5–27.

PART II

Specific Populations

CHAPTER 5

Children

JENNIFER L. HUDSON and PHILIP C. KENDALL

Mention of the word *homework* to children in therapy frequently elicits groans and subsequent sighs or thoughts of "Do I have to?" Children may be initially resistant to the idea of homework in therapy because they associate homework with school. For children with emotional and behavioral difficulties, homework in the school environment is frequently an issue of concern. The child with behavior problems may have daily struggles with his parents and teachers about school homework compliance. For the anxious child, homework may provoke fears of negative evaluation or concern over the accurate completion of the task. For parents too, the concept of homework tasks to monitor or complete might seem an unacceptable addition to an already busy and overwhelming schedule. Not surprisingly, the inclusion of homework tasks in treatment (i.e., cognitive behavioral therapy, or CBT) for children brings with it a number of obstacles to overcome in order to maintain a positive approach to out-of-session assignments.

Homework tasks are considered an integral component of CBT for children. One of the primary objectives of CBT is to teach children specific skills with which to manage their emotional or behavioral difficulties more effectively. Initially, it is the role of the therapist to assist the child in learning and applying these skills. As therapy progresses, the child is increasingly asked (and is able) to use the skills without the assistance of the therapist. Gradually the responsibility is shifted from the therapist to the child. Practice of the skills is considered crucial to the learning process. Rehearsal both in and out of the session is likely to increase the child's opportunity for repeated practice and increase the likelihood that the child will master the skills. First, the practice occurs in the session, in a less threatening and more supportive environment. With increased confidence, out-of-session practice follows, allowing the child to implement new skills in problematic settings at school, at home, and with peers.

Homework assignments allow the therapist to assess the child's grasp of the concepts. Homework gives the child an opportunity to demonstrate skill (without the guidance of the therapist) and allows the therapist to check the child's understanding of the material. Monitoring is particularly important when working with children. Although children may be overly compliant and eager to please and may agree with the therapist during the session without fully understanding the material, assessing and monitoring plays an important role in progress.

CBT for Childhood Disorders

There are a wide variety of CBT programs available for childhood disorders (see Kendall, 2000a). Although in this Chapter we cannot cover all of these programs, we will provide some as examples to illustrate selected points. Programs are available for parent training for children with oppositional behavior problems (Feldman & Kazdin, 1995; Southam-Gerow & Kendall, 1997; Webster-Stratton & Herbert, 1994; Wells & Egan, 1988) and for youth with anger problems (Lochman, Whidby, & FitzGerald, 2000) and depressed mood (Stark, Sander, Yancy, Bronik, & Hoke, 2000). Other treatments have shown efficacy for anxious children (e.g., Beidel, Turner, & Morris, 2000; Barrett, Dadds, & Rapee, 1996; Kendall, 1994, Kendall et al., 1997; Manassis et al., 2002), family anxiety management for anxiety in children (Barrett et al., 1996), exposure for specific phobia (Menzies & Clarke, 1993; Ollendick, Hagopian, & Huntzinger, 1991; Silverman et al., 1999), for childhood obesity (Epstein, Valoski, Wing, & McCurley 1994; Wheeler & Hess, 1976), and for enuresis (Houts, 1996; Houts, Berman, & Abramson, 1994). Although the overall efficacy of these programs has been evaluated, the specific role that homework plays in determining outcome has yet to be evaluated. Examples of homework assignments from some of these programs are reviewed further on, but first we must address the issues relating to homework that are not confined to a specific emotional or behavioral problem.

Assigning Homework Tasks

The CBT therapist typically assigns weekly take-home tasks for the child and/or parents to complete between sessions. The take-home tasks are based on the content covered in the session. Each week the homework tasks are assigned at the end of the therapy session and reviewed at the beginning of the next session. Although the content of the tasks varies from session to session, each week the child/family and the therapist discuss and plan the homework together. It is assigned, but it is a collaborative process. The child/family is likely given a notebook or monitoring form to record the out-of-session information, and the child is encouraged to record the homework experience as soon as possible after it occurs to prevent loss of information. Accurate recording of the homework allows the therapist to more carefully assess the child's experience and mastery. Homework tasks may also need to be modified depending on the child's developmental level. For example, the child may experience difficulty reading or writing and so the therapist may choose to ask the child to record her homework using pictures.

Homework assignments require forethought and planning: a central part of the session rather than a last minute addition as the child is rushing out of the therapy room. Tasks are designed to allow the child to have a positive experience and this, too, may require planning. Careful calibration of the difficulty of the task and the child's skill level combine as an important part of designing a successful homework assignment.

Introducing Self-Monitoring

Often the first task assigned to children and families in CBT is a simple self-monitoring task. The child may be asked to monitor his feelings, thoughts, or behaviors. Self-monitoring attunes the child to the specific cues or patterns that may be involved in the maintenance of the problem, in addition to providing information to the therapist about the frequency and severity of the problem from the child's perspective. Figure 5.1 provides an example of a monitoring form that asks the child to record a situation during the week, recording his feelings (and the severity) and thoughts. This form can be used to help children identify the link between thoughts and feelings.

Strategies for Effective Homework

One of the difficulties in using homework tasks is compliance. As already mentioned, this issue becomes even more salient in dealing with children. A number of features can be put into place that may increase the likelihood of the child's compliance. The following paragraphs provide a number of general strategies to increase homework compliance. The section entitled "Therapist's Responses to Noncompliance," later in this Chapter, also outlines

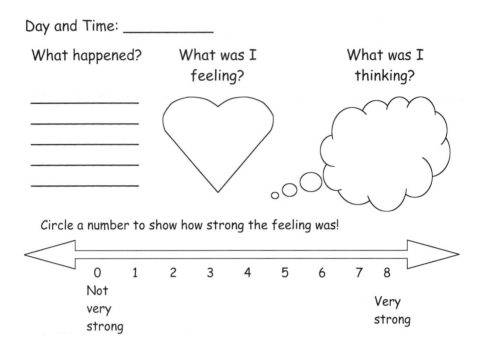

Day and Time: _____

What happened?   What was I feeling?   What was I thinking?

Circle a number to show how strong the feeling was!

0   1   2   3   4   5   6   7   8
Not very strong   Very strong

Fig. 5.1 Example of self-monitoring form for thoughts and feelings.

a number of examples of noncompliance and provides specific ways of responding.

Avoiding the Term Homework. How one refers to homework tasks can make a difference. An example comes from the "Coping Cat" program (Kendall, 2000b) used in the treatment of children with anxiety disorders. This program does not refer to the take-home tasks as homework. Rather, the child is asked to complete "Show That I Can" (STIC) tasks. The aim is to shift the focus away from the negative connotations associated with the term *homework* and toward tasks that demonstrate the child's mastery of new skills. Although research has not addressed this directly, use of the label "STIC task" does have fewer unwanted connotations and is therefore likely to be a beneficial strategy.

Using Rewards. An additional step taken to increase the likelihood of homework compliance is beginning with simple tasks to shape compliance and using positive reinforcement for each completed homework task. (This statement should be surprising to no one!) At the beginning of each session, the therapist reviews the child's homework. If the child has completed the task, he or she receives a reward previously negotiated. A token economy can be put in place, where the child is given points or tokens for completing homework tasks and then is able to exchange the points for a larger reward. In addition, the therapist uses social reinforcement by praising the child for completion or even partial completion of the tasks. In combination, these responses provide substantial motivation for the child to complete the homework tasks. Throughout the treatment program, if the balance between the salience of the rewards and the difficulty of the task is out of kilter, these rewards may need to be renegotiated.

If the child has not completed the homework, there is no punishment. Rather, the therapist takes time at the start of the session to do as much of the homework assignment with the child as possible right at that moment. For example, if a child were to report that she did not do the assigned task of watching others to try to determine their emotions, no punishments or rewards would be given, but the therapist could have the child do the assignment at that moment. The therapist and child might then discuss the obstacles the child encountered in completing the task at home. Once the therapist and child have determined the reasons for the child's non-compliance, the therapist can respond accordingly to enhance compliance in the following week. The section at the end of this Chapter outlines a number of probable reasons for noncompliance and provides a range of therapist responses to enhance the likelihood of homework completion.

Indeed, before deciding how to respond to a child's noncompletion of the homework, it is important to determine the reason for the child's failure to comply. A multitude of reasons for this may exist, and some may be quite legitimate. Inquiries, and an honest discussion, can sometimes reveal that, for reasons beyond the child's control, the task could not be completed.

Involving Parents. Another factor that may enhance the likelihood of homework completion is the involvement of parents in the process. Parent training is an integral component of a number of the CBT programs available for the treatment of children (Feldman & Kazdin, 1995; Webster-Stratton & Herbert, 1994). If they do so tactfully, parents can remind their children to complete their homework during the week rather than waiting until they see the therapist. Parents can also be involved in both designing appropriate tasks and scheduling a time to complete the tasks. This may be particularly important with younger children, for whom it is more difficult to work independently; it is also more difficult for the therapist to design suitable tasks for them, given the boundaries of a young child's environment. Involving the parents in the therapy and homework tasks not only allows the parents to be aware of the skills their child is learning but also enables the parents to serve as coaches and to be supportive as their child develops new skills.

In many cases, the family may play a crucial role in the maintenance of the child's difficulties. When the family is involved in therapy, the parents also learn new skills—in managing their own behavior as well as their child's. The parents are assigned homework tasks to monitor their own behavior and skill development. For example, the parents may be encouraging the child to avoid using public bathrooms owing to their belief that public bathrooms are "dirty" and "germ-ridden." The therapist might work with these parents to develop their own gradual exposure hierarchy for using public bathrooms. Once the parents' goal has been reached, they can then model the appropriate courageous behavior for their child.

The inclusion of parents may be less desirable with older clients (e.g., adolescents). As the therapist recognizes and supports the independence and autonomy of the youthful client, decisions inevitably arise as to whether or not to involve parents in out-of-sessions tasks.

Parents often have their own obstacles that affect their involvement in their child's homework, such as a busy schedule or perhaps lack of motivation or investment in the program. Some of the techniques described in this Chapter for the enhancement of child compliance are also useful to enhance parental compliance, such as enlisting help from a partner or friend or pairing the homework with a regular activity. In addition, therapist support may help the busy parent to remain focused on the program. For example, a midweek phone call from the therapist may serve as a reminder and aid the parent in resolving any difficulties with the homework.

Types of Homework

Having considered some of the general issues associated with the use of homework tasks, we now turn to some illustrative examples. There are many more programs that employ homework than there is space for us to describe them. Therefore our examples are illustrative rather than exhaustive. We encourage our readers not only to look for other examples but also to use homework in their own interventions with children. Our examples come from work with anxious youth, parent training programs, and impulsive children.

Homework Tasks in the Treatment of Youth With Anxiety Disorders. CBT for children and adolescents with anxiety disorders has been described, based on reviews of the literature, as a "probably efficacious" treatment (Kazdin & Weisz, 1998; Ollendick & King, 1998; 2000). The treatments have been evaluated in a number of randomized clinical trials (e.g., Kendall et al., 1997) and described in treatment manuals (Kendall, 2000b; Rapee, Wignall, Hudson, & Schniering, 2000). CBT for children with anxiety disorders focuses on building rapport, normalizing anxiety as a response, recognizing cues for anxious arousal, learning about emotion management, and teaching the child several skills to manage their anxiety more effectively. In the Coping Cat program, the child is taught a series of skills that are organized into the "FEAR plan" mnemonic:

Feeling frightened?: Recognition of affective and physiological cues
Expecting bad things to happen?: Identification of anxious thoughts
Attitudes and actions that will help?: Problem solving to apply less anxious cognitions and less avoidant coping
Results and rewards: Realistic evaluation and reward of efforts in using the FEAR plan

The first half of the program teaches the skills and organizes them into the FEAR plan; the use of homework (a STIC task) is a part of each session. Initially, the homework tasks are designed to be both easy and nonthreatening, so as to increase compliance for the first week and to establish a pattern of compliance for future, more challenging tasks. For example, the homework task for the initial session asks the child to record in the workbook a situation that felt "really great" (not worrisome) during the week. It is easier to describe fun/pleasant situations than those that are stressful and disturbing. Over the following weeks, the homework tasks focus on anxiety-provoking situations; eventually, the assignments have participants practicing the newly learned skills in at least one or two anxiety-provoking situations and recording the experience. The STIC tasks include monitoring bodily reactions to anxious situations, relaxation practice, recording anxious thoughts and coping thoughts, problem solving alternative responses to the situation, and evaluating and rewarding these efforts.

A core component of cognitive-behavioral treatment for anxious children is the exposure tasks that comprise the second half of the treatment. The exposure tasks are implemented in a gradual manner, and the exposure to feared situations takes place in sessions as well as out of sessions. Once the child has faced exposure tasks with the therapist, he or she is more able to cope with entering and facing other feared situations and eventually to entering formerly distressing contexts as part of an out-of-session STIC task (homework). As a part of the treatment, the child and therapist collaboratively develop a hierarchy of situations in which the child experiences distressing anxiety and/or situations the child has been avoiding.

STIC tasks (homework assignments) are important to the exposure portion of the therapy. The therapist constructs in-session exposure tasks for the child that are as close to real life as possible, but the fact remains that they are certainly removed from the child's school and home environment. For maximal benefit, it is essential for the child and therapist to arrange tasks between sessions that help the child gain increasing mastery (coping) in the real situation. Week by week, the therapist and child climb the child's hierarchy of anxiety-provoking situations, with the therapist balancing the level of anxious arousal with the child's mastery, as evidenced in previous situations. Creative, challenging, and reasonable STIC tasks (homework) contribute greatly to the achievement of compliance and to the eventual beneficial gains.

Homework Tasks in Parent-Management Training for Oppositional Behavioral Problems. Parent-management training programs (see Kazdin, 2000; Webster-Stratton, 2000) have received much attention in the literature, with numerous randomized clinical trials testing their efficacy. According to reviews of the literature, these programs are considered well established with respect to efficacy (Brestan & Eyberg, 1998). Follow-up of children whose parents received such training have shown that the benefits of the treatment can be maintained over 14 years (Long, Forehand, Wierson, & Morgan, 1994). Parent training programs differ a little from the other programs discussed in this Chapter, as the parents are the focus of treatment; the parents of the oppositional child are taught the principles and skills of social learning theory to manage their child's behavior more effectively. Out-of-session tasks assigned to the parents are among the most important components of the treatment program. In therapy sessions, the parents are taught the principles and skills primarily through therapist modeling and rehearsal; out of these sessions, the parents apply their new skills to increasingly difficult child behaviors. It is through the continual review and fine tuning of the homework tasks that the parents develop competence in managing their difficult child's behavior.

In parent-management training (PMT) (see Kazdin, 2000), parents are initially taught to monitor their child's behavior and encouraged to identify the child's target behaviors, such as tantrums or swearing. The homework consists of monitoring these behaviors during the week. Parents are then instructed to use reinforcement and punishment techniques consistently in response the child's target behaviors. The parents are encouraged to praise and reward the child for positive behaviors as well as to remove privileges and implement time out for negative behaviors. The therapist engages with the parent to develop a token reinforcement system to be implemented at home. For example, the parents may introduce a program at home whereby the child, whenever he packs away his toys nicely, is given specific verbal praise ("What a great job of putting away your toys") and a sticker on a special chart. Once the child has received three stickers, the stickers are exchanged for one reward on the child's special list, including choosing foods for dinner or dessert, watching a video with Mom and Dad, and going to the park with Dad. To begin with, the therapist sets the parents homework tasks involving less complex behaviors (e.g., putting the toys away). As the parents' skill level improves, the therapist increases the difficulty of the behaviors being targeted at home.

To help the parents implement these skills, the therapist acts as a coach out of session as well as in session. The therapist has weekly between-session contact with the parents to improve compliance to the treatment program and monitor accurate skill development. The contact serves as a reminder to the parents to implement the skills and as a support to deal with difficult situations as they arise. At each face-to-face session, the parent reports to the therapist on the progress of their skill development since last contact. The therapist provides feedback for the parent to enhance and refine the parent's skills as applied to increasingly difficult child behaviors.

Homework in the Treatment of Impulsive Children. Unlike both anxious youth, who may be prone to be compliant and self-reflective, and parents of oppositional youth, who perhaps participate in parent training programs by choice, impulsive youth are not known for their willingness to be self-reflective, their self-referral for treatment, or their tendency to remember to do homework assignments. Indeed, examples provided in this section may represent the most difficult of the applications discussed in this Chapter.

One program that works with impulsive children is called "Stop and Think" (Kendall, 1992). It strives to reduce acting without thinking by providing structured opportunities that have the child think before acting. To shape participation in homework tasks, the therapist might, for a first assignment, provide a small reward (fun time) if the child can remember the therapist's name at the second meeting. The therapist can make a reminder card or otherwise suggest a mnemonic strategy. At the second meeting, the therapist asks whether the child recalls the therapist's name —a simple task, but one that initiates homework on a good footing and is likely to be reasonably successful. As treatment progresses, the child is asked to recall and do increasingly challenging homework assignments.

Simple psychoeducational games and activities are used for the initial practice, but the skills (e.g., problem solving) are next applied to real-life situations. For example, a child may first learn to engage in three or four steps before giving an answer to a puzzle but will later be required to provide three or four options before engaging in a social behavior. A related homework activity would be for the therapist to assign the child the task of finding a situation during day (during the class period, during the week) to stop and think before acting. The child can complete the assignment by identifying situations from TV, from school or family activities, or from other contexts.

Interpersonal homework tasks can also be implemented. For example, the therapist and child go to the vending machines to purchase a snack. The therapist asks the child to pick a snack from among the choices but refrains from making the purchase until the child can name three choices that are appealing and can describe the taste of each one. This forced delay provides practice of "thinking before acting" in a fun context. The idea is to use sessions to introduce thinking into a stimulus-response sequence and to have homework tasks provide real and perhaps even pleasant opportunities to practice the same skills.

When a homework task (e.g., STIC task) is reviewed, the therapist is alert for (a) whether the homework was completed and (b) the quality of the homework. Inevitably, a child will not complete all homework tasks or not complete every task to its entirety. What to do?

When a participating child does not complete both a collaboratively designed and a therapist-assigned STIC task (homework), it is wise to refrain from judgment and avoid being in any way punitive; as noted earlier, the therapist simply completes the task at that very moment at the start of the session. This approach communicates to the child that it is important to complete the homework (either at home or in session), and often also communicates the expectation that the child will do better in the future.

When noncompliance occurs, rewards for homework are not given. When the child has made considerable effort to complete the task in session, a smaller or partial reward may be given. A partial reward may also be given when the child half-heartedly attempted part of the task or completed the task poorly. A positive child-therapist relationship is a part of all treatments, and this relationship may sometimes be called on to facilitate compliance.

Not all noncompletion is attributable to child noncompliance. Indeed, before deciding how to respond to a child's noncompletion of the homework, it is important to determine the reason for it. A multitude of reasons for the child's noncompliance exist, and some may be quite legitimate. Inquiries, and an honest discussion, can sometimes reveal that, for reasons beyond the child's control, the task could not be completed. For example, in one case the assignment was for the child to identify five different emotions expressed by sports figures in a sports magazine. The child who did not clip out pictures from magazines reported that his dad yelled at him and said he was not to cut up the magazine. Perhaps better planning on the part of the therapist could have avoided this situation, but it nevertheless illustrates that there are circumstances when the child's noncompletion is not noncompliance. These reasons, if likely to recur, need to be addressed and considered before future homework tasks are planned. The possible reasons for noncompliance are discussed collaboratively, providing possible solutions for each.

Common Barriers to Homework Completion

Some relatively common and recurring, if not characteristic, responses are offered by child clients who have not completed homework assignments. A discussion of some of these typical comments demonstrates how the therapist would respond.

"I Forgot!" Heard this before? If the child reports that she forgot to complete the homework task, and if this recurs, the therapist and child can collaborate and enlist a parent or sibling to remind the child during the week. Alternatively, the therapist can associate the homework task with another easy-to-remember activity like brushing teeth. The therapist may also consider a reminder card for the mirror, a note for the refrigerator door, or increasing the reward or modifying the reward to increase the child's motivation to remember.

"I Didn't Have Time." For families with busy schedules, additional weekly tasks might be easily lost in among the other family activities. Involving the parents in planning the homework tasks might assist in preventing noncompliance. The therapist and parent can discuss the possible obstacles to completing the tasks (e.g., schoolwork, religious training, family outing on the weekend). Discussing ways to remember and complete the task despite obstacles can lead to a greater commitment from the parent. As mentioned earlier, the integration of the therapy into the child's everyday activities is considered integral to achieving a positive outcome. Families in which this may not be possible despite the therapist's best attempts may have to consider continuing treatment at another time, when the family is more committed to change.

"I Didn't Want To!" Oppositional behavior in response to homework is likely to arise when oppositionality is also a problem in other areas of the child's life. If the child is not complying with tasks in the home or school environment, similar behavior in the therapy room are likely. In such a case, the therapist can set up a structure to manage the child's behavior within the therapy session. These contingencies can also be applied to

homework. Once the child is clear about the consequences of not doing the therapy homework (e.g., not getting the reward for completion), the therapist merely does his or her best, being consistent in offering and providing the reward when effort is seen and the assignments are done and not giving the rewards when the assignment is not completed. When necessary, the rewards may need to be rethought by the therapist and/or renegotiated with the child (i.e., deciding on a reward with adequate salience to motivate the child or playing a game together at the end of the session).

Therapists setting homework for children with behavioral problems may in fact find themselves faced with a number of the noncompliance excuses being discussed in this section. Hence, many of the other techniques suggested may also prove beneficial in encouraging the oppositional child to complete homework tasks. For example, these may include matching the child's skill level with the assigned task, enlisting parents in the homework, and working with the child collaboratively to design the task.

Consistent with patterns of avoidant behavior, anxious children may refuse to complete the STIC task because of the anxiety associated with the task (e.g., the child might think that the task must be completed 100% correctly and, rather than try, worries about making a mistake). Issues such as this can be addressed in the session using the skills the child has already developed.

An example of a therapist-child interaction regarding resistance to setting homework tasks is included below. In this example, the child is a 12-year-old boy receiving treatment for social anxiety with some oppositional behavior. Keep in mind that we refer to homework as a STIC task.

Therapist: This week I would like you to practice your relaxation three times before we meet again.

Child: Oh man. I have heaps of homework this week. This isn't fair. I can't do this too.

Therapist: Sounds like you think it is going to be difficult to do both the relaxation and your homework for school?

Child: Yep.

Therapist: Well let's think together about what might make it easier for you. Let's think about the reward. Did it make it easier to do your STIC task last week knowing you were getting a reward?

Child: A bit. But it's not that big of a deal. It's just a sticker.

Therapist: OK. Maybe we need to think up something more motivating—something that makes it worthwhile. How about we use the stickers but we also spend some extra time at the end of the session playing a game that you choose. What do you think?

Child: Yeah. What about a chocolate or something?

Therapist: Instead of the game?

Child: Yeah.

Therapist: I'm OK with that, and I bet your parents are too. Would it help you to get the STIC task done?

Child: Oh yeah. Can it be bubble gum instead? They have just brought out this new gum. You know the one with the pink and yellow wrapping? I saw it on TV.

Therapist: OK. Sounds like a good idea. Is it OK that I mention it to your parents…they'll be the ones to pass it along to you when the STIC task is done. OK? Can you think of anything else that might help you get it done, given you have a lot on this week?

Child: Nup.

Therapist: What about doing the practice just before you go to bed?

Child: I'd prefer to get it out of the way so that I didn't have to think about it.

Therapist: So how about after you have had a snack when you get home from school?

Child: I watch TV then.

Therapist: Until what time?

Child: 4:30.

Therapist: Could you do it at 4:30? On Mondays and Thursdays when you don't have baseball? And then maybe you could practice it on Sunday night too.

Child: That could work.

Therapist: Would it help if I sent you an e-mail to remind you to do it or asked Dad to remind you?

Child: My e-mail mailbox might be full. Try it, but maybe get Dad to remind me.

Therapist: OK. Sounds good.

"Everything Was Good." Another potential problem associated with completing homework is "faking good." The child may be concerned about the therapist's impression of the her and may report what she thinks the therapist's wants to hear rather than what actually took place. The child reports having completed the task and that all went well, but the therapist suspects (if not knows) that this is not the case. In such a situation, the therapist may choose, in a nonconfrontational manner, to go over the task

with the child in the session. Another twist, when perfectionism is an issue, is to design an exposure task in which the child has to incorrectly complete the homework for the therapist. The aim of this exposure would be to test out whether the child's negative predictions occurred and to eventually come to realize that even if she does the homework incorrectly she can cope!

"It Was Too Hard." Sometimes the homework task may have been too challenging for the child. If the task is too difficult, the child may not attempt the task or may not be able to complete it. Both of these outcomes are not desired. In legitimate instances of a task being too difficult, the therapist may renegotiate the task for the following week, calibrating it to the child's skill level. Making sure the task is adequately discussed with the child prior to its completion will allow the therapist to get a sense of the child's efficacy regarding task completion. To this end, the therapist can practice the task first with the child during a session. Tag-along procedures (e.g., Ollendick & Cerny, 1981), in which the therapist first demonstrates the skill and then gradually increases the child's involvement in the rehearsal, can be used to increase the child's mastery and understanding as well as the likelihood that the child will be able to complete the homework assignment.

Those children who simply do not want to make an attempt may also use the "it was too hard" excuse. The task may not, in fact, be too difficult for the child but instead may be associated with avoidance or oppositionality.

"It Was Too Easy, I Don't Need To Do It." We recognize that it may be difficult to identify a situation in which the child can practice. Finding the right balance between creating a success experience while also improving the child's mastery can be tricky. With some children, it might be difficult to ascertain the child's level of skill during the session, in which case the therapist may need to estimate the child's skill level and then calibrate it after hearing of the child's experience with the task during the following session.

A child might return for a subsequent session and report that she does not need to do the allocated homework task because she has already done it, so that it is now too easy. While this may be the case for some children, this could simply be a way of avoiding the task. The child may be responding to the therapist's suggestions with excuses as to why the homework task is not appropriate. In this case, as can be useful in other instances, the therapist could address the child's resistance by having the child engage in a similar task during the session—checking out, so to speak, the degree to which it is too easy.

"I Did It, but I Didn't Write It Down." This excuse is common. The child verbally reports having complied with the assignment but also states that he did not write it down in the workbook. Essentially, the writing down of the task is not as crucial as the completion of the task. If the child has actually completed the homework task, then the purpose of the task was achieved. Indeed, for some children, the interpersonal conflict and cost to the therapist-child relationship that is required to have the task written down may not be worth it. When deemed appropriate by the therapist, the child can be encouraged to do the practice without recording it, thereby reducing the demands of the task and associated pressure on the child.

"I Couldn't Be Bothered!" Children experiencing symptoms of depression such as fatigue, lack of energy, or lack of interest may find it difficult to be sufficiently motivated to complete a homework task. The therapist, parent(s), and child can schedule a time during the week to work on the task, perhaps planning a pleasant event immediately following the completion of the homework task. Designing short achievable homework tasks might also be important for these children.

"Oh Yeah, It Was All Right." Children may have trouble communicating the intricacies of the homework task and their emotional and interpersonal experiences with it. Such a situation leaves the therapist at a loss to know whether the task was a success, a complete disaster, or somewhere in between. Parents of the reticent child can act as an additional and valuable source of information regarding the child's progress. In addition, the therapist can develop imaginative ways of discussing the homework that might make it easier for the child—for example, by having specific questions to answer, rather than using an open-ended format.

Case Study 1

Andrew, an 11-year-old boy, and his parents sought help for Andrew's social anxiety. Andrew experienced significant anxiety when giving presentations at school, performing in front of others, and interacting with his peers. He was primarily concerned that the other children would think he was "an idiot" and that they would not want to be his friend. Prior to seeking help, Andrew experienced a brief episode of depressed and irritable mood that lasted about 3 days and was accompanied by fatigue, lethargy, and a loss of interest in his usual activities. The episode was triggered by an incident at school where he was asked a question in class to which he did not know the answer. He missed 2 days of school following this incident, and this led his parents to seek help. Andrew agreed with his parents that he would like to feel less worried about what others thought of him. He collaborated with the therapist in the first session to establish several therapy goals: (a) to complete the 15-minute speech for English class at the end of term and manage his feelings of anxiety, (b) to be able to have a conversation with someone he did not know, (c) to sign up to play in the band at school, (d) to be able to ask a question in class and not worry what the teacher or other children thought, and (e) to know how to handle feelings of depression. After introducing Andrew to the Coping Cat program, the therapist gave him his first STIC task: to report one time during the week when he did not feel worried. This task was designed to be easy and nonthreatening.

Andrew returned to therapy the following week not having completed his STIC task. He reported that "he couldn't think of anything to write." The therapist suggested that they think of something together and write it down in the notebook. The therapist asked Andrew to think of something he did on the weekend that he enjoyed. Andrew reported that he rode his bike with his little brother in the park. Andrew scribbled this event down in his notebook, covering his writing as he went. Given Andrew's social anxiety, the therapist was concerned that he was avoidant of the homework task due to fears that he would get it wrong and look silly. The therapist reassured Andrew that there were no right or wrong answers and that the STIC tasks were a chance to practice what he had learned during the session. Andrew was given one point rather than two points as a reward for the STIC task.

The next homework task involved writing about two situations: one in which Andrew felt nervous, worried, or scared and then another in which he felt relaxed. Andrew was able to complete the task during the following week but was reluctant to read it aloud to the therapist. The therapist acknowledged Andrew's reluctance and made a comparison to the anxiety he felt answering a question in class and his worry that he would say something stupid. Andrew agreed that he was "kind of" worried that he would sound like an idiot when he read out his STIC. The therapist suggested some alternatives that would make it easier for him to report on his homework while he was learning ways to manage his anxiety, such as having his mother tell the therapist about his STIC task at the beginning of the session or having the therapist read the STIC silently. Andrew decided that he would feel much better if he did not have to read out the STIC task, but he said that the therapist could read it to herself. For the next several sessions, Andrew was able to complete his homework, and he would let the therapist would read over his work. When it came time for the gradual exposure part of the program, Andrew and the therapist decided to develop a hierarchy where the goal was for Andrew to be able to read out his homework in front of other people (Table 5.1). The hierarchy was designed to help Andrew gradually face his fear that he would sound silly when he was reading out his homework. By using the FEAR plan, Andrew was able to reach step 7 on the hierarchy after two sessions. For the remainder of the therapy program, Andrew was able to complete his STIC task and read it out at the beginning of the session.

Case Study 2

Rosie, 8 years old, was referred to the "Stop and Think" program for help with her impulsive behavior. Rosie was experiencing significant difficulty waiting her turn at school. She would frequently interrupt the teacher and would start working on a task before she had received the teacher's full instructions. Her parents were becoming increasingly frustrated with this behavior at home and the teacher had also expressed her concern to Rosie's parents. One of the main goals of treatment was for Rosie to be able to think through a number of choices before deciding, rather than doing the first thing that came into her head. To increase Rosie's compliance, the therapist enlisted the help of Rosie's parents each week. The therapist would inform the parents of the task she needed to complete for the week. Together, the therapist, Rosie, and her parents would plan ahead when Rosie was going to complete her homework for the "Stop and Think" program. Rosie decided that she would remember her homework if she pinned it to the doorway of her bedroom. When a homework task was assigned, Rosie would write a reminder "My homework for this week is.... I agreed to do my homework at this time...." As soon as Rosie and her parents arrived home from the therapy session, they would go straight

TABLE 5.1 Andrew's Hierarchy for Reading Out His "Show That I Can" (STIC) Task

Goal: Read out my STIC task in front of other people.

Read aloud the STIC task from week 1 on my own in the therapy room.

Read aloud softly the STIC task from week 1 with the therapist in the room.

Read aloud in a strong voice the STIC task from week 1 with the therapist in the room.

Shout out the STIC task from week 1 with the therapist in the room.

Read aloud the STIC task from week 5 with the therapist in the room.

Read aloud the STIC task from week 5 with the therapist and Mom in the room.

Read aloud the STIC task from week 5 with the therapist, Mom and another therapist from the clinic in the room.

Read aloud the STIC task from week 5 BACKWARDS with the therapist, Mom and another therapist from the clinic in the room.

to her room and affix the reminder sheet to her doorway. Here is a list of some of the homework tasks that Rosie completed during the program:

1. Pay attention during the week and identify a time when someone else would be able to do something better if he or she were to stop and think first. In response, Rosie described a time when she and her dad and two friends were lost and, rather than driving around aimlessly, she reminded her dad about "Stop and think" and they stopped the car, asked directions, and proceeded purposefully to their destination.

2. Select a TV program to watch, but identify and consider three alternative programs before making a choice. Rosie's parents asked her each night to complete this task. Rosie would write down her three choices in addition to what she liked and did not like about each program. Her reward was being allowed to watch the TV show.

3. Decide on which time to begin schoolwork. Each afternoon when Rosie came home from school, her mother would ask her, "What homework do you have today?" Rosie would make a decision whether she wanted to do her homework before or after dinner. When she decided, she would plan out with her Mum how long it should take and whether she needed any special equipment for her homework (e.g., glue, special paper). Rosie's mother would then remind her when the time came.

Conclusion

Homework assignments are regularly used and are seen as an integral component of CBT with young people. The assignments provide opportunities for the treatment to take place out of the session. The therapist's approach and response to homework can be particularly important when the child does not comply, and we have discussed several examples to facilitate the effective use of homework tasks. Used well, homework can be a valuable tool that increases the child's sense of mastery and enhances the treatment's effectiveness.

References

Barrett, P. M., Dadds, M. R., & Rapee, R. M. (1996). Family treatment of childhood anxiety: A controlled trial. Journal of Consulting and Clinical Psychology, 64, 333–342.

Beidel, D. C, Turner, S. M., & Morris, T. L. (2000). Behavioral treatment of childhood social phobia. Journal of Consulting & Clinical Psychology, 68, 1072–1080.

Brestan E. V., & Eyberg, S. M. (1998). Effective psychosocial treatments of conduct-disordered children and adolescents: 29 years, 82 studies, and 5,272 kids. Journal of Clinical Child Psychology, 27, 180–189.

Epstein, L. H., Valoski, A., Wing, R. R., & McCurley, J. (1994). Ten-year outcomes of behavioral family-based treatment for childhood obesity. *Health Psychology, 13*, 373–383.

Feldman, J., & Kazdin, A. E. (1995). Parent management training for oppositional and conduct problem children. *The Clinical Psychologist, 48*, 3–5.

Houts, A. C. (1996). Behavioral treatment of enuresis. *The Clinical Psychologist, 49*, 5–6.

Houts, A. C., Berman, J.S., & Abramson, H. (1994). Effectiveness of psychological and pharmacological treatments for nocturnal enuresis. *Journal of Consulting and Clinical Psychology, 62*, 737–745.

Kazdin, A. E. (2000). Problem-Solving skills training and parent management training for conduct disorder. In P. C. Kendall (Ed.). *Child & adolescent therapy: Cognitive-behavioral procedures* (2nd ed., pp. 173–234). New York: Guilford Press.

Kazdin, A. E., & Weisz, J. (1998). Identifying and developing empirically supported child and adolescent treatments. *Journal of Consulting and Clinical Psychology, 66*, 100–110.

Kendall, P. C. (1992). *Cognitive-behavioral therapy for impulsive children: The manual* (2nd ed.). Ardmore, PA: Workbook Publishing. (www.workbookpublishing.com).

Kendall, P. C. (1994). Treating anxiety disorders in children: Results of a randomized clinical trial. *Journal of Consulting and Clinical Psychology, 62*, 100–110.

Kendall, P. C. (2000a). Guiding theory for therapy with children and adolescents. In Kendall, P. C. (Ed.), *Child and adolescent therapy: Cognitive-behavioral procedures* (2nd ed.). New York: Guilford Press.

Kendall, P. C. (2000b). *Cognitive-behavioral therapy for anxious children: Treatment manual* (2nd ed.). Ardmore, PA: Workbook Publishing. (www.workbookpublishing.com).

Kendall, P. C., Flannery-Schroeder, E., Panichelli-Mindel, S., Southam-Gerow, M., Henin, A., & Warman, M. (1997). Therapy for youth with anxiety disorders: A second randomized clinical trial. *Journal of Consulting & Clinical Psychology, 65*, 366–380.

Lochman, J. E., Whidby, J. M., & FitzGerald, D. G. (2000). Cognitive-behavioral assessment and treatment with aggressive children. In P. C. Kendall (Ed.), *Child & adolescent therapy: Cognitive-behavioral procedures* (2nd ed., pp. 31–87). New York: Guilford Press.

Long, P., Forhand, R., Wierson, M., & Morgan, A. (1994). Does parent training with young noncompliant children have long-term effects? *Behavior Research and Therapy, 32*, 101–107.

Manassis, K., Mendlowitz, S. L., Scapillato, D., Avery, D., Fiksenbaum, L., Freire, M., Monga, S., & Owens, M. (2002). Group and individual cognitive-behavioral therapy for childhood anxiety disorders. A randomized trial. *Journal of the American Academy of Child & Adolescent Psychiatry, 41*, 1423–1430.

Menzies, R. G., & Clarke, J. C. (1993). A comparison of *in vivo* and vicarious exposure in the treatment of childhood water phobia. *Behavior Research and Therapy, 31*, 9–15.

Ollendick, T. H. & Cerny, J. A. (1981). *Clinical behavior therapy with children.* New York: Plenum Press.

Ollendick, T. H., Hagopian, L. P., & Huntzinger, R. M. (1991). Cognitive-behavior therapy with nighttime fearful children. *Journal of Behavior Therapy & Experimental Psychiatry, 22*, 113–121.

Ollendick, T. H., & King, N. J. (1998). Empirically supported treatments for children with phobic and anxiety disorders: Current status. *Journal of Clinical Child Psychology, 27*, 156–167.

Ollendick, T. H., & King, N. J. (2000) Empirically supported treatments for children and adolescents. In P.C. Kendall (Ed.), *Child & adolescent therapy: Cognitive-behavioral procedures* (2nd ed., pp. 386–425). New York: Guilford Press.

Rapee, R. M., Wignall, A., Hudson, J. L., & Schniering, C. A. (2000). *Evidence-based treatment of child and adolescent anxiety disorders.* Oakland, CA: New Harbinger.

Silverman, W. K., Kurtines, W. M., Ginsburg, G. S., Weems, C.F., Rabian, B., & Serafini, L.T. (1999). Contingency management, self-control, and education support in the treatment of childhood phobic disorders: A randomized clinical trial. *Journal of Consulting & Clinical Psychology, 67*, 675–687.

Southam-Gerow, M., & Kendall, P. C. (1997). Parent-focused and cognitive-behavioral treatments of antisocial youth. In D. Stoff, J. Breiling, & J. D. Maser (Eds.), *Handbook of antisocial behavior.* New York: Wiley.

Stark, K. D., Sander, J. B., Yancy, M. G., Bronik, M. D., & Hoke, J. A. (2000). Treatment of depression in childhood and adolescence: Cognitive-behavioral procedures for the individual and family. In P. C. Kendall (Ed.), *Child & adolescent therapy: Cognitive-behavioral procedures* (2nd ed., pp. 173–234). New York: Guilford Press.

Webster-Stratton, C., & Herbert, M. (1994). *Troubled families-problem children: Working with parents: a collaborative process.* Chichester, England: Wiley.

Webster-Stratton, C. & Jamila Reid, M. (2000). The incredible years parents, teachers, and children training series: A multifaceted treatment approach for young children with conduct problems. In P. C. Kendall (Ed), *Child & adolescent therapy: Cognitive-behavioral procedures* (2nd ed., pp. 386–425). New York: Guilford Press.

Wells, K. C., & Egan, J. (1988). Social learning and systems family therapy for childhood oppositional disorder: Comparative treatment outcome. *Comprehensive Psychiatry, 29,* 138–146.

Wheeler, M. E., & Hess, K. W. (1976). Treatment of juvenile obesity by successive approximation control of eating. *Journal of Behavior Therapy and Experimental Psychiatry, 7,* 235–241.

CHAPTER 6

Adolescents

ROBERT D. FRIEDBERG and JESSICA M. MCCLURE

Many parents remark, "I don't know what happened to my kid. When she was 12, she was this sweet, compliant, motivated, respectful kid. Then, at 14, it was like she was snatched by aliens, and transformed into a self-absorbed monster designed to devour parents." Adolescence is a perplexing time that is confusing and troubling to teenagers and their parents. Teens feverishly search for identity, struggle with egocentrism, rebel against convention, and battle for autonomy. These developmental issues complicate the psychotherapy process and homework assignment.

Cognitive behavioral therapy is well suited to meet these clinical challenges. Collaborative empiricism and guided discovery allow therapists to intervene sensitively and effectively with teen clients who are struggling with autonomy, perceptions of control, and rebellion against authority. The goal-oriented, directive approach focuses on self-control and fosters a healthy self-identity. Cognitive therapy's emphasis on phenomenology respects the adolescents' subjective experiences yet balances them against objective reality. In this way, self-absorption may be decreased and broad self-identities reinforced.

Cognitive behavioral therapy enjoys empirical support for treating a variety of childhood problems. Cognitive behavioral approaches are effective in reducing symptoms of depression (Clarke, DeBar, & Lewinsohn, 2003; Lewinsohn, Clark, Rodhe, Hops, & Seeley, 1996; Weisz, Southam-Gerow, Gordis, & Connor-Smith, 2003) and anxiety (Albano & DiBartolo, 1997;

Ollendick & King, 1998; Velting, Setzer, & Albano, 2004). Additionally, disruptive behavior problems have also been effectively treated with cognitive behavioral methods (Bloomquist & Schnell, 2002; Feindler & Guttman, 1994; Kazdin, 2003; Lochman, Barry, & Pardini, 2003). Despite the favorable empirical findings, there is a lack of specific research examining the effectiveness of homework with adolescent patients.

This Chapter specifically addresses common barriers to homework in working with adolescent clients. Therapist and therapy-related problems such as lack of collaboration, the word *homework*, irrelevant homework assignments, vague tasks, leaving homework to the waning moments of a session, neglecting to write down assignments, and therapists' biased attitudes are described. Further, client barriers such as the nature of the adolescent's distress, misinterpretation or misunderstanding of the task, and skill deficits are discussed. Specific recommendations for overcoming these barriers follow and guide clinicians' problem-solving processes. Common homework assignments with adolescents are summarized, and the Chapter concludes with two case examples.

Common Barriers to Homework Assignments

Therapist and Therapy-Related Factors

Lack of Collaboration. Collaboration between clients and therapists is a central feature in cognitive therapy (A. T. Beck et al., 1979; J.S. Beck, 1995). Working together toward agreed-upon goals characterizes a team-oriented approach to treatment. However, when it comes to assigning homework, many therapists often neglect the therapeutic partnership and lean toward prescriptive assignments. This is particularly troublesome in working with adolescents.

Adolescents are trying on their individuality for size and are working hard to develop autonomy. Not surprisingly, they are resistant to authority figures ostensibly "controlling them." They do not want "adult" figures to co-opt their sense of choice and nascent freedom (Harris & Liebert, 1987). Therefore, we think it is best if homework comes directly from the teenager or if, at least, the youth has had significant input into the task. Therapists should avoid imposing assignments on adolescent clients.

The Word Homework. *Homework* is an emotionally loaded word that often carries negative implications for adolescents. They approach homework with dread and may work diligently to avoid anything associated with the term. Therefore, we suggest that therapists consider replacing *homework* with another term. Kendall and colleagues (Hudson & Kendall, 2002;

Kendall et al., 1992) offered the creative term *Show that I can* for homework assignments. Burns (1980) refers to homework as *self-help tasks*. We encourage therapists to adopt these terms and/or use their own imaginations to come up with alternative words for homework that are age appropriate.

Irrelevant, Meaningless Assignments. Homework assignments are intended to increase generalizability and behavioral rehearsal. They need to be practical and applicable. As any high school teacher knows, adolescents want to know how the material will help them in the future. If teen clients do not see how the homework can be meaningful to them, they will be less likely to complete it. Irrelevant assignments will be easily dismissed and quickly forgotten. Therapists must keep homework assignments real!

Relevance is influenced by many variables. First, what does the homework have to do with the adolescent's perceptions of the problem? If the youth believes she is in therapy because her mother "is a controlling bitch," keeping a mood log to track her angry outbursts will clearly be irrelevant to her. The therapist would have to design any assignment collaboratively so that it would approximate the client's view of her problem. If clients clearly see that completion of the homework is helping them with their problems (e.g., helping to convince a domineering mother to back away from her controlling behavior), their compliance and engagement in the homework task will likely increase.

Homework assignments with adolescents are always embedded in a familial and cultural context. Some homework assignments may be reinforced by caregivers, whereas others are not. Homework that is not encouraged by the family is unlikely to be completed. Therapists must ascertain the level of support for homework and therapeutic change within the family.

Homework assignments may unwittingly violate familial and/or cultural rules. Even an apparently simple task, such as monitoring and expressing negative feelings, may come up against a barrier. If the family, for personal or cultural reasons, sees anger as a taboo feeling, this task is doomed to failure. Friedberg and McClure (2002) suggest that developing an assignment that fosters greater autonomy when less autonomy is valued within the family's culture is an ill-advised therapeutic strategy. In assigning self-help tasks, the therapist must remain mindful of the family's cultural/ethnic identity and level of acculturation.

Vague, Abstract, and/or Difficult Tasks. Various cognitive behavioral therapists recommend that homework be broken down into small, discrete tasks (J.S. Beck, 1995; Spiegler & Guevremont, 1998). Adolescents need to know what is expected. If the task demand is too vague or abstract, they will not know what they are supposed to do. For instance, an apparently simple assignment such as "Keep track of your negative feelings" is way too vague. Which feelings? How do they know if their feelings are negative? How do they keep track of them?

When adolescents perceive that the task demands exceed their abilities, they are less likely to complete them. If a youngster is asked to complete a thought diary but does not yet know how to identify feelings or thoughts, the homework assignment is not likely to be effective. A graduated approach to homework matches the adolescent's skills to the task demands.

Leaving Homework to the Last Minute. Some therapists may leave homework to the last few waning moments of the session. Frequently this leads to a hurried assignment that more often than not misses the therapeutic mark. Additionally, it may foster increased noncompliance and ruptures in the therapeutic process.

Homework is central to cognitive therapy. When therapists leave homework to the last moment, it tends to be disembodied from the rest of the session rather than tied to a youngster's core problems (Friedberg & McClure, 2002). Moreover, the act of leaving homework to the last parts of the session is a metamessage to the young client. Not surprisingly, the client may think, "If the homework is so important, why is my therapist leaving it to the last minute?" Adolescents may feel rushed and consequently be less willing to ask questions about the assignment. Thus, confusion about the skills may be more likely. When the assignment is put off to the ending parts of the session, collaboration becomes difficult, and it is harder to write things down as a reminder or cue for completion. Additionally, potential obstacles cannot be discussed and solutions to these problems cannot be constructed.

Neglecting to Write Down Homework Assignments. Adolescents' lives are complex and replete with competing demands. These competing demands and varying attention levels contribute to forgetting about homework assignments. Therefore teenagers make use of multiple memory aides, Post-it notes, weekly calendars, and assignment books; they even write reminders on their palms! It is quite easy for busy teenagers to forget their therapy homework (Hudson & Kendall, 2002). Therefore neglecting to write down homework assignments may contribute to noncompliance.

Therapist Attitudes. In our experience of training and supervising doctoral students, therapists' attitudes to assigning homework can present obstacles to successful practice. Some therapists believe that homework places an unnecessary burden on the child. Other therapists think it ruptures therapeutic alliances and may simply believe homework is a bothersome task they would otherwise like to forget. Therapists may believe that assigning homework will reveal their own incompetence. In each of these general instances, the therapists' attitudes shape how homework is assigned and eventually completed. Ways of dealing with therapists' inaccurate beliefs about homework are presented in the following section on overcoming barriers to homework.

Client-Related Factors

Nature and Level of the Adolescent's Distress. An adolescent's psychological distress and presenting problems may create barriers to homework compliance. Depression, anxiety, rebelliousness, and psychological reactance may all contribute to difficulties with homework tasks. Emotional reasoning–based hopelessness, fearfulness, and anger can shape noncompliance. Fortunately, homework assignments can specifically target these obstacles.

A depressed teenager who is pessimistic and hopeless is likely to be noncompliant with homework assignments. Thoughts such as "Nothing will help," "Everything is useless," "I'm too depressed to do anything," "Even if I do homework, I'll do it wrong," and "This homework is too overwhelming for me" run through their minds. Anxious youngsters will avoid homework due to their fearfulness. They may believe "I can't do anything to cope," "Avoiding scary situations and feelings is better than dealing with them," and "Keeping track of my anxiety and noticing it are dangerous. It may make me worse."

Angry and rebellious youngsters may see homework as controlling and coercive. They may fight homework and engage in psychological combat with the therapist. Brehm's (1966) concept of psychological reactance is a particular way to explain this phenomenon. These youngsters believe that their freedom and sense of personal control is being thwarted by the homework assignment. Consequently, they will sabotage, avoid, and/or refuse homework as a way to preserve their autonomy.

Misunderstanding/Misinterpretation of the Task. Adolescents are not likely to do things they do not understand. Most adolescents demand to know the rationale for tasks they are given. Adolescents may also misinterpret assignments. Moreover, if they do not have a good grasp of the assignment, they may not attempt it because they fear failure. Finally, even if a task is tried with an inadequate understanding, the outcome is likely to be poor, which will undermine future compliance.

John is a depressed 16-year-old boy who was withdrawn, inactive, and avoidant of any perceived demands. Pleasant activity scheduling was assigned. In one instance, John came to the session without having completed the activity schedule. When the therapist processed the noncompliance with John, John said he thought he was not supposed to do anything that was unpleasant or demanding. This idiosyncratic misinterpretation compromised compliance.

Even an ostensibly clear assignment such as a daily thought record (DTR) can be open to misunderstanding and misinterpretation. Shelly, a 15-year-old angry and depressed girl, brought back a DTR with feelings listed in the thought column and thoughts recorded in the situation column. Simply, she did not know how to identify thoughts and the difference between situations, thoughts, and feelings.

Skill Deficits. Homework requires a certain level of skill level. If a teenager lacks the skills necessary to complete the task, he or she is unlikely to attempt the assignment. Some young clients have trouble reading or writing. Perhaps English is a second language for them. Others may have problems with abstract reasoning. Early in treatment, impulsive adolescents may lack the delay skills needed to "stop and think." When task demands exceed perceived or actual coping resources, distress occurs (Selye, 1974). Stress associated with the task and/or the client's perceived expectations from the therapist then will compromise the task. Thus, therapists need to develop assignments that are sensitive to adolescents' cognitive, behavioral, and emotional capacities.

Strategies for Effective Homework

Embed Homework in a Case Conceptualization. Cognitive behavioral therapy offers clinicians a robust conceptual model to understand and predict human behavior. The use of a case formulation to assign homework tasks helps the therapist to individualize treatment and places any technique in a proper clinical context. The case conceptualization helps the clinician to make effective choices regarding which assignment to use at what time. For example, if an adolescent is inactive, lethargic, and unable to access cognitions, behavioral assignments such as pleasant activity scheduling are first-rate alternatives. Further, if the DTR is not too difficult for a teenage client, moving on to self-instructional tasks seems indicated. On the other hand, if the client is detached from his thoughts and feelings, more work on self-monitoring aimed at identifying problematic thoughts and feelings is merited.

The case conceptualization also adds focus to homework assignment. For instance, a client may present in therapy due to social anxiety and avoidance. The social anxiety may be mediated primarily by problematic cognitions regarding fear of negative evaluation and social skills deficits, singly or both in combination. Case formulation yields data on which problems to target. Perhaps the skills deficit is primary. If this is the case, homework containing social skills practice, including overt and covert rehearsal, might be assigned. If the client's distortions compromise skill training, homework focusing on self-instruction, reattribution, or any rational analysis may be in order.

A case conceptualization gives clinicians ideas on *how* to assign tasks. If the case formulation reveals that the teen is quite passive, needy, and submissive during initial homework assignments the therapist might scoot a chair closer to the youngster, model the skill initially, or take a leadership position by beginning to write down the assignment. For other youngsters who are more autonomous and see others as overly controlling, more collaboration in homework assignment is indicated. The therapist might check in more frequently (e.g., "How does this idea seem to fit for you?"). Instead of scooting next to the client and writing on a tablet, the therapist might stand up and write on a dry-erase white board.

Finally, case formulations allow therapists to anticipate problems and obstacles in therapy (J. S. Beck, 1995; Persons, 1989). This is especially useful for homework assignments. For example, if, after formulating the case, the therapist predicts that the adolescent sees adults in authority as critical and punitive, he can anticipate that the young client may test him. The client may deliberately fail to complete an assignment so as to see the therapist's reaction. A conceptually prepared therapist is then ready to process the noncompliance with regard to the adolescent's interpersonal assumption. This strategy is likely to yield productive therapeutic results.

Processing Noncompliance. Noncompliance is common among patients in psychotherapy. Therefore we recommend that therapists be prepared to expect noncompliance with homework and to process problems with the assignment. Working through noncompliance serves several important purposes. First, it communicates to the adolescent that homework assignments are important and central to therapeutic change. Second, the processing of noncompliance exemplifies a collaborative approach to therapy. Through guided discovery, the therapist can explore the reasons behind noncompliance and try to see things from the youngster's perspective. Third, for many adolescent clients noncompliance with schoolwork or parental demands is part of the presenting problem. Not surprisingly, they may also avoid psychotherapy homework. By working through the noncompliance, therapists may begin to focus on core psychological features associated with the adolescent's presenting problems. Fourth, processing noncompliance with adolescent clients is a tangible way to reinforce the therapeutic alliance. It is a concrete way for therapists to show that they care.

Processing noncompliance with adolescents demonstrates that therapists take homework seriously and in a simple sense remember that homework is assigned. When therapists neglect to follow up on homework assignments, clients learn that therapy is not important. They may therefore tune out other assignments and a spiraling cycle of noncompliance may be established.

Be Collaborative Rather Than Punitive. In processing noncompliance, therapists are well advised to adopt a collaborative rather than punitive stance. Therapists should work to elicit the thoughts, feelings, behavior, and environmental circumstances surrounding the noncompliance. Questions such as "What is getting in your way?" "What was difficult?" and "What made it hard to check this out?" are examples of helpful questions.

Frequently, adolescents' noncompliance with homework reflects their core presenting problems. Noncompliance may be explained through fears of loss of control, rejection, disapproval, or feelings of shame, hopelessness, and embarrassment (Beck, 1995; Burns, 1989). Additionally, the young client may be rebellious and suspicious of the therapist's motives. Processing the noncompliance allows the cognitive therapist to work in the here and now with a concrete task. For instance, an adolescent might neglect to do homework because he is so depressed and pessimistic that he believes "nothing will change." This belief is not limited to homework assignments but rather reflects a general sense of helplessness and hopelessness. By collaboratively processing the noncompliance, therapists can elicit the belief and use guided discovery to test its accuracy. Thus, the therapist is not only managing the noncompliance but also chipping away at the youngster's negative cognitions.

Finally, processing noncompliance augments the therapeutic alliance. In our experience, adolescents respect therapists who mean what they say. If therapists say homework is important and believe it will be helpful yet leave noncompliance unaddressed, they are giving mixed messages to the youngster. This ambiguity will likely lead to increased anxiety and mistrust of the therapist. How can a trusting environment be created when therapists do not do what they say they are going to do?

Be Collaborative Rather Than Prescriptive. Collaborative empiricism and guided discovery, the central principles in cognitive therapy, are especially pivotal in homework assignment. Collaboration invites the adolescent to be a partner in the therapy. It helps the client make therapy her personal experience. Moreover, collaboration gives teen clients a voice in treatment. In our experience, most adolescents think adult authority figures are "know it alls" who enjoy constantly telling them what to do. A prescriptive approach where the adolescent has little say feeds right into this belief system. By collaborating and partnering with the adolescent, the therapist increases the youngster's perceived level of control. The more control adolescents believe they have, the more likely they are to comply with tasks.

Simplify Tasks and Use Graduated Assignments. In our clinical experience, difficult, ambiguous, and abstract tasks yield unproductive results and contribute to noncompliance. The method of "Just keep it simple, doctor" (JKIS) is recommended. Resist the urge to be overly sophisticated! For example, like J. S. Beck (1995), we recommend giving adolescents a thought diary in stages rather than having them complete the whole form at once. It is typical for us to initially assign the first three columns of a thought diary (e.g., situation, feeling, and thought). For some youngsters, this is too big a task. In these cases, we may assign one column at a time.

Reducing response demands on the adolescent is also a useful strategy. For example, in working with an angry adolescent who presents with aggressive behavior problems and is not a facile writer, the therapist may want to simplify a self-monitoring assignment. Rather than having the client write down all his potential angry triggers and provocative situations, the therapist might ask him about these circumstances, list the situations for him in simple language, and then ask him to just put a check by the ones he encounters during the coming week.

Begin the Task in the Session. As any procrastinator knows, there is nothing more daunting than a task left undone. Things appear overwhelming and often larger than they really are. When tasks are started during a session, they become more graduated and manageable. Further, if a homework assignment is begun in the session, the therapist can troubleshoot problem areas. Therapists can discern whether the adolescent really understands the task. The therapist and the client can deal with obstacles that may block task completion. Finally, an alert cognitive therapist can process the "here-and-now" thoughts and feelings a young client experiences in doing homework in session.

Writing Down Tasks. Regardless of the actual task, it is usually best to write homework assignments down on paper. Outcomes of homework assignments should also be recorded in some fashion. Certainly homework assignments should be noted in the client's chart. Adolescents could be given notebooks or agenda planners to keep track of their assignments. Many cognitive behavioral assignments—such as DTRs, pleasant activity schedules, and scales of subjective units of distress—are in work-sheet form and provide a readily available written record. For clients with reading and writing difficulties, therapists may have to reduce or eliminate the writing demands. Tape recorders and forms that include simple words and basic response demands (check marks, circles, etc.) may help (J. S. Beck, 1995).

Involving Parents and Establishing Contingencies. In typical outpatient therapy, clinicians see the adolescent for only about an hour per week. Parents and other caretakers should be enlisted as behavior managers. Parental involvement with homework is a real boost to the homework process. Therapists may need to work with parents to help them encourage their youngsters to complete homework tasks. Parents, adolescent clients, and therapists might establish contingency charts for homework assignments that the client completes. If the youngster reaches his or her goal for homework, a reward from the parents could follow.

Some youngsters need more than a weekly check-in to reinforce their homework completion. They simply need a schedule of reinforcement that richly rewards their efforts. For these young clients, therapists might invite them to call him or her with homework assignment results twice before the next session. If the clients and therapists enjoy computer access, youngsters could also e-mail the results to the therapist between sessions.

Involving parents in treatment is rarely a categorical decision for the therapist. Rather, it is a dimensional one. For us, it is not a matter of whether to involve parents in treatment but a question of how much to include them. Certainly when family systemic issues such as overprotectiveness, inconsistent discipline, or triangulation intrude on the adolescent's problem, family-oriented cognitive behavioral therapy is indicated. Typically, the client's behavior affects the family system. For example, a depressed youngster worries her parents. This increased worry may create greater tension and pressure at home. Involving the family in pleasant event scheduling may not only increase the youngster's mood but brighten the family climate as well.

While establishing contingencies may increase compliance, there are some potential risks to this approach. First, adolescents may feel pressured to comply by demanding adults. Second, they may become reactant to the perceived control of therapists and parents. Third, the idea of doing homework and being monitored by their parents may be overwhelming to already distressed youngsters. Finally, adolescents may resent parental intrusion into their therapy.

Parents should be included in a way that does not undermine an adolescent's budding psychological autonomy. In these instances, the adolescent could collaboratively determine when and how much to involve parents.

Working With Therapists' Attitudes Toward Homework. Therapists are not immune to dysfunctional attitudes. The use of DTRs, thought-testing techniques, and behavioral experiments will help. Giving therapists their own homework assignments facilitates empathic understanding of clients. Further, successful homework assignments gives therapists confidence in the process.

As supervisors, we initially elicit the therapists' cognitions and emotions regarding homework. Frequently, they worry that the adolescent will resent homework, dislike therapy, and disapprove of them. Once these thoughts and feelings are identified on the DTR, thought testing can occur.

Thought testing could include Socratic dialogues during supervision. Test of evidence and reattribution procedures might be started in supervision and continued as homework. Behavioral experiments where therapists try homework with their clients can be designed. Outcomes of the homework assignments should be recorded and analyzed. Finally, processing of therapists' thoughts and feelings accompanying the behavioral experiment is recommended.

Types of Homework

Introduction to Treatment

Adolescents may approach therapy with caution and even a degree of suspicion. Demystifying therapy is an important part of the therapeutic process. There are several homework assignments to facilitate an adolescent's introduction to treatment (Friedberg & McClure, 2002; Padesky, 1988). The "Dear Doctor" letter and problem list are two noteworthy examples.

The "Dear Doctor" letter (Padesky, 1988) gives adolescents a way of communicating their problems and goals for therapy. At home, the adolescent may craft a letter that supplies important information she or he forgot to tell the therapist or was uncomfortable expressing verbally. The letter helps the adolescent independently express perceptions of the problem and goals for treatment. Thus, the letter conveys the youngster's representation of the problem rather than the teacher's, parents', or therapist's view. The letter may add focus to the sessions and increase an adolescent's engagement in the task. If the client prefers, the letter may be recorded on tape rather than written.

The problem list (Padesky, 1988; Persons, 1989) asks the teen client to specify areas to change. Initially, adolescents may avoid responsibility for the problems and/or externalize blame. In the early phases of treatment, we suggest therapists accept this problem definition and work with the client to gradually internalize responsibility. Friedberg and McClure (2002) gave the example of a 15-year-old who described his main problem as being his mother's nagging. Gradually, the therapist shifted the focus from the mother's nagging to the child's behavior by using the problem list.

The problem list should carve the problems into cognitive, behavioral, interpersonal, physiological, and mood components. This specificity helps the therapist target salient symptoms. Moreover, the operationalized definition may also foster an adolescent's sense of control.

Simple Behavioral Tasks. Pleasant activity scheduling (A. T. Beck et al., 1979; Greenberger & Padesky, 1995; Stark, 1990) is designed to increase the level of positive reinforcement/pleasant activity in an adolescent's life. The pleasant activity schedule resembles a calendar or weekly planner with days of the week written across the top of the page and hours of the day down the left side. The youngster records the pleasant activity he or she attempted in the space corresponding to the day and time it was completed. Initially, adolescent clients may find it difficult to come up with pleasant activities. Stark (1990) provides lists of pleasant activities in the appendix of his book. Clients may want to choose activities from these lists.

In the therapy session, the therapist and client could scour a newspaper for ideas of pleasant events, then cut them out and put them in a box; then the youngster can choose an activity from the box three times during the week. He or she can then record the activity on the pleasant events scheduling form.

Relaxation training is a simple behavioral homework task. A sample assignment might involve the adolescent practicing relaxation for 20 minutes a day for 4 days of the week between sessions. Clients can then rate their mood prior to and after the relaxation practice.

Social skills assignments are also simple behavioral homework tasks. A teen client might be assigned the task of asking for help from a teacher or a peer in math class. The client may then record the situation, feelings, and thoughts accompanying the request. Additionally, the youngster might write down the reactions of peers and teachers. The adolescent might also record thoughts and feelings that arise after asking for help.

Self-Monitoring Tasks. Daily thought records or thought diaries are commonly used self-monitoring assignments (A. T. Beck et al., 1979; J. Beck, 1995; Greenberger & Padesky, 1995). In diaries, adolescents fill in columns describing problematic situations, distressing feelings, and automatic thoughts. In more advanced assignments, young clients may develop alternative thoughts to counter maladaptive beliefs and rerate their moods to assess the impact of the alternative response. Thought diaries are general assignments that are widely applicable to many adolescent problems, such as anxiety, depression, anger, aggression, shame, and guilt.

Subjective rating of distress (Masters, Burish, Hollon, & Rimm, 1987) tasks invite young clients to track their level of discomfort across various situations. The adolescent lists several distressing or provocative situations and then rates his or her subjective level of distress on a collaboratively determined scale (e.g., 1 to 5, 1 to 10, 1 to 100, etc.).

Hassle logs (Feindler & Ecton, 1986; Feindler & Guttman, 1994) are self-monitoring assignments used specifically for adolescents with aggressive behavior problems. They help youngsters record actual provocative situations, list the people involved, and track their physiological, cognitive, behavioral, and emotional responses. Most hassle logs include checklists on which adolescents simply check off items, making the task quite simple to complete.

Self-Instruction Tasks. Self-instruction is a basic cognitive change technique and is a homework staple. Generally, self-instruction follows assignments involving DTRs. Self-instruction provides adolescent clients with more adaptive and functional self-talk. The key is helping youngsters construct inner dialogues that counter their maladaptive thinking and that seem real to them. Making use of the adolescent's idiosyncratic language, slang, and idiom is a good strategy.

Meichenbaum (1985) offers clinicians and their clients some good examples of self-instructional statements. In general, there are several issues to consider in good self-instruction (Friedberg, Friedberg, & Friedberg, 2001). Effective self-instruction "makes sense of the event, seems believable to the child, and decreases negative feelings" (Friedberg et al., 2001, p. 82). Avoiding simplistic and Pollyannaish self-talk is strongly recommended. Ideally, coping thoughts should fully address the stressor, offer an alternative way of looking at it, and provide an active coping plan.

The typical process helps youngsters to come up with different things to say to themselves during times of distress. Depending on the client's capacity, the therapist may model some self-instructions. With many youngsters, the therapist may prompt the client by asking "What else could you say to yourself that would make you feel less depressed?" Once the youngster identifies some self-instruction, the therapist may proceed with a homework assignment. Sample homework assignments might include listing five additional coping statements. Another assignment might be completing the first three columns of the record by replacing the distressing thought with an adaptive response and then rerating the outcome. Coping statements could be recorded on pads or index cards.

Behavioral Experiments. Behavioral experiments are classical ways whereby youngsters can demonstrate their competence. Behavioral experiments test out a young client's predictions and hypotheses. In many cases, they may also be considered graduated exposure trials. The prediction of pleasure or anxiety is a common behavioral experiment.

Pleasure prediction is a way to test whether a depressed youngster's expectation that she will not enjoy any fun activity is accurate. Typically, these adolescents have some degree of anhedonia. In pleasure predicting, the teen constructs a list of pleasant activities that are planned for the following week. Next, they rate the degree of pleasure they anticipate getting from doing these activities. For homework, they actually do the activities and rate their degree of pleasure. Finally, they compare the actual to the anticipated pleasure. *Anxiety prediction* works in the same way. However, in anxiety prediction, actual anxiety ratings are compared to anticipated anxiety.

Behavioral experiments can be applied to troublesome thoughts, such as "I'm invisible. No one even notices me." In this instance, a homework assignment might include saying "Hi" to three people per day and then recording their reaction. Hudson and Kendall (2002) offer very creative homework assignments to challenge anxiety surrounding being the center of attention. Among many other assignments, they suggested wearing odd-colored socks to the shopping mall, asking to go to the bathroom in gym class, and returning an item to a store. Table 6.1 lists the therapy modules and their accompanying homework assignments.

Case Study 1

Trisha was brought to therapy by her mother because of "out-of-control behavior." Her mother reported defiance, oppositional behavior, arguing, and aggressive outbursts, which sometimes included throwing objects on the floor, pushing chairs, and on one occasion kicking her mother. Trisha lived with her biological parents and 12-year-old sister, who was moderately mentally retarded. Because of her sister's limitations, many responsibilities had fallen to Trisha, including caring for her sister and doing household chores. Trisha reported numerous depressive symptoms, including somatic complaints, fatigue, irritability, anhedonia, and vague suicidal ideation ("I wish I were never born.").

Given Trisha's level of irritability/depression, the therapist chose to begin treatment with behavioral activation. Because of Trisha's anger at her parents and low motivation for therapy, the first tasks needed to

TABLE 6.1 Therapy Modules and Accompanying Homework Assignments

Module	Homework Assignment
Socialization to treatment	"Dear Doctor" letter
	Problem list
Behavioral tasks	Pleasant activity scheduling
	Relaxation
	Social skills training
Self-monitoring	Daily thought records
	Subjective units of distress
	Hassle logs
Self-instruction	Coping statements
	Rational response diaries
	Coping cards
Behavioral experiments	Pleasure prediction
	Anxiety prediction

increase her positive affect. The first assignment was embedded in the case conceptualization based on Trisha's presentation of symptoms and expressed goals. Trisha's goals were discussed in detail. She complained that she "never has fun anymore, her parents never let her do anything, and they always make her watch her sister." Although these negative cognitions needed challenging, behavioral activation seemed like a better first step to both elevate Trisha's mood and make her more prepared for the tough cognitive work ahead. Moreover, it set the stage and provided data for subsequent thought testing.

Because of the time it took to initially establish rapport and discuss goals, the first therapy session was drawing to an end without fully introducing pleasant activity scheduling. Not wanting to rush the assignment and risk failure due to lack of understanding or overwhelming Trisha with too much homework, Trisha and the therapist agreed to start by making a list of previously enjoyed activities. During the interview, she had reported enjoying looking at fashion magazines at Barnes & Noble and watching reruns of the television show *Friends*. Those activities were added to the list during the session to help start the homework process. The therapist's flexibility with the homework helped maintain rapport and provided Trisha with an assignment with which she was familiar. Together, Trisha and the therapist agreed that she would complete the list for homework.

Trisha's oppositional and defiant behavioral pattern put her at risk for homework noncompliance. Thus, before ending the session, obstacles to completing the assignment were predicted and resolved. "What if you decide this is stupid and you aren't going to do it?" the therapist asked. Through discussion, Trisha generated self-instructional statements to help herself complete the tasks, including "I'll remind myself that we are doing this as an experiment to see if it works, and if it doesn't work, we can change it so it does."

Once Trisha's mood and motivation were raised through behavioral activation, she was enthusiastic and hopeful for the future, seeing how progress had occurred with past strategies. In the next few sessions, Trisha and her therapist again evaluated the cognitive model, keeping in mind the key areas of change. The following dialogue illustrates the progress:

Therapist: Well Trisha, I am sure you remember seeing this model a few weeks ago, and we have been talking about it as we reviewed your homework. What strikes you the most about the model now that you have seen it a few times and used some therapy strategies?

Trisha: Well, I remember the first day you talked about how all the areas are connected and when one changes, the others shift too. At the time, I thought that if we tried to change one to make me feel less sad, the other three would be still pulling to the sad side, and three outweighs one so....I was afraid it was a losing battle.

Therapist: That must have been a scary thought. It shows real strength and a desire to feel better that you still agreed to give it a try and see if you could help yourself, even with those beliefs.

Trisha: Thanks. I just told myself, it can't hurt to try, and if it doesn't work, I just won't do it any more.

Therapist: That self-talk really motivates you. So, looking at the model, what angle do you think we should attack your depression from from now on?

Trisha: Well, as I was doing the pleasant events scheduling, I noticed I do a lot of talking to myself that can really bring me down. Like, "This will never work, things will never get better, I'm such a loser." So whatever will help with those things.

Therapist: Well, look at the model. Which area do you think that would be?

Trisha: I don't know. I guess thoughts.

Therapist: That's right. Thoughts are the things we say in our heads. You are one step ahead because you already

started noticing your own thoughts when you were
completing the Pleasant Activity Schedule. By looking
at the thoughts in an organized way, we can figure out
what thoughts are true and which ones are not true.
The inaccurate thoughts can be changed, and we can
figure out ways to cope with the accurate ones.

Trisha: Yah, but what if the bad thoughts are actually true?
What if we look at them and find out that I really am
a loser, or that my parents do love my sister more
than they love me? I will feel horrible then!

Therapist: That's what we will be testing the thoughts to see. If
they are accurate, then I will help you learn ways to
solve the problem. But if they are not true, we will
work to modify them until they are.

Trisha: How will I know if they are true?

Therapist: I'm glad you asked. Let me show you what we call a
daily thought record.

Thus, the next homework assignment, DTRs, was closely tied to Trisha's
goals as well as session activities. The therapist and Trisha worked together
to complete a DTR. Since Trisha was familiar with the task of scheduling
pleasant activities, she easily identified events, feelings, and ratings.
She showed some skills in cognitive identification, and through therapy
learned to test her own thoughts and modify them as appropriate.
Together, the therapist and Trisha designed the DTR homework assignment. It was time to review the homework in the following session.

Therapist: So, how did it go with the thought diaries?

Trisha: I actually didn't have any thoughts to use so I didn't
do it.

Therapist: Wow, no thoughts in two weeks. That is curious. Tell
me more about what you mean.

Trisha: Well, I had thoughts, but none really like before. Plus,
I have been very busy and didn't really have the time
to write stuff down. School is starting, and I had to
watch my sister a few times. And, a friend had me
over for a night. I just ran out of time.

Therapist: What things did you try to help you get the work
done?

Trisha: I kept the worksheet on my desk like I always do so I
would see it every day. And I still have the sticky note

on my desk that reminds me, "It won't take as long as you think."

Therapist: So using those things, what still made it difficult to do the worksheet?

Trisha: I feel like the thoughts are true, and if I write them down it's just more proof of what a screw up I am.

By processing the noncompliance with Trisha, the therapist was able to uncover a belief that set up barriers for homework completion rather than just attributing the noncompliance to rebelliousness. Accordingly, the therapist and client were able to address Trisha's fears, work to set up more supports for homework completion, and complete a DTR in session about Trisha's fears.

Trisha's case illustrates several pivotal points. First, the therapist was genuinely *collaborative* in her approach to homework assignments. Second, homework assignments were embedded in a case formulation. Third, the assignments were specific and graduated. Finally, potential obstacles to homework were identified and strategies for overcoming these barriers developed.

Case Study 2

Carl is a 14-year-old adolescent presenting with significant social anxiety. At intake, his mother expressed concern because Carl "just sits in his room all day." He rarely saw peers outside of school and refused to join school activities. When pushed to engage in activities, Carl became angry with his parents, yelled, and cried. He often said, "Just leave me alone."

Carl presented for the initial session very defensively. He avoided eye contact, shrugged in response to questions, and rolled his eyes. The therapist was able to work with Carl during the session to establish rapport by acknowledging his anger at his parents and reflecting his resentment at being forced into therapy. The therapist worked collaboratively with Carl to make an agreement to try the therapy before making a decision about whether he wanted to participate in the future. Once therapy and confidentiality were described, Carl relaxed slightly. Since fear of negative evaluation was so present for Carl, the therapist adopted a graduated approach to therapy and expressiveness.

It was evident in the initial interview that Carl struggled with differentiating his feelings. At times, it was hard for him to distinguish between anger and anxiety. Situations that appeared to be anxiety-provoking for Carl often ended with outbursts of anger. Thus, building skill in identifying feelings was necessary for Carl to help him recognize what was uncomfortable about certain situations and thus to enable him to identify problems. The skills were discussed and taught in the session. Given Carl's high levels of anxiety and initial levels of avoidance, the therapist decided to begin homework assignments with plenty of time left in the session to ensure that it did not get cut short. Carl was very interested in video games and played his Xbox for hours. So the therapist talked with Carl about how he got better at games by practicing. The analogy was applied to therapy skills and homework was introduced. The following dialogue illustrates the process:

Therapist: Just like practice improves your performance on video games, practicing the things we do in here will improve your skills and help us reach your goals of not feeling "bad all the time." On this paper there are three categories: situation, feeling, and feeling rating. We are going to practice recording them just as we have been discussing them aloud.
[Therapist hands Carl the paper. Recognizing that his anxiety seems to be increasing, the therapist decides to have Carl simply write his responses so he does not increase his anxiety by saying them aloud. It seems to be triggering his fears of negative evaluation. Carl records an example and the therapist reads it aloud.]

Therapist: Great Carl, you are really getting the hang of this. Now, we need to decide how much practice would be helpful between now and next time we meet.

Carl: Whatever you think, doc.

Therapist: Well, we need to decide that together. We just did one in here, how long did that take?

Carl: Like two minutes.

Therapist: So how many would be helpful to do at home, but not take up too much time.

Carl: Maybe five?

Therapist: Okay, five. Now, what will help you remember to complete the paper and bring it back next session?

By solving the problem ahead of time, the therapist helps Carl predict obstacles to doing the homework and come up with a game plan for dealing with those obstacles. Then, if the obstacles present themselves, Carl will feel more confident in his ability to cope and complete the task. It also conveys the message that the work is important enough to discuss in detail and plan ahead for.

When Carl returned the next week for a therapy session, he smiled when he walked in the door carrying a folder. "I did the paper," he immediately said. The therapist praised him, and as they processed the homework experience, Carl was notably less anxious than he had been during the previous session. He described how he brought the worksheet home and put it on his bookshelf where he keeps his video games so that he would see it every time he played a game (which was every day). Carl described how he met some of the obstacles and overcame them with strategies discussed the previous week. By discussing the homework assignment as well as the process of completing it, the therapist sends the message that homework is a valuable part of therapy.

Working with Carl's fears of negative evaluation was a major focus of therapy. After he learned to accurately identify his thoughts and feelings, therapy shifted to modifying his inaccurate predictions of danger (e.g., "People will laugh at me. I'll embarrass myself. This will be humiliating.") Behavioral experiments were assigned in a graduated manner (e.g., getting a list of school activities, finding out where and when meetings were held, etc.) Whenever he did these tasks, Carl completed DTRs.

Finally, anxiety prediction was assigned. Carl predicted how much anxiety he would experience going to the meeting of the School Spirit Club. He also recorded the thoughts and feelings he experienced as he anticipated the meeting. ("All eyes will be on me. I'll feel terrified. I'll do something stupid and feel nervous.") Carl applied his newly acquired self-instructional skills to his anticipatory anxiety and came up with coping statements. ("It's unlikely people will see me as the center of attention. They are more likely to be paying attention to something else.")

Carl went to the club and rated his anxiety during and after the meeting. He compared his predicted anxiety rating to the actual distress and crafted a conclusion. ("Before the meeting, I thought it would be a lot worse than it was.") After he successfully completed the homework, he rewarded himself by playing his Xbox games for an extra 30 minutes.

Carl's case illustrates several key points. First, a modular approach to treatment characterized by graduated tasks was adopted. Second, knowing that initially Carl's fears of negative evaluation would compromise homework assignments, the therapist collaboratively helped Carl to solve the problem of obstacles to homework. Third, homework assignments specifically tailored to his presenting problems (e.g., going to school activities, etc.) were crafted.

Conclusion

Homework makes therapy portable for adolescents and their families. Homework assignments allow adolescent clients to practice their acquired skills in a natural context (e.g., home, school, etc.). It facilitates generalization and self-control. Despite these clear advantages, homework can be a tough "sell" to teenagers. In this Chapter, we presented common barriers to homework and potential strategies for overcoming these obstacles. Cognitive therapists are continually challenged to build homework assignments in creative and flexible ways. We hope that this Chapter will provide therapists with new ideas and methods to meet their clinical challenges with their adolescent clients.

References

Albano, A. M., & DiBartolo, P. M. (1997). Cognitive-behavioral treatment of obsessive-compulsive disorder and social phobia in children and adolescents. In L. Vandecreek, S. Knapp, & T. L. Jackson (Eds.), *Innovations in clinical practice: A source book* (pp. 41–58). Sarasota, FL: Professional Resource Press.

Beck, A. T., Rush, A. J., Shaw, B. F., & Emery, G. (1979). *Cognitive therapy of depression.* New York: Guilford Press.

Beck, J. S. (1995). *Cognitive therapy: Basics and beyond.* New York: Guilford Press.

Bloomquist, M. L., & Schnell, S. V. (2002). *Helping children with aggression and conduct problems: Best practices for intervention.* New York: Guilford Press.

Brehm, J. W. (1966). *A theory of psychological reactance.* New York: Academic Press.

Burns, D. D. (1980). *Feeling good: The new mood therapy.* New York: Signet.

Burns, D. D. (1989). *The feeling good workbook.* New York: William Morrow.

Clarke, G. N., DeBar, L. L., & Lewinsohn, P. M. (2003). Cognitive-behavioral group treatment for adolescent depression. In A. E. Kazdin, & J. R. Weisz (Eds.), *Evidence-based psychotherapies for children and adolescents* (pp.120–134). New York: Guilford Press.

Feindler, E. L., & Ecton, R. B. (1986). *Adolescent anger control: Cognitive-behavioral techniques.* New York: Pergamon Press.

Feindler, E. L., & Guttman, J. (1994). Cognitive-behavioral anger control training. In C. W. LeCroy (Ed.), *Handbook of child and adolescent treatment manuals* (pp. 170–199). New York: Lexington Books.

Friedberg, R. D., Friedberg, B. A., & Friedberg, R. J. (2001). *Therapeutic exercises for children: Guided self-discovery through cognitive-behavioral techniques.* Sarasota, FL: Professional Resource Press.

Friedberg, R. D., & McClure, J. M. (2002). *Clinical practice of cognitive therapy with children and adolescents: The nuts and bolts.* New York: Guilford Press.

Greenberger, D. P., & Padesky, C. A. (1995). *Mind over mood.* New York: Guilford Press.

Harris, J. R., & Liebert, R. M. (1987). *The child: Development from birth through adolescence* (2nd ed.). Englewood Cliffs, NJ: Prentice Hall.

Hudson, J. L., & Kendall, P. C. (2002). Showing you can do it: Homework in therapy for children and adolescents with anxiety disorders. *Journal of Clinical Psychology, 58*, 525–534.

Kazdin, A. E. (2003). Problem-solving skills training and parent management training for conduct disorder. In A. E. Kazdin, & J. R. Weisz (Eds.). *Evidence based psychotherapies for children and adolescents* (pp. 241–262). New York: Guilford Press.

Kendall, P. C., Chansky, T. E., Kane, M. T., Kim, R. S., Kortlander, E., Ronan, K. R., Sessa, F. M., & Siqueland, L. (1992). *Anxiety disorders in youth: Cognitive-behavioral interventions.* Boston: Allyn & Bacon.

Lewinsohn, P. M., Clarke, G. N., Rodhe, P., Hops, H. & Seeley, J. R. (1996). A course in coping: A cognitive-behavioral approach to the treatment of adolescent depression. In E. D. Hibbs, & P. S. Jensen (Eds.), *Psychosocial treatment for child and adolescent disorders: Empirically-based strategies for clinical practice* (pp. 109–136). Washington, DC: American Psychological Association.

Lochman, J. E., Barry, T. D., & Pardini, D. A. (2003). Anger control training for aggressive youth. In A. E. Kazdin, & J. R. Weisz (Eds.), *Evidence-based psychotherapies for children and adolescents* (pp. 263–281). New York: Guilford Press.

Masters, J. C., Burish, T. G., Hollon, S. D., & Rimm, D. C. (1987). *Behavioral therapy: Techniques and empirical findings* (2nd ed.). San Diego, CA: Harcourt, Brace, Jovanovich.

Meichenbaum, D. H. (1985). *Stress inoculation training.* New York: Pergamon Press.

Ollendick, T. O., & King, N. J. (1998). Empirically-supported treatments for children with phobic and anxiety-disorders: Current status. *Journal of Clinical Child Psychology, 27,* 156–167.

Padesky, C. A. (1988). *Intensive training series in cognitive therapy.* Workshop series presented at Newport Beach, CA.

Persons, J. B. (1989). *Cognitive therapy in practice: A case formulation approach.* New York: Norton.

Selye, H. (1974). *Stress without distress.* New York: Signet.

Spiegler, M. D., & Guevremon, D. C. (1998). *Contemporary behavior therapy* (3rd ed.). Pacific Grove, CA: Brooks/Cole.

Stark, K. D. (1990). *Childhood depression: School-based intervention.* New York: Guilford Press.

Velting, O., Setzer, N., & Albano, A. M. (2004). Update on and advances in assessment and cognitive behavioral therapy of anxiety disorders in children and adolescents. *Professional Psychology, 35,* 42–54.

Weisz, J. R., Southam-Gerow, M. A., Gordis, E. B., & Connor-Smith, J. (2003). Primary and secondary control enhancement training for youth depression: Applying the deployment-focused model of treatment development and testing. In A. E. Kazdin, & J. R. Weisz (Eds.), *Evidence-based psychotherapies for children and adolescents* (pp.165–186). New York: Guilford Press.

CHAPTER 7

Older Adults

DAVID W. COON, YARON G. RABINOWITZ, LARRY W. THOMPSON,
and DOLORES GALLAGHER-THOMPSON

Clearly the introduction of cognitive, behavioral, and cognitive behavioral therapies (CBT) into psychological practice and clinical intervention research has helped to encourage the consistent use of homework or self-help assignments in psychotherapy (e.g., Beck, Rush, Shaw, & Emery, 1979; Ellis, 1962; Kanfer & Phillips, 1966; Lewinsohn, 1974). The skills-based nature of these theories builds on an underlying assumption that homework directly reduces emotional distress by teaching patients skills to identify and modify unhelpful thinking and behavior patterns. CBT also hypothesizes that homework can help change patients' behavior and support therapeutic gains between psychotherapy sessions, serving as a kind of between-session "maintenance of gains strategy." As a result, homework has remained both a traditional and integral component of contemporary manual-based CBT approaches.

More pertinent to the current Chapter is growing evidence helping to firmly establish CBT as an efficacious intervention for a variety of mental health disorders in later life. This evidence is not only synthesized in recent reviews of the treatment literature (e.g., DeVries & Coon, 2002; Gatz et al., 1998; Pinquart & Sörensen, 2001; Teri & McCurry, 2000) but also presented in new outcome studies addressing later life depression (e.g., Gallagher-Thompson & Steffen, 1994; Thompson, Coon, Gallagher-Thompson, Sommer, & Koin, 2001) and generalized anxiety disorder (e.g., Mohlman et al., 2003; Stanley et al., 2003; Wetherell, Gatz, & Craske, 2003), as well as family caregiver distress (e.g., Coon, Gallagher-Thompson, & Thompson, 2003; Coon, Thompson, Steffen, Sorocco, & Gallagher-Thompson, 2003; Gallagher-Thompson, Coon, Solano, Ambler, Rabinowitz, & Thompson, 2003; Gallagher-Thompson, Lovett, et al., 2000).

However, even though homework is usually a central feature of CBT treatment protocols with these clients, the literature examining the actual use of homework with older adults remains very sparse. To our knowledge, only a couple of studies have investigated the relationship between homework compliance and older adults (Coon & Thompson, 2003; Thompson & Gallagher-Thompson, 1994). The results of these two investigations indicate that older adults' perception of homework helpfulness is significantly related to improvement ratings in mood and overall functioning posttreatment, and that depressed older adults who complete more homework report significantly greater reductions in their depression than those who are less compliant with homework assignments. These findings also suggest that therapists need to address homework compliance issues immediately and implement strategies to overcome obstacles to homework completion across the course of treatment. Clearly, additional studies exploring the role of homework in CBT with both younger and older adults are needed, including those that help (a) determine whether or not homework is more useful for particular client problems, (b) investigate the relative effectiveness of different types of homework assignments, (c) identify therapist behaviors that enhance homework effects, and (d) examine homework-related issues among diverse populations of older adults (Coon & Thompson, 2003; Kazantzis et al., 2000).

The remainder of this Chapter focuses on the facilitation of homework completion among older adults struggling with later life affective distress and builds on our experience utilizing CBT with older adults who are being seen in a variety of outpatient settings. It includes a brief description of the CBT framework within which we use homework to foster the type of skill development that we find necessary for effective therapeutic change with older adults. This Chapter also provides a substantive discussion of themes and strategies often used to facilitate homework completion with older adults, and it presents two case examples to help illustrate our key points.

CBT and Homework for Late-Life Distress

Many of the concepts and examples in this Chapter draw heavily from our work with empirically supported clinical protocols developed by Thompson and Gallagher-Thompson and their colleagues for use with depressed older adults (e.g., Coon, Rider, Gallagher-Thompson, & Thompson, 1999; Coon & Thompson, 2003; Gallagher-Thompson & Steffen, 1994; Laidlaw, Thompson, Dick-Siskin, & Gallagher-Thompson, 2003; Thompson et al., 2001) and distressed family caregivers of older adults (e.g., Coon et al., 2003; Gallagher-Thompson, Lovett, et al., 2001; Gallagher-Thompson et al., 2003). These protocols have been implemented over the past two decades with several hundred older adults and family caregivers at the Older Adult & Family Center (OAFC) of the VA Palo Alto Health Care System and Stanford University School of Medicine. The protocols are only briefly reviewed in this Chapter, given its focus on issues of homework and homework compliance with older adults; therefore readers are referred to other sources on both the CBT clinical protocol for individual treatment of late-life depression (e.g., Dick, Gallagher-Thompson, Coon, Powers, & Thompson, 1996; Thompson, Gallagher-Thompson, & Dick, 1996; Thompson et al., 2001) and the CBT-based psychoeducational skill-building classes to help alleviate family caregiver distress (e.g., Gallagher-Thompson et al., 1992; Gallagher-Thompson, Ossinalde, & Thompson, 1996), culturally tailored to meet the needs of European American, Latino/Hispanic, and Chinese caregivers.

This 16- to 20-session individual therapy clinical protocol for late-life depression modifies and extends the work of Beck (Beck et al., 1979), Lewinsohn (Lewinsohn et al., 1986), and other CBT theorists (e.g., Burns, 1980; Young, 1999) to meet the needs of older adults. Our use of CBT integrates two complementary theories resting on the rationale that client maladaptive thoughts and behavior occurring either singly or in combination can trigger and sustain late-life emotional distress. In brief, this approach balances Beck's theory emphasizing the role of unhelpful or dysfunctional cognitions in the origin and maintenance of depression (Beck et al., 1979) with Lewinsohn's theory (Lewinsohn et al., 1986) stressing the interrelationship between maladaptive behavior and negative emotional states. Emotional distress, according to Beck, results from consistently held negative thoughts, attitudes, and beliefs about oneself, one's experiences, and the future. These negative thoughts create a negative lens that distorts how clients evaluate the world, which in turn leads to erroneous thinking arising automatically. Intervention strategies and techniques focus on teaching clients to identify their negative thinking patterns and then systematically challenge these negative cognitions. As a result, clients learn to develop more adaptive ways of viewing both themselves and their situations.

Lewinsohn's approach, in contrast to Beck's, argues that depression results from repeated lack of pleasant events or activities in a client's life.

In sum, less positive social interaction occurs for a client as her frequency of pleasant or adaptive behavior decreases; as a result, she experiences less overall pleasure on a daily basis. This pattern of behavioral withdrawal can become reinforced over time, creating a vicious downward cycle into "the blues," where the client does less and feels worse and consequently does even less and less. Interventions are designed to help clients recognize the strong link between their involvement in pleasant activities and the successful maintenance of positive mood states. Clients are ultimately encouraged to increase their rates of engagement in, and enjoyment of, everyday pleasant activities, so that their negative patterns of withdrawal can be interrupted and effectively altered.

Phases of Treatment

The OAFC protocol builds on a directive, structured, time-limited approach tailored to give older adults skills applicable to their daily lives. This approach consists of several phases of treatment. The *socialization phase* encourages therapists to recognize the need to "socialize" many older adult clients into treatment. Socialization helps to effectively establish a solid therapeutic relationship and to allow both client and therapist to take an active role in the client's problem identification, goal definition, and appropriate intervention approaches and homework assignments. During the *early and middle treatment phases*, each CBT session always includes a structured agenda constructed collaboratively with the client. Sessions generally begin with a review of current distress level and homework assignments. The core of each session focuses on developing specific cognitive and behavioral skills to address the client's target complaints and associated goals. Sessions end with positive reinforcement of the client and written reminders of homework activities and the next appointment. Our *termination and "booster" phase* of treatment suggests that therapy end in a gradual and systematic way, by spacing out the final few sessions to a biweekly or monthly basis, and we encourage building in "booster" or check-in sessions at 3, 6, and 12 months after the last more formal session. This spacing of sessions can be particularly important for severely depressed or formerly suicidal older adults who are physically frail or socially isolated, since the therapeutic relationship may be one of the client's few close relationships.

Booster sessions can help to facilitate maintenance of therapeutic gains by assessing how well clients continue to use the skills taught in therapy and by reinforcing skill use. Therapists spend the final few sessions developing a written maintenance guide in collaboration with clients to be used as a relapse-prevention aid. The guide is designed to delineate therapeutic successes by summarizing specific skills learned and implemented effectively during therapy and by brainstorming future stressful situations. Step-by-step plans are then developed to manage those situations, drawing on the CBT skills the client has learned and practiced. Given the current Chapter's focus on homework, we refer readers interested in more details of the protocols to the reference list and the current OAFC therapist and client treatment manuals available through the OAFC.

Types of Homework

A variety of both cognitive and behavioral focused homework activities ranging from bibliotherapy activities to the practice and reinforcement of more "active" skills are useful across the various treatment phases. The identification of target complaints and their translation to relevant goals are often constructive homework assignments for older adults during the socialization phase. The ongoing, systematic monitoring of goal progress in tangible terms also can prove to be an invaluable homework assignment to help evaluate the intervention strategies used. The range of these types of assignments is broad, from tracking frequency and severity of problems or identifying and rating recent coping strategies to monitoring change in self-reports of distress or increases in positive target behaviors.

To address the cognitive component of CBT, we have tailored a variety of well-established techniques (e.g., Beck et al., 1979; Young, 1999) designed to teach older clients to identify, challenge and modify their unhelpful thoughts. Central to our approach is the use of the *daily thought record* as one specific technique we have found particularly useful with older adults suffering from a variety of late-life stressors. Like all techniques and strategies, the pencil-and-paper thought record is presented and practiced in the session and then assigned as homework to reinforce skill development. Daily thought records ask patients to identify and challenge unhelpful thinking in their lives through five columns or steps, in which they learn to (a) describe a situation that led to their unpleasant emotions, (b) identify and record their cognitions in the situation, (c) identify and record their related feelings, (d) challenge and replace any negative cognitions associated with the situation with more adaptive thinking and write them down, and (e) identify and record changes in mood after challenging their negative cognitions. Our protocol and accompanying manuals expand on similar discussions with younger clients (e.g., Beck et al., 1979; Burns, 1980) by identifying negative thought patterns frequently exhibited by older clients (e.g., Coon & Gallagher-Thompson, 2002; Coon et al., 1999; Dick et al., 1996; Thompson et al., 1996).

In terms of the behavioral components of our protocol for older adults, we employ a variety of specific behavioral management techniques depending on the individual client's needs, including relaxation techniques (e.g., meditation, imagery, progressive muscle relaxation, breathing exercises, and physical exercise), time-management techniques, assertive communication skills, and problem-solving strategies. In contrast, arousal hierarchies, including descriptions of anxiety triggers and the practice of graded exposure exercises, as well as the use of worry time activities, are frequent assignments used in the treatment of anxiety. One key component of our protocol for late-life depression is the Older Person's Pleasant Events Schedule (OPPES) (Gallagher & Thompson, 1981) (Figure 7.1), drawn from Lewinsohn's work (e.g., Lewinsohn et al., 1986). The OPPES helps clients identify pleasurable activities they are currently not incorporating into their lives. This tool is based on the rationale that if we can convince distressed older adults to increase their level of pleasant activities on a daily basis, their mood will improve. This technique is particularly suited to help distract older adults from ruminative negative thinking and to increase their social integration. Most OPPES activities are inexpensive activities that are acceptable to many cultural groups; therefore the OPPES can be a particularly useful component for therapists with clients from different cultural backgrounds. Finally, many of the components of the maintenance guide developed during the termination phase can be turned into useful homework assignments, such as brainstorming potentially stressful situations, identifying danger signals and developing action plans, and using daily thought records to address thoughts and concerns about termination.

Strategies for Effective Homework

Therapists can employ a variety of strategies to effectively address challenges to homework completion and promote homework compliance with older adults, ranging from issues related to the process of homework prioritization and the joint construction of assignments to the design of both goal relevant and realistic homework activities. Many factors—such as physical health limitations, family caregiving responsibilities, financial constraints, and transportation concerns that interfere with older clients' commitment to regularly scheduled therapy—can also create additional challenges to older clients' homework completion or even the active engagement of older adults in the homework process altogether. As a result, increasing homework compliance with older adults demands considerable planning, practice, and persistence on the part of both clinicians and their older clients themselves.

The following pages present common barriers to homework compliance and discuss themes and strategies relevant to homework completion with older clients. This material is drawn from work with both older adults (e.g., Coon & Gallagher-Thompson, 2002; Grant & Casey, 1995; Laidlaw et al., 2003; Rybarczyk et al., 1992) and other populations that we find applicable with today's elders (e.g., Bryant, Simons, & Thase, 1999; Hay & Kinnier, 1998; Organista & Muñoz, 1996; Tompkins, 2002). Since the material is grounded in the principles of cognitive (e.g., Beck et al., 1979) and behavioral psychotherapy theory (Lewinsohn et al., 1986), key aspects of these themes and suggested strategies will sound familiar to more experienced CBT practitioners. However, we expand on many of the established principles of homework by addressing some of the most frequent challenges we encounter in encouraging homework compliance among older adults. We begin our discussion with prioritization, collaboration, and homework relevance as the cornerstones of successful homework completion, on which other themes are firmly established. We continue by addressing some of the nuts and bolts of successful homework, including its need to be realistic, time-limited, and manageable; we then reinforce its "learning laboratory" nature and underscore the importance of tailoring assignments to meet the needs of older clients within their particular sociocultural contexts. We incorporate relevant case examples and conclude with a discussion of additional strategies to address homework noncompliance.

Prioritization of Homework

Unfortunately, therapists and clients all too often fall into the trap of seeing homework assignments as either "unnecessary add-ons" or "extra-credit exercises" rather than as central components of effective treatment. Several strategies are particularly important to help ease older clients into the process of homework, establish homework as a priority, and foster ongoing adherence. Therapists must prioritize homework without hesitation, believe at the very least in its overall utility, and emphasize to their clients its relationship to positive treatment outcomes as demonstrated in clinical research findings, including those involving older adults (e.g., Coon & Thompson, 2003; Thompson et al., 2001). In addition, one simple but incredibly valuable strategy is the consistent presence of homework on each session's agenda, both in terms of the review of previously assigned homework as well as the development and reinforcement of the next week's homework assignment. We and other clinical researchers (e.g., Secker, Kazantzis, & Pachana, 2004) also find that an agenda helps to challenge many older clients' outmoded beliefs about what constitutes psychotherapy in general, while at the same time it helps to effectively guide the session and reinforce the prioritization of homework. Review of the preceding week's assignment after obtaining a quick consensus on the current session's agenda provides a structure and rhythm across sessions that is useful in working with all types of older clients, especially those struggling with memory complaints, depression, or anxiety. A seemingly trivial part of the agenda, often overlooked in working with older adults, is the strategy of asking clients to repeat back in their own words their understanding of their homework assignment. This strategy helps to validate consensus on the assignment. Clients can also be encouraged to record homework assignments in their therapy notebooks or calendars or to use another appropriate means that captures assignments, such as audiotapes or videotapes of therapy sessions. Session recordings can be particularly useful for clients with certain cognitive or physical limitations.

Therapists also need to call their clients' attention to the limited amount of time they actually spend in a single session compared to the rest of their week, emphasizing the fact that homework is a useful way of extending therapy beyond the office by practicing new ways of thinking and behaving in the course of daily living. Again, we also find that periodically reviewing and reinforcing homework's priority is another way of dispelling older clients' misperceptions of therapy by revealing that research shows CBT to be most effective when older clients regularly practice what they have learned out in the real world, as opposed to just talking about how things could be different (e.g., Coon & Gallagher-Thompson, 2002; Laidlaw et al., 2003). Moreover, clients need to be reminded throughout therapy that homework assignments are crucial to the development of skills that have practical value in their daily lives, with therapists pointing out ways in which assignments support self-monitoring and evaluation, promote the development and mastery of new skills, and teach clients healthy ways in which to encourage and reward themselves.

Clinicians can establish homework's importance from the very beginning of therapy by asking older clients to complete various forms or materials at home to facilitate therapy's socialization phase and assist with problem identification. These assignments might include providing a short list of their current expectations for psychotherapy and/or prior experiences with psychotherapy and the completion of intake packets as well as certain key questionnaires and measures that will be used to monitor therapeutic progress (such as a depression symptom inventory or other symptom checklist). We find that these early assignments are particularly useful in identifying and brainstorming necessary modifications for both homework and in-session activities and materials (e.g., using large-print material for the visually impaired) and to quickly identify, discuss, and solve potential problems with homework compliance.

Finally, therapists need to be sensitive to the term *homework* from its first introduction into therapy. For some older adults, particularly for clients with little formal education or those who did poorly in school, *homework* can hold unpleasant connotations or be construed as somewhat demeaning. Moreover, primary and secondary education systems often varied greatly in availability and comparability across countries and by cohorts for older adult immigrants. Therefore therapists need to be prepared to adjust assignments to meet each client's particular skill set. Homework may also exacerbate worry or anxiety for older adults with sensory limitations that impede reading and writing assignments when modifications have yet to be introduced. Thus, we encourage therapists to work collaboratively with clients, when necessary, to find more palatable terms for homework by using their clients' own language and experience as a backdrop for the discussion. Finding substitute phrases for the *process* of homework such as "between-session practice," "handling their job," "working on assignments," "testing experiments," or "learning new habits" and referring to homework *assignments* as "experiments," "practice sheets," "journal writing," "mind exercises," or "mind pushups" can often help reduce fears about criticism and foster homework completion (Coon et al., 1999; DeVries & Coon, 2002).

Collaboration

Drawing on the collaborative nature of CBT, homework tasks should be shaped in consultation with the client, building on session content, process, and activities. Clearly, therapists have the training and skill to design and suggest homework strategies that have been effective with clients in similar situations; however, they must avoid the tendency to impose assignments without allowing clients to play an active role in designing the final products. Still, even the process of collaboration must be considered within the sociocultural context of the older adult client and tailored to meet his or her needs. Simple Socratic questioning is often a useful process to set the stage for homework collaboration, and is essential in helping to demonstrate respect for older clients. For example, *How can we* (or *What would be a good way to) take what we are talking about and have you practice it at home (at work? ..with your partner? ..in these situations that bother you?). How have you handled this in the past that worked for you? What do you think might work now?* Even if therapists suggest a basic assignment (e.g., using a daily thought record or flash card of alternative, less punitive self-statements), gathering input through a series of questions can help minimize resentment or demotivation and enhance likelihood of success. Using *How, Who, What, When, Where,* and *Why* questions can help focus the discussion on particular elements that need resolution: *How can you practice the relaxation strategies we have covered to help you while in the situation? Where can you practice the self-statements (or alternative more helpful thoughts) prior to the situation? Where afterwards? Who would you like to ask to sit with your husband while you go to the doctor? If you feel like you need to leave the situation, what can you say or do to excuse yourself that you think and feel would be ok with you? What will you do to reward yourself for attempting this task? What else would you want to know before practicing this activity at home (...work?...school?...in these situations?).* This interrogative process not only fosters client "buy-in", but also models constructive steps relevant for both skill-building and enhancing self-efficacy.

Goal-Relevant Homework

Homework also works best when the activity is closely tied to the client's particular target complaints and overarching goals for therapy. Moreover, it is very helpful to base homework in a theme covered during the current or at least a recent session. Still, therapists will frequently need to clarify the relationship between the assignment and the client's individual treatment goals. If the therapist cannot explain or justify the relationship, the assignment probably lacks validity and should be revamped or even abandoned if deemed inappropriate. We find that all of the underpinnings designed to maximize homework success can be easily undermined if the older client does not understand and accept the rationale or potential utility of the homework assignment. Answers to questions like *What do you see as the purpose of this exercise?* and *What is the reason you see for completing it?* can help legitimize and solidify a homework activity or expose misinterpretations and fatal flaws. Another strategy that is closely aligned with goal relevance and that often facilitates the homework process involves brainstorming ways to enhance the assignment's personal relevance or importance. Therefore, we find it useful to ask older adults directly: *How do you see this experiment as related to your goals for therapy? How important (e.g., on a scale of 1 to 10) is completing this activity to you? What might you gain or get out of doing this? How might it be helpful to you?*

If the client's response is lackluster, rote, or hesitant, we follow-up with questions like: *What would you change about this activity that would make it more important or valuable to you?* Certainly, not all assignments will be nor can they necessarily be rated a 10. In fact, it can actually be beneficial at times to "lower the stakes" of an assignment. For example, when clients are just learning a new skill and need additional practice, they typically should not try out that skill in situations that are especially complicated or emotionally loaded until after they have achieved at least a basic level of skill mastery.

Realistic and Specific Homework Assignments

Client' homework, like their treatment goals, must be not only important to them as older adults but also realistic for them to achieve during the time allotted and measurable in terms of its successful completion. Thus, central to its development are time limitations as well as specific instructions and parameters that are manageable and do-able by clients within their own sociocultural contexts. Too often, clinicians hold ageist stereotypes about the amount of leisure time older adults have at their disposal and translate those stereotypes into homework of unrealistic length and duration, with tasks involving too much detail or frequency. *What is the older client's schedule for the next week? What obligations does she or he have? What opportunities exist for what type of assignments?* Well-planned, shorter assignments that are completed successfully are much more likely to be beneficial (Hay & Kinnier, 1998) than longer, more complicated assignments that an older client leaves unfinished. This strategy is particularly worthwhile at the beginning of therapy when clients need to develop positive views of homework and its utility (Coon & Gallagher-Thompson, 2002), and proves especially important in introducing the older client to a new activity or new skill.

Nevertheless, both the therapist and client sometimes "bite off more than the client can chew", and through reevaluation and collaboration, the assignment needs to be broken down into smaller, more manageable steps. Although the ability to effectively break down valuable assignments into more manageable steps comes with practice and experience, the design of effective backup plans for homework assignments can model a proactive approach for clients. As part of a backup plan, we encourage therapists to practice a basic problem-solving model with older clients to address potential barriers, such as the following: (a) brainstorm barriers or problems that might interfere with homework, (b) write down problems that are among the most likely to occur, (c) brainstorm strategies to counteract each of these problems, (d) identify strategies assumed to be most useful for each and record them in response to their associated problems, (e) try them out as needed and keep track of what worked and did not work, and (f) save a record of the most successful ways to overcome barriers for future use. Therapists should be prepared for the possibility that this brainstorming process and the joint development of a backup plan might uncover the need to modify or even abandon an assignment and ask the client to first monitor a particular problem he or she is not yet ready to tackle (Tompkins, 2002).

Finally, we caution therapists that assigning only one or two small homework activities requires ongoing assessment of the client's capacity to do more homework as well as ongoing evaluation of progress toward treatment goals and the client's commitment to therapy and homework activities. Clearly, some clients would consistently choose to do only one small activity if not challenged to attempt more. Open, honest communication with clients and regular review of treatment progress can help therapists determine how much homework to assign and when to push older clients to try to complete more.

Lessons in a Learning Laboratory

Homework, like therapy itself, is an ongoing learning process, extending skills learned in the "practice room" of therapy out into the "learning laboratory" of everyday life. Remember, one of the chief purposes of homework is to do just that—to learn more. Therefore we encourage therapists to set up homework as a "win-win" or at least a "no-lose" experiments (Laidlaw et al., 2003), where lack of compliance or partial homework completion is useful fodder for in-session discussion, role playing, or other practice and can be used for the revision or refinement of homework assignments. With such a philosophy, the client obviously reaps homework's benefits when the assignment is successful; however, when it is unsuccessful in terms of compliance or derived benefits, then the session's "homework review" time should be spent investigating what did not work, what was learned (if anything), and how the assignment could be improved. In such a framework, homework difficulties become new learning possibilities for both the client and therapist and afford additional opportunities for clients to learn to recognize and reward themselves for each successful step they take (Coon & Gallagher-Thompson, 2002).

We also find that older adult clients often begin therapy believing that if homework is not "easy" or "immediately successful" or if they have not completed it "perfectly," nothing has been accomplished. By drawing on a psychoeducational skill-building approach, we teach clients that homework progress, just like goal progress, seldom grows steadily in a positive direction. Instead, homework is more likely to proceed in sawtooth curve fashion through a process of successive approximations. Homework with older adults needs to be viewed as a series of skill-building opportunities that take into account the client's current level of functioning. This current level of functioning, particularly older clients' physical and cognitive functioning, often encompasses more complex situations when compared to that of most younger adults.

Homework and Individual Differences Among Older Adult Clients

Contrary to pervasive stereotypes about aging and older people, diversity actually increases rather than decreases with age. Stereotypical prototypes of older adults can quickly fade as we consider the wide range of personal histories and sociocultural contexts of today's older clients. This diversity is reflected not only in our older clients' current physical health, cognitive functioning, mental health, and socioeconomic situations but also in their individual sociocultural contexts and personal histories. Maximization of homework compliance demands that therapists value these personal histories and contexts in order to more effectively collaborate with older clients in the development of suitable homework assignments. This is especially important to keep in mind, since individual difference variables can easily shape help-seeking behavior and substantially affect the enactment of prevention, surveillance and intervention activities, including homework activities (Coon & Gallagher-Thompson, 2002; Organista & Muñoz, 1996).

Tailoring Homework for Late-Life Physical Challenges. Successful homework completion with physically ill, disabled, or frail older adult clients requires the development of new skills and perspectives for most therapists, including greater sensitivity to the medical context of psychotherapy with older adults; increased knowledge of common illnesses and functional impairments; more frequent and effective contact with health care providers; greater flexibility in session locations and meeting times, including nursing homes, hospitals, clinics, and family residences; and an additional emphasis on teamwork among both the formal and informal support systems (Haley, 1996). All of these skills and perspectives can facilitate implementation of treatment strategies, including the design and delivery of homework assignments. The medical, support system, and contextual considerations that arise with physically impaired older clients require an even greater amount of close collaboration between therapist and client in the development of homework assignments. These considerations also raise issues of confidentiality and privacy typically not faced when working with more able-bodied clients; as a result, therapists need to consider how and when to obtain permission to contact both formal and informal support network members whose assistance may be needed to facilitate homework compliance. For example, network members may be needed to help write down information, set up audiovisual or other equipment, assist with trips to a park or other pleasant activities, or dial the telephone for information or social calls. Clearly, therapists need to help these older clients with physical challenges maintain their dignity by respecting their confidentiality and privacy and by avoiding the development of any coercive systems or tactics to promote homework compliance.

To help maximize homework completion and success with older clients facing physical challenges, we build on the principles outlined by Grant and Casey (1995) and Rybarczyk and colleagues (1992): (a) working in tandem with clients and their support systems to resolve any practical barriers to homework participation (e.g., providing large-print material or tape recordings for the visually impaired or supplying in-session amplifiers, taping sessions to amplify at home, or identifying bibliotherapy material for the hearing impaired); (b) modifying the goals and pace of therapy and related homework assignments, starting with modest steps to foster success and then adjusting the pace to match patient progress; (c) developing backup plans and breaking assignments into several simple steps or components; and (d) conducting shorter, more frequent sessions and designing homework assignments that minimize fatigue, discomfort or overload.

Homework will often need to focus on three key issues: (a) helping clients and their support systems to determine if excess disability is occurring (i.e., whether or not additional amounts of disability beyond that imposed by the disease or physical impairment are being experienced as a result of the clients' emotional distress), (b) educating clients and their support systems that depression and other forms of late-life distress are reversible problems that can be distinguished from their physical challenges, and (c) working together to challenge the older adult's perception of self as only "a burden" to others.

Adaptations for Mild to Moderate Cognitively Impaired Older Adults. Similarly, we have discovered several modifications to homework strategies that can be used to enhance homework activities for individuals with mild cognitive impairment: (a) simplify and reduce the number of concepts used, and then reuse and reinforce them consistently, (b) provide audiotapes of therapy sessions for clients to review at home, (c) create an intact notebook/calendar to hold both intervention and homework material and to schedule sessions (but keep it simple), (d) develop structured and simple activity schedules collaboratively and enter them in the notebook/calendar, (e) limit the amount of material housed in the notebook calendar ("identify the best and remove the rest"), (f) identify with the client and a family member one place in the house to repeatedly place the notebook/calendar, and (g) discourage the use of other reminder notebooks, calendars, or notes. For example, we have discovered that even a five-column daily thought record can be effectively reduced to three columns of "thought, feeling, and new thought" for clients with mild cognitive impairment (Coon & Gallagher-Thompson, 2002).

In a somewhat different approach than for much of our work, Teri and her colleagues (1997) demonstrated that behaviorally oriented interventions can improve depressed mood in both outpatient individuals with dementia and their family caregivers. Their results suggest that therapists and family caregivers can work together to help caregivers learn to practice and implement a program at home with depressed dementia patients through the following elements: (a) identifying and then avoiding or decreasing topics and situations unpleasant to the patient, (b) identifying the patient's cognitive deficits and minimize situations that exacerbate them, (c) increasing the patient's social and other pleasant activities (as well as increasing shared pleasant events), and (d) giving greater attention to the patient during nondepressive moments.

Valuing the Personal Histories and Sociocultural Contexts of Clients. Multiple layers of powerful sociocultural influences, ranging from clients' families and peers to their community and cultural backgrounds, can ultimately shape their personal histories; these layers can, in turn, shape the signs and symptoms of emotional distress, leading many older adults to view this distress as a somatic problem, a spiritual difficulty, or even an untreatable, shameful mental illness rather than as a warning sign of treatable psychological distress. Thus, the sociocultural contexts and personal histories of our older clients can significantly influence their health and mental health beliefs and values as well as their thoughts, behaviors, and feelings, including their views about themselves, others, and the environment—all of which are key components of CBT interventions. However, these interventions are based predominantly on approaches developed with western Caucasian clients; little is still known about the effectiveness of CBT approaches with elders belonging to racial and ethnic minorities (Gallagher-Thompson, Arean, Coon, et al., 2000; Organista, 2000; Thompson, Powers, Coon, et al., 2000), much less about the effective development of culturally appropriate homework activities for diverse elders. Moreover, our clients' personal histories and contexts can also modify their help-seeking behavior and substantially affect their engagement in treatment activities, including homework acceptability and compliance (Coon et al., 1999).

Cultural influences are all too often ignored or minimized in the development of treatment and homework, with too few therapists becoming actively engaged in a creative intervention process that is grounded in CBT principles but culturally tailored to the more effective development of relevant engagement techniques targeting complaints and goals, intervention strategies, and homework assignments (Organista, 2000). However the demonstration of a basic and fundamental respect for older clients and their personal stories can serve as the cornerstone of this creative intervention process regardless of one's cultural background and ethnic heritage. We recommend that therapists encourage clients to share their personal stories using their own descriptors for distress and problem definition, and we remind therapists to remain sensitive to the term *homework*, especially with clients whose native language may differ from that of the majority culture and who may, as a result, have experienced educational and other forms of discrimination. Respect encompasses at least two other key issues that can facilitate or impede homework completion. First, therapists need to gain a clear understanding of the client's respect for and acceptance of the views significant others hold about the conceptualization, assessment, and treatment of mental health problems, including the use of homework assignments. How important or influential are the beliefs of family, extended family, community leaders, and cultural institutions? For example, we have found that homework assignments with Latina family caregivers that either require them to practice assertiveness skills to enlist additional family members' support for caregiving activities or ask them to increase the frequency of their own participation in pleasurable activities may require additional time or additional cultural tailoring or modifications. These assignments typically ask these women to "take time out for themselves," a practice that is often incongruent with strong cultural traditions dictating that women must put the needs of their family members ahead of their own (Organista & Muñoz, 1996; Organista, 2000).

A second key issue asks therapists to increase their understanding of and respect for the use of religion and other spiritual practices, including the routine use of more "nontraditional" therapies, such as culturally defined healers and helpers (e.g., acupuncturists, herbalists, spiritual advisers, and psychic readers) in tandem with traditional Western health/ mental health practices. For instance, homework activities intricately tied to religious or spiritual activities may enhance the efficacy of CBT interventions and increase the retention rates and homework compliance for the religious or spiritually inclined older client (Mausbach, Coon, Cardenas, & Thompson, 2003; Thompson et al., 2002).

Finally, therapists need to be careful not to make automatic assumptions about what will and will not work as homework with older adults; rather, they should take things slowly, gather the necessary information from the client and other reliable sources, and check in with clients about their homework assignments repeatedly along the way while remaining mindful always to work within the client's sociocultural context (Gallagher-Thompson et al., 2000).

Multiple Modalities

Older adults typically benefit from homework assignments presented through multiple learning modalities, with therapists helping clients find ways to "say it, show it, do it" (Zeiss & Steffen, 1996). For example, the therapist might do the following: (a) introduce and explain the rationale for the three-column daily thought record; (b) work with clients in session, showing them how to fill it out and using an example from that session or a recent session; (c) ask the client to repeat the rationale and the steps to filling out another thought record using a different example, with the therapist providing coaching as necessary; and (d) have the client take it home as an assignment to complete with a situation that arises before the next session. Using multiple modalities is especially powerful for building new skills and transferring established skills to particularly loaded contexts and situations. Role-playing techniques, in which client and therapist dramatize situations involving the client and significant others in stressful situations, are another example of strategies that combine the "say it, show it, do it" components. In our role-plays with older clients, we spend extra time going over and processing the experience, helping to model, coach, and reinforce the clients' development of more effective responses by increasing their assertive communication skills and developing successful challenges to their maladaptive thinking.

Multiple modalities should also be incorporated into older clients' actual homework assignments while recognizing the limitations of their sociocultural contexts and current levels of functioning. Within these contexts, the types of assignments may range from behaviorally based experiments such as relaxation exercises, pleasant events schedules, and "respite" or "don't do anything" exercises (often useful for overextended family caregivers) to written exercises like journal keeping, thought records and bibliotherapy, as well as video viewing and Internet research, depending on the client's access to technology. These assignments can be enhanced further by creating assignments that teach new skills in one area while building on the older client's particular strengths, comfort, and preferences in another. For example, if older clients have strong interpersonal/communication skills as well as the core value of "giving back" and "teaching others," they may choose to incorporate opportunities to use these skills in their pleasant event or activity schedules.

Common Barriers to the Completion of Homework Assignments

Numerous issues can affect homework compliance. When our older clients avoid or fail to finish homework assignments, we talk with them about this directly and then work with them to find strategies to enhance homework completion. We prefer to deal with the issue rather than label noncompliance as resistance. Thus, we find it useful to give both older and younger clients the benefit of the doubt regarding homework compliance, at least initially. If they avoid homework, we engage clients in dialogues around the specific homework tasks and then work together to find strategies to enhance compliance. However, if problems continue to occur, a more thorough evaluation of the situation is warranted. In any case, noncompliance is typically useful fodder for therapy, and incomplete homework is frequently a reflection of some aspect of the client's target complaints or therapeutic goals. For example, many older adults must balance just as many or more role conflicts and demands on their time as their younger counterparts. As a result, they may have difficulty organizing their time and daily tasks. In response, the therapist and client often need to work together to help clients manage distractions and organize a specific time and place to get their homework done.

The following are key questions to explore with older adult clients regarding homework compliance or completion issues. Once again, we find this type of Socratic questioning to be critical in gaining insight into various barriers to homework compliance.

Was the assignment unclear, unrealistic, or lacking in specificity? If so, the therapist can work more collaboratively to help the client gain a better understanding of the what, how, and why of particular assignments.

Did the client forget to do the assignment or forget how to do all or some part of the assignment? In our experience, written assignments are more likely to be completed than those just talked about and not recorded. Reminder or interim check-ins about homework between sessions can be useful in some situations. Scheduling specific times and places for homework can also enhance compliance in these situations. Of course, therapists should also consider whether or not there is the need for a memory screen or related workup.

Is the therapist inconsistent in reviewing homework assignments? Homework needs to be prioritized each and every session to help clients grasp its importance and to maximize compliance.

Was the rationale clear or did the client decide that the assignment lacked value or importance? If so, how can the therapist remember to check in more consistently with the client about the "why" of homework? Moreover, what changes or modifications need to be made to salvage the assignment, or is a completely new approach warranted?

Was the homework "assigned"? That is, did the assignment lack necessary input from and collaboration with the client?

Did unanticipated practical barriers arise, or does the older client need help in structuring his time or environment to make it more conducive to homework?

Is noncompliance a reflection of some other issue or view of the self? For example, some clients can hold perfectionistic standards about homework, completing either "all" or "nothing." The use of an in-session thought record exploring the situation can help identify unhelpful thinking and develop counterarguments to help enhance compliance.

What stopped the client? This question can be useful in identifying many of the issues described thus far, as well as several others, and provides another opportunity to use a thought record to explore clients' thoughts and feelings about themselves, their assignments, their significant others, and the therapist. We encourage clients to view the Socratic questioning of "What stopped you?" as a learning opportunity to identify and begin to address barriers to compliance.

What will the outcome look like? How does the client see it impacting others? How will the client handle that? How will the client feel if she succeeds? Sometimes clients are concerned about how the changes they are making in therapy will impact their surroundings and significant others. Explorations into these areas are very useful in enhancing compliance and clarifying the ways in which clients will view their progress to their therapeutic goals.

Finally, we also use the following series of steps to help maximize homework compliance, building on similar processes used with other populations (e.g., Hay & Kinnier, 1998; Tompkins, 2002) by integrating key issues raised in this Chapter:

1. Gather client input to reach an agreement or a mutual understanding of the key points of the session.

2. Work together to draw additional relationships between the work in the current session and the client's overall treatment goals, pointing out and asking for client insight on how the work builds on previous learning or skill development.

3. Help the client tie the summary and overall treatment goals to previous homework assignments and their modifications as appropriate. Seize opportunities to point out interrelationships and reinforce the utility of previous efforts at homework completion or homework attempts.

4. Link potential homework assignments to the client's summary and overall treatment goals, helping the client frame any new assignment as an opportunity to refine or extend previous work.

5. Build in backup plans that break potential assignments into steps or components that can be tackled individually or in smaller groups, as warranted.
6. Explore with clients how the potential assignments fit into their sociocultural contexts. Remain open and sensitive to cultural differences and tailor assignments accordingly.
7. Get final input into the design of the assignment as well as agreement from the older client about its value or importance and the potential for its completion.
8. Frequently during this process or at least as a final activity, ask the older client to summarize the session, its relevance, and the homework assignment in her own words.

Moreover, potential homework assignments often emerge early or in the middle of a session and therapists must consider the "rhythm" of the session and decide whether or not the steps just outlined should be raised and addressed at the end of the session or as they arise. However, consistent structure can be especially useful with older adults and the elderly, particularly in the beginning of therapy with clients unfamiliar with or uneasy with mental health treatment, as well as with those struggling with memory complaints. In any case, therapists must allot time to identify potential barriers to homework compliance that need to be addressed and clients should be given ample opportunity to air any concerns about what, when, where, how, and why the assignment is to be done.

Therapists and Their Homework Beliefs

Interwoven across therapy is the need for therapists not only to remain mindful that psychotherapy is framed within the sociocultural contexts of their clients' lives and current situations, but also to acknowledge that the sociocultural histories of therapists themselves create a lens through which we as therapists see psychotherapy unfold. Through these lenses, therapists observe, envision, interpret, and comprehend their clients and their clients' target complaints, the therapeutic process, their clients' progress toward stated goals, and the effective development and completion of homework strategies. Thus, therapists' beliefs can either enhance or constrain the ultimate efficacy of CBT (Padesky, 1988; Persons, 1989), and we believe that their attitudes about homework and its prioritization is central to that efficacy with older clients (Coon & Gallagher-Thompson, 2002; Laidlaw et al., 2003). However, increased awareness of the influence of our own lenses as therapists is not enough. Continuing education and training as well as case consultation are necessary to help therapists move from heightened awareness to increased competence and ongoing professional development.

In our experience of training new therapists, some trainees have questioned the use of homework assignments with older persons, saying, for example, that "Homework only increases the burden on already overwhelmed older clients (especially those with physical impairments)." Or "How can I expect her to try this out at home, given her memory problems?" "I feel I am being disrespectful [coercive or overbearing] when I assign homework to older clients." Or "He has done it this way for over 60 years; how can I expect him to change?" (A modification of the old adage "You can't teach an old dog to try new tricks!") However, therapists need to be prepared to recognize how their particular views shape the ageist assumptions behind these questions and should confront them directly, since such assumptions can easily lead to therapist pessimism that, in turn, can quickly derail treatment content, process, and outcome. Therapists working with older clients need to ask themselves: *What evidence is there that an older client cannot complete homework appropriately tailored and accommodated to meet their individual needs? What evidence is there that homework developed collaboratively cannot be presented with respect to elders, taking into account their situations and the sociocultural contexts in which they live and function?* Thus, we find it very helpful to continue to examine our own lenses as part of the identification of barriers to homework compliance that arise with older clients and to pay close attention to ageist assumptions and patronizing attitudes that in the end limit older adults' access to the full range of treatment strategies, including useful homework activities.

Group Therapy and Psychoeducational Skill Building

Up to this point, we have framed this homework discussion within the context of individual therapy. However, our experience and that of other clinical researchers (e.g., Beutler, Scogin, Kinkish, et al., 1987; Yost, Beutler, Corbishley, & Allender, 1986) suggests that similar homework principles apply both with time-limited group therapy for late-life affective disorders (e.g., DeVries & Coon, 2002; Thompson et al., 2000), as well as short-term CBT-based psychoeducational skill-building classes, such as those designed to reduce emotional distress among family caregivers (e.g., Coon, Thompson, Steffen, Socorro, & Gallagher-Thompson, 2003; Gallagher-Thompson, Lovett, et al., 2000; Gallagher-Thompson, Coon, Solano, Ambler, Rabinowitz, & Thompson, 2003). CBT-based groups can not only facilitate positive clinical change but also improve the quality of life for older adults by reducing their sense of social isolation, sharing their struggles with peers, gaining new insights, and developing strategies for handling their problems through peer interactions. CBT skill-based group interventions may also hold social significance (Schulz et al., 2002) by increasing cost-effectiveness and reducing case backlogs for therapists and their agencies (Coon et al., 2003; Thompson et al., 2000). Moreover, CBT's framework, strategies, and techniques provide considerable potential to tailor group factors—such as the primary content and the number of sessions—to meet the special needs of a variety of elders, including the cognitively impaired, the physically frail, those suffering from chronic pain, or the bereaved, as well as older adults and their family caregivers from different cultural backgrounds (Gallagher-Thompson, Arean, Rivera, & Thompson, 2001; Gallagher-Thompson et al., 2003; Thompson et al., 2000). We refer readers to other sources (see DeVries & Coon, 2002; Thompson et al., 2000; Zeiss & Steffen, 1996) for additional information on group and psychoeducational CBT-based approaches that rely heavily on homework for the treatment of other later-life problems, including anxiety disorders, grief, insomnia, and sexual dysfunction.

As with individual therapy, homework remains an essential part of CBT-based group interventions across the entire course of treatment and should be used to both teach and reinforce adaptive coping skills. Fortunately, many of the homework assignments integrated into individual therapy—from mood monitoring, thought records, and pleasant events schedules to relaxation exercises, scheduling of "worry time," and the development of maintenance guides—can easily be adapted for group treatment. But the process of review and discussion often needs to be modified for the group context. Therapists may also want to consider gathering input from group participants within the first couple of sessions for the process of renaming homework, given the objections to this term that have already been raised. This process can serve a dual purpose in the group by providing the therapist with a platform to emphasize the important role of homework in behavioral change, state it as a group "norm," answer questions about home practice, and assuage clients' concerns about how it will be used.

Therefore therapists should encourage group members to share their homework throughout treatment as part of a planned agenda item at the beginning of each session (e.g., by way of a "home practice review"). Sharing of the struggles and successes of homework affords the opportunity for participants to compare experiences and learn from one another, and these interactions create a natural opportunity for therapists to clarify skills or techniques, develop new homework assignments, or deal with obstacles to homework completion (DeVries & Coon, 2002). However, it is even more important within group treatment to avoid criticizing clients with homework difficulties. Rather, therapists and clients need to work collaboratively within the group to help clients identify activities relevant to their specific goals and create homework assignments that are likely not only to foster skill development but also to empower clients by building a greater sense of self-efficacy. Just as in individual treatment, therapists need to point out steps toward success and help clients successfully identify and dismantle barriers to homework completion.

Over the years, current and former OAFC staff have developed several 8- to 10-session psychoeducational classes with accompanying manuals (available from Dolores Gallagher-Thompson, one of the present authors, on request) for small groups of 6 to 10 individuals. These classes, grounded in CBT and its change strategies, are designed to reduce depressive symptoms in older adults (e.g., Thompson, Gallagher-Thompson, & Lovett, 1992) or to reduce distress in family caregivers of impaired elders (e.g., Gallagher-Thompson, Rose, Florsheim, et al., 1992; Gallagher-Thompson, Ossinalde, & Thompson, 1996). In our opinion, these psychoeducational skill-building classes are structured in ways that differentiate them from most other group therapy. In contrast to more traditional group therapy, psychoeducational classes can be distinguished in the following ways: (a) they are always time-limited (with the length depending upon the target audience and class goals), (b) they employ a very detailed agenda for each meeting which outlines the class's goals and the steps to be taken in class to achieve those goals, and (c) they use a great deal of active in-class participation in role-plays and skill demonstrations to learn and practice the material (Coon et al., 1999).

In addition, these short-term psychoeducational skill-building classes, in contrast to most group therapy approaches, make even more extensive use of homework assignments to encourage practice of new skills outside the classroom. Difficulties with homework completion are approached as beneficial for the entire class by drawing relationships between members' particular situations, issues, or backgrounds and helping them resolve obstacles to homework completion. Many times, class participants have proven to be very effective in helping one another identify unhelpful thinking patterns and barriers to engagement in pleasant events as well as in brainstorming ways to effectively challenge these patterns.

Recent empirical research indicates that these psychoeducational skill-building approaches for family caregivers who are dealing with dementia are effective in reducing caregiver symptoms of depression and anger/hostility and in increasing adaptive coping and caregiver self-efficacy (Coon et al., 2003; Gallagher-Thompson, Lovett, et al., 2000). Moreover, the content and homework assignments used in these classes can be effectively tailored for different cultural groups (e.g., Gallagher-Thompson et al., 2001; Gallagher-Thompson et al., 2003). For example, our recent "coping with caregiving" class (CWC) (Gallagher-Thompson et al., 1996) is designed to teach mood management skills through two fundamental CBT approaches: (a) an emphasis on decreasing negative affect by learning how to relax in stressful situations, appraise the care-recipient's behavior more realistically, and communicate assertively and, (b) an emphasis on increasing positive affect through the acquisition of such skills as learning the contingency between mood and events and activities, developing strategies to engage in more small, pleasant everyday activities, and

TABLE 7.1 Coping With Caregiving Psychoeducational Skill Building and Related Homework Assignments

Phase/Class	Goals	Homework
Phase one		
Class 1	Overview of dementia, understanding frustration and caregiver stress, practicing relaxation.	Daily relaxation practice and relaxation diary.
Classes 2 to 4	Identifying antecedents, beliefs, and consequences of frustrating caregiving situations. Identifying unhelpful thoughts about caregiving, changing unhelpful thoughts into adaptive thoughts and linking to new adaptive behaviors.	Relaxation practice and relaxation diary, daily thought records and behavior logs.
Phase two		
Classes 5 to 6	Understanding different types of communication styles and practicing how to be more assertive in caregiving situations, with professionals and with family members.	Practice assertive communication and Assertiveness Practice Sheet. Daily relaxation practice and daily thought records.

(continued)

TABLE 7.1 Coping With Caregiving Psychoeducational Skill Building and Related Homework Assignments *(continued)*

Phase/Class	Goals	Homework
Phase three		
Classes 6 to 9	Understanding depressive symptoms and monitoring mood. Identifying and tracking pleasant events and activities, and understanding and overcoming personal barriers to increasing pleasant events to help improve mood. Identify pleasant events to do with care recipient.	Daily mood rating, pleasant events tracking form including obstacles to events. Relaxation diary.
Class 10	Review of major skills taught, listing of problem areas in which skills can be used in the future. Identification of most relevant skills for participants' particular caregiving situations. Discussion of termination and review booster agendas.	Encourage use of all homework, especially that identified as most relevant for caregivers' particular situations.
Phase four		
Eight monthly boosters	Maintain skills learned and fine tune skills.	Apply skills and use homework material and strategies in everyday situations and as new stressors develop.

establishing self-change goals and rewards for accomplishments along the way (Gallagher-Thompson et al., 2003). Table 7.1 outlines the CWC's key phases and classes as well as their related goals and the homework assignments designed to help achieve those goals. Each class begins with a review of the previous week's homework assignments, ranging from relaxation exercises and relaxation diaries to daily thought records, assertive communication practice sheets, pleasant events tracking, and mood monitoring. Each session ends with a review of the newly introduced material and its relationship to other skills introduced in the class as well as a discussion of the next week's homework assignment. Our emphasis on homework and skill building in these classes extends to contacting participants who miss a session in order to provide a "make-up" class, either in person or on the phone, to make sure that they do not miss ongoing opportunities for learning and practice. Finally, all participants receive a class manual complete with basic homework assignments as well as all necessary forms and paperwork to facilitate completion. Use of these comprehensive manuals has greatly enhanced homework compliance among the family caregivers in our groups; it also gives them a record of the skills they learned between sessions and at the end of treatment. Manuals (particularly the final sections, which provide a personal review of skills and strategies most helpful to the individual) serve a similar purpose as the maintenance guide offered in individual therapy (Coon et al., 1999; Coon & Gallagher-Thompson, 2002).

Case Study 1

Mr. R., a 71-year-old man, is serving as caregiver for his 69-year-old wife, who is bedridden with a crippling arthritic disorder. Both Mr. R. and his wife are college graduates, and both were actively employed until each retired at age 65. They met in college and were married immediately after their graduation. Mr. R. worked as an accountant for many years for a local company and then began his own business. His wife worked in marketing for a national fashion company for many years and had not wanted to retire but was forced to do so because of her illness.

Mr. R. came to the clinic in response to an advertisement offering free therapy through a research study for persons who were suffering from depression. Mr. R. met criteria for Major Depressive Disorder according to DSM-IV-R. His Beck Depression Theory (BDI-II) was 35, and he complained of excessive worry and rumination. However, his hopelessness scale was below 10, and there was no evidence of suicidal ideation. Mr. R. had been taking medication (Zoloft) prescribed by his private practitioner for approximately 3 months, but this was not improving his depression; as a result, he decided to try psychotherapy.

Mr. R. was accepted as a patient in the research program and began a trial of CBT using our manualized protocol. He found mood monitoring to be helpful, and seeing the connection between pleasant events and mood shifts gave him substantial encouragement that he could do something about his depression. His depression decreased, and by the fifth session, his BDI-II score had dropped to 21.

Early on, Mr. R.'s therapist picked up on his distaste for the term *home-work*. They then brainstormed together and Mr. R. chose "job assignment" to describe his out-of-session practice activities. He liked the idea of having important work to do, even though he had retired. During the fifth session, he expressed concern that while he was doing better, his wife still seemed to be feeling great distress about her low level of functioning and pain. His job assignments for the sixth session were to continue monitoring his mood, practice the relaxation technique he was learning, and make a list of activities that he and his wife would enjoy doing together. While Mr. R. was successfully completing at least a couple of assignments each week, the therapist and Mr. R. always developed a backup plan, prioritizing each of the job assignments (e.g., for the sixth session, mood monitoring would be first, followed by relaxation practice and then pleasant event identification).

Mr. R.: came for the sixth session and immediately said, "You're going to scold me!!"

Therapist: Why is that?

Mr. R.: I haven't done most of my job assignments this week. I only practiced my relaxation.

Therapist: OK. Well, let's set up our agenda for today and put that on the agenda with some other things that we talked about doing this week.

Mr. R.: *[Nods in agreement.]*

Therapist: We talked last week about seeing how the relaxation practice is going and discussed the idea of finding ways to shorten it. So why don't we do that first, and talk about how to use just one word to initiate the relaxation sequence in situations where you can't do a prolonged relaxation. Then, we can come back to talk about what got in the way of doing the other assignments.

The therapist and Mr. R. worked together through the "say it, show it, do it" sequence, helping Mr. R. identify a calming word to initiate the relaxation sequence and then demonstrating and practicing the sequence several times. Afterwards, Mr. R. remarked that he felt less tense, and even though worrisome thoughts would come up during the relaxation exercise, he was able to just put them away and continue focusing on the task. The therapist reinforced the positive aspects of this behavior, asked Mr. R. for additional questions and feedback on the new relaxation strategy, and then returned to the agenda.

The therapist asked Mr. R. to talk about what problems had come up that made it difficult for him to complete all of his assignments: *Were there too many assignments? Did any seem inappropriate or unimportant? Were the rationales not explained well?* Mr. R. thought everything was fine; that he just had not felt up to doing it. Then, his therapist began to explore other activities that might have interfered or stopped Mr. R. from completing his assignments during the week. Mr. R. in turn reported an unusually busy week, making several trips to the city on the bus for personal business, running several errands to get prescriptions refilled and insurance mistakes cleared up for his wife, and helping their daughter move and paint one of the rooms in her new apartment. In addition, Mr. R. completed many of his regular chores, such as doing the laundry, cleaning the house, shopping for groceries, preparing meals, and spending some quality time with his wife reading and discussing some of the personal business issues he had to tackle. He also remarked that he was obsessing over various things that had to be done. Many times when he started to do the relaxation technique, he would think of something that had to be done and therefore could not focus.

By nighttime, he was just too tired to even think about his mood monitoring or pleasant activities that both he and his wife could do. He was pleased with the shortened relaxation technique they had just practiced, but he was still concerned about all his worry over the personal business issues and his wife's failing health. His therapist responded with empathy and remarked that it was understandable that Mr. R. did not feel up to all his job assignments. The therapist gently pushed on the idea that she wanted him to get all he could out of therapy and it was important that he continue to try to do those job assignments that they would agree on and to remember to break assignments down into manageable steps.

They then both agreed to change the agenda based on a suggestion by the therapist to talk about how to bring more organization into Mr. R.'s life so he could free up time to complete important job assignments at home. Through a basic brainstorming and problem-solving process, they developed a general schedule of daily activities, including a block of "protected time" for Mr. R. to complete his assignments. During the process, the therapist also introduced the idea of a specified worry time for Mr. R. to think about, identify, and write down all his concerns each day. Mr. R. agreed to try the experiment and said the best time for worry time would be in the morning, when he could prioritize. So he agreed that during the day, when things came up that were not on the schedule, he would assign them to worry time so that he could concentrate on whatever his current schedule required. Finally, they prioritized the assignments, brainstormed potential obstacles to completing his job assignments and potential ways to overcome those difficulties, including asking his daughter for more assistance.

At the seventh session, Mr. R. reported that the worry time had been very helpful, particularly when he was practicing the relaxation, and that the abbreviated relaxation was working well. He liked the fact that he had more time to get other things done. He felt he was now ready to work on the pleasant things that both he and his wife could do together but was not sure how to begin, given his wife's physical limitations. Many of the activities they used to enjoy were now difficult for her. To facilitate this activity, the therapist and Mr. R. decided to have him help his wife complete the OPPES (see Figure 7.1 for sample questions) as well for him as complete the instrument himself and then to compare activities and brainstorm any additions. This job assignment was entered into his activity schedule and successfully completed.

Mr. R. continued to improve across the course of therapy, scoring within normal limits on the BDI-II for the last phase of therapy and maintaining these gains at subsequent booster sessions. He had increased his engagement in pleasant events both on his own as well as in conjunction with his wife and still made use of worry time and a structured activity schedule. At his last booster, he reported that his daughter was spending more time with his wife and came to help cook and visit for at least one family meal on the weekend. He also had joined a family support group for spouses of people with debilitating illnesses and took pride in helping others who were facing similar problems. In fact, Mr. R. said he had taught the group the short relaxation technique he had learned in therapy.

Case Study 2

Mrs. M. is a 52-year-old Mexican American and mother of three adult children. She and her husband have been married for over 30 years and were the first children in their respective families to be born in the United States. Their two daughters are both married and raising families of their own. One is a teacher and the other a stay-at-home mom. Their only son has survived a serious car accident but is partially paralyzed and struggles to manage his physical pain. According to Mrs. M., her son has always been a bit "wild" and still struggles with alcohol abuse more than she cares to think about. She says she prays especially hard for him every day. Mrs. M. had worked part-time for a number of years as a bookkeeper but cut her work hours dramatically 2 years ago to stay home with her mother, who was diagnosed with dementia. Between her mother and her son, Mrs. M. has assumed major caregiving responsibilities that she simply describes as "part of life." Mrs. M. learned through her son's case manager about

Please circle one number in each column for each item.	*How often in the past month?*			*How pleasant was it or would it have been?*		
	0 = Not at all *1 = 1 – 6 times* *2 = 7 or more times*			*0 = Not pleasant* *1 = Somewhat pleasant* *2 = Very pleasant*		
Looking at the stars or the moon	0	1	2	0	1	2
Exploring new areas	0	1	2	0	1	2
Meditating	0	1	2	0	1	2
Planning trips or vacations	0	1	2	0	1	2
Creative crafts	0	1	2	0	1	2
Gardening	0	1	2	0	1	2
Church religious services	0	1	2	0	1	2
Seeing beautiful scenery	0	1	2	0	1	2
Listening to music	0	1	2	0	1	2
Visiting a museum	0	1	2	0	1	2

Fig. 7.1 Sample items from the older person's pleasant events schedule.

local "coping with caregiving" classes being conducted for Latinas caring for loved ones with dementia and contacted our center. She had come to recognize that she was becoming increasingly stressed, irritable, and sad and was concerned about her physical health, especially her diabetes. Mrs. M. also had dropped many of her regular activities at church and with friends and was becoming increasingly isolated.

Mrs. M. welcomed the opportunity to learn more about dementia and enjoyed meeting with other Latinas facing similar situations. During one of the class sessions immediately after she had successfully completed a five-column thought record, Mrs. M., after reporting that she had endured a very stressful week, shared thoughts and feelings from this document. Old friends were visiting from out of town, her mother had developed some bladder accidents, and when her son needed transportation to a medical appointment, he smelled of alcohol. In the meantime, she felt criticized by her husband and daughters, who all complained that she gave too much help to her son. Even though Mrs. M. had developed more adaptive thoughts to challenge her negative thinking and help lift her feelings of disappointment and frustration, Mrs. M. told the class leader and participants that she often felt unappreciated by her family and that they never offered to help her. She believed all the stress was affecting her physical health. In fact, she felt it was exacerbating her current cold.

Mrs. M. felt comforted when several other women in the class reported also feeling unappreciated and unsupported in their caregiving situations. However, the class leader took the opportunity as part of the homework review to ask Mrs. M. "What stops you from asking your daughters... your husband...and even your son for help?" This process not only generated several different family situations to help identify distorted thought patterns but also reinforced Mrs. M.'s emerging skills in challenging her unhelpful thoughts. Most notably, Mrs. M. realized she automatically assumed her family knew what she needed, even when they had not been asked, and that she blamed them for not meeting these assumptions. Mrs. M. decided this came in part from having always served as the family caregiver, providing help and assistance at every turn. She believed she knew what they needed; why didn't they know what she needed? Many of the other caregivers expressed similar thoughts and feelings, leading to a discussion of the Latino cultural values of *familismo* dictating that Latinas must often put the needs of their family above their own. Ultimately, Mrs. M. was gently chided by the class leader and several fellow participants about the importance of taking time to care for herself. Caregivers are often reminded that caregiving is stressful and takes it toll, and that taking care of oneself is one way to help hold onto the caregiving role if they should want to do so.

This class discussion provided a nice transition into that week's mini lecture on the use of assertive communication skills with family members and professionals. Mrs. M. actively participated in the discussion following the lecture and made a point of thanking the class leader for the opportunity to role play how to ask her family members for help. She and other class members were encouraged to try out the new skill as a homework assignment with family members in the upcoming week.

Mrs. M. had a busy schedule the next week, including hosting a dinner party for the visiting friends, taking her mother to the doctor, and provid-

A - ANTECEDENT OR SITUATION	B - BELIEFS OR THOUGHTS	C - CONSEQUENCE OR EMOTION	D - DEVELOPING ADAPTIVE RESPONSES	E - EFFECTS OR OUTCOME
Describe the event or experience leading up to your unpleasant emotions	*Write down your negative thoughts and/or negative self-talk that occurred with the event or experience just described. Rate your degree of belief in the thoughts or self-talk, from 0 to 100%*	*Write down what you are feeling (sad, anxious, angry, etc.) Rate degree of emotion from 1 to 100%*	*Try to challenge your negative thoughts or self-talk. Thank about: What is the evidence for the idea? What are its pros and cons? Can I think of an alternative?*	*Re-rate your belief in your original negative thoughts, from 0 to 100%*
DATE: Two days before party			*Rate how much you believe these new thoughts, from 0 to 100%*	*Specify and rate your emotions NOW, from 1 to 100%*
"We" are hosting a dinner for friends we've not seen for 2 years. I will run late because none of my family will be there to help. I haven't had a chance to discuss Mom's memory problems with our friends and I'm afraid that she will be embarrassed.	No-one is here for me when I need help. If my family cared they would be here helping me. They just care about food and my support. Mom will be sad because she won't be able to answer questions they ask her. It's my fault for not telling them, ahead of time. I will not enjoy myself because the party will be a disaster. Everything will be late and taste bad.	Irritable (a lot! 75%) Worried (50%) Frustrated (70%) Disappointed (90%)	My family loves me. I can ask each one to help in some way. I won't know, if I don't ask. My husband can pick up my son. My son can spend time with Mom. My daughters like to cook. I can ask if they can come over early and help. I can call my friend and let her know about Mom's memory. I don't have to explain everything. They are kind people and will understand. People like my cooking, especially these friends.	Irritable (30%) Worried (30%) Frustrated (20%) Disappointed (don't know yet!)

Fig. 7.2 Daily thought record.

ing transportation for her son to see his case manager. During the home-work review at the next class, Mrs. M. asked if she could present the thought record she had completed two nights before the dinner party. This record (Figure 7.2) focused on her anticipation of preparing the dinner party with no assistance from anyone in her family. These thoughts led to feelings of frustration, irritability, disappointment, and worry. However, Mrs. M. reported that practicing the assertive communication skills gave her ideas and hope to challenge these thoughts and to create a "real list" of what to ask each family member to do for her. She also trusted that her friends would understand her mother's situation, especially when she reminded herself of their sincerity and compassion. Mrs. M.'s friends actu-ally called her first to ask what they could bring to the dinner, and the call gave her the opportunity to briefly discuss her mother's memory prob-lems. Mrs. M. told the class that while the dinner was not the best meal she had ever cooked, she thought it was "the best" because she saw just how much her family would help her when she asked them.

In the classes ahead, Mrs. M. also reported that, with the help of other class members, she found new ways to engage in pleasant activities outside of class. She made a commitment with her best friend, as part of a home-work assignment, to watch their favorite soap opera regularly and then chat on the phone and occasionally in person over coffee about it. Mrs. M. and her husband also made a "date" to take walks together three nights a week, and she got her family members to rotate staying with her mother several times a month so she could attend the women's prayer meeting at her church. At the end of the class meetings, Mrs. M. reported substantially less stress, sadness, and irritability; at booster follow-ups, reported ongoing use of and satisfaction with many of the skill-building homework activities.

Conclusion

Growing empirical and clinical case evidence suggests that homework is essential to skill reinforcement and generalization for both older and younger adult clients. However, the design and delivery of effective home-work for older adults requires not only significant forethought and cre-ativity but also considerable patience, persistence, problem solving, and advance planning on the part of both therapist and client to successfully dismantle attitudinal and logistical barriers (Coon & Gallagher-Thompson, 2002). The most effective homework will most likely incorporate the themes raised in this Chapter, including assignments that are closely tied to client target complaints and treatment goals, exercises that build on in-session themes, and tasks that the clients perceive as both realistic and valuable to complete. Moreover successful homework must be developed as a treatment priority in collaboration with the older adult; it must be tailored to address their particular problems and framed as an opportunity for skill development and learning that is applicable to their individual sociocultural context. There remains a good deal for us to learn about to homework and its use with older adult clients, particularly in regard to its effective use with ethnic minority elders. Thus, we encourage CBT practitioners to continue to share the creative homework activities they design and develop for older adults, and we ask clinical intervention researchers to continue to investigate the utility of homework strategies with various populations, including groups of culturally diverse older adults.

References

Beck, A. T., Rush, A. J., Shaw, B. F., & Emery, G. (1979). *Cognitive therapy of depression.* New York: Guilford Press.

Beutler, L. W., Scogin, F., Kinkish, P., Schretlen, D., Corbishley, A., et al. (1987). Group cognitive therapy and alprazolam in the treatment of depression in older adults. *Journal of Consulting and Clinical Psychology, 55,* 550–556.

Bryant, M. J., Simons, A. D., & Thase, M. E. (1999). Therapist skill and patient variables in homework compliance. Controlling an uncontrolled variable in cognitive therapy outcome research. *Cognitive Therapy and Research, 23,* 381–399.

Burns, D. D. (1980). *Feeling good: The new mood therapy.* New York: Signet.

Coon, D. W., & Gallagher-Thompson, D. (2002). Encouraging homework completion among older adults in therapy. *Journal of Clinical Psychology/In Session: Psychotherapy in Practice, 58,* 549–563.

Coon, D. W., Gallagher-Thompson, D., & Thompson, L. (Eds.). (2003). *Innovative interventions to reduce dementia caregiver distress: A clinical guide.* New York: Springer.

Coon, D. W., Rider, K., Gallagher-Thompson, D., & Thompson, L. (1999). Cognitive-behavioral therapy for the treatment of late-life distress. In M. Duffy (Ed.), *Handbook of counseling and psychotherapy with older adults* (pp. 487–510). New York: Wiley.

Coon, D. W., & Thompson, L. W. (2003). Association between homework compliance and treatment outcome among older adult outpatients with depression. *American Journal of Geriatric Psychiatry, 11,* 53–61.

Coon, D. W., Thompson, L. W., Steffen. A., Sorocco, K., & Gallagher-Thompson, D. (2003). Anger and depression management: Psychoeducational skill training interventions for women caregivers of a relative with dementia. *The Gerontologist, 43,* 678–689.

DeVries, H. M., & Coon, D. W. (2002). Cognitive/behavioral group therapy with older adults. In F. W. Kaslow & T. Patterson (Eds.), *Comprehensive handbook of psychotherapy,* Vol. 2: *Cognitive- behavioral approaches* (pp. 547–567). New York: Wiley.

Dick, L., Gallagher-Thompson, D., Coon, D., Powers, D., & Thompson, L. W. (1996). *Cognitive-behavioral therapy for late-life depression: A patient's manual.* Stanford, CA: VA Palo Alto Health Care System and Stanford University.

Ellis, A. (1962). *Reason and emotion in psychotherapy.* Secaucus, NJ: Lyle Stuart.

Gallagher, D., & Thompson, L. W. (1981). *Depression in the elderly: A behavioral treatment manual.* Los Angeles: University of Southern California Press.

Gallagher-Thompson, D., Arean, P., Rivera, P., & Thompson, L. W. (2001). Reducing distress in Hispanic family caregivers using a psychoeductional intervention. *Clinical Gerontologist, 23,* 17–32.

Gallagher-Thompson, D., Arean, P., Coon, D., Menendez, A., Takagi, K., Haley, W., Arguelles, T., Rubert, M., Loewenstein, D., & Szapocznik, J. (2000). Development and implementation of intervention strategies for culturally diverse caregiving populations. In R. Schulz (Ed.), *Handbook on dementia caregiving* (pp. 151–185). New York: Springer.

Gallagher-Thompson, D., Coon, D., Solano, N., Ambler, C., Rabinowitz, R., & Thompson, L. (2003). Change in indices of distress among Latina and Anglo female caregivers of elderly relatives with dementia: Site specific results from the REACH National Collaborative Study. *The Gerontologist, 43,* 580–591.

Gallagher-Thompson, D., Lovett, S., Rose, J. McKibbin, C., Coon, D. W., Futterman, A., & Thompson, L. W. (2000). Impact of psychoeducational interventions on distressed family caregivers. *Journal of Clinical Geropsychology, 6,* 91–110.

Gallagher-Thompson, D., Ossinalde, C., & Thompson, L. W. (1996). *Coping with caregiving: A class for family caregivers.* Palo Alto, CA: VA Palo Alto Health Care System.

Gallagher-Thompson, D., Rose, J., Florsheim, M., Jacome, P., DelMaestro, S., Peters, L., Gantz, F., Arguello, D., Johnson, C., Moorehead, R. S., Polich, T. M., Chesney, M., & Thompson, L. W. (1992). *Controlling your frustration: A class for caregivers.* Palo Alto, CA: VA Palo Alto Health Care System [Note: This refers to two English-language manuals: a class leader and a class participant version.]

Gallagher-Thompson, D., & Steffen, A. M. (1994). Comparative effects of cognitive behavioral and brief psychodynamic psychotherapies for depressed family caregivers. *Journal of Consulting and Clinical Psychology, 62,* 543–549.

Gatz, M., Fiske, A., Fox, L. S., Kaskie, B., Kasl-Godley, J. E., McCallum, T. J., & Wetherell, J. L. (1998). Empirically validated psychological treatments for older adults. *Journal of Mental Health and Aging, 4,* 9–46.

Grant, R. W., & Casey, D. A. (1995). Adapting cognitive behavioral therapy for the frail elderly. *International Psychogeriatrics, 7,* 561–571.

Haley, W. (1996). The medical context of psychotherapy with the elderly. In S. Zarit & B. Knight (Eds.), *A guide to psychotherapy and aging* (pp. 221–239). Washington, DC: American Psychological Association.

Hay, C. E., & Kinnier, R. T. (1998). Homework in counseling. *Journal of Mental Health Counseling, 20,* 122–132.

Kanfer, F., & Phillips, J. (1966). A survey of current behavior and proposal for classification. *Archives of General Psychiatry, 15,* 114–128.

Kazantzis, N., Deane, F. P., & Ronan, K. R. (2000). Homework assignments in cognitive and behavioral therapy: A meta-analysis. *Clinical Psychology: Science and Practice, 7,* 189–202.

Kazantzis, N., Pachana, N. A., & Secker, D. L. (2003). Cognitive-behavioral therapy for older adults: Practical guidelines for the use of homework assignments. *Cognitive and Behavioral Practice, 10,* 325–333.

Laidlaw, K., Thompson, L. W., Dick-Siskin, L., & Gallagher-Thompson, D. (2003). *Cognitive behaviour therapy with older people.* West Sussex, UK: Wiley.

Lewinsohn, P. M. (1974). A behavioral approach to depression. In R. Friedman & M. Katz (Eds.), *The psychology of depression: Contemporary theory and research* (pp. 154–176). New York: Wiley.

Lewinsohn, P. M., Muñoz, R. F., Youngren, M. A., & Zeiss, A. M. (1986). *Control your depression.* New York: Prentice Hall.

Mausbach, B., Coon, D. W., Cardenas, V., & Thompson, L. W. (2003). Religious coping among Caucasian and Latina dementia caregivers. *Journal of Mental Health and Aging, 9,* 97–110.

Mohlman, J., Gorenstein, E. E., Kleber, M., de Jesus, M., Gorman, J. M., & Papp, L. A. (2003). Standard and enhanced cognitive-behavior therapy for late-life generalized anxiety disorder: Two pilot investigations. *American Journal of Geriatric Psychiatry, 11,* 24–32.

Organista, K. C. (2000). Latinos. In J. R. White & A. S. Freeman (Eds.), *Cognitive-behavioral group therapy for specific problems and populations* (pp. 218–303). Washington, DC: American Psychological Association.

Organista, K. C., & Muñoz, R. F. (1996). Cognitive behavioral therapy with Latinos. *Cognitive and Behavioral Practice, 3,* 255–270.

Padesky, C. A. (1998). *Protocols and personalities: The therapist in cognitive therapy.* Keynote address at the European Association for Behavioural and Cognitive Therapies (EABCT), Annual Conference, Cork, Ireland.

Persons, J. B. (1989). *Cognitive therapy in practice: A case formulation approach.* New York: Norton.

Pinquart, M., & Sörensen, S. (2001). How effective are psychotherapeutic and other psychosocial interventions with older adults? A meta-analysis. *Journal of Mental Health and Aging, 7,* 207–243.

Rybarczyk, B., Gallagher-Thompson, D., Rodman, J., Zeiss, A., Gantz, F., & Yesavage, J. (1992). Applying cognitive-behavioral psychotherapy to the chronically ill elderly: Treatment issues and case illustrations. *International Psychogeriatrics, 4,* 127–140.

Schulz, R., O'Brien, A., Czaja, S., Ory, M., Norris, R., Martire, L. M., Belle, S., Burgio, L., Gitlin, L., Coon, D., Burns, R., Gallagher-Thompson, D., & Stevens, A. (2002). Dementia caregiver intervention research: In search of clinical significance. *The Gerontologist, 42,* 589–602.

Secker, D. L., Kazantzis, N., Pachana, N .A. (2004). Adapting cognitive therapy for use with older adults: The issue of structure. *Journal of Rationale-Emotive and Cognitive Behavior Therapy, 22,* 93–109.

Stanley, M. A., Beck, J. G., Novy, D. M., Averill, P. M., Swann, A. C., Diefenbach, G. J., & Hopko, D. R. (2003). Cognitive-behavioral treatment of late-life generalized anxiety disorder. *Journal of Consulting and Clinical Psychology, 71,* 309–319.

Teri, L., Logsdon, R. G., Uomoto, J., & McCurry, S. M. (1997). Behavioral treatment of depression in dementia patients: A controlled clinical trial. *Journal of Gerontology: Psychological Sciences, 52B,* 159–166.

Teri, L., & McCurry, S. (2000). Psychosocial therapies. In C. E. Coffey & J. L. Cummings, (Eds.), *Textbook of geriatric neuropsychiatry* (2nd ed., pp. 861–890). Washington, DC: American Psychiatric Press.

Thompson, L. W., Coon, D. W., Gallagher-Thompson, D., Sommer, B. R., & Koin, D. (2001). Comparison of desipramine and cognitive/behavioral therapy in the treatment of elderly outpatients with mild-to-moderate depression. *American Journal of Geriatric Psychiatry, 9,* 225–240.

Thompson, L. W., & Gallagher, D. (1984). Efficacy of psychotherapy in the treatment of late-life depression. *Advances in Behaviour Research and Therapy, 6,* 127–139.

Thompson, L. W., Gallagher-Thompson, D., & Dick, L. (1996). *Cognitive-behavioral therapy for late-life depression: A therapist's manual.* Stanford, CA: VA Palo Alto Health Care System and Stanford University.

Thompson, L. W., Gallagher-Thompson, D., & Lovett, S. (1992). *Increasing life satisfaction class leaders' and participant manuals* (revised version). Palo Alto, CA: Department of Veterans Affairs Medical Center and Stanford University.

Thompson, L., Powers, D., Coon, D., Takagi, K., McKibbin, C., & Gallagher-Thompson, D. (2000). Older adults. In J. R. White & A. S. Freeman (Eds.), *Cognitive behavioral group therapy for specific problems and populations* (pp. 235–261). Washington, DC: American Psychological Association.

Thompson, L., Solano, N., Kinoshita, L., Coon, D. W., Mausbach, B., & Gallagher-Thompson, D. (2002). Pleasurable activities and mood: Differences between Latina and Caucasian dementia family caregivers. *Journal of Mental Health and Aging, 8,* 211–224.

Tompkins, M. A. (2002). Guidelines for enhancing homework compliance. *Journal of Clinical Psychology/In Session: Psychotherapy in Practice, 58,* 565–576.

Wetherell, J. L., Gatz, M., & Craske, M. G. (2003). Treatment of generalized anxiety disorder in older adults. *Journal of Consulting and Clinical Psychology, 71,* 31–40.

Yost, E. B., Beutler, L. E., Corbishley, M. A., & Allender, J. R. (1986). *Group cognitive therapy: A treatment approach for depressed older adults.* New York: Pergamon Press.

Young J. E. (1999). *Cognitive therapy for personality disorders: A schema-focused approach* (3rd ed.). Sarasota, FL: Professional Resource Press.

Zeiss, A. M., & Steffen, A. (1996). Treatment issues with elder clients. *Cognitive and Behavioral Practice, 3,* 371–389.

CHAPTER **8**

Couples

FRANK M. DATTILIO

Many professionals in the field of couples and family therapy believe that one of the main components that makes treatment effective is the armamentarium of techniques. One important tool is the ability to select assignments both inside and outside of the therapy session.

Couples therapists, no matter their theoretical orientations, usually expect to fortify in-session treatment with out-of-session assignments. These assignments are commonly referred to as "homework" (Primakoff, Epstein, & Covi, 1986; Schultheis, O'Hanlon, & O'Hanlon, 1999). In the field of cognitive behavioral therapy (CBT), homework assignments have become the hallmark of treatment and are considered a critical component of change with such disorders as anxiety and depression as well as with couples and family problems (Beck, Rush, Shaw, & Emery, 1979; Dattilio & Epstein, 2003; Dattilio & Padesky, 1990). In the latest results of the Delphi Poll, which is conducted every 10 years, therapist didactic direction, such as homework assignments, was predicted to significantly increase in the next decade (Norcross, Hedges, & Prochaska, 2002).

Although the efficacy of homework assignments is not universally accepted, most criticism is actually based on semantics. Many clinicians feel that the term *homework* carries a negative connotation and that a therapist using it runs the risk of turning people off, especially if the assignment is imposed in a directive fashion. In fact, an entire special edition of the *Journal of Clinical Psychology* was dedicated to the use of homework in psychotherapy; a consistent thread throughout this edition was the suggestion that clients have negative perceptions of homework assignments (May, 2002). Homework may invoke negative associations with experiences of hierarchy and punishment as well as boredom and futility (Rampage, 2000), no doubt related to memories of school. It follows, then, that clients will assume that something called homework is going to be unpleasant. For this reason, some therapists have replaced *homework* with something else, such as *out-of-session assignments* or *experiments*. Others have used *data collection* or *task assignments*, and Rampage (2000) refers to "the more oblique suggestion of something that may be worth noticing."

Regardless of the semantics, the majority of couples therapists admit that out-of-session assignments or homework are an integral part of their treatment process. In fact, some theories argue in favor of using written homework assignments in order to help couples assume greater responsibility for changes in their relationships (L'Abate, 2003).

A recent project undertaken by Dattilio and Bevilacqua (2000) involved assembling 18 of some of the most prominent theorists of diverse orientations of couples therapy to contribute to a text titled *Comparative Treatments for Relationship Dysfunction*. In this work, the contributors were provided with a detailed case history of a couple in conflict and asked to answer a series of questions in terms of how they would approach the couple's problems and their circumstance from their own therapeutic perspective. One of the standard categories that they were asked about involved the use of homework assignments during the process of treatment. The authors were specifically asked, "Would you assign homework to this couple, and if so, how often and under what circumstance would the assignments be given?" All of the authors admitted recommending homework. Some said they would introduce assignments more tacitly than others and with a less directive approach. Many theorists believed that they should avoid "telling the couple what they should do." In only one case (object relations) did the authors believe that homework or special assignments would not be used, unless, of course, "sex therapy exercises were found to be necessary" (p. 99). This distinction appears elsewhere in the professional literature as well (Weeks & Gambescia, 2000, p. 108). However, it is not uncommon in couples work from an object relations standpoint to suggest that couples "make time between sessions to talk to each other" (Scharff & deBarela, 2000), which might be interpreted as an out-of-session assignment of sorts.

So, even in a case of the more "nondirective approach," there is usually some suggestion of out-of-session assignments. And how could there not be given the need to extend the work accomplished in the therapy session to the other 167 hours of the couple's week. Homework provides the opportunity to expand on what was accomplished during the course of the session and to test it out in the real world.

Homework is an important part of CBT with couples, since the skills that are acquired in treatment become more ingrained with the right assignments and the chance to process enacting behaviors. In fact, CBT's working with couples rely on these assignments to galvanize the work accomplished during the course of the therapy session. Research in CBT has indicated that clients who engage in homework activities display greater and more rapid improvement than those who do not (Primakoff, Epstein, & Covi, 1986). The rationale for assigning homework is that spouses often learn best by doing. Homework assignments can often facilitate small changes in one or more of the areas discussed during the course of treatment in order to lead to some of the larger changes that may need to occur.

Types of Homework

There are several types of homework assignments in CBT with couples. Two of the more common ones involve observational assignments (OAs) and experimental learning tasks (ELTs).

Observational Assignments

As the term *observational* implies, this is a passive, more consummative assignment that involves collecting information. OAs involve recording one's feelings and automatic thoughts leading to beliefs about oneself or one's spouse. By keeping track of positive gains or problem behaviors, spouses become more acutely aware of what is happening in the relationship. Specific assignments may include observing one's spouse to notice similarities or differences in behavioral speaking patterns or maintaining a time journal to see whether patterns exist and if they are linked to any particular time of the day, specific activities, or moods. OAs can actually continue throughout the course of treatment and are designed to become part of a permanent repertoire for couples. Couples are encouraged to eventually adopt this technique as part of the repertoire for fostering growth in their relationship on an ongoing basis.

A good example of an OA during the course of therapy is offered in the following case. Bob and Alice were a couple in their mid-forties who had been married 21 years. Bob complained that for years Alice never acknowledged any of the positive things that he did. The two key words in this complaint are "positive" and "never." Consequently, the first task assignment was for Bob and Alice to collect some data on their respective behaviors. For homework, it was suggested that Bob keep track of the times that he did something that he believed was positive and also to record his perception of Alice's reaction, but not to assign a "positive" or "negative" value to it. This was a "learning task assignment," through which both partners developed a great deal of insight about the frequency with which they did things. Bob came to realize that the term *never* was an exaggeration and that the description stemmed from his anger toward Alice. He also learned that he was misreading Alice's facial expressions. This was the start of the cognitive restructuring process for Bob, which would eventually benefit Alice as well. Alice also learned that she had a tendency to display conflicting behaviors at times, which could be very confusing to Bob. Consequently, Alice needed to remain more conscious of the images that she was sending to Bob.

OAs may also involve having a couple observe other couples in their interactions. For example, both spouses may be asked to observe other couples' interactions while out at social events and then to compare notes about what they saw and the impressions that they got from those interactions. This experience serves to take them out of the spotlight and give them something to do together, in addition to learning something about how others interact. The main goal of OAs is to gather information, learn to be observant, and become less impulsive in the process. It is through such assignments that couples may also learn to collect all of the facts rather than responding to pure emotion and to filter out some of the destructive content that contributes to conflict.

Journal Writing and Other Writing

Journal writing is another type of OA, which allows partners to maintain a continuous log of their feelings about what unfolds during the course of treatment and about interactions with each other. Other useful information may also come to mind during the process. In addition, because writing can be a cathartic exercise, one may experience a release of tension that leads to greater focus and clarity (Esterling, L'Abate, Murray, & Pennebaker, 1999). If spouses are open to the idea, they are encouraged to write in a journal as much as possible, keeping in mind that women are more apt to do so than men. Although journals are usually private, parts of the journal entires may be shared with the spouses or in a particular session. Progoff (1975) classified journals with diaries in that they require the least structure.

So-called focused writing sets a specific amount of time in which spouses may be instructed to write about particular aspects of their hurts or emotions (Esterling, L'Abate, Murray, & Pennebaker, 1999). A good example of focused writing is the case of Rita, who would often become so angry with her husband that she would spout off hurtful statements, which would alienate her husband and make him stop communicating. After she had calmed down, she would often regret her words, but then it was generally too late. Therefore she was encouraged to sit down and put into writing whatever came to her mind (to serve as sort of a cathartic exercise) in order to purge her anger. Once she had done this, she was then to confront her husband with a more respectful yet honest account of her feelings. L'Abate (2003) talks about two other types of writing in this context: *guided writing*, which involves answering specific questions for later review, and *programmed writing*, as presented in workbooks when a series of homework assignments are devoted to a single topic.

Experimental Learning Tasks

Experimental learning tasks (ELTs) differ from OAs in that they are actually tasks designed to be implemented directly, whereas OAs are passive activities in which spouses conserve energy and consume. ELTs vary depending on the couple's problems and the nature of their dysfunction. Having a couple try out a new behavior or communication style and then record the outcome of the trial is an example of a learning task. ELTs may also involve completing an automatic thought record and determining whether this process reduces distressing emotions. The couple may be asked to try out new problem-solving strategies around a particular issue and to keep track of their thoughts and feelings about it.

ELTs may be brought into treatment with the therapist casually suggesting, "Why don't we try a little experiment?" A good example of a context-specific ELT is the pad-and-pencil technique, which is introduced to help spouses refrain from interrupting each other during heated conversations or arguments. This technique, first developed by Dattilio (1996; 1999), involves having each spouse take notes on the spontaneous thoughts that emerge while the other spouse is talking. One reason couples interrupt each other is that they fear they will not remember or be able to express the automatic thoughts that came up for them. Interruptions may also be a result of poor impulse control, or they may serve as a means of exerting power or control over the spouse. All of these possibilities must be investigated, but in the interim the pad-and-pencil technique allows clients to channel their automatic thoughts so that they do not hinder the therapeutic process. Thus the spouses have an alternative behavior to interrupting, and they can also feel reassured that they will not lose the important thoughts or emotions that they are having. They are later given a full opportunity to express verbally what they have captured on paper.

As homework, the technique is first tried out during a session; then it is prescribed for use at home during discussions or arguments. The goal is to allow for a more fluid exchange of emotions and to reduce friction between spouses as well as to alleviate stress for the therapist, who can easily become fatigued by the role of referee.

Individual or Conjoint Assignments

Homework assignments in general may be given individually or to the couple conjointly and usually involve assessing focus on thoughts, feelings, behaviors, physiology, and the pattern of interactions. Whether to assign individual or joint homework assignments depends on the situation, even though many therapists may be concerned about suggesting an assignment to one spouse but not the other. However, assignments should be collaboratively designed around relevant issues in the couple's relationship, and they also need to take into account what is occurring at the moment in treatment. In CBT, homework assignments are critical for achieving the goals of changing specific core beliefs that contribute to dysfunction and modifying destructive interactional patterns. They are also essential if a couple plans on acquiring new skills with which to deal more effectively with themselves and the stressors of their relationship. It is important for the therapist and client to be aware that certain homework assignments may require continued practice or experimentation over a period of time before they yield any reliable results. The following example of Kelly and Ardith, a gay couple who had lived together for 15 years, illustrates how separate homework assignments can be effective in reducing tension in a relationship.

Kelly, who has always been a rather fastidious individual, likes things to be in their place. This comes down to even having certain items lined up properly in the refrigerator. Ardith, on the other hand, describes himself as an outright "slob" who throws clothes on the floor and leaves them lying around for days. Obviously, this drives Kelly "nuts," the tension of which has alienated them from each other.

Hence, a homework assignment might involve having them each modify their behaviors in a small way each day without verbally announcing what they have done. Each individual would also be asked to record any changes that is seen with the other and bring that record in to the following session.

The Collaborative Nature of Assignments

A collaborative approach is believed to be one of the essential features that makes CBT so effective. When couples have an equal part in devising their assignments, the assignments are usually more effective. First, when clients have an instrumental role in developing the plan it ensures a focus on an area that is of interest to them. Therapists should also use the couples' unique language and their metaphors as the homework process takes shape so that the partners can relate to it.

Second, couples are more likely to comply with homework assignments they help create. It is thought that one of the many reasons for noncompliance is that one or both spouses disagree with the assignments or perceive them to be silly or ridiculous. If, therefore, the spouses are working alongside the therapist, it makes a major difference in their response. The therapist can also use positive language that assumes compliance, such as, "When you complete this assignment, we'll go over how it affected you." It is also important to stress to each spouse that not completing homework assignments may also be giving the other, and the therapist, a nonverbal message.

Bibliotherapy

It is not clear where the term *bibliotherapy* came from, although it literally means "therapy from a book," which is not exactly the intention in this context. Supplemental reading, as opposed to self-help, is closer to what the term is intended to convey and, in most cases, is how it is used during the course of treatment. Supplemental reading assignments are used by many couples therapists, often as part of homework assignments.

Typically, it is suggested that both spouses read segments of a certain book (or in some cases an entire book) in order to bolster certain concepts or skills addressed in therapy. Bibliotherapy may also be used to stimulate or provoke thought. One of the most popular books assigned currently is *Fighting for Your Marriage*, by Markman, Stanley, and Blumberg (1994). Couples are typically asked to read specific Chapters of this book at given times so as to support what is being addressed in treatment (i.e., problem solving, communication training). Reading also helps to galvanize what was addressed during the course of the sessions and keeps the techniques fresh in the spouses' minds between sessions. It also allows them to see that they are not alone in their relationship struggles and that others wrestle with similar problems.

If one or both spouses have difficulty reading or simply do not like to read, an alternative may be for them to listen to the given book on tape. Both partners can listen at the same time and compare notes, and most popular books are available on cassettes. When spouses set aside time at home or in the car on long drives to listen to a book, they not only learn from the content but also have a chance to do something together. They can start and stop the tape as desired, discuss the contents, and report on it at the subsequent session.

Sometimes, specific readings may be prescribed, as in the event of a trauma or a circumstance involving children or family members. For example, *After the Affair*, by Spring (1996), is often assigned as mandatory reading for couples early in treatment when they are attempting to recover from an extramarital relationship. Both spouses are urged to read the book, after which specific content will be discussed in subsequent sessions.

Therapists are cautioned not to use bibliotherapy randomly or simply to "give the couple something to do," as assignments proposed in a vacuum are likely to wear thin. Assigned readings should be selectively chosen and evenly paced so as to serve as an effective supplement to the work done in the actual therapy session.

Strategies for Effective Homework

The Language of Homework Assignments

Returning to the all-important issue of semantics, how an assignment is communicated will affect how it is received by the couple. There are times when assignments should be suggested or "tacitly implied," and there are other times when they should be directly prescribed or required. The choice of terms given the who, what, when, where, and why is important. Sometimes, couples may actually ask for homework assignments in their zeal for results. It is important, however, not to assign homework prematurely or in excess, and it is essential to take the lead in the decision.

Timing and Pacing of Homework Assignments

The timing and pacing of assignments is almost as important as their content. Assignments should be used differently in various stages of treatment and should never be introduced prematurely or abruptly. They can do more harm than good if used at the wrong time. An illustration of bad timing is offered by the case of Tom and Vivian, who sought marital treatment because they were arguing all the time. Each complained that the other did not follow through on promises. For example, Vivian had been "harping" at Tom about having the chimney of their house fixed because some of the brickwork needed to be repointed. Tom kept promising that he would "get somebody out to estimate the job" but failed to do so. Each time, Vivian would fly into a tirade and say that Tom just didn't care and only gave her "lip service."

In this case, the therapist suggested a homework assignment that required Tom to take steps to get the job done as soon as possible. In the session, they outlined certain things that he would do and made him sign an agreement. Vivian also signed an agreement stating that she would not harp at Tom and that she would allow him time to complete the task. Unfortunately, the homework assignment was unsuccessful, mostly because it had been introduced too soon in the treatment process. The therapist had failed to investigate the reasons for Tom's lack of follow-through more deeply before presenting the assignment. It was only later that Tom's resistance was linked to his anger toward Vivian. The effect then was that when the therapist pushed the issue, Tom only became more stalwart and, in a sense, also retaliated against the therapist by not completing the assignment. This assignment might have been more successful if the therapist had introduced it later on, after Tom's core beliefs about Vivian were uncovered, along with his anger toward her and what it was all about. It was not so much the content but the timing of this assignment that doomed it to failure. In this case, the therapist failed to conceptualize Tom's difficulty with expressing his anger, which would have come out later during the course of treatment. Assignments are often unsuccessful due to client sabotage, at times because of misguided anger.

Homework as Part of the Assessment Phase

Sometimes, homework may be used to help the therapist assess various dynamics of the relationship, such as the couple's stamina or ability to comply or to work together. Also, how well couples take direction together and carry out assignments tells a therapist a lot about how cohesively they function and how they might fare in treatment. For instance, a couple may claim that they cannot seem to do anything together, yet they complete an assignment successfully and without incident. Even though they retort by saying that they did so because they were told to by the therapist, their ability to see the assignment through is quite telling about how their relationship works.

On the other hand, a couple who actually ask a therapist to give them some homework together and then fail to complete it or have difficulty with it may need to be reassigned homework separately. It may also clue the therapist in to the possibility that perhaps this couple are engaging in "magical thinking" or are unrealistic about what they can accomplish.

Usually, the first homework task assigned to couples during the assessment phase is the completion of questionnaires or inventories. A host of questions have been designed to tap into various aspects of thoughts, behaviors, and emotions. These are outlined in Dattilio (1998). In addition, how spouses attempt the completion of such inventories is also very important for a therapist to note, providing possible hints about directions to explore during the process of therapy.

Homework Assignments as Part of the Treatment, Enactment, and Follow-up Phase

Even though, with many cases, assessment never truly ends, there comes a point when homework is used more as a means to acquire or solidify behaviors learned in therapy than solely as an assessment tool. Early on in the initial assessment phase, homework may elicit results that are used in developing a "road map" of how treatment might unfold; later, it is used to support or enhance learning.

The homework used in the treatment intervention phase is usually constructed to help with change. Therefore the homework assignments may be more repetitive and reflective of permanent change as opposed to exploratory or experimental. In every phase, the stumbling blocks that occur may serve as a diagnostic aid as to what is dysfunctional in the relationship. This is seen most commonly with communication techniques, which often have to be reinforced repeatedly with a couple. However, the more they practice, the more skillful they become.

Noncompliance with Assignments

One of the problems with a modality that relies on homework assignments is that when one or both spouses fail to comply with an assignment, the treatment process is interrupted. Such noncompliance is usually accounted for by some type of resistance, and there are various views as to the reasons for it. Nichols and Schwartz (2001) suggest that early family therapists interpreted resistance as homeostasis or a force that opposed change in systems, regardless of whether the system involves a couple or a family relationship. Most theories of family therapy recognize that all human systems are resistant to changes that involve any type of risk, and most recognize that families should resist change until they are sure that the change is safe and the therapist can be trusted. Thus the perspective has shifted among some theorists in the field from "resistance as homeostasis" to "resistance as [to some extent] self-protection." Some approaches basically extend the view from individual therapy to couples or families, including psychoanalytic, cognitive behavioral, and experiential family therapies. These views of resistance closely parallel those of their respective individual therapies.

For years, CBT therapists tended to shy away from the use of terms that have any associations with psychodynamic models, such as *resistance*. CBT therapists do not deny that couples may engage in behaviors that interfere with progress in therapy, but they prefer to deal with the behaviors as they arise rather than grouping them into a pattern, which they may refer to as "roadblocks" (Dattilio, 2003).

Sometimes, noncompliance has to do with schemata that involve danger or risk of some sort, such as revealing certain things that may render an individual vulnerable. CBT therapists tend to look at schemata that center around noncompliance as a result of essential beliefs that need to be challenged, according to evidence from the given individual's life. Certainly much resistance or noncompliance may rest on an individual's dysfunctional belief system; other issues or environmental factors may also be salient. Beck and Freeman (1990) outline a number of issues in their work to explain why individuals are noncollaborative. Their lengthy list encompasses a range of ideas regarding the clients, the therapist, and other variables: the couple or family members may lack the skills to be collaborative, ideas and beliefs may be in place regarding potential failure in treatment or the effects of the couple's change on others, there is secondary gain from maintaining dysfunctional patterns, there is the timing of interventions introduced by the therapist, the couple and family members lack motivation, lack of trust between patient and therapist, frustration about slow progress of treatment on the part of the therapist or patient, and others.

The view of resistance and noncompliance as a reflection of underlying dysfunctional and distorted thinking has been elaborated on and modified by other CBT therapists, including Goldfried and Davison (1976) and Leahy (2002). In some cases, the couple may sense the therapist's doubt or negative expectations about the couple's ability to change, which may, in turn, affect their compliance. The therapist's ability to adequately conceptualize what a couple requires and what needs to be accomplished may also play a significant role in their noncompliance. A final explanation may also lie with more significant psychopathology that exists with one or both spouses, such as Axis I or II content or depression, which may interfere with their ability to comply with homework assignments.

Noncompliance may come in one of two forms: outright refusal or passive resistance. Couples who engage in outright refusal usually have a very specific reason for their noncompliance. They may believe that it is unnecessary to do outside work or they simply do not like to be assigned anything to do outside of the session. These responses may stem from a basic personality structure or from the need to have the therapist show what he or she can do for them in the session first. Whatever the reason, it is suggested that the therapist back off and perhaps reintroduce the assignment or an alternative at a later date. If noncompliance or partial compliance is still an issue, the matter of resistance needs to be explored as a part of the therapeutic process. It has also been found that couples tend to be more compliant with homework assignments when the task is designed to be consistent with therapy than when the link is unclear (Jacobson, 1981). A therapist may have a couple actually do the assignment right in the therapy session and then ask that they complete a small portion of the task at home. Sometimes, this type of "jump start" is just what they need to be successful in undertaking the assignment.

The more difficult form of noncompliance is the passive-resistant form, when spouses nod affirmatively, as though they have every intention of completing the assignment, but then never actually do it. This may send a far more important message to the therapist than that of disinterest, such as that they tend to say what others need or want to hear. Therapy with couples of this type is likely to be much more arduous and lengthy. A discussion about being "up front" along with encouragement of full disclosure is warranted and may serve to set therapy on a different course if it is addressed early on. The nature of the collaboration between the couple and the therapist also needs to be explored in greater detail.

Case Study

The following case illustrates how homework can be used all the way through the treatment process with a couple in crisis, including the three phases of treatment; assessment, intervention, and follow-up.

Tony and Jette were a young couple in their early to mid-thirties, married 10 years. They had two children, a girl, age 7, and a boy, age 5. They were referred for marital counseling by their minister because of a trauma that had recently occurred in the relationship. Tony learned that Jette had engaged in an extramarital affair with a coworker, which turned the marriage upside down. Obviously, Tony had a very negative reaction to his wife's infidelity and needed to see his family physician for medication to help him sleep. Apparently Jette had confessed to the affair after Tony sensed that something was wrong and kept harping at it. Jette lied to Tony several times before revealing the truth. She was not able to tell him why she had the affair but stated that this man had paid attention to her at work and "one thing led to the other." Jette contended that she liked the attention and that she "felt special" as a result.

Upon gathering this information, it became clear that there had been some tension in the relationship long before the affair started. Jette always felt that Tony was very controlling, and she detested it. Tony stated that, over the preceding 10 years, he had only tried to make his wife happy; he felt that nothing he did was ever good enough for her. By the time they presented for treatment, Tony and Jette said they were tired of rehashing the same things. Tony was relentless in questioning Jette about details of the affair. He also wanted to confront the married man with whom she had the affair with and divulge the indiscretion to *his* spouse and family as a means of retaliation.

This couple reported was that things would periodically settle down between them and then flare up again. Tony and Jette would both attempt to heal, but then Tony would start up about specific details, especially after something had triggered his emotions. For example, Tony told about lying in bed in the couple's bedroom, waiting for Jette to come out of the shower.

She came into the bedroom, and as he watched her drying off, he became aroused. However, his arousal was quickly mediated by the intrusive thought, "I'm not the only one who has seen her naked." With this, he flew into a tirade, making resentful comments about how she violated the marriage and her family when she became sexually involved with another man. The experience also sparked a great deal of insecurity in Tony about his own masculinity. Both Tony and Jette were attractive people. Jette was a tall, slender Scandinavian who carried herself with an air of sophistication. Tony was a handsome Italian with a muscular build who worked in construction.

Selecting homework assignments for this couple was somewhat of a challenge at first, especially during this period of crisis. Initially, Tony and Jette were asked to read *After the Affair* (Spring, 1996). The primary objective for assigning this book was to help them realize they were not alone as well as to validate their feelings about the infidelity and its effect on their relationship. Reinforcing the fact that neither would be able to forget the circumstances easily and that their relationship was in turmoil was very important. While the book usually receives acclaim from those who have been assigned to read it, it annoyed Tony because of the section that talks about it being normal for the offending spouse to continue to maintain loving feelings for the person with whom he or she had the affair.

When it came to this discussion, Tony was very short-fused, throwing his hands up and saying, "Fine, if she is going to still have feelings for that sonofabitch, there's no use in going forward; we're through." Some work had to be done in the therapy session in order to help Tony understand that his wife stepped out of the marital relationship because she was looking for something she felt she was not getting in the marriage. The point made by the book had to be reframed: "What kind of person would Jette be if she didn't have any feelings for the person with whom she had been sexually involved?" Part of this cognitive restructuring process took place in the session; it was then assigned to Tony to do on his own. He was to repeat the idea to himself and to try to think through the circumstances of the affair without being overwhelmed by his immediate emotions, making an effort to understand why the affair occurred. Therefore homework was very strategic in the beginning and mapped out in the session. In addition, the therapist met frequently (every 4 or 5 days) with the couple, so that not too much time elapsed between homework assignments. The pacing of sessions was intended to mitigate the couple's tendency to wander into conflictual interactions or arguments that would likely detract from what was being accomplished during the therapy sessions.

Interestingly, homework was assigned separately to this couple in the initial phase of treatment, since they were not ready to interact cohesively.

Jette's homework assignments were designed to help prepare her to deal with the fact that, during the healing process, Tony would have outbursts in which he would regress and make shortsighted statements, such as "I'm out of here. I want out of this marriage." Learning how to be patient with her husband in the aftermath of her affair was part of Jette's taking responsibility for her behavior.

As the crisis began to settle down, a second homework assignment was devised to continue with the assessment phase. At this point, the therapist still needed to know about the family of origin of each spouse as well as about some of the dynamics that evolved over the course of their 10-year relationship and what may have contributed to the infidelity. Both spouses were asked to develop a genogram so that the therapist could gain a better understanding of what occurred in their upbringing and in their familial line. The genograms of both spouses were reviewed in the session so that both could listen in and learn more about their respective backgrounds. Jette shared that she came from a divorced family, in which her father was the one who had an affair and violated her mother's trust. Jette recalled being devastated by her father's infidelity at the time. On the other hand, Tony came from a family in which his father died early, and he was raised by his mother and his two sisters. Since he was the "man" of the house, he took it upon himself to protect his mother and sisters. Tony's mother never remarried. The genogram homework assignment provided an opportunity for the therapist to begin to build some connections between normal needs and roles in relationships and the fact that, given their backgrounds, Tony and Jette were ill prepared to deal with conflicts in their married life. The suggestion was also made that Jette may have engaged in the affair in order to beat Tony to the punch; that is, her behaviors were an attempt to protect herself lest Tony violate their relationship as her father had done with her mother. Jette later revealed that she had always worried that Tony would be unfaithful, although he had never given her any reason to do so. Aside from this, Jette was also in need of more attention than Tony was giving her.

At times, this couple had trouble complying with assignments. Jette was especially prone to becoming sour about the entire process of treatment. She would frequently state that it was a waste of time, that they were not getting anywhere, and that she did not see how the homework assignments fit into the therapy. Despite the fact that she wanted very much to salvage the marriage, she often undermined the efforts. Part of this was recognized as her resistance and fear of moving forward, which was made clear to her. She also responded in this way because of her feeling about being told what to do, particularly since it paralleled her experience with Tony. Jette felt that Tony was controlling, always laying everything out for her. She stated that the homework assignments had a tendency to trigger the same reaction in her. This was remedied by having Jette become more actively involved in generating the ideas for homework assignments herself. The philosophy behind out-of-session assignments was clarified with the explanation of how they helped to fortify the work that is accomplished during the session. One assignment had Jette examine some of her resistance, at one point even having her explore whether or not she wanted to remain in the relationship with Tony. Jette had been assigned the task of listing the reasons why she wanted to remain married to Tony. After several unsuccessful attempts, she was instructed to do the reverse and list reasons why she should leave him. This forced some of her resistance to the surface.

As the therapy sessions progressed, Tony and Jette were able to outline the three areas that needed to be addressed, over and above healing from the extramarital affair. One goal was to learn how to argue constructively. Neither felt that they had ever learned to do this, so their arguments went off on tangents. Another goal was to learn to communicate effectively. And the third aim was to be able to express loving feelings toward each other without losing focus. This was particularly important for Tony, who had a tendency to ruminate about whether or not Jette was fantasizing about being with the other man.

One of the most elaborate homework assignments for this couple involved the use of the daily dysfunctional thought record, which is a cornerstone of the CBT approach. The use of cognitive restructuring of dysfunctional thoughts was essential in helping Tony to overcome his intrusive thoughts, which so often contributed to the couple's backslides. One of the persistent thoughts was his own fantasy of confronting the other man face to face. Tony had convinced himself that it would make him feel better to do this, and he wanted to get a look at the man for himself, to see what he had that Tony himself did not.

Since this was a particular problem for Tony, he was urged to use the thought record in Figure 8.1, which is commonly employed to help couples restructure dysfunctional thoughts. Tony was asked to record the time, date, and situation or actual events that led to an unpleasant emotion or stream of thought. He was then asked to isolate his automatic thoughts about the situation, describe the emotion in detail, and gauge how much it affected him. Once he had done this, he was to bring the homework assignment into the session, where the therapist and Tony would proceed by labeling any distortions that existed with his thoughts and then collaboratively come up with some alternative responses that might intercept such thinking, so that it could be restructured to achieve some sense of balance. The rationale is to mediate irrationality and determine how much is fueled by cognition and emotion and then weigh whether or not the action would be something that would be in his and Jette's best interest. As can be seen in Figure 8.1, Tony's thoughts were structured nicely, which provided him with some sense of coping until this period of high emotionality passed. His restructured thoughts served to reduce his anger.

As we can see from this case, Tony was helped to mitigate some of his anger and frustration by restructuring his thinking. However, repetition is important, and this is one reason why homework is so important. The more something is practiced, the more it will become a permanent part of one's repertoire.

Similar assignments were used with Jette, given her feeling that she was not able to take any more of Tony's ranting and raving, that she was being punished excessively, and that they should just get on with their lives. Her restructuring involved preparing for the cycle to last for a while because Tony was angry and had a right to be angry. It had to take its course, and part of the healing process would involve her being patient with him and letting it pass.

In addition, a number of other homework assignments were given to help Tony and Jette rebuild their relationship. For example, during the course of the assessment and later in treatment, both were asked "Aside

DYSFUNCTIONAL THOUGHT RECORD

DIRECTIONS: WHEN YOU NOTICE YOUR MOOD GETTING WORSE, ASK YOURSELF, "WHAT'S GOING THROUGH MY MIND RIGHT NOW?" AND AS SOON AS POSSIBLE JOT DOWN THE THOUGHT OR MENTAL IMAGE IN THE AUTOMATIC THOUGHT COLUMN.

D A T E T I M E	SITUATION	AUTOMATIC THOUGHTS	EMOTION(S)	DISTORTION	ALTERNATIVE RESPONSE	OUTCOME
	DESCRIBE: 1. Actual event leading to unpleasant emotion, or 2. Stream of thoughts, day dreams, or recollection, leading to an unpleasant emotion, or 3. Distressing physical sensations.	1. Write automatic though(s) that preceded emotion(s). 2. Rate belief in automatic thought(s) 0-100%	DESCRIBE: 1. Specify sad, anxious/angry, etc. 2. Rate degree of emotion 0-100%	1 ALL OR NOTHING THINKING 2 OVERGENERALIZATION 3 MENTAL FILTER 4 DISQUALIFYING THE POSITIVE 5 JUMPING TO CONCLUSIONS 6 MAGNIFICATION OR MINIMIZATION 7 EMOTIONAL REASONING 8. SHOULD STATEMENTS 9 LABELING AND MISLABELING 10 PERSONALIZATION	1. Write rational response to automatic thoughts(s). 2. Rate belief in alternative response 0-100%	1. Re-rate belief in automatic thought(s) 0-100% 2. Specify and rate subsequent emotions 0-100%
4/5/00	At work, during lunch break, sitting in the cafeteria.	Suddenly start thinking about how, while I was hard at work, my wife is off having an affair with this jerk. Obviously, he had something that I didn't. Maybe he's more of a man than I am.	Anxious, weak, sensitive, feeling vulnerable, and bad about myself.	2, 4, 6	What my wife did had nothing to do with my manhood. It has more to do with boundary issues and her anger and low self-esteem. I need to remind myself that regardless of how much of a man I am, this may have still happened and it's something that we have to work through regarding our relationship and her self-esteem and anger toward me	1. 80%. 2. 75% improvement

Questions to help formulate the ALTERNATIVE RESPONSE: (1) What is the evidence that the automatic thought is true? Not true? (2) Is there an alternative explanation? (3) what's the worst that could happen? Could I live through it? What's the best that could happen? What's the most realistic outcome? (4) What should I do about it? (5) What's the effect of my believing the automatic thought? What could be the effect of changing my thinking? (6) If ___Tony___ _____ was in this situation and had this thought, what would I tell him/her?

Fig. 8.1 Daily dysfunctional thought record for Tony.

from the negative things that have occurred, what works in your relationship? In other words, despite all of the turmoil, what is still positive about this relationship?" The first part of the homework assignment was for them to make separate lists of the positive aspects of their relationship. They were to bring their lists to the next session and discuss them with the therapist. The second part of the assignment was for them to combine their lists in the session so that they could come up with one joint list that they could both agree on. They were then asked to pick out an item from the list and accentuate it.

Other homework assignments involved having the couple keep track of positive aspects that they noticed about each other during the course of their day and to feel free to acknowledge those aspects verbally. Being able to engage in this type of interaction was a break from the negative pattern that had been established following disclosure of the affair.

The follow-up phase of homework focused on further strengthening many of the milestones that were achieved during the course of treatment. Tony was urged to address negative thoughts about his wife's infidelity immediately as they came up so as not to allow himself to backslide. Also, any time one or both started to weaken or pay less attention, that was the time to call a joint meeting to sit down and revisit relevant issues.

The preceding case presents just a smattering of some of the many homework techniques that might be used with couples and how they might be implemented to bolster advances made during the course of treatment. This challenging case illustrates the need for and the value of homework assignments to supplement the in-session work.

Common Barriers to Homework Assignments

Despite the fact that the majority of modalities of marriage and family therapy strongly recommend the use of homework assignments, it can have drawbacks. Couples therapists may encounter couples whose resistance, for instance, makes relying on homework assignments an ineffective strategy. There are cases in which certain spouses simply refuse to do out-of-session assignments; therefore the therapist has to have other approaches available to make sure that change in the treatment process occurs within the parameters of the therapy session. Perhaps, homework assignments can simply be modified to be done during therapy sessions; the couple can then be scheduled for more frequent treatment (i.e., every 3 to 4 days versus every 7 to 10 days). Such accommodations might help fill the gap created by a couple's lack of completed out-of-session assignments.

Finally, it cannot be emphasized enough that using the wrong type of homework assignment too early (or too late) in the treatment process may also prove detrimental. Homework assignments need to be strategically selected, carefully timed and paced, and tailored to the couple's style and issues as well as to what is happening in the therapy if they are going to be successful in helping couples move toward a more rewarding relationship.

References

Beck, A. T., & Freeman, A. (1990). *Cognitive therapy of personality disorders.* New York: Guilford Press.

Beck, A. T., Rush, A. J., Shaw, B. F., & Emery, G. (1979). *Cognitive therapy of depression.* New York: Guilford Press.

Dattilio, F. M. (1996). Videotape. *Cognitive therapy with couples: Initial phase of treatment.* Sarasota, FL: Professional Resource Press, 56 minutes.

Dattilio, F. M. (Ed.). (1998). *Case studies in couple and family therapy: Systemic and cognitive perspectives.* New York: Guilford Press.

Dattilio, F. M. (1999). Pad and pencil technique. *Journal of Family Psychotherapy, 10(1),* 75–78.

Dattilio, F. M. (2003). Techniques in family therapy. In R. E. Leahy (Ed.), *Overcoming roadblocks in cognitive therapy.* New York: Guilford Press.

Dattilio, F. M., & Bevilacqua, L. J. (2000). *Comparative treatments of relationship dysfunction.* New York: Springer.

Dattilio, F. M., & Epstein, N. B. (2003). Cognitive-behavioral couples and family therapy. In G. Weeks, T. L. Sexton, M. Robbins (Eds.), *The family therapy handbook.* (pp. 147–175) New York: Routledge.

Dattilio, F. M., & Padesky, C. A. (1990). *Cognitive therapy with couples.* Sarasota, FL: Professional Resource Exchange.

Esterling, B. A., L'Abate, L., Murray, E., & Pennebaker, J. M. (1999). Empirical foundations for writing in prevention and psychotherapy: Mental and physical outcomes. *Clinical Psychology Review, 19,* 79–96.

Goldfried, M. R., & Davison, G. C. (1976). *Clinical behavior therapy.* New York: Holt, Rinehart, and Winston.

L'Abate, L. (2003). Treatment through writing: A unique new direction. In G. Weeks, T. L. Sexton, M. Robbins (Eds.), *The family therapy handbook* (pp. 397–409). New York: Brunner Routledge.

Leahy, R. L. (2002). *Overcoming resistance in cognitive therapy.* New York: Guilford Press.

Markman, H. J., Stanley, S. M., & Blumberg, S. L. (1994). *Fighting for your marriage.* San Francisco: Jossey-Bass.

Nichols, M. P., & Schwartz, R. (2001). *Family therapy: Concepts and methods* (5th ed.). New York: Allyn & Bacon.

Norcross, J. C., Hedges, M., & Prochaska, J. O. (2002). The face of 2010: A Delphi Poll on the future of psychotherapy. *Professional Psychology: Research and Practice, 33,* 316–322.

Primakoff, L., Epstein, N. B., & Covi, L. (1986). Homework compliance: An uncontrolled variable in cognitive therapy outcome research. *Behavior Therapy, 17,* 433–446.

Progoff, I. (1975). *At a journal's workshop.* New York: Dialogue House Library.

Rampage, C. (2000). Feminist couples therapy. In F. M. Dattilio & L. J. Bevilacqua (Eds.), *Comparative treatments for relationship dysfunction* (pp. 325–341). New York: Springer.

Scharff, J. S., & de Varela, Y. (2000). Object relations therapy. In F. M. Dattilio & L. J. Bevilacqua (Eds.), *Comparative treatments for relationship dysfunction* (pp. 81–101). New York: Springer.

Schultheis, G. M., O'Hanlon, B., & O'Hanlon, S. (1999). *Brief couples therapy homework planner.* New York: Wiley.

Spring, J. A. (1996). *After the affair.* New York: Harper Collins.

Weeks, G. R., & Gambescia, N. (2000). *Erectile dysfunction: Integrating couple therapy, sex therapy and medical treatment.* New York: Norton.

CHAPTER 9

Families

FRANK M. DATTILIO, LUCIANO L'ABATE, and FRANK P. DEANE

Despite the fact that homework assignments are reported as being a major thrust in the armamentarium of therapeutic techniques, very little has appeared in the professional literature regarding its use with families (Dattilio, 2002; Van Noppen, 1999). A recent authoritative compendium that includes major schools of family therapy (Sexton, Weeks, & Robbins, 2003) failed to contain any references about homework assignments or task prescriptions except for one Chapter on cognitive behavioral therapy and written homework assignments. Hence, the often-repeated claim that most family therapists do use homework assignments or task prescriptions does not find any support, at least in this recent publication. However, there have been more frequent references to homework in texts that focus on more cognitive behavioral family therapy approaches (e.g., Falloon, 1988; Falloon, Laporta, Fadden & Graham-Hole, 1993). For example, in describing communication training with families, Falloon et al., state that the way that homework involving "real-life practice" is organized is of vital importance to the success of behavioral family therapy. Cognitive behavioral couples and family therapists have touted homework assignments as being a cornerstone of treatment (Dattilio, 1998, 2001; Dattilio & Padesky, 1990).

Homework and "out-of-session assignments" have also been endorsed by systemic, structural, psychodynamic, integrative and postmodern approaches. It appears that this would be a standard, since so much is predicated on what occurs in between therapy sessions (Dattilio, 1998).

This is particularly the case for cognitive and behaviorally oriented family therapy approaches that broadly include interventions such as contingency contracting, behavior exchange, problem solving, communication training, parent-management training, and cognitive restructuring approaches (Falloon, 1988). One possible reason for the lack of empirical research into the effects of homework in CBT approaches to family therapy may be that homework is so central to the approach that it is not seen as necessary to extract the important components. However, there are usually multiple types of homework assignments that can be recommended for similar clusters of problems and varying levels of systematic administration that might make homework more or less effective. Understanding these variants may lead to more effective implementation within the CBT approach. Certainly there appears a need to clarify the extent that between session homework contributes to outcomes in family therapy. The little that does appear in the professional literature seems to indicate that, for years, homework assignments have been thought of as an important part of training programs for family therapy. Originally, L'Abate (1986) contracted with all respondents, after they signed an informed-consent form, that they would match one homework assignment for one face-to-face therapy session. With families who could not afford weekly therapy sessions, the number of homework assignments increased to fill the void between face-to-face sessions. If a family was seen once a month, for instance, family members had to complete weekly assignments individually and then come together at preset family conferences to compare and discuss their responses. Homework assignments in L'Abate's practice consisted specifically of written questions or tasks to be answered by family members in writing. They did not include the array of homework assignments listed below. To ensure maximum involvement in the process of homework, families were initially told that if they did not agree to complete systematically written homework assignments (SHWAs), the therapist could not see them professionally. Face-to-face talk, therefore, was made contingent on families agreeing and completing SHWAs (L'Abate, 2003).

Benefits of Homework in Family Therapy

There are a number of benefits in using homework in the treatment of families. For one, a family in crisis or amid dysfunction is often a volatile situation. Due to the multiple dynamics, structure is often a very important component of the therapeutic process. The systematic use of homework assignments transforms the therapeutic process into a 24-hour experience. That is, the majority of time occurs outside of the session within the original environment from which the dysfunction often emanates. Therefore homework, or out-of-session assignments, serves to keep the content of therapy sessions fresh in family members' minds during the interim periods and promotes a transfer from the therapy session to day-to-day living.

Homework is also important because it helps to move the family into active involvement, signifying that they have already acknowledged the notion that change is beneficial at both the personal and interpersonal levels (Prochaska, DiClemente, & Norcross, 1992). For example, suggesting that a family consider attending an outing together, in which they will engage in a physical task where they will need to rely on one another to achieve a goal, is a form of acknowledging that each member can be relied on.

Another benefit of homework is that the assignments give individuals in therapy an opportunity to implement and evaluate insights for coping behaviors that have been discussed during the treatment process. Hence, practice serves to heighten awareness of various issues that have unfolded in treatment. Furthermore, homework can increase the expectations to follow through with making changes rather than simply discussing change during the therapy session. Exercises usually require participation and a degree of cooperation, which can create a sense that family members are taking active steps toward change. Alternatively, homework can also set the stage for trial experiences. Such experiences can be reintroduced in the next session for further processing. As a result, modifications can be made to thoughts, feelings, or behaviors as the homework is processed in the therapy session.

Since cognitive behavioral therapy (CBT) with families is typically guided by an agenda, adding homework assignments can reenergize treatment by reinforcing focus and structure. It can also provide content for fruitful discussion in subsequent sessions. Moreover, homework can increase the family members' motivation to change because it gives them something specific to work on and allows the theme of therapy to remain fluid.

Two other additional benefits include the increased involvement of family members and significant others in the process of treatment. This is accomplished by way of assignments that call for the participation of others and the promotion of more efficient treatment by encouraging the participants to actively develop insights, positive self-talk, and coping behaviors between therapy sessions (Bevilacqua & Dattilio, 2001). Homework strategies are promoted initially when families interact in the therapy session. They are later instructed to modify their interaction outside of the therapy session. It is important for the clinician to take into account the couple's or family's ability, tolerance, and motivation to maximize the potential for the successful completion of specific homework tasks.

Types of Homework

Some of the more common homework assignments used are listed below. It should be noted that some assignments might be more suitable early in the treatment process (i.e., videotaping, self-monitoring, etc.), whereas others should be introduced later (i.e., action oriented assignments, cognitive restructuring, etc.). A number of manuals have been introduced into the professional literature that capitalize on the use of homework assignments and various out-of-session assignments with families (Bevilacqua & Dattilio, 2001). The reader is referred to this reference for a number of additional homework assignments.

Bibliotherapy Assignments

As can be seen in Chapter 17, bibliotherapy assignments are more common in couples therapy. This is particularly relevant since it is more difficult for an entire family, especially with young children, to complete assigned readings. Families may also benefit from homework assignments such as those found in the *Brief Family Therapy Homework Planner* by Bevilacqua and Dattilio (2001). When implemented, bibliotherapy may focus on a circumscribed topic, such as separation or divorce, or even the death of a member of an extended family, such as a grandparent. Such books as *The Dinosaurs Divorce* (Brown & Brown, 1998) or *The Fall of Freddy the Leaf* (Buscalglia, 1983) can be read out loud to children by parents in a group setting and then discussed. There are other topics that can be discussed or processed during the course of therapy sessions as well. Bibliotherapy reinforces the content covered during therapy sessions and keeps family members active between sessions. Assigned readings are usually germane to the content focused on in the course of treatment.

Audio- or Videotaping Out-of-Session Interaction

Audio- or videotaping interaction outside of the session allows both therapist and family members to review some of the interaction that occurs more spontaneously in natural environments. This interaction affords the opportunity to review important ideas to develop as well as the content of discussions in sessions. During the in-session review of the tape, clinicians can ask family members for their retrospective opinion about their behaviors as well as their afterthoughts and discuss alternative coping strategies and/or interactions. An example of this may be for a family to videotape a meeting at home, or even a heated argument, so that positive and negative aspects of the exchange can be observed and it can be determined where the break-down of communication occurs. In this respect, videotaping has an advantage over audiotaping in that important nonverbal behaviors and body language can be observed. The beauty of observing footage of a family in the middle of a heated argument is that the therapist can review the tape with them and ask "What was going through your mind at that particular moment?" Family members can also observe their behaviors, which may sometimes even be embarrassing and sobering.

Activity Scheduling

The use of activity scheduling for emphasis on communication, improved interactions, and the development of problem-solving skills is extremely important in conducting family therapy. Activity scheduling is intended to diagnose dysfunction as well as help family members to acquire new behaviors. An example of this might be for a family to try out a new activity together (e.g., water rafting) and observe how each member reacts to an unfamiliar situation and how they also assist each other. Do they stick together and work as a team, or do they become disengaged?

Activity schedules can also be used to help families keep track of their activities on a regular basis. If there are negative interactions or symptoms within these systems, they may benefit from less demanding forms of activity, such as maintaining a list of activities that occurred during the day or talking about tasks that were completed. Activity schedules should include a subjective rating for those activities that provide the most achievement and pleasure as opposed to those that do not.

A useful strategy is to incorporate pleasure and mastery ratings into activity schedules. Families can use these scales to rate activities from 0 (no sense of pleasure or mastery) to 10 (a total sense of pleasure or mastery). The activity schedules and rating scales combined usually encourage individuals to focus on activities that provide a sense of achievement and pleasure. They are also designed to develop and enhance cohesiveness in the family. So, for example, in one of the aforementioned cases in which a family embarked on an activity in which they needed to rely on one another, a follow-up question during therapy might be for each family member to rate how he or she felt when someone with whom they had been experiencing tension helped them with a particular task.

Self-Monitoring

In traditional CBT, members of a family unit are usually asked to complete thought or mood assessments between sessions (Dattilio, 1998; Dattilio & Padesky, 1990). Monitoring exercises are usually designed to provide the clinician with accurate information about family members' particular struggles or conflicts. Participants are also asked to concentrate on the thoughts and beliefs they experience automatically during the course of these exercises and activities. The thrust of self-monitoring involves helping members get in touch with exactly how they think and behave and how this affects their individual dynamics. One example of this is the use of the daily thought record (Beck, Rush, Shaw, & Emery, 1979), in which individuals are asked to record their thoughts during arguments or family activities and point out how these thoughts affect their moods and behaviors. These thought records provide a means whereby families can reevaluate their thinking styles, and they are often used to support cognitive restructuring of dysfunctional thoughts.

Behavioral Task Assignments

The use of homework in the treatment of communication, problem solving, and relationship tensions can often enable individuals to better cope with their circumstances through the practice of techniques acquired in treatment. Behavioral assignments may involve having family members use restructured self-talk and to search for alternative explanations for their own or others' behaviors. Such behavioral assignments may also involve locating common bonds among the participants. For example, when one family member is either emotionally or physically hurt, how do the others react?

Homework assignments are often most effective when family members are involved in the design and planning of assignments. Such planning might include the timing of the assignment and deciding who will be involved. It would also determine how frequently it should be conducted and the length of time required for completion.

Homework assignments should also be scheduled for review upon completion, with a discussion of any difficulties the family members had in completing it. If there are problems with completion of the assignment, an attempt to analyze roadblocks should be made so that future difficulties can be identified and effectively dealt with in treatment (Dattilio, 2003).

Some of the more popular "behavioral task assignments" include mutual exchange or positive reciprocity exercises (e.g., to notice your family member doing or saying something nice and letting him or her know about it), pleasing behaviors, behavioral rehearsal, assertiveness exercises, and role reversal.

Systematically Written Homework Assignments (SWHAs)

L'Abate (2002; L'Abate & De Giacomo, 2003) has advocated the use of distance writing and homework administration of workbooks, to individuals, couples, and families. This practice is in part supported by the research of Pennebaker (2001) as reviewed by Esterling, L'Abate, Murray, and Pennebaker (1999). L'Abate has contended, with some evidence (Smyth & L'Abate, 2001), that workbooks are cost-effective, mass-producible, versatile, and specific. This last advantage allows workbook interventions to be matched with the reason for referral or diagnosis in a way that is often difficult to achieve verbally. The versatility of workbooks is shown by their application in primary, secondary, and tertiary prevention (L'Abate, 2003). They can be used by themselves in marriage education (L'Abate, 2003), in conjunction with preventative approaches with families, and before, during, or after crisis interventions and psychotherapy (L'Abate, 1986). Combined with computers and the Internet (L'Abate, 1992, 1996, 2001a), workbooks will allow professionals to reach many more families in need of help than would otherwise be possible through face-to-face talk.

L'Abate has classified writing, among other dimensions, according to four levels of structure: (a) *open-ended*, as in diaries and journal writing; (b) *focused*, as in the expressive writing paradigm developed by Pennebaker and colleagues (Lepore & Smyth, 2002; Pennebaker, 2001) and in auto-biographies; (c) *guided*, as in writing a series of questions to be responded to also in writing ("We have read your autobiography and we have written several questions that come out from reading it. We would like for you to answer them in writing"); and (d) *programmed*, as in workbooks, consisting of a series of written homework assignments focused on a specific topic, such as family negotiation and problem solving, relationship styles, and others (L'Abate, 2002). A meta-analysis of workbook studies (Smyth & L'Abate, 2001) found a mean effect size estimate of .44, which is a consi-derable outcome, considering that costs for the administration of these workbooks were negligible. L'Abate (2004c) also summarized effect sizes for 10 studies conducted with workbooks for couples that produced a wide range of effect size estimates. As shown in Table 9.1, workbooks can be classified according to a variety of dimensions (L'Abate, 2003; L'Abate & De Giacomo, 2003. Lately, L'Abate (2005) has stressed the importance of using workbooks as interactive instruments of theory or model testing, especially when a workbook has been derived directly from a list of items (L'Abate, 2002).

An analysis of 25 years of part-time clinical practice with individuals, couples, and families with and without SHWAs showed that contrary to predictions about the cost-effectiveness of workbooks, their administra-tion significantly prolonged the length of therapy for families, couples, and single adults (L'Abate, L'Abate, & Maino, 2005). Unfortunately there was no way to evaluate whether the increase in the number of therapy sessions meant an increase in effectiveness.

TABLE 9.1 Toward a Classification of Self-Help, Mental Health Workbooks (L'Abate, 2004b)

Respondent composition:	Children, Adolescents, Single Adults, Couples, Families
Theoretical background:	Cognitive-behavioral, empirical, existential/humanistic, rational/emotive, psychoanalytic, interpersonal competence.
Relationship to theory:	Independent, related, derived or driven.
Level of functionality:	Normative, externalizations, internalizations, and severe psychopathology.
Style:	Straightforward/linear versus circular/paradoxical
Format:	Nomothetic (same for all) versus idiographic (specific to one respondent and to no one else, or both)
Content:	Specific to the reason for referral or to the diagnosis

Hugging, Holding, Huddling, and Cuddling

L'Abate (2001, 2003; L'Abate & De Giacomo, 2003) developed a theory-derived generic prescription and homework assignment consisting of teaching families to be together without talking. Instead families utilize a nonverbal modality of being together through hugging, holding, huddling, and cuddling (3HC) each other without any demands for performance, production, perfection, or problem solving. After initiating and demonstrating this task in the therapist's office, family members or couples perform it at home at preset intervals (15 minutes) and days (two or three times a week or every day). Specific and replicable instructions to families on how to perform this homework assignment are available in L'Abate (2001). Unfortunately, only four case studies are presented, two with low-income, low-education single mothers with three children each, one upper-class family, and one middle-class couple. All were followed up after 1 year and all four reported positive outcomes. Hence, broad evidence to support the usefulness of this prescription is not available and will have to derive support from sources other than the original one.

Strategies for Effective Homework

The strategic selection of homework assignments that are germane to the family and the focus in therapy is a key objective. Often, clinicians are guilty of randomly assigning homework ad hoc simply for the sake of issuing an assignment. Choosing and designing specific assignments is crucial. Nelson and Trepper (1993) have produced two volumes of family therapy interventions, many of which include homework assignments that can be utilized during treatment. Choosing the timing of an assignment so that it does not come too early in the treatment process is also essential if treatment benefits are to be maximized.

In implementing homework assignments, it is suggested that clinicians think about how they wish to suggest the use of assignments during the course of treatment and what point in the treatment process may offer an good opportunity to intervene. They also need to think about what they want to accomplish in assigning homework. This goal, of course, will vary and is left to the clinical judgment of the therapist. Falloon et al., (1993) specify five major components of the homework process in working with families: (a) providing a rationale for the homework; (b) outlining the steps to completing the task, using appropriate diary-style work sheets; (c) checking to make sure that all participants understand the task; (d) organizing the display of prompt sheets and work sheets to remind family members to complete the homework; and (e) reviewing real-life practice at the beginning of the next session. In addition, the guidelines for systematic implementation of homework that apply to individuals generally also apply to families (e.g., Kazantzis & Deane, 1999; Shelton & Levy, 1981). Forgetting and distorting of verbal instructions by family members, no matter how clearly enunciated by therapists, led L'Abate (1986) to start issuing instructions in writing.

There may be added complexities in working with family members. For example, specific steps should be taken to review each assignment with the family members so that they understand exactly what the objective of the assignment is and, more importantly, know exactly what they are to do and why. Often clients will nod their heads acknowledging that they understand homework assignments when, in fact, they are confused about the specific request but are reluctant to voice their uncertainty. The process of checking for understanding with more participants requires both additional time and care as compared to working with an individual client. The more clearly a particular homework assignment is compatible with the families' goals for therapy, the more straightforward the checking process is. Similarly, the closer the homework assignment is to activities that are conducted in the course of therapy sessions, the easier it becomes to clarify the rationale. If therapists dedicate adequate time to a problem formulation and conceptualization of the family problem, this should set the groundwork for appropriate homework assignments. It is also common in family therapy to have families rehearse the skills of a specific homework assignment in the session before it is assigned as a way of preparing for a successful outcome.

Homework administration with families also offers some advantages over working with individuals. As with other forms of public commitment, getting several individuals to commit to completion of a particular between-session activity increases opportunities for prompting each other, positively reinforcing attempts to complete a task, and dealing with difficulties that might interfere with completion. In multifamily therapy, therapists also have the opportunity to capitalize on wider group processes to reinforce the role of homework. This includes wider expectations in the group that homework is to be completed and presented as a core component of each group session. Homework review also offers the opportunity for all families to learn from each other's homework experiences as well as opportunities for problem solving and positive social reinforcement for attempts at homework completion. Therapists working with families should attempt to maximize these strengths when negotiating, planning, and reviewing assignments. For example, it has been suggested that, in a group context, those who completed the homework assignment rather than those who did not should receive more of the therapist's attention (Fichter & Postpischil, 1988).

Common Barriers to Homework Assignments

Recent research has supported the importance of inquiring about homework assignments. Bryant, Simons, and Thase (1999) rated therapy tapes regarding homework assignments and compliance. The strongest predictor of homework compliance in their study was therapists' behavior in reviewing assigned homework tasks. Following up on the results of homework assignments is obviously very important. It is strongly recommended that this be considered an agenda item for the subsequent visit, unless, of course, the family members request more time to complete the task. Ensuring follow-up on the results of homework will also provide an indirect message to the family that these assignments are crucial and are not administered in order to fill time or to give the therapist something with which to occupy their time outside of the therapy session. General therapeutic skills also predicted homework compliance in the study of Bryant et al. Presumably these general skills would include collaboration in establishing the homework and providing positive reinforcement in the form of encouragement and praise for all efforts at homework completion. The research—though conducted with individual clients—underscores the importance in family therapy as well.

The role of homework practice is seen as essential to CBT family therapy, so much so that the Falloon et al. (1993, p. 178) state the following: "Any evidence of suboptimal performance of this task is viewed as a potential crisis by the therapist, requiring immediate action." Where there are concerns about adherence to homework practice, therapists should review the steps previously outlined and, in addition, consider the perceived relevance of the homework to the family, further reinforcing its rationale and connection with therapy goals. When families have not completed their homework, Falloon et al. also recommend delaying the start of the session to allow them to do so. For example, with communication training assignments, "the therapist may request that the household convenes for the missed family meeting at this time. This use of therapy time reinforces the BFT view that the real-life practice is at least of equal value as therapist coaching" (p. 179).

During the process of securing an agreement from each family member that they will at least try an assignment, the clinician may encounter situations in which some participants may think that the assignment is silly or simply not a good idea. These issues need to be addressed during the course of the treatment process. The more agreement that is achieved between family members about completing the homework, the more likely the assignment is to be successful. The resistance to homework assignments, be it overt or passive, is "grist for the mill." In other words, a therapist can assign the task of having the family openly discuss why the homework failed to be completed. At least some cohesiveness may emanate from this discussion and the owning of responsibility. Sometimes, families communicate more with us by the ways in which they fail to complete assignments or resist them. This is always fertile ground for exploration.

Resistance

One of the most common difficulties is the resistance of certain family members in completing homework assignments. This resistance may often occur despite the fact that the family has agreed to the assignment and acknowledged that it would be helpful. This resistance may have its roots in more complicated dynamics of the family, or it may be as simple as the fact that the assignments are being referred to as "homework," which carries a negative connotation for some. Clinicians may choose to consider changing the term *homework* to either *task* or *experiment*. Homework assignments are better received when family members are asked "Suppose we try an experiment?" Usually there is something intriguing about the term *experiment* and, for many, its use is less threatening or dictatorial than the term *homework assignment*.

Tactful handling of resistance in completing homework assignments is essential. Possibly, family members who avoid completing homework assignments may be providing the clinician with important information about the effect that change may have on them. These may include difficulties with communication, working together as a unit, or simply the awkwardness about change in the relationship. Regardless of the reason, it is important to explore both the dynamics behind resistance and the alternatives that may be utilized in dealing with it. In particular, therapists should carefully consider secondary gains to various family members if they do not carry out the assignment (Birchler, 1988). Secondary gain may involve an attempt to stall treatment in order to maintain power and control. This analysis should include consideration of the effects of homework noncompletion on significant others. On discussing this issue in detail, the therapist may decide to reassign the same or a different exercise or defer the idea completely until another time.

Resistance is not specific to families alone. All of us are fearful of change ("The devil I have is better than the devil I might get."). However, under stress or as a result of chronically rigid relational patterns, change may be perceived as dangerous and threatening, such as loss of power. There are several other strategies that may reduce the probability that resistance to homework will become a major therapeutic stumbling block. Discussion about the certainty of assigning homework should take place from the very first session. ("This is my style of practice. However, if you would prefer to see another professional who does not assign homework, I will be glad to give you the names of three highly qualified ones.") This preliminary discussion will uncover resistances in individual family members that need to be addressed from the outset. Usually, this resistance is not just directed specifically against homework assignments per se, but it is also an expression of general opposition against the perceived power of those family members who do want change for the better.

Consequently, preliminary discussion of homework assignments allows evaluation of how power is (or is not) distributed in the family. Unless this issue is discussed from the outset, the resistant family member(s) will sabotage the entire process of homework assignments. This is why paradoxical prescriptions of the positively reframed symptomatic behavior (e.g., "You really care for each other because you are so involved with each other!") may be necessary as part of targeting opposition or skewed power structure through homework assignments (Weeks & L'Abate, 1982). The following statement provides an example of a paradoxical prescription:

> Before we go on even to talk about homework assignments, we need to acknowledge that some of you have certain well-founded reservations about them. Why don't you continue to hold these reservations, because the more you hold on to them, the more power you will have over your family, to make sure that changes

for the better will take place in this family. How long would you like to hold on to your reservations ?

Failure to discuss from the very outset the use of homework assignments as part and parcel of therapy may produce negative reactions not only in selected family members but in the whole family, to the point that some families may drop out of treatment altogether.

Other authors have also suggested that paradoxical techniques may be helpful in family therapy, particularly "when resistance to homework assignments is significant and persistent" (Birchler, 1988, p. 150). In describing family approaches to treating alcoholism Fichter and Postpischil (1988) suggested the following: "When patient and spouse repeatedly show noncompliance concerning homework assignments, the therapist may point out to the couple that the disturbance of their relationship is so severe that they will not be able to carry out homework assignments; a remark of this kind may induce paradoxical reactions" (p. 365). However, many authors also warn that the elicitation of paradoxical responses to poor homework compliance should be done cautiously. The therapist needs to first be clear that he or she has tried to systematically administer homework using recommended strategies (e.g., collaboratively negotiated, clear rationale, graded tasks, written and specific instructions, review and reinforcement of all attempts).

Finally, another preventative strategy for managing resistance involves anticipating relapses or setbacks, particularly related to homework completion, as a normal part of the change process. It has been argued that by anticipating setbacks, therapists enhance their credibility and increase the family members' sense of control (Birchler, 1988).

Case Study

This is a case of a very tumultuous family that was referred for treatment by their family physician and the local school counselor because of acting-out behaviors of the adolescent son.

The parents, both in their mid-40s, had two sons, Robert, age 19, and Luke, age 16. The family submitted for treatment in crisis, initiating with the father, who contended that he was struggling with anxiety and depression over the problems that they were having with Luke. The father stated that the boy was out of hand and completely disrespectful. The parents were at a loss as to how to control him. The older son, Robert, was away at college but had now returned and was residing at home while attending the local community college.

This is a very interesting case of a father who appeared at the initial visit to be very nervous and agitated. "I am a complete wreck and feel totally out of control," he cried in the initial interview. His wife, on the other hand, was a very passive and mild individual, almost withdrawn. The major complaint was the tension between father and son. Luke, on the other hand, felt that his father was unreasonable and acting "like an idiot." On meeting with this family for the first time, it was very clear to the therapist that the dynamics between father and son were very similar to what is typically seen with sibling rivalry. They would badger one another to the point where they would actually set off a physical altercation. Each would say that the other was making faces and taunting him behind his back, all of which seemed to disgust the mother, who remained silent and disengaged. It was at that point that the mother also began to inform me that her husband would become very irate with her because she would not support him and take his side against Luke. She then stated that the father would become angry and would sometimes put a board (a 2-by-4) between them in bed to delineate their respective spaces. The father admitted doing this and claims that he did it to retaliate because he felt that his wife would desert him by sticking up for Luke.

In the initial family meeting, the parents admitted jointly that they were guilty of having allowed their Luke to manipulate them. Robert, the older son, refused to attend the family sessions, stating that he did not have time for such nonsense.

The father presented as the more forceful parent. The mother was the one taking the weaker posture but at times was almost passive-aggressive, undermining her husband because she felt that he did things that reminded her of her own mother, who was rigid and strict during her childhood. This exacerbated the problems, which trickled down to the immediate family. Surprisingly, it did not affect Robert as much as it did Luke. Luke was more emotional and "feisty," which is probably why the family's problems became focused on him. The father's complaint was that his wife never backed him up and was unsupportive. The mother claimed that it was always because her husband was so unfair and unreasonable. Despite this, both parents stated that they loved each other, which is why they remained married. They also contended that they loved their children.

With regard to Luke, he clearly stated that he just felt that his father was a "dick" and that "He acts more immature than I do." There were also some reported problems with low grades in school, which Luke blamed on the family dysfunction at home. At times, the father stated that he felt that he was like "the monkey in the middle," between his wife and son, neither of whom was supportive or willing to empower him as the father figure. Ironically, mother argued that she was more the monkey, pulled between her husband and Luke.

Because this family was so volatile, the therapist took an unusual course and met with the family members individually in order to complete the initial assessment. One of the first homework assignments was to have mother and father complete a family-of-origin questionnaire, which allowed for the development of insight as to where they came from and how they were raised. During this time, Luke was also given a homework assignment of writing a letter to each of his parents titled "Why I am so angry with you." This was designed to help Luke get in touch with his thoughts and feelings, but in a way that would not be in his parents' faces for a while so that the therapist could gather some background information about the parents' respective families of origin. Luke was asked to be as detailed as possible in composing his letter and to think through everything carefully. The family of origin information revealed that the mother grew up in a situation in which her father was never around. He worked the "graveyard shift" and was also a bartender. He was also a heavy consumer of alcohol. Her mother was the head of the household and was "always the boss." This is something that the mother came to despise, since she felt that it was a terrible imbalance. She claims that she and her siblings always listened to her mother. She denies being angry with her father for not having been around, but she admitted that she did not love him either. She never knew him as anyone significant in her life. She recalls that there were really no behavioral problems. Mostly, the three children did what they were told and it was a rather uneventful life. On the other hand, Luke's father explained that his father also worked second shift and was never home. He showed very little emotion and had little contact with the family. He claims that his mother was very loving, but his father could be "a real S.O.B." He recalls that on one occasion his father would not give him a ride home from work and simply abandoned him. He was therefore forced to walk home from work at 4 o'clock in the morning. He recalls that he had a very tumultuous upbringing and has bad memories of his own father's tyrannical behaviors.

During the session, we reviewed the parents' homework assignment and then tried to discuss how the family of origin of each spouse affected their joint parenting. The father admitted that his wife was not the type of woman that he wanted her to be. She was not loving in the sense that she was supportive of him; felt that she disempowered him by her silence in siding with Luke. The mother, on the other hand, resented her husband's dominant stance in the relationship. At the same time, she did not like the fact that her mother was the boss and had hoped that both she and her husband could parent on a more passive level as opposed to what she had known as a child. This, unfortunately, was not the case.

When asked about the problems in the family, both parents agreed that things went fairly well and everyone was close until Luke was approximately 14 or 15 years of age. It was at that point that the mother found a letter, written by Luke, stating that he felt that his father did not love him and that the father showed favoritism toward his older brother, Robert. The father, of course, denied this, but the mother felt that it was true, because Robert was more enthusiastic about being with his dad. He was also easier to handle. The father claimed that he did chase after Luke to be with him more, but that he pushed Luke to succeed and Luke was not interested. The father reports that he was involved in all types of sports with both boys, but Luke simply never seemed to be receptive; he viewed this as reflecting his son's disinterest in him. Both parents agreed that the situation within the family was clearly "out of control" and that they were very worried. The father also admitted that he would become overly excited at times, but at the same time he believed that he was justified in that Luke was simply downright disrespectful to him. He also complained that his wife was not supportive, which did not help matters. The mother feels that the father is just as immature as Luke and that he just handles the entire situation poorly.

The homework of tracing the family of origin was very helpful with this family in that it allowed both parents to see that they came from dysfunctional situations that contributed to their current problems. This set the stage for us to go forward and rebuild a new union between the two.

In the meantime, Luke's homework assignment yielded a great deal of insight from his perspective. His letter to his father suggested that he recalled his father punishing him and hitting him with a belt, or grabbing him by the throat, ever since he was small. He resented this but could not do anything about it. He agreed that he was now retaliating for what had occurred in the past. He also claimed that his mother would not believe him until many years later. Luke stated that it was not the fact that he was punished but the manner in which his father tried to exert his power that angered him. Luke had good insight into the fact that he was getting older and, in his later teenage years, was beginning to retaliate against his father and challenge his authority. Luke also admitted that he viewed his mother's passive role as an indirect way of supporting him and that he was doing the right thing by acting out against his father. Luke also recalled that his father would taunt him by saying such things as, "Ha, Ha, Mom's not home now. What are you going to do? Nothing." Luke also felt that his father paid more attention to his brother, Robert, which he resented. Luke stated that his father's behaviors were immature and childish, showing that "he is not half the man that he thinks he is." Luke would frequently complain about the fact that his mother would take his father's side sometimes, which really angered him. He also admitted that his mother has been placed in the middle of this conflict. Luke's letter to his mother included his complaints that he was angry with her because his father reduced himself to fighting with him as though he were his sibling, and he felt that his mother never did anything to intervene. In essence, Luke voiced his anger over his mother's passive role and the general imbalance in the family.

When the family was all together, the therapist pointed out that it appeared that mother was empowering Luke, unknowingly, to assert his power against his father as a means of symbolically asserting her power against her own parents. In many ways, she did not want to be the center of conflict, but unfortunately this was the case, whether she liked it or not. She was truly the "monkey in the middle," as she would often state it.

Many of the homework assignments during the course of treatment involved steps that would allow this family to attempt to rearrange their positions based on insight into the dynamics that the parents brought from the family of origin and the misappropriated empowerment that was instilled in Luke during his early development because of the parents' disharmony.

This was a very difficult situation in which homework assignments needed to be strategic. One of the milestones in this case was to get Luke to admit that he really did not want the power that he had and that he was willing to relinquish it. Homework assignments for the parents consisted in realigning the power and control, learning to take steps to communicate with each other and also to parent together, which was very difficult for them, particularly since they had not seen this during their own upbringing.

Homework assignments for both Luke and his father involved helping them take a look at their tendencies to allow the situation to escalate. An exercise for Luke and his father was to look at "what happens to each of us when we become angry." They were given an exercise to monitor the physiological aspects, such as body tension, accelerated heart rate, thoughts that went through their minds about justification, and also a fear of being overwhelmed by the other.

Once again, a typical course of utilizing cognitive behavioral strategies involved thought restructuring, whereby each participant was taught to refer the dysfunctional thought record (see Figure 17.1 in Chapter 17). In this particular case, all members of the family was asked to utilize the thought records in processing their thinking and identifying distortions. By having each member review their thinking about the matter, they were able to weigh the alternatives and to consider alternative behaviors.

Additional behavioral strategies involved time-out procedures so that each could cool down.

With cases such as the one above, a series of in-session and out-of-session assignments would be prescribed to help re-engage the family. The assignments would start simultaneously with the parents and son, but, separately and slowly, eventually bringing them together.

Obviously, family therapy would need to be augmented with individual therapy for family members. The treatment would also need to be coordinated among the various therapists. An alternative to having different therapists in addition to one for the family is to assign specific workbooks for individual family members or for the parents. For instance, one family could receive assignments about arguing and fighting. If a father acknowledges being depressed while the wife admits to being anxious, both could receive individual assignments, which, however, after completion, they would have to share with one another (L'Abate, 2002). A theory-derived parenting workbook could be administered to parents whose skills in this area need bolstering (L'Abate, 2005).

Conclusion

Homework is often crucial in facilitating changes in difficult family systems, as in the aforementioned case example. Therapists are urged to include a cadre of assignments in their repertoire in order to augment their in-session work. Homework will also continue to grow into self-adaptive behaviors for the family long after the therapy process terminates.

References

Beck, A. T., Rush, J. A., Shaw, B. F., & Emery, G. (1979). *Cognitive therapy of depression.* New York: Guilford Press.

Bevilacqua, L. J., & Dattilio, F. M. (2001). *Brief family therapy homework planner.* New York: Wiley.

Birchler, G. R. (1988). Handling resistance to change. In I. R. H. Falloon (Ed.), *The handbook of Behavioral Family Therapy* (pp. 128–155). New York: Guilford Press.

Brown, L. K., & Brown, M. (1998). *Dinosaurs divorce: A guide for changing families.* New York: DEMCO Media.

Bryant, M. J., Simons, A. D., & Thase, M. E. (1999). Therapist skill and patient variables in homework compliance: Controlling the uncontrolled variable in cognitive therapy outcome research. *Cognitive Therapy and Research, 23,* 381–399.

Buscaglia, L. F. (1983). *The fall of Freddie the Leaf.* New York: Holt Rinehart & Winston.

Dattilio, F. M. (Ed.). (1998). *Case studies in couple and family therapy: Systemic and cognitive perceptions.* New York: Guilford Press.

Dattilio, F. M. (2000). Graphic perceptions. In R. E. Watts (Ed.), *Techniques in marriage and family counseling* (pp. 49–52). Alexandra, VA: American Counseling Association.

Dattilio, F. M. (2001). Cognitive-behavior therapy: Contemporary myths and misconceptions. *Contemporary Family Therapy, 23,* 3–18.

Dattilio, F. M. (2002). Homework assignments in couple and family therapy. *Journal of Clinical Psychology, 58,* 570–583.

Dattilio, F. M (2003). Techniques in family therapy. In R. E. Leahy (Ed.), *Overcoming roadblocks in cognitive therapy.* New York: Guilford Press.

Dattilio, F. M., & Padesky, C. A. (1990). *Cognitive therapy with couples.* Sarasota, FL: Professional Resource Exchange.

Dunlap, K. (1932). *Habits, their making and unmaking.* New York: Liveright.

Esterling, B. A., L'Abate, L., Murray, E., & Pennebaker, J. W. (1999). Empirical foundations for writing in prevention and psychotherapy: Mental and physical outcomes. *Clinical Psychology Review, 19,* 79–96.

Falloon, I. R. H. (Ed.). (1988). *The handbook of Behavioral Family Therapy.* New York: Guilford Press.

Falloon, I. R. H., Laporta, M., Fadden, G., & Graham-Hole, V. (1993). *Managing stress in families: Cognitive and behavioral strategies for enhancing coping skills.* London: Routledge.

Fichter, M. M., & Postpischil, F. (1988). Alcoholism. In I. R. H. Falloon (Ed.), *The handbook of behavioral family therapy* (pp. 350–371). New York: Guilford Press.

Kazantzis, N., & Deane, F. P. (1999). Psychologists' use of homework assignments in clinical practice. *Professional Psychology: Research and Practice, 30,* 581–585.

L'Abate, L. (1986). *Systematic family therapy.* New York: Brunner/Mazel.

L'Abate, L. (1992). *Programmed writing: A self-administered approach for interventions for individuals, couples, and families.* Pacific Grove, CA: Brooks/Cole.

L'Abate, L. (1996). *Workbooks for better living.* http://www.mentalhealthhelp.com/

L'Abate, L. (Ed.). (2001a). *Distance writing and computer-assisted interventions in psychiatry and mental health.* Westport, CT: Ablex.

L'Abate, L. (2001b). Hugging, holding, huddling, and cuddling (*3HC*): A task prescription in couple and family therapy. *The Journal of Clinical Activities, Assignments, & Handouts in Psychotherapy Practice, 1,* 5–18.

L'Abate, L. (2005). *Beyond psychotherapy: Programmed writing and structured computer-assisted interventions.* Newport, CT: Ablex.

L'Abate, L. (2003). Treatment through writing: A unique new direction. In T. K. Sexton, G. Weeks, & M. Robbins (Eds.), *The handbook of family therapy.* (pp. 397–409). New York: Springer, Verlag.

L'Abate, L. (2004a). *A guide to self-help workbooks for clinicians and researchers.* Binghamton, NY: Haworth.

L'Abate, L. (2004b). *Workbooks in prevention and psychotherapy: A guide for clinicians and researchers.* Binghamton, NY: Haworth.

L'Abate, L. (2005). *Personality in intimate relationships: Socialization and psychopathology.* New York: Springer/Verlag.

L'Abate, L., & De Giacomo, P. (2003). *Intimate relationships and how to improve them: Integrating theory with preventive and psychotherapeutic interventions.* Westport, CT: Praeger.

L'Abate, L., L'Abate, B. L., & Maino, E. (2005). Written homework assignments and length of therapy. *American Journal of Family Therapy, 33,* 19–31.

Lepore, S. J., & Smyth, J. M. (Eds.). (2002). *The writing cure: How expressive writing promotes health and well-being.* Washington, DC: American Psychological Association.

Nelson, T. S., & Trepper, T. S. (Eds.). (1993). *101 interventions in family therapy.* New York: Haworth.

Pennebaker, J. W. (2001). Explorations into the health benefits of disclosure: Inhibitory, cognitive, and social processes. In L. L'Abate (Ed.), *Distance writing and computer-assisted interventions in psychiatry and mental health* (pp. 33–44). Westport, CT: Ablex.

Prochaska, J. O., DiClemente, C. C., & Norcross, J. C. (1992). In search of how people change: Applications to addictive behaviors. *American Psychologist, 47,* 1102–1114.

Sexton, T. K., Weeks, G., & Robbins, M. (Eds.). (2003). *The handbook of family therapy.* New York: Brunner-Routledge.

Shelton, J. L., & Levy, R. L. (1981). *Behavioral assignments and treatment compliance: A handbook of clinical strategies.* Champaign, IL: Research Press.

Smyth, J., & L'Abate, L. (2001). A meta-analytic evaluation of workbook effectiveness in physical and mental health. In L. L'Abate (Ed.), *Distance writing and computer-assisted interventions in psychiatry and mental health* (pp. 77–90). Westport, CT: Ablex.

Talyarkhan, A., Deane, F. P., Lambert, G., & Pickard, J. (2003). *Homework adherence in multiple family therapy for schizophrenia.* Manuscript 2005.

Van Noppen, B. (1999). Multi-family behavioral treatment (MFBT) for obsessive compulsive disorder. *Crisis Intervention and Time Limited Treatment, 5*(1–2), 3–24.

Weeks, G., & L'Abate, L. (1982). *Paradoxical psychotherapy: Theory and practice with individuals, couples, and families.* New York: Brunner/Mazel.

PART **III**
Specific Problems

CHAPTER 10

Panic, Agoraphobia, and Generalized Anxiety

ROBERT L. LEAHY

Common Barriers to Homework Assignments

Noncompliance and Resistance to Change

Cognitive behavioral therapy (CBT) presents many opportunities for noncompliance or resistance to change. Whereas psychodynamic therapy "requires" openness to the stream of thoughts and emotions but places the patient in a relatively passive role, with CBT the patient is expected to actively engage in challenging negative thoughts and behavioral exposure to anxiety-provoking situations. A number of points of noncompliance or resistance as "procedural resistance"—where the noncompliance focuses on the specific procedures or interventions implicit in the cognitive model—have been discussed elsewhere (i.e., Leahy, 2001). The clinician can anticipate the possibility of noncompliance by relying on psychoeducation, clarifying homework assignments, shaping, modeling, utilizing rewards, increasing contingency, or using response cost (Leahy, 2001).

Specific patient characteristics also affect noncompliance. For example, patients who view themselves as "special people" may believe that the homework is beneath them, while patients with schemas of helplessness and dependency may believe that they are incompetent to help themselves and that the therapist needs to rescue them. Other patients may have risk-averse strategies—quickly defining any negative as a downward spiral or believing that they need perfect information prior to making a change. Still others may self-handicap or view themselves as requiring extensive validation for their troubles. These specific patient characteristics are described in my book *Overcoming Resistance in Cognitive Therapy* (Leahy, 2001) and may be important elements in noncompliance for any patient—including the panic-disordered and generalized anxiety–disordered patients described in the current Chapter.

The focus in this Chapter is on the procedural resistance to homework or to in-session behaviors that are viewed as important components for the patient in CBT. The assumption, of course, is that CBT involves specific procedures and follows an agenda for each session. Given the high efficacy of CBT for panic disorder and for generalized anxiety disorder (GAD), it is essential that the therapist not abandon the CBT model in favor of the patient's noncompliance. To understand and rectify these problems, this Chapter reviews each of these anxiety disorders, briefly describes a standard of treatment, outlines points of noncompliance, and suggest strategies for intervention.

Panic Disorder and Agoraphobia

Panic disorder is characterized by the occurrence of panic attacks, which appear suddenly with great intensity and are marked by intense physical sensations (heart palpitations, shakiness, sweating, shortness of breath, sensation of choking, chest pain, nausea, dizziness) feelings of detachment or unreality (depersonalization or derealization), fear of losing control or going insane, fear of a medical crisis (e.g., heart attack), numbness or tingling, and hot or cold flashes (American Psychiatric Association, 2000). The primary fear is of the sensations and experiences of the panic—such as the fear of dying, losing control, or going insane. This is distinguished from social anxiety disorder, where the fear is that the symptoms of anxiety will be visible to others, thereby humiliating the patient. Many patients with panic disorder also develop agoraphobia, which is characterized by fear of open spaces, places where exit is blocked, or other stimuli (such as heights, bright sunlight), where the fear is that the situation may elicit a panic attack. The lifetime prevalence of panic disorder is 1.5 to 3.8%, with females twice as likely to manifest this disorder. Age of onset for panic disorder with agoraphobia is in the early twenties.

Many of the situations that are feared by the agoraphobic are situations that might confer greater danger in an evolutionary adaptive environment (Leahy & Holland, 2000). For example, situations that might elicit panic attacks are open spaces (greater vulnerability to predators), closed spaces (vulnerability to suffocation or being trapped), bright sunlight (more visible to predators), and heights (danger of falling). Panic disorder relates to the fear of the consequences of one's own anxiety symptoms (that is, the fear of going insane, losing control, or a medical crisis). It may be that this "fear of fear"—elicited in these specific situations was adaptive to primitive ancestors. The nature of these sensations and the situations that elicit panic is important in the cognitive behavioral treatment of this disorder. Individuals with this disorder misinterpret these sensations, which are viewed as predictive of catastrophic consequences that "must be avoided" or eliminated completely.

The cognitive behavioral theoretical model is shown in Figure 10.1. It is derived from the work of Barlow (1988), Beck, Emery, and Greenberg (1985) and Clark (1986). The initial "panic attack" is accompanied by a catastrophic interpretation—"I am going crazy"—leading to hypervigilance for other signs of anxious arousal. This increased self-focus on one's own arousal increases the likelihood of arousal being detected or escalated— leading to false confirmations that another panic attack is imminent. Many panickers rely on "safety behaviors," such as being accompanied by another person, stiffening their posture, or "taking deep breaths" (which augment the hyperventilation syndrome). Situations that trigger increased arousal—such as open spaces, heights, closed spaces, or behaviors that trigger arousal (exercise)—are anticipated with dread or tolerated with increased discomfort.

The general CBT plan of treatment involves differential diagnosis (e.g., "Is this panic disorder or social anxiety disorder?"), identification of safety behaviors, identifying triggers for panic and agoraphobic avoidance, bibliotherapy, socialization to treatment, establishing a therapeutic contract, construction of a fear hierarchy, anxiety management training, rebreathing training, exposure to "interoceptive sensations" (e.g., hyperventilation), panic induction, training in rational responses to panic, and exposure to hierarchy. As part of treatment, the clinician will examine the patient's reliance on drugs or alcohol, which he or she may use to inhibit anxiety, or the use of caffeine or stimulants that increase anxiety.

A meta-analysis of 48 controlled studies of cognitive behavioral treatment of panic disorder with agoraphobia indicates that CBT was highly effective in yielding panic-free outcomes, with an effect size of .88 (compared to an effect size of .47 for pharmacological treatment) (Gould, Otto, & Pollack, 1995). The range of patients who received CBT who were panic-free after treatment was between 32% and 100%. In most of the studies reviewed, the percentage of panic-free patients exceeded 80%.

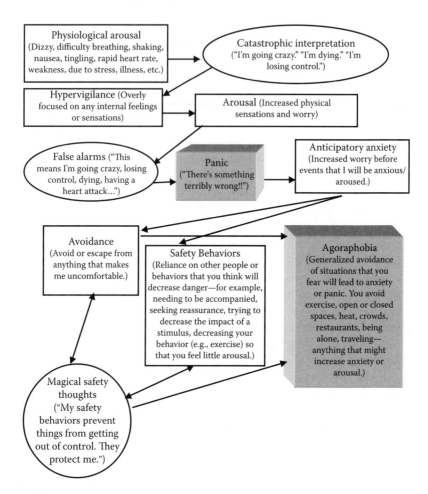

Fig. 10.1 Cognitive behavioral model of panic and agoraphobia. Copyright © Robert L. Leahy, Ph.D. 2000.

Types of Homework

Typical homework assignments involve practicing anxiety management techniques (such as deep breathing, muscle relaxation, and mindfulness training), monitoring anxiety levels, constructing exposure hierarchies, engaging in exposure, identifying and challenging automatic thoughts about arousal and panic, inducing panic attacks in and outside of sessions, and examining and modifying beliefs about absolute control over "symptoms." In addition, identifying and relinquishing safety behaviors during exposure will also be a significant component of cognitive behavioral treatment for panic and agoraphobia.

Strategies for Effective Homework

Reasons for Noncompliance

Indeed, homework compliance—involving both behavioral and experiential exposure and cognitive disputation—is viewed as so central to effective treatment of panic disorder that the patient may feel a bit overwhelmed by the task at hand. Thoughts about being overwhelmed, losing control, inducing catastrophic experiences, or becoming more sensitized to panic by utilizing exposure are common objections and concerns of patients presenting with this problem in CBT. In fact, the importance of self-help homework—with continued exposure to sensations and experiences that the patient would otherwise avoid—can be viewed as an added "inoculation" to relapse: the patient can be informed that one reason patients with panic and agoraphobia maintain their gains after treatment has been completed is that they continue their "treatment" after they stop seeing the therapist. This is similar to the added benefits of exercising and following a prudent diet after a "crash diet" (treatment) has been completed. Maintenance of gains is viewed as maintaining the self-help homework.

There are several opportunities for noncompliance in the treatment of panic and agoraphobia, since the treatment approach and conceptualization involve numerous points for intervention. The clinician should be mindful that the panic patient feels bewildered by these sensations, interprets his problem as catastrophic, and relies on avoidance and escape as coping mechanisms. Since the essential aspect of panic disorder is "fear of fear," the patient may naturally view CBT as a frightening and destabilizing experience. The therapy may be viewed by the patient as an attempt to deprive her of essential coping tools and that this will leave her defenseless. Moreover, even though the cognitive behavioral model is sophisticated and empirically based, the patient may view it as simplistic and overly optimistic. Thus we begin our discussion of noncompliance by focusing on the psychoeducational component of treatment. The therapist needs to explain to the patient that the goal of therapy is not to eliminate sensations but to change the patient's interpretation of these sensations. Thus, we cannot eliminate a rapid heart rate, but we can modify the interpretation. Analogies to sensations (such as rapid heart rate) that are present during aerobic exercise—but are benignly interpreted—can help modify catastrophic interpretations. Utilizing "coping cards" that exhibit neutral or decatastrophizing statements—for example, "a rapid heart rate means that I am excited"—can be helpful. The clinician can engage the patient in practicing these coping statements within sessions, utilizing imaginal exposures to feared sensations, with the therapist "modeling" a panic attack while using coping statements or "barbing" the patient with automatic thoughts that the patient challenges. These interventions can be helpful in reducing noncompliance with in vivo exposure.

Case Study 1

Debbie, a young single woman, developed panic disorder with agoraphobia 3 years before coming in for treatment. She reported fearing that she would have a panic attack, marked by hyperventilation, dizziness, and the fear of collapsing, in situations where exit was blocked (crowded theaters and shopping malls) or on the open street if there was significant crowding that would block her escape. She indicated that she had fears that she would collapse and make a fool of herself and that she needed to have assurances that there would be safety exits nearby or stores to which she could retreat from the open avenues. Like many panickers, she believed that she might have deep-seated problems that she feared would interfere with the life that she hoped to live.

Misunderstanding Panic Disorder

Noncompliance with homework can occur at any point in the treatment plan. For example, some patients even disagree with the diagnosis, believing that they have "deep-seated problems"—that they may, for example, have an incipient schizophrenia. These extreme interpretations are often reinforced by other therapists who have viewed panic disorder as reflective of severe personality dysfunction. Utilizing the DSM-IV-TR with the patient—with a checklist of symptoms and a comparison to social anxiety disorder (which is sometimes confused with panic disorder) and with schizophrenia (which is sometimes the patient's fear)—can be helpful in establishing the appropriate diagnosis with the patient.

Other patients may be hesitant to agree to a therapeutic contract that involves exposure to feared sensations and situations, arguing that they must be "ready" or "relaxed and confident" before they can engage in exposure. Rebreathing training or relaxation training can, in some cases, actually induce panic attacks, as the patient feels that his "guard is down" during relaxation. Detailed socialization and bibliotherapy are essential components in anticipating these points of resistance. We provide patients with the Patient Information Form from the Leahy and Holland (2000) book, which explains the essential role of exposure and inducing anxiety and panic in the treatment of panic disorder.

The evolutionary model of panic disorder and agoraphobia has considerable appeal to patients. We have found that this model helps patients understand why they would fear situations such as open spaces, heights, bridges and tunnels, since these stimuli would suggest danger in a primitive environment. By viewing their panic as the "right response at the wrong time" (from the evolutionary perspective), patients feel less "pathologized," since their responses reflect "adaptation." Indeed, a rapid heart rate and hyperventilation are responses consistent with motoric escape—running away from danger—a response that is blocked in many agoraphobic situations. Moreover, the use of the schematic in Figure 10.1 often results in patients saying, "This is exactly how I think."

Debbie found the patient handouts, the schematic on panic disorder, and the evolutionary explanation to be significantly reassuring. She indicated that "now my panic makes sense," and that she had never thought of the adaptive nature of panic and agoraphobia as suggested by the evolutionary model. Moreover, the identification of safety behaviors was an important recognition, she said, that the therapist had competence in treating panic, since she had never discussed these safety behaviors with anyone and she was therefore surprised that the therapist could anticipate their existence.

Beliefs That Panic Reflects "Deep-Seated" Problems

Many of our panic-disordered patients have sought treatment with psychodynamically oriented therapists who have interpreted their symptoms as reflective of severe underlying pathology that appears mysterious and confusing to the patient. Indeed, the persistence of panic disorder and agoraphobia for years in some patients lends itself to this "pathologizing" interpretation. The patient reasons that "If this were not a deep-seated, horrible problem, it would not persist."

The psychoeducational component in the treatment of panic is essential. As indicated, we stress both the ethological model—which emphasizes the evolutionary adaptive value of agoraphobic fears (e.g., open spaces, closed spaces, bridges, tunnels)—and the cognitive behavioral model depicted in Figure 10.1. The "conservation" of anxiety, through the continued avoidance of feared stimuli, results in the inability to disconfirm the "panic beliefs"—such as "If I have a panic attack, I will go crazy." Continued avoidance (or, as we shall see, reliance on safety behaviors) reinforces the belief that panic attacks can only be avoided, rather than the new belief that these "symptoms" can be reinterpreted and experienced safely.

A major part of the psychoeducational component is emphasis on the misinterpretation of "symptoms." Patients can identify their automatic thoughts about their panic symptoms ("I will lose control"—fortune telling; "I will go crazy"—catastrophizing) and can see that these misinterpretations are part of the panic disorder. Moreover, the patients' underlying assumptions, such as "I must eliminate all negative sensations" or "I must always be in control," can also be identified through psychoeducation.

Comparisons to the reliance on alcohol to reduce anxiety are useful. The therapist can point out that if you use alcohol every time you feel anxious, you will learn that the only way you can cope with anxiety is to drink. Thus drinking will increase and the anxiety will keep reappearing when you are not drinking. Persistence of a fear is not equivalent to either the deep-seated nature of the fear or to its resistance to proper treatment.

Debbie's view of her panic disorder was inconsistent with her view that she was a generally well-adjusted person. She had feared that there might be some unknown problems from which she was suffering. A thorough psychological assessment—especially a detailed history—ruled out any significant comorbidity. This collaborative component of CBT is often quite helpful for patients who may view psychotherapy as "opening a can of worms." Helping the patient obtain an accurate diagnosis demystifies the problems to be addressed and results in a greater sense of control on the part of the patient.

Too Rapid Movement in the Exposure Hierarchy

Although it is often possible to move a patient rapidly up an anxiety hierarchy, the clinician should use judgment and caution with extremely fearful patients. Some patients will not allow any exposure until they obtain a "total guarantee" that they will be OK. This demand for certainty and intolerance of discomfort needs to be negotiated in each new therapeutic contract for exposure. Thus, the patient can be given the overall instruction that therapy involves exposure and the experience of discomfort and the pros and cons of this exposure can be explored. With patients who are reluctant to take on more demanding exposures, the therapist can utilize imaginal exposure or have the patient observe the therapist mimicking the experiences of a panic attack, utilizing rational responses along the way.

Interventions to counteract too rapid movement in the hierarchy include the following: (a) Ensure that the patient knows that he or she can indicate that the exposure is too difficult at this time. This allows the patient the freedom to feel in control of the process. (b) As a matter of course, go to lower points in the hierarchy as "refresher" exposures. This can be used to warm up or practice before elements higher in the hierarchy are reached. (c) Elicit specific predictions about what will happen with this next exposure. "Will you go crazy?" or "Will you collapse?" The clinician can then examine whether similar predictions have been made before. Rational responses, placed on coping cards and rehearsed in session, can be utilized to counter these thoughts and predictions. Furthermore, some patients may benefit from the freedom to employ "self-guided" exposure, such that they determine the rate and intensity of exposure.

We have found it helpful to provide the patient with a model of tolerating discomfort in the pursuit of getting better. The following example can be helpful: "Let's imagine that I am your physician and there is a terrible flu epidemic, but I have an inoculation here that can prevent you from getting the flu. However, I don't want to cause you any pain with this injection so I tell you that I am not going to inject you, but only place this syringe on the table next to you and hope that somehow that will be effective. What would you think?" Patients are quite familiar with the idea that a little bit of discomfort now can prevent a lot of discomfort later. Furthermore, patients can be instructed that feelings of effectiveness and empowerment come from enduring discomfort, giving one a sense that he or she is overcoming obstacles. We have found that reframing discomfort tolerance as empowerment has beneficial effects.

In Debbie's case, initial exposure was somewhat anxiety-provoking. This was due to the fact that options for "escape" on crowded New York streets were somewhat unpredictable However, the therapist rehearsed in session the possible catastrophic thoughts and safety behaviors that she might utilize, which helped reduce her reluctance to confront the feared situations.

Belief That You Need to "Control" Anxiety and Sensations

Negative emotional beliefs—such as the belief that one has to control all anxiety and arousal—can interfere with exposure homework that is aimed to increase arousal. The patient may refuse to carry out the homework because arousal is viewed as entirely "negative." The patient can be asked to consider the costs and benefits of these beliefs about arousal and to identify both neutral and positive kinds of intense arousal. For example, the patient can indicate what the costs and benefits of arousal from excitement, exercise, surprise, or sexual experiences might be. The therapist can ask the patient to attempt to "go crazy" or to "overbreathe," in order to test out the idea that arousal and anxiety will go out of control. Finally, the patient's "post hoc" explanations for why he or she has not "gone crazy" or "lost control" may often include the recognition that the patient is "catching" himself or herself before the dreaded outcome is experienced. We suggest to patients that they catch themselves catching themselves and then attempt to intensify the arousal to see if the dreaded outcome occurs. The therapist can ask, "Why don't you go crazy?" and examine the patient's belief that insanity is a consequence of panic attacks or that death is a consequence of a rapid heart rate. Since the patient has experienced numerous panic attacks and has not gone insane or had a medical crisis, the causal beliefs can be tested by inducing these "symptoms" and maintaining the level of arousal sufficiently long enough.

Debbie was highly focused on wanting to be rational and in control of her emotions, thereby leading her to jump to conclusions about her anxiety and arousal. Initially, she was skeptical about the value of exposure and believed that increases in anxiety would "always be bad." This reluctance was addressed by "normalizing" the arousal by linking it to prepared responses from an evolutionary model and by equating anxious arousal with physiological arousal similar to the arousal one experiences with aerobic exercise. Panic induction, through hyperventilation, in session helped reduce her fear of these sensations, as did indicating that increased arousal does not lead to fainting, since the blood pressure is increasing.

Overreliance on Safety Behaviors

The recognition that safety behaviors often maintain the dysfunctional beliefs underlying panic disorder is an important contribution to understanding that "exposure" is not always as effective as one would hope it would be (see Clark, 1999; Wells, 1997). Patients who claim that they have engaged in exposure with little benefit may often be utilizing overt or covert safety behaviors, such as leaning against a wall to avoid collapsing, tensing their hands, repeating self-assurance statements, praying, or attempting to distract themselves. These safety behaviors are often unintentional rituals that neutralize exposure and therefore interfere with the homework that is being assigned. A full inventory of safety behaviors needs to be taken—for example, directly inquiring as to the reliance on any behaviors, images, statements, or other strategies that the patient uses in order to "feel more comfortable." Many patients do not spontaneously describe these safety behaviors, so the clinician can provide them with a list of possible safety behaviors. These behaviors include changes in breathing (holding the breath or breathing deeply or rapidly to "catch your breath so you don't suffocate"), tensing the body, narrowing of visual focus on "signs of danger" or "safety places," needing to be accompanied by someone ("In case I can't get out by myself"), repeating "self-assurance" statements, clutching objects, walking rapidly, or other covert and overt behaviors. The patient may be consciously or unconsciously resistant to relinquishing these behaviors "because they make me feel safe now." This "felt sense" of safety, by relying on magical safety behaviors, is an important part of noncompliance that can be examined and tested: "You seem to believe that you need these behaviors to be safe because you feel safer when you use them. How do you account for the fact that you have not gone insane (or collapsed) when you do not use these behaviors?" Would you be willing to test out your belief that you need these behaviors by experimenting with not using them a few times in these situations? What do you predict will happen?"

Asking the patient to experiment with exposure while either relinquishing the safety behavior or even engaging in the opposite behavior can serve as an effective demonstration that safety behaviors are not only unnecessary but that they maintain the panic beliefs. For example, a woman who had a fear of having a panic attack while walking along an open street noted that she fixed her gaze intensely on the sidewalk in front of her. She believed that this would stabilize her, but her fixed gaze only contributed to greater vertigo. She was instructed to catch herself in this fixed gaze and to "do the opposite"—in this case, directing her eyes toward objects or people in the periphery or through her entire range of vision. This substantially reduced her anxiety.

Generalized Anxiety Disorder

The essential features of GAD are physical symptoms and apprehensive worry. The GAD patient worries about several different issues and reports difficulty controlling worry. Symptoms often include restlessness, irritability, fatigue, difficulty concentrating, muscle tension, and insomnia. The patient is worried about a variety of events, unlike in other disorders where worry is confined to specific stimuli or issues. Lifetime prevalence of GAD varies between 5.8% and 9%, with greater risk for women (the male/female ratio being 2.5:1), young adults, and blacks (Blazer, George, & Winfield, 1991; Breslau & Davis, 1985). Patients presenting with GAD often relate that onset has been gradual and that they have been anxious since childhood. Some studies indicate the average length of this problem to be 25 years prior to treatment (Butler, Fennell, Robson, & Gelder, 1991; Craske, Rapee, Jackel, & Barlow, 1989). Because of its chronicity, its self-perpetuating quality, and its frequent nonresponse to treatment, some clinicians and researchers view GAD as a lifelong illness, similar to diabetes or essential hypertension.

The cognitive model of GAD is outlined below, with a specific focus on the metacognitive model of worry (see Leahy, 2004; Wells, 1997, 2000). We then examine a number of factors that interfere with self-help homework compliance and examine how cognitive behavioral techniques and conceptualization can help the patient to overcome these problems.

There is now promising evidence that a cognitive behavioral treatment of GAD is effective and that these gains are maintained after treatment has been terminated. Butler, Fennell, Robson, and Gelder (1991) found significant improvement in patients utilizing a combination of evaluation of automatic thoughts, activity scheduling, and graded task assignments. Öst and Breitholtz (2000) found cognitive therapy to be equivalent to behavioral therapy for GAD, producing 62% clinically significant improvement.

Dugas, Buhr, and Ladacoeur (2004) found significant improvement with a CBT package targeting intolerance of uncertainty. Borkovec, Newman, Pincus, and Lytle (2002) also found significant improvement utilizing cognitive and behavioral treatments for GAD. In a recent meta-analysis of CBT for GAD, Gould, Safren, Washington, and Otto (2003) concluded that CBT offers significant advantages over no treatment, pill placebo, or nondirective controls.

The cognitive behavioral model of anxiety has traditionally focused on two aspects of GAD: physiological arousal and worry (Barlow, 1988; Borkovec & Roemer, 1994). Individuals with GAD are often higher in anxiety sensitivity than the general population, reflecting their overall higher level of arousal and their tendency to focus on this arousal with negative interpretations. Physiological arousal is often addressed using breathing exercises and relaxation, with the assumption that relaxation is incompatible with anxiety. GAD poses a problem for the simple arousal model in that the worries that characterize this disorder focus on a variety of possible problems, many of which never occur.

The initial cognitive model of worry, proposed by Beck and associates (1985), emphasized the tendency of these individuals to overestimate the probability and negativity of possible outcomes. Like Richard Lazarus's (1966) appraisal model, which proposed that anxious individuals overestimate threat and underestimate their ability to cope, the cognitive model advocated by Beck and colleagues viewed GAD as a reflection of the anxiety schemas of threat and the self-schemas of incompetence in coping with threat. This schema model stresses the typical automatic thought distortions characteristic of depression: fortune-telling ("I will fail"), personalizing ("If I do, it's all my fault"), catastrophizing ("It would be terrible if I didn't do well"), and mind reading ("He thinks I am a loser"). Interventions focus on having the worried patient stipulate her negative predictions ("I am going to get fired"), examine the costs and benefits of these predictions, weigh the evidence for and against (e.g., the patient often uses her emotions as evidence—"I feel anxious, therefore it's likely to happen"), and then evaluate coping strategies ("If I get fired, then I can get a new job") (Barlow, 1988).

Borkovec's (1994) model stresses the patient's belief that worry is *out of control* and that this will lead to sickness or insanity. Beliefs in the uncontrollability of worry are addressed by having the patient assign "worry time," such that a specific time and place is set aside daily for intensive worry. This helps the patient recognize that worries are controllable and the content of worries is limited to a few repeated themes (e.g., finances, sickness, interpersonal conflicts). Other methods of demonstrating control include interrupting worry with distraction techniques; for example, asking the patient to describe all the objects in the office.

Borkovec's (1994) model marked the beginning of what may be called a "metacognitive" model of worry, although this is not a term associated with Borkovec's model. *Metacognitive* refers to beliefs about how the mind or emotions function. For example, the belief that "my worry will drive me crazy" is a metacognitive belief. Wells and associates have expanded beyond this model to propose that worriers maintain beliefs that their worrying prepares them, helps them find solutions, prevents bad things from happening, and is uncontrollable (Papageorgiou & Wells, 2001; Wells, 1997; Wells & Carter, 2001). Moreover, the worries are often expressed as "possible" statements about which the patient worries—"I might lose my job"—thereby making them resistant to disconfirmation. Since almost none of the worries come true, the patient may hold a tacit belief that "My worrying kept it from happening." Some patients indicate that they fear not worrying, lest they tempt the "Evil Eye"—that is, lest they become so confident that they either tempt the fates or let their guard down about possible danger.

Because of the patient's belief that worrying prepares, protects, and prevents bad things from happening, these individuals are reluctant or unable to relinquish these cognitive "strategies" (Leahy, 2001). Indeed, pointing out that the events about which they worry are improbable often elicits the strategy "Even if it is improbable, it still is possible and I should make sure it never occurs. I could be that one in a million." From the patient's emotional perspective, the worry must be "working," since the bad things never happen.

Recent work by Borkovec and others indicates that worry inhibits emotional processing and serves as a means of emotional avoidance (Borkovec, Alcaine, & Behar, 2004). Thus, when individuals are actively engaged in the abstract linguistic process of worrying, their physical arousal is reduced, only to be incubated during worry and to rebound as free-floating anxiety after the worry has subsided. Thus, worry is reinforced by the reduction of anxiety in the short term.

Finally, an intriguing new approach to worry stresses the individual's intolerance of uncertainty, with worriers equating uncertainty with an unacceptable aspect of reality (Dugas, Buhr, & Ladouceur, 2004). Indeed, some worriers would rather know that something is definitely bad than to be uncertain about the outcome. Dugas and colleagues have developed a highly effective treatment approach that distinguishes between current worries that can be addressed by taking action in the present and "uncertainty" worries that require repeated exposure to the visual imagery and detailed stories of "possible negative outcomes." For example, worrying about how you will get from New York to Boston may be resolved immediately by scheduling a train reservation, whereas worrying that the train will break down on the way will necessitate repeated exposure to image of the train stalled on the tracks. This has proven to be a highly effective treatment for GAD in both individual and group formats.

Common Barriers to the Use of Homework Assignments

Reasons for Noncompliance

The different cognitive behavioral models of GAD and its treatment all lend themselves to a variety of points of intervention. Feeling overwhelmed with arousal is an important component of GAD for many patients, and CBT may be viewed as another source of unpleasant arousal and thoughts. The reliance on worry as a problem-solving strategy or as a means of avoiding unpleasant emotions can also lead to noncompliance, since CBT requires abandoning the worry as a general problem-solving strategy and induces worry exposure (through worry time or through uncertainty training). Leahy and Holland (2000) have identified additional reasons for noncompliance; these include (a) excessive focus on negative feelings, (b) difficulty identifying automatic thoughts, (c) demand for immediate results, (d) perfectionist beliefs about anxiety reduction, (e) demands for certainty, and (f) beliefs that the worries are realistic. Below, some of the more common reasons for noncompliance are examined, as are interventions that may prove helpful in reducing these problems.

Case Study 2

Tom, an accountant in private practice, reported having difficulty with work, decision making, procrastination, self-esteem, regrets, social skills, assertion, obsessive thoughts, suicidality, anxiety, and depression. He indicated that he worried about not completing his own tax returns, not finishing the work for his clients, his clients getting angry with him, losing clients, going bankrupt, never achieving anything, and being viewed as a failure. He reported regrets about past investments and personal decisions in relationships and was afraid to make decisions now lest he regret them later.

From the meta-cognitive model of worry, Tom's belief was that he needed to worry to avoid exposing himself to making bad decisions; that is, "Worry protects and prepares." However, he also believed that he had no control over worry, and he worried about this. His tendency to procrastinate was based on a number of his beliefs: (a) he would make a mistake if he took action; (b) if he carried out the action, it would lead to worse consequences; (c) these anticipated, often unnamed consequences would be catastrophic; (d) he needed to be absolutely sure—therefore, he must collect as much information as possible before taking action; (e) he was unique with his worries and problems and therefore highly defective; (f) he needed to ventilate with the therapist how bad things were to make himself clear; and (g) he had "deeper issues" that would need to be resolved before he could change his behavior.

Given his history of making catastrophic predictions and his use of avoidance and procrastination as coping mechanisms, Tom was likely to be noncompliant with self-help homework assignments. However, the therapeutic strategy would be to use his noncompliance as a window into his general problem and to use homework assignments to test his negative beliefs. Therapy focused on identifying specific tasks to be accomplished; for example, completing his own taxes, completing his clients' work, billing clients, and developing marketing plans. Each task was broken down into smaller steps and would be assigned as homework tasks to be completed. Noncompliance with these task requirements would be used as a way of eliciting his negative thoughts and challenging them. Individuals with generalized anxiety believe that their worry may protect them; at the same time, their worry is out of control. Therefore therapy is best focused on examining and testing these beliefs by using cost-benefit analysis, examining evidence (to address the positive views of worry), and testing the client's belief in the uncontrollability of worry by imposing delays and constraints on worry.

Positive Views of Worry

A central reason for noncompliance with homework for GAD patients involves their "positive views" of worry. These positive views are reflected by beliefs that worry prepares, protects, and prevents bad things from happening. Worry is viewed by these individuals as a problem-solving strategy. The protective function of worry is reinforced by the fact that bad things are generally not happening, thereby leading to the implicit belief that worry has in fact served to prevent and protect. As a consequence of these beliefs in the *positive* function of worry, many patients may resist changing their patterns of worry.

We have found it helpful to distinguish between productive and unproductive worry, with the former referring to worry that actually leads to a solution and an action that can be taken immediately, whereas unproductive worry is "possible" or "what-iffing" worry (Dugas et al., 2004; Leahy, 2004; Wells, 1997). The therapist can ask, "What specific action can you take right now?" If the patient cannot identify one, then it is characterized as unproductive worry that can either be delayed or used for uncertainty exposure, as described above. The therapist can also address the metacognitive theory of worry as a form of problem solving or prevention by asking the patient to identify specific problems that have been avoided because of worry and to ask for examples of positive outcomes that the individual was surprised by. The therapist can examine with the patient the costs and benefits of this continual worry about potential problems that almost never occur.

Furthermore, underlying the belief that one needs to worry to solve problems is the corresponding belief that one cannot cope with unforeseen problems that might arise. This coping model of stress and anxiety can be examined by asking the patient to describe real problems that have arisen that were unforeseen and how the patient viewed herself in coping with these problems. In the specific case of Tom, his belief that his worry protected him and prevented bad things from happening could be evaluated by examining the countervailing evidence that his worry had not solved his problems of procrastination on his taxes, contacting clients, or asserting himself. Indeed, the worry had only added to his problems. Moreover, in his past history as an employee at an accounting firm, he recognized it was the things that he did not worry about that he actually solved. Worry and problem solving appeared to be antagonistic processes, and his worry only added to his catastrophic predictions that if he actually attempted to solve the problem, the solution would be impossible to attain.

Excessive Focus on Negative Feelings

Excessive focus on negative feelings is part of the self-focus and ruminative bias of these patients, such that the self-focus dramatically increases the accessibility of negative beliefs and anxious sensations (Wells & Matthews, 1994). Thus, people who focus on their negative thoughts and feelings will find it easier to experience increasingly negative thoughts and feelings. This is similar to opening up a file labeled "danger" and reading everything in the file, only to notice later how anxious you feel. If you had opened additional files named "quiet country scenes" or "pictures of puppies," you might come away with more relaxed and pleasant feelings. Self-focus in worry increases the accessibility of the negative thoughts and feelings. This is a major goal of CBT—to modify the self-focus on negative thoughts and feelings into more productive, often action-oriented behaviors. The implication for homework noncompliance is that patients may focus on how bad they feel, ruminating about their emotions and their problems rather than focusing on how their situations might be changed. The therapist may explore with the patient the costs and benefits of this self-focused rumination. Many worried individuals believe that their anxious rumination is a type of problem solving rather than being a type of problem magnification.

Interventions for this bias include examining positive beliefs about self-focus (for example, "worry prepares me"), evaluating the costs and benefits, and examining the evidence that this self-focus has actually prevented anything bad from happening. This is the first step in modifying the "emotional schemas" that the patient employs—that is, the patient's beliefs and strategies about how to handle an unpleasant emotion (Leahy, 2003). Individuals who are prone to feel anxious are more likely to ruminate and focus on their negative feelings and to believe that their feelings and thoughts are out of control.

Tom displayed great emotional intensity in discussing his problems. This preoccupation with feelings rather than on changing behavior was reflected in his noncompliance with homework. For example, he indicated that gathering information about his taxes made him feel anxious, resulting in his avoidance of working on his taxes. We examined a number of "off task" behaviors that he pursued rather than working on his own taxes. These included perfectionistic and obsessive work on a client's taxes, watching television, and sitting and ruminating. Like many people who ruminate, he indicated that his belief that worrying about his problems might lead to a solution. I suggested that ruminating made him think that his problems were worse than they were in actuality. An alternative would be, "Break down the problem into steps, take one step at a time, even if you are anxious, and carry out the steps. If you take action on your problems, they might seem more manageable." Since he had been focusing on his feelings rather than his actions, he made little progress and his problems seemed worse, thereby justifying more procrastination.

Another implication of his focus on negative feelings was that Tom used his emotions as evidence that things were going badly. This focus on negative feelings would impede homework compliance, since self-help required his ability to step back from his feelings, identify his thoughts and challenge them, or take action that might cause discomfort. Thus, when he considered doing the homework of collecting information for his tax returns, he became anxious and chose not to do the homework. He then jumped to the conclusion that his anxiety was a good predictor of bad outcomes. In order to increase homework compliance, I asked him to monitor his anxiety every hour and to write down any anxious thoughts. We then examined whether the evidence for his negative thoughts was based on his feelings or the facts that were available. Tom said, "I realized that I didn't have any facts a lot of the time—just my feelings. But I used my feelings as if they were facts." This circularity kept him locked in avoidance, procrastination, and worry.

Difficulty Identifying Automatic Thoughts

Some worried patients have difficulty identifying automatic thoughts. This presents difficulty in homework compliance in that such patients will not be able to challenge thoughts they cannot identify. Part of the problem is that patients are so focused on feelings that they have difficulty slowing down their reflection to their thoughts. Another problem is that anxious thoughts come up very rapidly, and the patient may therefore simply notice the outcome—that is, the anxious feelings—because they are both more accessible and more uncomfortable. Helpful interventions include experiential or emotional evocation techniques, such as having the patient, in session, close his eyes, imagine a situation associated with anxiety, describe as many physical and sensation details as possible, and project visual images onto an imaginary screen. The therapist can encourage the patient to project a series of images and examine the thoughts and feelings associated with them. In addition, the therapist can suggest to the patient that there may be certain thoughts that may be arising and thus tentatively asking the patient if these may be the thoughts she is having (e.g., "Could you be thinking that you'll fail?") (J. S. Beck, 1995).

Tom sometimes appeared to focus so much on his emotions—intensifying them in session—that he appeared to be not only anxious but also histrionic. This histrionic and cathartic style had been reinforced in other psychodynamically oriented therapy that he had pursued, therapy that emphasized "expression" rather than thinking. Slowing down the process of identifying these thoughts—as well as engaging in imagery to elicit these thoughts—was helpful to Tom. Moreover, clearly distinguishing thoughts from feelings was an important step for him, since he was good at reporting feelings but tended to confuse these with automatic thoughts.

For Tom, the automatic thoughts were "I'll never get better" (fortune telling), "I'll lose everything" (catastrophizing), "I'm a total loser" (all or nothing, labeling), "You think I'm a failure" (mind reading), "Nothing I've done counts if I don't get my taxes done" (discounting positives), and "My client is angry, so I must have failed" (personalizing). His assumptions were "I should always do it perfectly," "It's terrible if people are angry at me," "If I don't do everything right, then I am a failure," and "I should do things only if I'm certain about the outcome and I'm not anxious." His coping rules were "I should wait for all the information before taking action," "I should reduce my anxiety immediately by avoiding action," "I can appease my clients by not asking for payment," and "I can satisfy clients only if I do extra work for which I don't charge them." His personal beliefs or schemas about himself included *defective, incompetent,* and *pathetic.* His beliefs about others were that they were *judgmental* and *rejecting.*

Demand for Immediate Results

A frequent demand for immediate results may appear ironic to the therapist, who can note to the patient that the anxiety has persisted for years and that it may be unrealistic to expect immediate results. These demands for immediate results often discourage patients from completing thought records or engaging in exposure or assertion. The therapist can utilize this demand as an example showing that anxiety persists. Since patients are demanding immediate results that are not forthcoming, they tend to give up quickly, thereby convincing themselves that things are hopeless. The therapist and patient can develop measurable criteria for "progress"; for example, subjective ratings of anxiety each hour for each day, a decreased percentage of belief in automatic thoughts, and self-monitoring of effective behavior.

The demand for immediate results can be addressed by asking the patient, "Specifically what will happen if you do not get immediate results?" In addition, the therapist can say, "Did you have immediate results in obtaining your education? In learning how to do your job? In learning sports?" Hopelessness predictions—often based on excessive task difficulty or incompetence—underlie these demands for immediate results: "If I don't get what I want right now, I never will. It's impossible."

Demands for Certainty

The patient's demand for certainty is related to the foregoing. As part of the emotional and cognitive perfectionism of these individuals, this demand further exacerbates the anxiety and serves to discourage homework compliance. The patient's beliefs about certainty can be examined by asking questions such as the following:

- What are the costs and benefits of demanding certainty?
- Does anyone have certainty?
- What will happen if you do not have certainty?
- What are some things that you have done in the past for which you did not have certainty?
- What is the probability of something bad happening?
- Where do you get evidence about probabilities?

The latter questions about probabilities are central in reducing anxious predictions and modifying homework noncompliance. A patient who says "I may have cancer" (because she has a headache) or "I may lose everything" (because of a 20% drop in his stock portfolio) can be asked to look at the population "base rates" for that particular problem. For example, "What percentage of people in New York City have headaches today and how many of them will have a brain tumor?" The demand for certainty is often reflected in the belief that "rational" responses cannot provide a guarantee and therefore are not relevant. These noncompliant beliefs can be examined for their contribution to anxiety proneness.

When Tom considered the steps to be taken in getting his tax returns completed, he responded with a series of "What if?" statements: "What if they don't allow me to file now? What if they take away my license? What if I lose my practice? What if I go bankrupt?" When he considered doing his cognitive therapy homework, he procrastinated because of these "what-ifs." I pointed out that his rule seemed to be "If it is uncertain, it must be bad." I suggested that we could consider the following: "Uncertainty is neutral." This actually proved to be a revolutionary concept for him—one that he repeated to me for the next 3 months in therapy. He had automatically assumed that any uncertainty was automatically negative, leading him to require complete information and emotional readiness before making a decision. We examined the many things that he did for which he did not have certainty—taking his licensing examination, asking women out, even coming to therapy with me.

Uncertainty was reframed as "collecting information, making progress, changing a bad situation, surprise, challenge, and something that could be interesting." Examples of uncertainty were collected from everyday life: "Not knowing what will happen next in a sports event. Not knowing what my date will say next. Not knowing what the next person will look like who gets on the elevator." Exposure to uncertainty was accomplished through developing a written vignette of his feared outcome ("going to prison") and replaying this image for 20 minutes each day until it became boring.

Beliefs That Worries Are Realistic
Most GAD patients believe that their worries are realistic. This may lead them to either not challenge their negative thoughts or to view the challenges as a form of denial, conferring the risk of being caught off guard. The therapist does not want to find herself in the position of Pollyanna, claiming that everything will work out. We have found it useful to have patients distinguish between "productive" and "unproductive" worry, such that the former refers to predictions or concerns with a higher probability and for which one can take action; for example, "April 15 is rolling around, so I should take some action about my taxes." Unproductive worries are often expressed as "what ifs," often reflecting low-probability, implausible

events over which one has no control, such as, "What if the plane crashes?" or "What if I overlook something?"

Tom indicated that he worried about not completing his own tax returns, not finishing the work for his clients, his clients getting angry with him, losing clients, going bankrupt, never achieving anything, and being viewed as a failure. He reported regrets about past investments and personal decisions in relationships and was afraid to make decisions now lest he regret them later. Tom indicated that he believed that he needed to worry about these things to avoid making future mistakes. On the other hand, he indicated that his worry was "out of control" and he worried that he was making himself incapable of taking any action if he worried. When he considered doing things that might be productive, such as completing his tax returns or contacting a client about an unpaid bill, he reported feeling anxious and subsequently avoided doing these things.

His belief that his worries were realistic—and that these consequences would be so overwhelming that he would not be able to cope—was addressed by collecting the evidence. This was done by having the Tom collect the necessary information about his own expenses and income and consulting with a tax attorney. A step-by-step program of collecting information, learning about his rights, and eventually making a proposal to the Internal Revenue Service (IRS) dramatically reduced his anxiety.

Catastrophic Predictions

Many patients are reluctant to engage in productive behavior because they believe that the consequences will be catastrophic. This was also true for Tom. His first homework assignment was to collect information about what steps needed to be taken to get his tax returns completed. This assignment was not completed. His automatic thoughts were, "It's too late," "The IRS will accuse me of tax evasion," and "I'll lose my license." These catastrophic predictions led him to avoid doing anything about his taxes, adding further to his avoidance. We examined the evidence that his predictions might not be true. At this point, he had no evidence either way.

Since Tom had been rehearsing stories about negative outcomes, I suggested that he needed to construct some detailed stories about positive outcomes. His homework assignment was to develop a detailed story about first, how his tax situation could be resolved satisfactorily, and second, how he could build his practice. I suggested that his worried thoughts often led him to go off onto tangents of catastrophic predictions and frightening narratives and that this made him even more sure that things were really terrible. He had to come up with new stories about positive outcomes that began with, "What if things really do work out well for me? How could that happen?" This intervention proved helpful to him since he had automatically begun stories with "What if it doesn't work out?" and either jumped to catastrophic visions of bad outcomes or distracted himself with off-task behaviors.

Another challenge to his catastrophic predictions included "coping" possibilities. Since he believed that there were no solutions to the terrible problems facing him, he was reluctant to gather the information he needed to pursue his tax filing. We examined his prediction that he might be penalized for not filing on time. He had read about a case of an accountant who was penalized by having his license suspended for 6 months (for violations more excessive than Tom's), and he knew of several cases where the accountant had simply been reprimanded without any penalty. In examining the possibility that his license could be revoked, he considered the possibility that he could work for someone else for a year, which would only mean having less income for that period. This reduced the negative implication of his predictions.

Avoidance of Anxiety

As Borkovec's model of worry suggests, individuals with GAD often attempt to avoid anxiety. We have found it useful to examine the patient's beliefs about what will happen if he allows himself to feel anxious, sad, or angry. Negative emotional schemas—such as, "My anxiety will last forever," "It will overwhelm me," or "I can't stand this anxiety"—are not uncommon for GAD patients. Maladaptive strategies for handling these emotions can be identified; for example, utilizing worry, procrastination, or avoidance as coping strategies.

This avoidance of negative emotions contributed to Tom's procrastination. In our behavioral plan to address his tax problem, we had agreed that the next step was to get legal advice. He indicated that he could contact legal counsel associated with his professional organization. However, the next two sessions revealed that he had not done anything about this. He indicated that thinking about it made him anxious and he avoided calling because he thought it would make him more upset. We examined his noncompliance and procrastination rule, "If it makes me anxious, then I must avoid it." This procrastination and avoidance rule applied to a number of his problem areas, including the tax returns, requesting payments from clients, marketing his practice, making investments, and making a commitment to a woman.

Many anxious individuals appear to be "nearsighted" about their anxiety; they believe that they must reduce their anxiety immediately. Therefore they have a difficult time doing things while they are anxious. Since his highest priority was to avoid an increase of discomfort, Tom would avoid doing things that might raise his level of anxiety. Thus, when he considered collecting information for his tax returns, as a homework assignment, he avoided doing this. His thoughts were, "This makes me anxious" and "I don't want to do this." We identified an "anxiety rule" that Tom employed: "If it makes me uncomfortable, then I must avoid doing it." We examined the costs and benefits of this belief. He noted that the costs of this belief were that he never got these things done, it lowered his self-esteem, and it made him more anxious later. The benefit was that he could reduce his immediate level of anxiety. I compared this to the use of alcohol as a short-term solution for anxiety that becomes a long-term problem—one which contributes to low self-esteem and more anxiety. I suggested a new anxiety rule: "Identify things you need to do. If they make you anxious, do them anyway." We examined the costs and benefits of this new rule and he concluded that although it might make him anxious over the short term, it might help him immensely over the long term. We identified a number of things that he had accomplished when he was anxious—for example, in competitive sports (he had been an accomplished athlete), in passing his licensing examination, and in asking women out.

I asked him, "What would happen if you did something and it made you anxious? What will the anxiety do to you that's so terrible?" This proved to be a very helpful question for him to consider. He recognized that it would make him uncomfortable but that the discomfort might decline over time. This was then assigned as a homework task: "Do something every day that makes you anxious and then write down the outcome." In the next session, he indicated that he had collected some information about his past taxes and that he had called legal counsel regarding his tax liability. He described himself as feeling somewhat less anxious and depressed.

"Writing Down My Thoughts Will Make Me More Anxious"

The CBT approach involves writing down negative thoughts—either in worry time or in rational responses. A common belief among anxious patients is that writing these thoughts down will make them more powerful and upsetting. This is similar to the belief that negative emotions must be avoided at all costs. Tom's reluctance to write down his thoughts and challenge them reflected his belief that confronting his problems would only make him feel worse. We examined this in the session by having him write down his thought "I am a complete failure," identify his level of anxiety (95%), and then examine the evidence for and against this thought. The evidence in favor was that he was not making as much money as some people he knew and that he had problems with depression and anxiety. The evidence against his thought was that he was self-supporting, had a nice apartment, a girlfriend he liked, lots of friends, and that he was in excellent physical condition. He then rerated his anxiety at 35%. I asked him, "How is this consistent with your prediction that writing down your thoughts will make you feel worse?" He acknowledged that he felt better, but indicated that at home he often felt worse as he began focusing on his negative thoughts. I then said to him:

> There is a difference between challenging your thoughts and just dwelling on how bad you think and feel. We call this rumination. It's like chewing over the same negative stuff over and over. It only makes you feel worse. So, you are right. You do feel worse when you ruminate and dwell on things. The question is whether you will feel better if you challenge or even attack your negative thoughts with logic, evidence, and action to solve your problems.

Belief That Worry Is Out of Control

Many worried individuals believe that their worry is out of control and will make them physically ill or lead to insanity. If the therapist then asks the patient to write down worries and challenge them, this attitude can lead to noncompliance. Consequently, establishing that control can be manifested is essential. This was accomplished by identifying Tom's beliefs: "I worry all the time" and "I have no control over these worries—they seem to happen to me." Next, I asked Tom to do two things: (a) set aside a *worry time* every day at 4:30 p.m. for 30 minutes and write down his worries, and (b) categorize his worries—for example, worries that "I won't get my taxes done" and "that I will lose my clients." The advantage of this assignment is that the patient learns that he can delay most worries until worry time, his worries appear limited in number, and he can use the other time for productive behavior. This establishes some sense of control. It is also important to examine the ideas that control is not "all or nothing." Control can be viewed along a continuum from 0% to 100%, and the perception of control of worry also varies.

Putting Self-Esteem and Readiness Before Change

Like many individuals who have been in insight-oriented therapy, Tom held the belief that "deeper changes" in his self-esteem would have to occur before he could change his behavior, and that he needed to feel ready to change. We examined these noncompliant assumptions for their advantages and disadvantages. The advantages of readiness and self-esteem requirements were that he believed he would be less anxious when he finally did something and that it would assure that things would work out. The disadvantages were that nothing changed, nothing got done, and that he felt worse about himself. I indicated to him that the cognitive therapy approach was the opposite of readiness demands: "In this kind of therapy we encourage you to do things that you don't feel ready to do and that make you anxious. We view self-esteem as a consequence of facing your fears, not as a prerequisite." We examined the costs and benefits of this approach. He indicated that a major benefit was that it gave him something concrete that he could do and that his other approach had failed him anyway. We also examined evidence of times that he acted against his anxiety and things improved—for example, when he first learned how to drive, when he took the licensing examination, and when he first asked his girlfriend for a date.

Conclusion

In this Chapter, several components of procedural resistance—or noncompliance—for panic disorder and GAD have been identified. Indeed, the specific aspects of noncompliance actually reflect underlying cognitive schemata that these patients have about their emotional problems and how to cope with them. The patient with panic disorder may be noncompliant because of catastrophic ideas about intense emotion. These beliefs about emotion—and about one's underlying psychological or physical vulnerability—will occur in the context of exposure treatment and panic induction. In fact, the noncompliance is a natural part of the psychological disorder.

The same can be said for noncompliance with GAD. These chronic worriers believe that their worry prepares and protects—so reducing it may lead them to feel more vulnerable. Moreover, the belief that worry is out of control and dangerous can lead to noncompliance with worry time or with uncertainty exposure. In the examples outlined in this Chapter, the clinician can view the noncompliance with homework as another source of information about the patient's beliefs as to how to cope; the therapist may then use the noncompliance as an opportunity to modify these core coping beliefs. Rather than view this noncompliance as interfering with treatment, we can view it as enhancing a better understanding of cognitive and emotional strategies that the patient uses and that, ironically, only perpetuate the problem.

References

American Psychiatric Association. (2000). *Diagnostic and statistical manual of mental disorders: Text revision* (4th ed.). Washington, DC: Author.

Barlow, D. H. (1988). *Anxiety and its disorders: The nature and treatment of anxiety and panic.* New York: Guilford Press.

Beck, A. T., Emery, G., & Greenberg, R. L. (1985). *Anxiety disorders and phobias: A cognitive perspective.* New York: Basic Books.

Beck, J. S. (1995). *Cognitive therapy: Basics and beyond.* New York: Guilford Press.

Blazer, D., George, L., & Winfield, I. (1991). Epidemiologic data and planning mental health services. A tale of two surveys. *Social Psychiatry and Psychiatric Epidemiology, 26,* 21–27.

Borkovec, T. D. (1994). The nature, functions, and origins of worry. In G. C. L. Davey & F. Tallis (Eds.), *Worrying: Perspectives on theory, assessment and treatment* (pp. 5–33). Chichester, UK: Wiley.

Borkovec, T. D., Alcaine, O. M., & Behar, E. (2004). Avoidance theory of worry and generalized anxiety disorder. In R. G. Heimberg, C. L. Turk, & D. S. Mennin (Eds.), *Generalized anxiety disorder: Advances in research and practice.* New York: Guilford Press.

Borkovec, T. D., Newman, M. G., Pincus, A., & Lytle, R. (2002). A component analysis of cognitive behavioral therapy for generalized anxiety disorder and the role of interpersonal problems. *Journal of Consulting and Clinical Psychology, 70,* 288–298.

Borkovec, T. D., & Roemer, L. (1994). Generalized anxiety disorder. In M. Hersen & R. T. Ammerman (Eds.), *Handbook of prescriptive treatments for adults* (pp. 261–281). New York: Plenum Press.

Breslau, N., & Davis, G. C. (1985). DSM-III generalized anxiety disorder: An empirical investigation of more stringent criteria. *Psychiatry Research, 15,* 231–238.

Butler, G., Fennell, M., Robson, P., & Gelder, M. (1991). Comparison of behavior therapy and cognitive behavior therapy in the treatment of generalized anxiety disorder. *Journal of Consulting and Clinical Psychology, 59,* 167–175.

Clark, D. M. (1986). A cognitive approach to panic. *Behaviour Research & Therapy, 24,* 461–470.

Clark, D. M. (1999). Anxiety disorders: Why they persist and how to treat them. *Behaviour Research and Therapy, 37,* 5–27.

Craske, M. G., Rapee, R. M., Jackel, L., & Barlow, D. H. (1989). Qualitative dimensions of worry in DSM-III-R generalized anxiety disorder subjects and nonanxious controls. *Behaviour Research and Therapy, 27,* 397–402.

Dugas, M. J., Buhr, K., & Ladouceur, R. (2004). The role of intolerance of uncertainty in the etiology and maintenance of generalized anxiety disorder. In Heimberg, R., Turk, C. Mennin, D. (Eds.), *Generalized anxiety disorder: Advances in research and practice.* New York: Guilford Press.

Gould, R. A., Otto, M. W., & Pollack, M. H. (1995). A meta-analysis of treatment outcome for panic disorder. *Clinical Psychology Review, 15,* 819–844.

Gould, R. A., Safren, S. A., Washington, D. O., & Otto, M. W. (2003) Cognitive-behavioral treatments for generalized anxiety disorder: A meta-analytic review. In Heimberg, R., Turk, C. Mennin, D. (Eds.), *Generalized anxiety disorder: Advances in research and practice.* New York: Guilford Press.

Lazarus, R. S. (1966). *Psychological stress and the coping process.* New York: McGraw-Hill.

Leahy, R. L. (2001). *Overcoming resistance in cognitive therapy.* New York: Guilford Press.

Leahy, R. L. (2003). Emotional Schemas and resistance. In R. L. Leahy (Ed.), *Rondblocks in cognitive-behavioral therapy: Transforming challenges into opportunities for change* (pp.91–115). New York: Guilford Press.

Leahy, R. L. (2004). Cognitive-behavioral therapy for generalized anxiety disorder. In R. G. Heimberg, C. L. Turk, & D. S. Mennin (Eds.), *Generalized anxiety disorder: Advances in research and practice.* New York: Guilford Press.

Leahy, R. L., & Holland, S. J. (2000). *Treatment plans and interventions for depression and anxiety disorders.* New York: Guilford Press.

Öst, L. G., & Breitholtz, E. (2000). Applied relaxation vs. cognitive therapy in the treatmentof generalized anxiety disorder. *Behaviour Research & Therapy, 38,* 777–790.

Papageorgiou, C., & Wells, A. (2001). Metacognitive beliefs about remination in major depression. Cognitive and Behavioral Practice, 8, 160–163.

Wells, A. (1997). *Cognitive therapy of anxiety disorders: A practice manual and conceptual guide.* New York: Wiley.

Wells, A. (2000). *Emotional disorders and metacognition: Innovative cognitive therapy.* New York: Wiley.

Wells, A., & Carter, K. (2001) Further tests of a cognitive model of generalized anxiety disorder. Metacognitions and worry in gad, panic disorder, social phobia, depression, and non patient. *Behavior Therapy,* 32(1).

Wells, A., & Matthews, G. (1994). *Attention and emotion: A clinical perspective.* Hillsdale, NJ: Erlbaum.

CHAPTER 11

Obsessions and Compulsions

MARTIN E. FRANKLIN, JONATHAN D. HUPPERT, and
DEBORAH ROTH LEDLEY

Cognitive behavioral therapy (CBT) involving exposure and response (ritual) prevention (EX/RP) is an empirically based treatment of established efficacy for obsessive-compulsive disorder (OCD). (For a review see Franklin & Foa, 2002.) Exposure to feared thoughts and situations is a fundamental component of this treatment, as is the voluntary abstinence from rituals and other forms of passive avoidance (e.g., wearing gloves in order to touch doorknobs). Although avoidant strategies can seem helpful in the short run because they alleviate anxiety temporarily, such avoidance has long-term consequences of maintaining anxiety by preventing the client from learning that the feared consequences of confronting situations are unlikely to occur and that anxiety would habituate over time even without rituals. Thus, in treating clients with OCD, it is essential to use exposure to feared thoughts and stimuli and to encourage cessation of all rituals and overt avoidance in order to maximize the effect of CBT involving EX/RP. Further, because treatment sessions typically last only 2 hours each day (Kozak & Foa, 1997), it is imperative to assign exposure and response prevention exercises for clients to complete between treatment sessions; this approach is even more crucial when treatment sessions are shorter and conducted less frequently (e.g., 60-minute sessions held once a week).

Within EX/RP, two types of exercises are used: in vivo and imaginal exposures. Between-sessions homework usually includes repeating the

219

exposures that were conducted in session or conducting variations of the in-session exercises. In vivo exposure entails systematic and gradual confrontation of external situations, places, or activities that trigger obsessional distress. The exact nature of in vivo exposures depends on the client's particular concerns. For example, consider a client with OCD who has fears about contracting a dreaded disease. Exposure for such a client might include instruction to confront numerous things in a hospital setting (e.g., door handles, phones, shaking hands with medical personnel, etc.). It is crucial that along with instructions to do exposures feared situations, clients are also told to refrain from handwashing and other rituals, as well as passive avoidance. By doing so, the client would observe that his anxiety would decrease without engaging in rituals and would show him that visiting the hospital does not inevitably cause illness.

Imaginal exposure involves having the client vividly imagine a feared situation and its consequences and, as with in vivo exposure, not avoiding or escaping the resulting anxiety. Imaginal exposure for OCD is most useful when the client believes that specific feared consequences will result from refraining from rituals and avoidance. For example, an OCD client who fears killing a pedestrian while driving would be asked to create a brief script in which driving without ritualizing did indeed result in this feared consequence. The script would then be used to create an audiotape in which the client would listen to his worst-case scenario repeatedly; habituation with repeated exposure would follow, and the client would therefore learn that anxiety does not persist indefinitely and that the occurrence of a feared thought does not necessarily mean that the fear is credible. Clearly, encouraging clients to listen to imaginal exposure scripts for homework is challenging and, in our view, requires a cogent rationale.

Whether conducted imaginally or in vivo, exposure is often characterized as a behavioral technique, yet it would be inaccurate to presume that cognitions are ignored in most EX/RP protocols. Informal discussion about likelihood and consequences of anticipated harm or other costs often takes place before, during, and/or after the exposure exercises to in order to promote disconfirmation of erroneous beliefs. Often, cognitive techniques are used to challenge irrational beliefs, particularly if such beliefs are holding clients back from doing exposures. Accordingly, clients in EX/RP are sometimes assigned cognitive exercises for homework, such as calculating the realistic probability of a specific feared outcome. In the context of EX/RP, cognitive homework is usually assigned to supplement exposure and response prevention assignments; in more cognitively oriented protocols, these cognitive assignments are more strongly emphasized.

Types of Homework

Early Assignments

Homework is typically a part of EX/RP from the first session, and as such, it helps demonstrate the integral role that homework plays in treatment. Furthermore, assigning homework early encourages a tone of collaborative empiricism in which therapist and client are working together to understand and treat OCD. The rationale for other aspects of the treatment is described in more detail below. Clients can be given handouts to read about OCD and its treatment, or they can be started on initial self-monitoring of rituals. It is important to determine, before making such an assignment, whether the client's symptoms are likely to interfere with compliance. For example, some clients with contamination fears may be reluctant to touch a paper given to them in the first session by the therapist. As routine practice, we recommend inquiring whether the client will be able to receive materials from the therapist and bring them into her home at the very outset of therapy. Another common example of an initial homework assignment gone awry is the use of a self-monitoring sheet with clients who fear providing insufficient detail in response to questions. With these clients, we recommend providing very clear instructions about what to include and what not to include on the monitoring sheet. This is helpful in ensuring that the client does not spend excessive time and energy recording irrelevant behaviors that require valuable therapy time to discuss.

Assigning monitoring as an early homework assignment is especially important, as it allows the therapist and the client to get a clearer sense of the specific nature of the problem. This can be especially useful with clients who find it very difficult to report on their symptoms, particularly when the rituals are largely automatic or pervade much of client's day. Self-monitoring also helps clients to see how the concepts discussed in session depict the reality of their lives. This is an excellent way for the therapist to know that the client understands the treatment rationale. For example, early sessions involve explaining to clients the role that rituals play in the maintenance of obsessions. After clients learn about this functional relationship, self-monitoring often helps to illuminate the relevance of this in their own specific OCD symptom presentation. One client in our center came in stating that he had been unaware of the connection between his obsessions and compulsions, but that every time he washed, he had a thought about contamination prior to the ritual. Sometimes the thought of contamination was triggered by another thought, and he did not realize that he did not need a contaminant immediately in front of him to trigger the obsession that led to the compulsion. Similarly, another client with fears of causing a fire in her home because of her own carelessness learned that these fears were much more prominent during the work week, when her teenage children would be home without her for several hours after school; this led to increased concern that failure to check the oven and other appliances would result in their deaths.

Clinicians should be aware that self-monitoring can be anxiety provoking to OCD clients. This is not seen as a drawback, but a natural process of the treatment because exposure to anxiety is encouraged throughout the treatment. By monitoring their anxiety, some OCD clients are focusing on their anxiety for the first time instead of making their usual attempts to neutralize an obsession (e.g., replacing bad thoughts with good ones) or using other methods to avoid thinking about it (e.g., distraction). This focus on specific obsessions and on the resulting rituals can indeed be anxiety provoking and is an excellent introduction to the concept of exposure. Monitoring can also be anxiety provoking if clients believe that they must complete it perfectly, and this is certainly a vulnerability for anxious clients in general and for OCD clients specifically (Antony, Purdon, Huta, & Swinson. 1998). Clients with OCD might need their monitoring to be written perfectly or might become anxious about recording just the "right" thing. In such situations, we may include "doing homework incompletely" into the hierarchy intentionally. The therapist's normalization of errors made in homework during early sessions is important for all clients and especially useful for those who are especially perfectionistic. Regardless, the two key concepts regarding the first posthomework session is to positively reinforce whatever has been completed and to help the client see how the homework will be used to his or her advantage.

Assigning Exposure Exercises for Homework

Once clients grasp the theoretical foundation of EX/RP, exposure therapy can truly begin. Even the most intensive EX/RP protocols allow for only a few hours of client contact per day, however, and the reality is that most people who receive EX/RP will do so with even less intensive regimens. There are several reasons why in-session exposures are not sufficient for successful treatment, and these should be communicated clearly to clients. By presenting a rationale for the assignment and successful completion of exposure homework, client compliance is likely to be improved and thus outcome enhanced. We tend to emphasize the following points about exposure homework within EX/RP:

First, in order to maximize treatment effects, clients need much more exposure to their fears than they will get in weekly (or even daily) EX/RP sessions. Sometimes this involves exposure to different stimuli, but it also involves repeated exposure to the same items in various contexts (e.g., touching trash cans in the therapist's office, at work, and at public restaurants), which animal models suggest is important to promote retention of new learning (e.g., Bouton, 1994). Indeed, clients often need to have repeated experiences in order to form new beliefs about a given situation. For example, after leaving the office at work without checking the door once, one of our clients remained convinced that a break-in would occur if this exposure were done repeatedly. Her subsequent homework assignment was to leave the office without checking the door every evening for a week. By the end of that week, she was much more convinced that her fear was unfounded, even if she still felt slightly anxious in simply shutting the door and leaving for the evening.

Another reason for having clients engage in exposure homework outside of sessions is that they can come to view the presence of the therapist, as well as the clinic, as "safe," leading them to discount the outcome of in-session exposures and thus continue to avoid feared situations outside of sessions. These "safety beliefs" can take on many forms. For example, one of our adolescent clients who was afraid that a flood would occur if he did not check the faucets was asked to use every sink in the unit and then shut off the water without checking as an in-session exposure. The therapist accompanied the client during these exposures, and the client came to believe that if the therapist noticed any problems with the sinks, he would come back after the session and address the problem, and thus a serious flood would be averted. Only by conducting these same exposures without the therapist present were we able to expose the client to his ultimate fear, which was that *his* insufficient care would result in serious flood damage. Thus, the exposure was conducted again with the client repeating the circuit of unit sinks while the therapist remained in his office; the next logical step was to have the client conduct the same exposure in his own home, which was the exposure assignment given after the client completed the in-session sink exposure. This approach gave the client an opportunity to practice what he had done in session but also to take an important next step by conducting the exposure in his own home rather than in the clinic. By carrying out this homework assignment without the supervision of his parents, the exposure activity enabled the client to successfully evaluate the utility of his fear-related belief.

Another reason given for the importance of assigning exposures for homework is essentially to teach clients to be their own therapists. EX/RP is a short-term therapy; its overt goal is to help clients learn to deal with their OCD successfully on their own so that they can maintain treatment gains long after active treatment has ended. Homework gives clients opportunities to get used to this role and also allows them to begin designing their own exposures while still receiving formal coaching from an expert.

Once a client in our clinic has demonstrated competence in implementing assigned exposure homework, we often begin assigning "wild card" homework created by the client based on the general principles of EX/RP and in light of the current symptom targets; these assignments give the client more room for creativity and also allow the therapist the opportunity to check in on the client's conceptual understanding of how to select and conduct exposures.

Strategies for Effective Homework

Designing Homework Assignments

As already noted, most homework assignments in EX/RP involve some form of exposure. Frequently, exposures are conducted in a hierarchical fashion, with thoughts and stimuli evoking moderate obsessional distress being addressed first, followed by more and more distress-evoking areas. The specific situations to be targeted are discussed with the client throughout treatment. Situations are chosen by balancing the importance of confronting anxiety with the client's willingness to remain engaged in the exposure. There is no strong theoretical rationale for doing exposure in a hierarchical manner, but the practical implications are clear: if exposure assignments selected by the therapist are too challenging initially, the client may become overwhelmed and then noncompliant. Clients who are selecting their own homework sometimes make the opposite error of picking exposure targets that are too easy, which then retards progress in confronting the most difficult items. Ideally, exposure exercises, whether in session or as homework, should be created collaboratively to balance these imperatives. In addition, we sometimes provide a bit less direction in creating exposure homework for our more perfectionistic clients, in order to create more ambiguity and thus improve their tolerance for uncertainty.

Exposures are typically completed for the first time in the therapy sessions themselves, and the therapist then assigns a similar variant for homework. In designing these homework assignments, there are two major considerations: to consolidate the gains the client has made in session through rehearsal and to assign tasks that cannot be or are better accomplished without the presence of the therapist. The former is accomplished by assigning repetition of in-session exposures. The latter is best achieved by tailoring the exposures to increase anxiety in a variety of situations throughout the client's life. For example, a client with primary hoarding might be asked to bring in a box of hoarded printed matter that can be discarded and discussed in session, and the homework assignment emanating from that exposure session might be to sort that day's mail using the same principles taught in the session.

Earlier in treatment, we often suggest that clients focus on exposures assigned by the therapist. As treatment progresses, however, clients should be instructed to seize every opportunity for exposure exercises that naturally occur. This helps them obtain naturally occurring environmental reinforcers, thereby increasing the generalization of adaptive skills. For example, one of our clients had four sessions of EX/RP that focused primarily on driving without checking to see if she had accidentally run over a pedestrian. During the first week of her intensive treatment, a snowfall, ice storm, and subsequent snow removal efforts had resulted in a significant increase in potholes along one of the local roads, and the client decided that she should begin taking that road to and from session instead of the interstate highway during the second week of treatment because this increase in potholes increased the number of times that her car would hit bumps, prompting her obsessional distress about having run over a pedestrian. When clients look for and then take advantage of such opportunities, it indicates strong motivation and good comprehension of the rationale for EX/RP, facilitating the goal of becoming their own EX/RP therapists.

Encouraging Homework Compliance

In introducing the general concept of homework, the metaphor of learning a language can be used and may facilitate compliance. For example, clients can be told: "Learning to treat your anxiety is like learning a new language. Did you take a second language in school? What language was it? How did you do? Can you speak it now? If so, what factors led to you retaining it? What makes one fluent in a language? What is a sign that you are fluent?" Each of these questions are discussed in a way that engages the client. We lead them to the idea that "fluency" can be best demonstrated by being able to argue and dream in a language. Only constant practice can lead to such fluency. In fact, the best way to learn a language is to get some of the basics, and then to immerse oneself completely in that language: if you want become fluent in French, go to France and live among the French. We finish the metaphor with the following:

> Basically, we are going to work on learning a new language: OCD management. This language is difficult to learn, and requires immersion. In sessions, we will work on the basics: the grammar and the vocabulary. The good news is that this is the easy part, there is one major principal in this language: exposure to your anxiety. The other side of that coin is to stop any rituals or avoidance behaviors

that you have been engaging in that interfere with exposure. We will be doing a number of things in session to help you learn this, and the more that you apply what we do at home, the better off you will be.

If the language metaphor does not resonate with clients, the therapist should find an example that does, such as learning a new sport or hobby.

In assigning specific homework assignments, compliance can be facilitated both by the way that homework is assigned and the way in which it is integrated into the subsequent treatment session. With respect to the way that OCD homework is assigned specifically, it should, where possible, be made relevant to clients' long-term goals for how they want to live their lives. For example, one of our clients was asked to clean his boat without ritualizing; when he balked about doing an "inadequate" job, we reminded him that last summer the boat sat in dry dock all year because he could not bring himself even to try attempt to clean it, and thus an entire summer of fun with his family on the water was lost to OCD. He explicitly told us during the intake that this was an example of something he wished to do differently, and we simply reminded him that this was a stated goal of his from the outset. The client was then able to summon up the courage to clean the boat "inadequately," and soon thereafter he was able to take his daughter and her friends for a ride on a pleasant summer evening. After homework is assigned, it is also essential that it be reviewed carefully at the beginning of the next session, in order to underscore its importance to the treatment process.

Working with OCD in Childhood

In treating younger clients, it is imperative that the process of assigning homework maintain a collaborative spirit. Children and adolescents already have ample homework without the addition of homework from their therapy, and they may be especially sensitive to additional demands being placed on their time by adults in authority. In order to prevent this tone from developing, we first emphasize the collaborative process early on in EX/RP, encouraging our young clients to be part of a team with the task of fighting back against OCD (for a comprehensive review of these procedures, see March & Mulle, 1998; Wagner, 2003). Young clients in EX/RP are encouraged to choose from among similarly ranked items from the hierarchy, are given primary responsibility for "bossing back" OCD while the therapist serves as a coach, and are asked to make use of their allies in the battle, typically their parents and perhaps siblings as well.

Homework compliance can also be facilitated by engaging the child in a discussion about how homework can be made more fun for him or her:

Therapist: So, this week in school, our goal is to really boss the OCD around. OCD is going to tell you to go back and correct your work lots of times, or rewrite your letters till they look perfect, or reread stuff to make sure you really understand. But, you want to tell OCD that it's a pain. How do you figure we could keep track of how many times you beat OCD and how many times OCD beat you?

Client: I guess I should write it down. But, there's so much to write down in school anyway. What if I miss something important when I am working on my OCD?

Therapist: That's a great question. I'm glad you brought that up. Do we actually have to write much of anything?

Client: Well, how will I keep track?

Therapist: What about a little symbol? Something quick and easy?

Client: I know! What if I made two columns, one for me winning and one for the OCD winning? And, I could put a check mark when I win and a big "X" when OCD wins?

Therapist: That's such a cool idea.

Client: And, you know, I got this really neat paper for my birthday and some cool markers. Should I use them?

Therapist: I think that's a really good idea. Some of this homework stuff is hard, so if you can make it a little more fun for yourself, that's great. I remember you telling me about those great markers. I'll bet it's going to be really fun to look at your homework when you're done!

Children also respond well to rewards, even those they give to themselves. For example, we often encourage children to do their homework before a fun activity like playing on the computer or watching a favorite TV program. This kind of reward system can help motivate children to do their homework and adds some structure to their days, so that homework does not fall by the wayside (e.g., "My favorite show comes on at 6 p.m., so I am going to spend from 5:30 to 6:00 each day doing my homework").

While homework, and treatment in general, is a serious matter, it is our experience that many children and adolescents actually enjoy completing their homework. They feel good about taking an active role in planning assignments (since they do not get this opportunity in school!) and are proud to report back to the therapist about successfully completed homework.

Parental Involvement

With respect to parental involvement, the EX/RP program we recently evaluated for pediatric OCD (Franklin, Foa, & March, 2003; March, Franklin, Nelson, & Foa, 2001) specifies that parents are included for all of sessions 1, 7, and 11 in the 14-week, 12-session acute treatment phase. Parental involvement within that structure depends largely upon the developmental stage of the child, the specific nature of the OCD (e.g., presence of reassurance rituals involving parents directly), and the quality of past and present interaction about OCD and in general between the child and his or her parents. In cases where instructing the parent directly is viewed as necessary to promote the child's homework compliance between sessions, we invite parents to attend some of the EX/RP sessions to provide them with an opportunity for direct observation of how to conduct exposures with their child. Regardless of the method, parental involvement is essential.

One area in which parental involvement is essential with children (and partner involvement in adults) is reassurance seeking, a common problem with OCD. For example, children who are concerned about contracting an illness might constantly ask their parents whether they should engage in a behavior that might be dangerous (e.g., "Mom, if I eat these leftovers, will I get the stomach flu?") or whether they already did something to put themselves at risk (e.g., "Dad, I touched Jimmy's desk at school today. Am I going to get sick?"). Reassurance seeking is a ritual, and parents must be given strategies to apply at home to help rein this in. We have a number of such techniques that can be helpful. After the client and parent are clear about the negative role of reassurance, we will ask the client and parents to come up with responses to use when clients slip and ask for reassurance. These responses cannot be pejorative or angry but should be guiding. Such responses as, "Your OCD must be pretty strong right now," "Is that question an OCD question?," or "We agreed in the doctor's office that I shouldn't answer OCD's questions, right?" can be helpful for some. For some children, we have provided them with "reassurance cards" if absolute prevention was too difficult. The idea is that they would be allotted a certain number of passes to ask for reassurance, the number of which are then tapered weekly until the client refrains completely.

With respect to homework compliance specifically, parents can play an enormously important role but can also undermine the child's taking responsibility for the treatment; therefore this situation must be managed artfully. At the end of every session we invite the parent in and then ask the child to describe the homework assignment to the parent. This procedure allows the therapist to check on whether the child grasps the assignment and its conceptual underpinnings, and also reinforces for the whole family that the child is primarily responsible for the treatment. With our youngest clients (below age 8), we often make the homework assignment collaborative, but only if the parents have been coached in how to manage negative affect during exposure and if they agree not to push the child past the point of their competence/confidence. Exceptions to this general approach are made on a case-by-case basis, but in our view it is essential that homework completion be the primary responsibility of the child rather than the parent whenever feasible, as it is the child who will have to learn how to employ the EX/RP principles in response to uncontrived exposures that so often occur (e.g., spill of a "contaminated" substance in the cafeteria).

Common Barriers to Homework Assignments

There are many forms of homework noncompliance that have the potential to compromise EX/RP outcomes. Below we address four common types of noncompliance that occur when assigning exposure assignments to clients with OCD: (a) misunderstanding the assignment, (b) outright refusal, (c) repeatedly explaining why homework was not completed, and (d) partial compliance. We address each in turn, briefly discussing key principles that are then demonstrated specifically via case examples.

When a client fails to complete a homework assignment, it is important to be open to multiple interpretations of such behavior. As cognitive behaviorally oriented therapists, we do not assume that noncompliance is symbolic of resistance or a sign of passive aggressiveness. One of the best ways to promote assumption of a neutral stance is by determining whether the client fully understood the assignment, and, if not, to assume some responsibility for the lack of clarity. Then, the therapist can help the client consider ways to improve compliance in the future. A dialogue about homework compliance could proceed as follows:

Therapist: So, how did the homework go this week?
Client: Well, you know, I never really got around to it.
Therapist: Did any particular thing get in the way for you?
Client: I really just didn't feel like it. It just seemed overwhelming.
Therapist: Okay. Well, let's start out by reviewing what the assignment was, and then talk about why it felt overwhelming to you.
Client: Well, you told me to use a public bathroom at least once a day. And, to not wash my hands afterward.
Therapist: Yup. That's a tricky one. Can you reconstruct why we chose this assignment?

Therapist: So, any thoughts on what you could do if a difficult homework assignment comes up again?

Client: Well, I could call you. Or, I could try to select a similar assignment that is a little less difficult that I can do.

Therapist: Sounds like an excellent plan.

This example demonstrated how in-session work (e.g., seeking out relatively clean bathrooms for exposure homework) can be used to demonstrate homework assignments, thereby increasing not only compliance but also the utility of the homework. As another example, one of our clients came in after her first imaginal exposure homework assignment stating that she did not feel anything when listening to the tape of losing control and harming her child. Puzzled by the incongruity of the affective response to the same tape during session versus what the client was now reporting, the therapist first inquired about the frequency and duration of listening to the tape and also about what the client was doing while listening to the tape. The client responded that she had listened to the imaginal exposure tape while driving to and from work in order to maximize efficiency. The therapist apologized for not having been more careful in her explanation of how to do imaginal exposure, and then explained that the client should be in a quiet place where she would not be interrupted for an extended period of time. The rationale for imaginal exposure was reviewed, and the client completed the homework assignment properly after the following session. At the next session, the client reported having this time felt fully engaged in the imaginal exposure and, as in the last few treatment sessions, had habituated somewhat to its content.

A final issue about noncompliance deserves mention. Homework, and therapy in general, should be designed with the client's cultural/religious background in mind. It is inappropriate to assign exposures that are inconsistent with religious law. As an example, many clients with OCD experience intrusive sexual thoughts. They worry that these thoughts mean that they are "bad" people, that they might want to act on the thoughts, or that they will actually act on the thoughts if they allow themselves to think about them enough. In response to these concerns, patients try to suppress sexual thoughts and avoid stimuli that bring these thoughts on in the first place. We would encourage clients like these to actually attend to these thoughts and to do exposures to stimuli that bring them on. For example, we treated a married man who often experienced sexual thoughts about women as he passed them on the street. After having these thoughts, he would feel terribly guilty, leading him to "confess" to his wife that he had been unfaithful. He feared that if he did not do this, he would become unbearably anxious and then the anxiety would never go away. Following similar in-session work, he was asked for homework to sit in the park and look at women he found attractive and think of all the attributes about them that were attractive to him. He was to then refrain from confessing anything to his wife. With continued exposure, his anxiety in response to these thoughts did indeed recede, without having to engage in rituals. After a few weeks, his spontaneously occurring thoughts about other women started to decrease significantly too.

We treated another patient with very similar concerns who was so worried about having intrusive sexual thoughts about women that he avoided leaving his house, and when he did have to go out, he would look only at the ground, risking injury to himself and others. His case was complicated by the fact that he was a devout Muslim. According to the teachings of his religion, he was not permitted to look at women or have lustful thoughts. Assigning the same homework assignment (purposefully thinking lustful thoughts) to this young man would have forced him to disobey the laws of his religion. Instead, we gradually helped him to walk outside looking straight ahead and eventually had him describe nonsexual attributes of women (e.g., "She has brown hair," "She has a red skirt on"). Through these exposures, he was instructed to refrain from neutralizing sexual thoughts that might spontaneously occur and to refrain from confessing the sin of looking at women to his clergyman. We were not able to tap into this client's concerns to the same degree as we were with our other client, but we worked as best we could within the constraints of his culture.

The bottom line is that clients should not be coerced into doing homework assignments; even if they acquiesce, it is very unlikely that in such instances the follow through will be optimal. Instead, it is suggested that the therapist review the rationale for the assignment and then work with the client to achieve a compromise that will not attenuate EX/RP outcome. For example, a client with OCD with contamination concerns conducted an in-session exposure of putting bits of paper from the therapist's office trash can on her clothes and body. However, she was unwilling at that time to take the paper home and use it to contaminate her belongings there. She said she understood that this step was necessary ultimately to reduce her obsessional distress, but she felt that she would be too overwhelmed to complete this assignment at home. In the end, she agreed to leave the paper in the car the first day, then to bring it to one area of the house that was already deemed contaminated. Bringing the paper to the rest of the house did not happen for homework but later during a therapist visit to the house. We have also written in detail elsewhere (Abramowitz, Franklin, & Cahill, 2003) of a client who reported that he would be unable to comply with the strict ritual-prevention homework that had originally been assigned to him (remove all gloves and touch items in home with contaminated hands). Here again we used the same principles to achieve a compromise: the client, who had been wearing triple gloves for years at home, agreed that he would be able to remove one pair of gloves per day and then gradually expose items in his home to the less and less "protected" hands. It was emphasized during the discussion that the goal of complete ritual abstinence had not and should not be changed but that the speed with which it was to be achieved was somewhat flexible.

Years after completion of this case the therapist conducted a long-term follow-up with this same client, who stated that he specifically recalled the original discussion of ritual abstinence. He said during the follow-up (but not during the original discussion) that he would have dropped out of the therapy the next day if the assignment had not been adjusted. Giving up on the assignment would have compromised the therapy, but adjusting it allowed a client to remain in treatment long enough to benefit.

Clients with OCD may hold their beliefs about the consequences of confronting their feared object to the point where they appear to be delusional, which has been referred to in the OCD literature as overvalued ideation (OVI; Kozak & Foa, 1994). OVI has been found predictive of poorer EX/ RP outcome (Foa et al., 1999), and the likely mediator of this relationship is homework noncompliance. If clients refuse to engage in an exposure for homework because they believe it will truly be harmful, more emphasis should be placed on in-session exposure, modeling the exposure, and challenging the clients' motivation for change. For such clients, as is the case for many homework issues, the noncompliance is a reflection of a greater therapy issue that needs to be addressed carefully during the therapy session. For example, a client concerned about getting AIDS from touching the doorknob of a bathroom reluctantly engaged in the exposure with the therapist's guidance. However, when this task was assigned for homework, the client refused outright. Further exploration led the therapist to realize that the client believed that the doors selected for in vivo exposure must have been predetermined to be "safe," because as a reasonable person the therapist would not put the client in harm's way or risk litigation for having done so. However, he still believed even after the exposures that most bathrooms are in fact contaminated and that he would contract AIDS if he touched doorknobs. The therapist had the client randomly pick five bathrooms throughout the area and then the therapist went with the client to the bathrooms, modeling exposures and having the client engage in them. The client was then more willing to engage in the exposures for homework.

If a client repeatedly gives reasons for not doing homework, this should be considered carefully in order to allow the client the benefit of the doubt while still helping him or her to see that it is a problem. The conversation that ensues from this initial interaction often ends up being about choice and motivation for change. A young client with whom we worked came in stating that he had not conducted any of the homework exercises assigned to him regarding confronting his fears of the devil. The therapist asked what prevented him from doing them, and the client said that he was busy with schoolwork until late every night and was too tired to listen to the imaginal exposure tapes or to do the written exercises that had been assigned. The therapist acknowledged that it is difficult to do exposures when life is busy with so many other demands. Then the therapist said, "So, it must be hard working so much that you don't have any time for yourself. Were you able to do anything outside of school this week?" The client replied that he had gone to a movie with friends, had watched a football game on television, and played basketball twice. The therapist then asked how the client might have been able to incorporate the homework assignments into his busy school day and among his pleasure activities. After the client came up with a few ideas, the therapist complimented him for his creative thinking and suggested that the more the client could do such problem solving independently, the more likely he would be to improve. The client said he understood and completed a substantially greater proportion of the assigned homework over the next few sessions.

More so than outright refusal, partial completion of homework is very common among OCD clients. Some clients complete only the self-monitoring and lower-level exposures, some will not complete monitoring at all, and others may engage in their exposures but continue to conduct their avoidance behaviors or compulsions, or vice versa. Notably, Abramowitz et al. (2002) found that while therapist-rated client compliance with in-session exposure and homework assignments was related to EX/RP outcome after treatment, compliance with self-monitoring of rituals was not. Partial compliance can be due to a combination of factors raised earlier in this Chapter (misunderstanding, lack of motivation, anxiety, and so on). It is important to reinforce the client for completion of any part of an assigned homework that was in fact completed, but then to carefully examine the factors associated with noncompliance with the rest of the assignment. For example, one client verbally reported completing all of his exposures but continuously refused to complete any monitoring of his assignments. English was his second language, and completing the forms was difficult for him, even in his native language. However, he also had difficulties with doing things imperfectly, and because he was unsure he could complete his monitoring forms correctly he was reluctant to try. Accordingly, imperfect completion of these monitoring forms was added to the stimulus hierarchy, and became a focus at the beginning of each subsequent session.

Another client reported completing all of her exposures to contaminants in her hierarchy but was not habituating. A careful analysis by the therapist determined that the client was continuing to engage in mental rituals immediately after engaging in the exposure, which led to maintenance of anxiety between sessions. After reiterating and discussing the rationale for ritual prevention, the client was asked to do one of the exposures assigned for homework during a treatment session while refraining from all mental rituals. The client noticed that this exposure was more anxiety-provoking than when she had tried it previously, and habituation occurred between homework exercises once she ceased doing any mental rituals during the assigned exercises. She generalized this principle to uncontrived exposures, and found that here too these exposures became less anxiety-provoking over time when the mental rituals were dropped.

Conclusion

Our extensive clinical experience conducting EX/RP across the developmental spectrum and the extant literature on the relationship between homework compliance and outcome in CBT more generally suggest the importance of successful homework assignment and completion in promoting a good immediate and long-term outcome for the anxiety disorders. Homework compliance is representative in part of motivation for change and comprehension of the treatment rationale and helps the client generalize and consolidate gains made in treatment sessions. As in all other aspects of treatment, flexibility must be used to shape the homework to the individual client's needs and stage of treatment. Promoting homework compliance with pediatric clients involves successfully installing the youngster as the captain of the team, with therapist and family playing ancillary yet important roles as coaches and allies, respectively.

References

Abramowitz, J. S., Franklin, M. E., & Cahill, S. P. (2003). Exposure and ritual prevention for OCD: Beyond the treatment manual. *Cognitive and Behavioral Practice, 10,* 14–21.

Antony, M. M., Purdon, C., Huta, V., & Swinson, R. (1998). Dimensions of perfectionism across the anxiety disorders. *Behaviour Research and Therapy, 36,* 1143–1154.

Bouton M. E. (1994). Context, ambiguity, and classical conditioning. *Current Directions in Psychological Science, 3,* 49–53.

Foa, E. B., Abramowitz, J. S., Franklin, M. E., & Kozak, M. J. (1999). Feared consequences, fixity of belief, and treatment outcome in OCD. *Behavior Therapy, 30,* 717–724.

Franklin, M. E., & Foa, E. B. (2002). Cognitive-behavioral treatment of obsessive compulsive disorder. In P. Nathan & J. Gorman (Eds.), *A guide to treatments that work* (2nd ed., pp. 367–386). Oxford, UK: Oxford University Press.

Franklin, M. E., Foa, E. B., & March, J. S. (2003). The Pediatric OCD Treatment Study (POTS): Rationale, design and methods. *Journal of Child and Adolescent Psychopharmacology, 13 (suppl. 1),* 39–52.

Kozak, M.J., & Foa, E.B. (1994). Obsessions, overvalued ideas, and delusions in obsessive-compulsive disorder. *Behaviour Research and Therapy, 32,* 342–353.

Kozak, M. J., & Foa, E. B. (1997). *Mastery of obsessive-compulsive disorder: A cognitive-behavioral approach.* San Antonio, TX: Psychological Corporation.

March, J. S., Franklin, M. E., Nelson, A. H., & Foa, E. B. (2001). Cognitive-behavioral psychotherapy for pediatric obsessive-compulsive disorder. *Journal of Clinical Child Psychology, 30,* 8–18.

March, J., & Mulle, K. (1998). *OCD in children and adolescents: A cognitive-behavioral treatment manual.* New York: Guilford Press.

Wagner, A. P. (2003). *Treatment of OCD in children and adolescents: A cognitive-behavioral therapy manual.* Rochester, NY: Lighthouse Press.

CHAPTER 12

Depression

ANNE GARLAND AND JAN SCOTT

EXTRACTS FROM A DAY IN THE LIFE OF A COGNITIVE BEHAVIORAL THERAPIST:

Raymond is a 48-year-old man with a 20-year history of depression. At the beginning of each session Raymond removes his therapy folder from his rucksack. The folder contains the summarized contents of the cognitive therapy sessions with the therapist. Everything is in order, the top sheet being the homework negotiated at the previous session. Raymond, looking ashamed, sighs and says, "I've not written anything down. I've not read anything we talked about. I'm so useless. You must be so fed up with me. I don't know why you bother; this is all a waste of time. I wish I could feel differently; then I'd be able to do it." You may not be surprised to know that Raymond attends every session and is reasonably active during therapy. But, as he often observes, "Everything we talk about here makes sense, but as soon as I leave it is wiped out and I sink into a black hole where everything is pointless, and as a result, I just sit and do nothing, and my mind is full of everything that has ever gone wrong."

Joanna is a 42-year-old woman with a 3-year history of persistent depression. Joanna carries a therapy file with all handouts, diary sheets, and homework outcomes individually filed in polyethylene pockets. Ask her about any homework assignment and she can turn to it in her folder. Every assignment is dutifully completed, learning identified, and the results summarized on a separate sheet that Joanna has specifically constructed for this purpose. After five sessions of cognitive therapy, Joanna's depression rating on the Beck Depression Inventory (Beck et al., 1961) dropped from 48 (out of a maximum of 63) down to 38; however, between sessions 6 to 10, her depression rating has remained static. Joanna attends every session and always appears bright and breezy, telling jokes and reporting her successes in the completion of homework of the previous week. However, discussions during the session often reveal a multitude of negative thoughts that Joanna has actively chosen not to write down and/or modify because the thoughts are too painful to contemplate. It also becomes apparent that Joanna has avoided tackling a range of difficult situations. When this topic comes up, she initially begins to cry and then becomes silent. When encouraged by her therapist to speak, Joanna will typically say: "I just don't want to think about how bad I feel." "If only I could control all this, then it would be okay." "I'm sorry for crying." She will then begin to flick through her therapy folder to move the focus away from her overt distress.

Angela is a 28-year-old woman with a 5-year history of major depression. Angela's homework sheet is invariably filed in whichever coat or bag she brought to the previous session, neither of which has been brought to the current session. Indeed, she has never provided written results from any homework assignment but each week carries out one or two behavioral experiments relevant to the work of the previous session. Angela is proactive during treatment sessions and participates actively in negotiating homework assignments. She seems to have a ready capacity for internalizing learning at an experiential level and acting on that learning accordingly. If the therapist tries to ask Angela about her therapy folder and the results of her homework assignments, Angela will say, "Oh, sorry, I've never been good at keeping things in one place and writing things down. Do other people you see do that? Gosh, no; I just prefer to get on with doing things."

And so the day continues…

Setting the Scene: What Is the Purpose of Homework in Cognitive Therapy

Homework assignments are a core element of cognitive therapy for depression. These tasks form a bridge between sessions, offering clients a link between the work undertaken in therapy sessions and the realities of their daily lives. It also provides the therapist with crucial insights into the clients' behaviors and experiences in their relationships outside therapy. The process of designing and agreeing on homework assignments also provides a useful snapshot of the working relationship between the client and the therapist and of their attitudes to and expectations of therapy and the therapeutic relationship. In this respect it is important to give consideration not only to the clients' attitudes and expectations of therapy and the therapeutic relationship but also to those of the therapist. Increasingly, students of cognitive therapy are being encouraged as part of their training experience to pay attention to their own automatic thoughts, beliefs, and attitudes in working with clients (Bennett-Levy, Lee, Travers, et al., 2003) and to consider the impact these may have not only on the therapeutic interaction but also on the use of cognitive therapy interventions, one of which is the homework assignment.

For example, the vignettes outlined above may elicit a range of automatic thoughts in different therapists. For example, for Raymond: the hopelessness reflected by his thoughts (e.g., "This is all pointless," "I am never going to get better," "I might as well give up now") may lead the therapist dealing with Raymond to feel despondent herself and be less active in treatment. However, a different therapist may note feelings of anger in her interactions with Raymond, accompanied by automatic thoughts such as "He just isn't trying," "He is wasting my time," "He enjoys being miserable." As a consequence, this therapist might discharge him from treatment. A further response may be feelings of guilt, as a result of which, the therapist concludes "I'm not trying hard enough to help him," "It is up to me to sort out his problems," and "If he had a more skilled therapist, he would be better by now." This therapist might then make more strident attempts to help Raymond complete his homework. It may also be that some therapists in their interaction with Raymond might react with automatic thoughts such as "Poor man, he is really suffering," "He has such a terrible illness," "He really deserves my time and attention," and "If we persist, we will get somewhere in the end."

The same considerations can be given to the types of automatic thoughts an encounter with Joanna or Angela might elicit. With Joanna, it would be easy to be lulled into an initial false sense of security with thoughts such as "She is working really hard," "She is very committed to this therapy," and "She is going to do really well in treatment." However, as progress comes to a halt, the therapist might then begin to doubt his abilities with thoughts such as "She is such a good case to treat; I must be useless if I can't help her with her problems."

Similarly, Angela's approach to homework may lead the therapist to take a critical stance: "She doesn't listen to what I ask her to do," "How can she hope to get better if she doesn't do her homework properly," or a more helpful position, such as "She seems to be making good use of the therapy and using it in her own way; that's what counts." Giving consideration to our own emotional responses and automatic thoughts in relation to the activity of homework can lead to a deeper understanding of how to negotiate potential obstacles to homework completion and to maximize the potential benefits of this important cognitive therapy intervention.

So before proceeding, you may wish to reread the case vignettes given above and note your observations and tentative hypotheses about the characteristics of the client. In addition, you may want to reflect on your own emotional reaction to the clinical descriptions in the vignettes and note any automatic thoughts that run through your mind as you read.

The development of meaningful homework assignments has received surprisingly little attention in the cognitive therapy literature. Indeed, guidance regarding the attitudes, knowledge, and skills required by therapists to successfully integrate homework into therapy are often relegated to the position of a postscript at the end of a Chapter, a training workshop, or supervisory session. In this Chapter we review how homework assignments reflect the goals and principles of cognitive therapy and why such tasks are important. In addition, we give consideration to how the clients' responses to homework assignments can be integrated within the therapy framework to help in the development of a cognitive case formulation of their problems. Finally, we explore the key elements of beneficial homework assignments and the possible client and therapist reactions that may increase or decrease the clinical utility of these tasks.

Main Goals of Homework in Cognitive Therapy

Taken at face value, it is easy to conclude that the main goal of homework in cognitive therapy is task completion. That is to say, the client engages in the completion of homework assignments in a prescriptive fashion and in the fullness of time recovers from her depression. In reality, homework serves a variety of functions within the overall treatment rationale and, when used effectively, can deeply enrich the process of therapeutic learning for therapist as well as client. For example, how a client approaches a homework assignment and whether it is completed or not can yield important information about his perceptions of himself and others and how he generally approaches his problems. This provides useful data for the overall formulation of the client's problems. In this respect, whether homework is completed or not is secondary to the fact that homework assignments can be viewed as an important mechanism of change in cognitive therapy and therefore need to play a central role in each session. Homework also acts as a bridge between the work of the session and the client's everyday life and is the method by which in-session learning is applied and generalized to tackle problem situations in the client's life.

Approaching the task of homework can also give useful insight into the therapist's own belief system and how this affects the therapy process. Consider, for example, a therapist who had a belief system similar to Joanna's. What would be the helpful and unhelpful aspects of this therapeutic alliance? What steps might the therapist have to take in order to monitor the impact of her own beliefs on the therapy process and optimize the benefits of cognitive therapy? From this brief discussion it is possible to see that within the cognitive therapy treatment rationale, homework serves a variety of goals; being mindful of these during the course of treatment can exert a powerful influence over the course and outcome of therapy.

Homework and the Cognitive Model of Depression

In the 1960s, cognitive therapy emerged as an intervention specifically designed for the treatment of mild to moderate acute depression. More recently, this application has been extended to be used in the treatment of more chronic and severe depression (Paykel et al., 1999). Its founder, A. T. Beck (1967), describes cognitive therapy as a problem-solving, structured, short-term (15 to 18 sessions) treatment based on the assumption that it is not situations in themselves that make us happy, sad, anxious, or guilty but the view that we take of them. Emotional responses are mediated by perceptions of the event or experience rather than the actual event or experience, and these appraisals and feelings largely dictate an individual's behavior (Beck, Rush, Shaw, & Emery, 1979).

The cognitive model also identifies core cognitive structures and cognitive processes that increase the individual's vulnerability to the onset of depression or the persistence of depressive symptoms once they arise. The model suggests that learning experiences during childhood and adolescence may lead some individuals to develop maladaptive beliefs or unduly rigid rules about how they should act and react in certain situations, their view of self and self in relation to others, their relationships with others, and the world in which they live. The cognitive model suggests that emotional disorders arise when these beliefs are activated by events that have specific personal meaning for that individual, whereby the critical incidents that trigger these beliefs in some way mirror the circumstances that shaped the development of the beliefs. Thus, such beliefs represent a psychological vulnerability to depression, which when activated gives rise to depressive symptoms. Further, a major feature of depression is the presence of cognitive processing biases. Such biases lead depressed persons to be prone to negative appraisals of their day-to-day experiences, which in turn leads to further lowering of mood. The effect of this downturn in mood is to increase the accessibility of negative memories of past experiences, which further enhance negative appraisals of current situations and increase the frequency of negative predictions about the future. These biased appraisals influence the individual's emotional responses and behaviors, and so a vicious cycle is set in motion. A fundamental principle of the therapy is to break into this cycle by identifying the links between thoughts, emotion, and behavior and, via a range of interventions, to modify these cognitive biases and maladaptive beliefs.

It is important to bear in mind the cultural origins of the model that is being proffered in working with clients. Like many psychotherapy models, cognitive therapy is predicated on the societal norms of white, western middle-class culture. There is a strong emphasis on autonomy, individualism, and self-determination. Other influences include many of the traditions inherent to western medicine and specifically psychiatry. In this respect it is important to give consideration to cultural and subcultural norms that may stand outside of this frame of reference and therefore potentially clash with the philosophical principles that are a part of cognitive therapy but often go unarticulated. Obvious examples include attitudes and values that stem from race, ethnicity, and creed. There may also be specific considerations regarding sexual orientation, gender, and social class, or combinations of the above. This is true for both client and therapist.

These values may influence how homework is approached and valued by the patient, and indeed, whether it is completed at all. For example, a central aspect of therapy in treating depression is tackling approval-based beliefs. This may include behavioral experiments around asserting one's rights in particular situations, prioritizing one's own needs, and putting oneself first. In western culture, these are acceptable goals and are generally considered healthy behaviors. However, in Chinese/Asian culture, deferring to the wants and needs of others is always primary, and to put one's own needs first would be socially unacceptable. Therefore treatment goals that target this type of behavior may be inappropriate in some contexts. It is important that treatment be sensitive to such cultural differences, and any negotiated homework tasks must take these differences into consideration. These cultural and subcultural norms are often subtle and must be carefully considered both in therapy and in setting meaningful and appropriate homework assignments.

Identifying the Vicious Cycle: The Event-Thought-Feeling-Behavior Link

When Raymond fails to complete his homework, he reports negative automatic thoughts such as "I'm so useless," "You must be so sick of me," "This is all a waste of time." Such automatic thoughts represent his appraisal of the situation at hand, in this instance reviewing homework assignments. These situation-specific appraisals are accompanied by feelings of sadness, anxiety, and guilt; Raymond's behavior in the session then changes and he becomes withdrawn and inactive. Contrast Raymond's reported thoughts with those of Angela, who also never fully completes her homework assignments in the manner originally negotiated. Her appraisal of the same situation is as follows: "I've never been good at writing things down, I just prefer to get on and do things." She does not report any notable affective change other than surprise that some clients actually keep written records of their homework assignments. Her behavioral response in this situation was to begin the task of agenda setting for the session. Meanwhile, Joanna always appears to complete homework to a very high standard in exactly the way negotiated at the previous session. It is very important to Joanna that the therapist review homework assignments, and she spontaneously produces an immaculately completed homework diary at the beginning of each session. The statement "I've done my homework and this is what I've learned" often accompanies this action. Behaviorally Joanna is keen to press on with the session and talk about what she has been doing during the intervening week. This is often presented in an overly familiar fashion, as if she were trying to keep the conversation chatty and informal. However, if the therapist retains a focus on the homework, it is usually easy to uncover evidence that Joanna has undertaken most work on activities that are emotionally "safe"; she has selectively avoided tackling activities that would be likely to cause her distress.

Using the Vicious Cycle to Develop Hypotheses About Underlying Beliefs

The reactions noted when each individual reports on attempts to undertake the same activity (i.e., homework completion) raise an important question: *What determines our different individual emotional responses to the same situation or event?* Cognitive theory suggests that the mediating factor is the individuals' beliefs, values, and attitudes. It is hypothesized that these are developed during childhood and adolescence and further elaborated during our adult lives. Certain types of beliefs are viewed as particularly unhelpful or maladaptive because the person concerned adheres to them rigidly. These beliefs differ from automatic thoughts in that the latter represent our appraisal of a specific situation, but beliefs are applied inflexibly across many situations. Cognitive theory suggests that the underlying beliefs are critical to the emergence of the specific automatic thoughts. Thus, helping an individual identify automatic (situation-specific) thoughts enables the identification of recurring themes that in turn allow the identification of key underlying beliefs. The nature and content of the individual's belief system represent a psychological vulnerability to depression. For example, Raymond and Joanna both have exacting standards and endorse the belief "If I can't do something properly, there is no point in doing it at all."

Raymond was raised in a large family and on the whole was left to his own devices during his childhood. He had an especially difficult time at school. He was not academically talented and was often ridiculed and humiliated by teachers for his poor grammar and spelling. Raymond often cited his inability to spell and his fear of being viewed as foolish as barriers to the completion of written homework assignments. Fundamentally Raymond believes that he is "insignificant" and "a failure," that others are judgmental and rejecting, and that the world is a hostile place. For Raymond, being able to do things properly is a measure of personal effectiveness (success) and also acceptance from others. However, his fear of failure and the consequent reinforcement of his negative self-image—combined with his predictions that others will ridicule him if he fails to achieve an appropriate standard—account in part for his procrastination and avoidance of completing his homework. Not doing the agreed tasks has an immediate benefit for him in that he avoids confirming his beliefs about himself as well as the possibility of being judged by others. However, when he arrives at the session without having completed the homework, this is taken by him as evidence of failure, and his mind becomes dominated by automatic thoughts about himself (as useless and a failure) and others (who, he believes, see him as a waste of time). As a result he feels anxious, guilty, and depressed. Extrapolating from this specific scenario (noncompletion of homework) to a more general level, we can hypothesize that Raymond perceives that he never has and never will be able to do anything as it should be done, and we can now learn something about his rigid and strict criteria of what doing something "properly" entails. We can use this information and evidence to help Raymond understand that his beliefs about himself influence his emotions and behaviors in such a way that the beliefs become a self-fulfilling prophecy, which over the course of his life have had a pernicious effect on his work and personal relationships and played a significant role in the onset and maintenance of his depression.

Joanna grew up in a family where social acceptability and the maintenance of high standards were considered imperatives. When Joanna succeeded in living up to these principles, she was praised and gained the approval of her parents and teachers. The continued operation of this belief was readily observed in her conscientious approach to the completion of homework and was also reflected in her production of ordered records immaculately kept in a therapy folder. Like Raymond, Joanna held the belief that she should always do things properly with a high degree of conviction, and this principle was applied rigidly across all situations, often with equally detrimental effects. For Joanna, praise for her perfectionistic approach reinforced the idea that love and approval were contingent on maintaining high standards. At a more fundamental level, Joanna had a fragile self-image, viewing herself as worthless, others as potentially critical (she felt that if she did not maintain high standards, they would reject her), and the world as a place in which one is judged. Joanna's need for approval ruled out the possibility of not producing homework records for the therapist, and she engaged in this task diligently. However, she clearly found aspects of treatment very difficult, and she adopted a coping strategy of undertaking only those homework tasks that were related to less emotive situations. In fact, Joanna actively avoided activities and situations that triggered a strong emotional reaction in her—for example, she never recorded her most distressing automatic thoughts for fear that the therapist might not approve of them. The lack of "hot" cognitions to evaluate and modify was probably an important determinant of the persistence of her depression and her failure to make observable progress.

Angela was raised in a family where she was encouraged to do her best but always felt accepted and cared for no matter what her actual achievements were. Angela did not describe a rigidly held belief about any need to reach predetermined standards but endorsed the idea that "If I give something a go, then I can always learn from it." Once again, this could be observed in her approach to homework. She did not see it as important to tackle activities in a prescribed way and, unlike Raymond and Joanna, did not anticipate negative judgments, ridicule, or disapproval from others if she did not carry out tasks as agreed, or indeed, if things did not go according to plan. This meant that Angela was readily able to complete homework assignments and did not perceive any risks if she completed these in her own way. At a more fundamental level, Angela viewed herself as a worthwhile individual and her expectation of herself was that she should try to do her best. She experienced others as her equals and strongly endorsed the idea that the world should be a fair place. It was this latter belief alone that had been implicated in the onset of her depression.

In the examples above, two types of belief are expressed. The first is described as a conditional belief or rule, usually expressed as an "if/then" statement (e.g., "If I'm not in control, then something bad will happen"), which essentially acts as a rule governing behavior. The second type of belief is described as an unconditional belief defined in terms of "I am, people are, and the world is…" (e.g., "I am a failure," "people are judgmental," and "The world is a hostile place").

From the clinical vignettes, it can be seen that the different outcomes observed in response to homework provide rich evidence about the form and content of each individual's automatic thoughts, their conditional and unconditional beliefs, and how these influence their emotional responses and behaviors. Part of the therapeutic process in cognitive therapy is to work with the client to identify these beliefs in order to understand the development and maintenance of depression. The clinical examples demonstrate that these beliefs continually shape the person's experiences both within and outside of therapy sessions. As homework forms a bridge between these two environments, it is clear that this provides a means to actively understanding and modifying the impact of such beliefs. Identification of the emotions, thoughts and behaviors associated with completion or noncompletion of homework represents one of the most effective ways of beginning the process of case formulation and hypothesizing about conditional and unconditional beliefs. However, this can happen only if the therapist recognizes that exploration of the client's responses to homework is a high priority and ensures that the relevant information is evaluated not only from the obvious perspective of "did the client complete the homework task with the expected results?" but also considers the evidence gathered at a metalevel. This requires evaluating the outcome of the homework assignment within the framework of the cognitive model, that is: "Did the client's reaction to the specific tasks reflect his emotional and behavioral responses in other similar situations, and if so what conditional and unconditional beliefs may be operating?" To do this, the therapist must make sure that he forms an objective view of what occurred during the attempted completion of the homework assignment, reflects on how that information is reported back, and reviews the client's reaction to this process. For example, does the client become anxious because she thinks the therapist will judge her? Does the client appear frustrated and discount the successful completion of a task because he now regards the specified goal as too simple?

How Homework Reflects the Goals of Cognitive Therapy

As stated previously, cognitive therapy is a structured intervention. Specific strategies are used at specific points in treatment in order to tackle specific problems. The treatment protocol for acute depression is summarized in Beck et al. (1979) and incorporates a number of practical strategies to achieve three broad aims:

- Alleviate the distressing and disabling effects of depressive symptoms
- Equip the client with a range of practical strategies to improve day to day functioning and reduce the likelihood that symptoms persist or worsen
- Modify unhelpful conditional and unconditional beliefs to reduce the individual's vulnerability to future depressive relapse

Each therapy session is highly structured with set items, such as agenda setting and client feedback. The style of therapy is one of client and therapist working together as a team in order to solve problems. In this respect the therapist and client are seen as equal partners and use a variety of strategies to tackle problems that have arisen as a result of depression. This may involve keeping a record of the automatic thoughts described previously and engaging in exercises aimed at modifying these thoughts, devising behavioral experiments to test the validity of these thoughts, and making written summaries of learning from these experiments. It may also involve using interventions such as in-session role-playing to rehearse how to act or cope with interpersonal situations or how to implement certain strategies outside the therapy session. Thus, key targets for change are unhelpful or maladaptive cognitions (automatic thoughts and conditional beliefs), problematic behaviors, and affect regulation. These targets are addressed during cognitive therapy sessions. Within-session learning is then transposed into the client's real-world environment via the process of repetition outside the therapy sessions, which is best achieved through homework assignments.

Why Is Homework Important?

There are two main reasons to regarded homework assignments as crucial components of cognitive therapy. First, the trajectory of improvement in depression is likely to be accelerated not only if clients are practicing skills outside of therapy sessions but also if they are gathering vital evidence to bring to future sessions, which then informs the process of therapy. Second, there is empirical evidence to suggest that depression-prone individuals show some trait deficits in their ability to solve problems and in the way in which they process information. As such, certain types of homework assignments may help them to make connections between events, thoughts, emotional responses, and behaviors; in addition, the methods used to identify such links (e.g., daily thought records and weekly activity schedules) may enable clients to acquire skills they previously lacked.

Depression

There is robust evidence supporting the use of cognitive therapy in the treatment of both acute and chronic depression (Scott, 1996; Scott, 2000). Research has also shown that duration of therapy, therapist competence, and the therapist's adherence to the treatment protocol are important factors in determining treatment outcome (Scott, 2000).

Homework as a Method of Skills Development

A number of cognitive processing deficits are recognized as trait characteristics of individuals at risk of developing depression (Scott, House, Harrington, & Ferrier, 1996; Garland, Harrington, House, & Scott, 2000). For example, individuals who develop depression are more likely to demonstrate deficits in basic problem-solving skills and also have more difficulty in recalling specific personal memories when presented with emotional cue words (e.g., depressed individuals are more likely to recall overly general memories in response to cue words, such as *happy*). Williams et al. (1997) present a comprehensive review of these deficits, which suggests that depressed individuals in comparison to nondepressed controls:

- Take longer to register a stimulus than nondepressed controls
- Have reduced abstracting ability
- Retrieve more negative and overly general autobiographical memories
- Have significantly poorer problem-solving skills
- Have a lower self-appraisal of their ability to solve problems

These deficits in cognitive functioning can be viewed as symptoms of depression, which are overtly manifest in working with the depressed client and may account for much of the negativity that characterizes the disorder. However, if many of these deficits predate the onset of depression, it can quickly be seen that teaching an individual how to resolve a specific problem may also be teaching her the principles of problem solving for the first time. Likewise, asking an individual to record automatic thoughts may help her recognize how to make connections between her emotions and specific thoughts. For example, while completing a diary to identify these links may be the primary goal of homework, the process of recording each specific thought may give the client a new skill that overcomes the tendency to register overly general autobiographical memories in response to emotional cues. As such, homework assignments, particularly in individuals with chronic depression, may have a dual role (Moore & Garland, 2003).

From the depressed clients' perspective their overall ability to process information is retarded, and the predominant content of their thinking is negative. They often lack the specificity of detail that is a prerequisite of being able to solve problems. In addition, in trying to utilize a problem-solving approach, a depressed client will more frequently focus attention on what can go wrong, why it will not work, and his or her own shortcomings in implementing the plan. Raymond's description of the impact of his depressive mind set on his approach to homework typifies this style of information processing. In working with Raymond to try and actively overcome the obstacles to homework completion, his usual response is that "my mind is blank" or a sigh followed by a resigned "I don't know." He was readily able to recall times when his attempts to complete homework assignments had gone wrong and required repeated prompting from the therapist to access information that provided evidence of benefits derived from previously completed homework tasks.

Adopting a problem-solving stance in reviewing homework with Raymond was equally challenging for both client and therapist. Raymond would often fail to answer questions and sit in silence; when prompted by the therapist, he would give monosyllabic replies. As might be anticipated, this process quickly led Raymond to access his conditional belief about doing things properly and elicited automatic thoughts that he was useless.

deficits were symptoms of depression that significantly interfered with his mental processes, rather than being evidence of Raymond's "inherent stupidity," was important. It enabled Raymond to take an initial step toward attempting some homework assignments.

How Is Homework Integrated Into a Cognitive Therapy Session?

A number of factors need to be given consideration in order to maximize the effectiveness of homework assignments in working with depression. These include a coherent rationale for each homework assignment; the pacing of homework tasks (which need to be appropriate to the stage of therapy and relevant to the work of the session and overall goals of treatment); and finally identifying tasks that are achievable given the client's current level of depression. As already highlighted, both therapist and client play an important role in how these factors are managed during the process of therapy.

Guiding Principles for Integrating Homework into Sessions

A fundamental principle of cognitive therapy is that homework is an integral component of each treatment session (Detweiler & Wishman, 1999; Beck et al., 1979). A key role of the therapist is to establish a routine at the start of each session whereby previous homework is reviewed. This process builds a bridge between sessions and ensures that what has been learned from homework assignments is explicitly articulated and built upon in subsequent assignments. This discussion is ideally concluded with a written action plan for how new learning is to be applied in real-life situations or a brief summary made for what has been discovered or understood from the experiment. Writing such summaries makes the task or learning point "real" to the client and gives her a point of reference to return to at a later date (for evidence, see Cox, Tisdelle, & Culbert, 1988).

Therapists need to be mindful of the impact of depressive symptoms on the individual and to take into account the influence of the biased cognitive processing in negotiating assignments. However, if homework is viewed as an exercise in understanding, there is no such thing as an unsuccessful homework assignment, because each task is presented as an experiment. Thus, whether the intended outcome is achieved or whether there are barriers that prevent attainment of the goal, the objective is still to reflect on what has been learned during the process of engaging in the homework task or to elicit what new information is now available to the client once he or she has attempted the task. Typically the therapist spends 5 to 10 minutes during each session in reviewing homework. However, in the early stages of therapy up to 20 minutes may be devoted to this aspect of the session. Sessions during which a homework assignment is not reviewed should be seen as exceptions. It is likely that the client has put a great deal of effort into the activity and indeed may have struggled to complete the homework assignment. For example, if the therapist were to omit the customary review of a diary or activity record that Raymond or Joanna had spent time and effort completing (this would be demoralizing for most people), it might reinforce Raymond's view that he and his efforts are insignificant or Joanna's view that she is worthless. At the very least the therapist's failure to review homework could reduce the engagement or investment of both clients in homework assignments. In addition, such an omission could be perceived as rejection or as a sign that the assignment had not been completed correctly. Therapists need to be aware that, in working with clients with conditional beliefs about doing things properly, there is huge potential for homework assignments to become a source of stress and pressure. Indeed, the client may become focused on the idea that they are being judged or criticized; thus the concept that homework is a tool for understanding and overcoming their depression is totally undermined.

Optimizing Homework Completion

There are key aspects of the process of cognitive therapy for depression that optimize the likelihood that homework will be completed and the client will derive benefit from the activity.

Giving a Rationale for Homework That Emphasizes the "No Lose" Scenario

This is most readily achieved by couching the homework assignment as an experiment, not a test. If the homework task is completed, it is a step toward understanding the client's problems and working toward the goals of therapy. However, it is vital to emphasize to the client that it is just as important, or indeed even more important, to understand the obstacles to completion of a particular homework task. This provides important information about unhelpful patterns of thinking and behavior that may maintain the client's depression. As might be anticipated, in the course of therapy with Raymond, he failed to complete 70% of the negotiated homework assignments at the first attempt in the early stages of treatment. However, careful and repeated examination of the reasons for not completing homework eventually helped him overcome his fear of failure and improved his overall homework concordance. This enabled ... and his avoidance of ...ions and activities where he might potentially risk being judged. This, for Raymond proved something of a revelation.

Making a Homework Assignment Achievable

Breaking tasks down into manageable steps is an important aspect of the problem-solving rationale inherent in cognitive therapy. If a specific task is not achievable because it is beyond the capacity of a client who is depressed, then the chances of attempting the task, let alone completing it, are significantly reduced. For example, in working with Joanna, she stated she felt overwhelmed at the prospect of trying to record her thoughts on a diary sheet. Discussion with the therapist revealed Joanna's belief that, to gain maximum benefit from the exercise of recording automatic thoughts, she would have to write down every automatic thought she experienced. Given the frequency with which negative thoughts are experienced, recording them all would indeed be impossible. Through discussion and negotiation, Joanna and her therapist agreed she would aim to record a maximum of four upsetting automatic thoughts between weekly therapy sessions. From Joanna's perspective, this immediately made the task more achievable as well as providing a behavioral test that directly contravened

Joanna's conditional belief that she must do everything properly (that is, writing down *every* automatic thought she experienced).

Making Use of the Structured Approach to Therapy

As stated, the first agenda item of any session is ideally a review of previous homework. The use of a standardized format, alongside strategies such as completion of homework summary sheets that explicitly identify key learning points from each homework activity, helps to reinforce the central role of homework in the process of recovery. In addition, the establishment of such routines within the session minimizes the impact of depressive symptoms and cognitive biases on the structure and process of therapy.

As well as reviewing previous homework, the therapist needs to allow sufficient time during each session to negotiate future homework. The overall goal is to make sure that the work that has been carried out in the session forms the basis of the homework assignment. It is preferable that homework tasks be agreed on jointly as the session progresses rather than addressed as an afterthought at the end of the treatment hour. Homework assignments need to be appropriate to the stage of therapy and must take into consideration factors such as how well engaged the client is in the therapy process, his level of skill in utilizing cognitive therapy interventions, and the degree of functional impairment that he is currently experiencing as a consequence of depressive symptoms. Tasks should be as simple and clear as possible and written guidance provided wherever possible.

Using Audiotapes, Handouts, and Written Summaries

Clients often cite the concentration and memory deficits that characterize depression as reasons for not completing homework assignments. Beck et al. (1979), in their original treatment protocol for acute depression, recommended that therapists could routinely provide the client with an audiotape recording of the therapy session to listen to between sessions. This approach is highly recommended, as it enables the client to review the session's content and to clarify any aspects of the homework task that she cannot immediately recall or understand. Similarly, written summaries of in-session learning (Moore & Garland, 2003) and handouts that provide information and guidance on how to practice specific cognitive therapy skills (Fennell, 1990) improve clients' chances of completing homework assignments. In using written handouts, it is important to consider the client's preferred language, her reading ability, and the cultural relevance and/or general accessibility of the material. Ideally any written information needs to be brief and should use simple, straightforward language to convey the intended message. Materials that are illustrated with practical examples are of greatest utility.

Modeling the Skills Required for Task Completion Within Sessions

A commonly cited reason for not completing homework is that the client was unclear about how to complete a task—for example, a written record such as a diary sheet. The impact of this can be minimized by modeling the skills required for completion of the task, such as writing a diary sheet during the session. A useful rule of thumb is to try to ensure that the client has had an opportunity to practice the skills required to complete a homework task before applying the skills outside therapy. The client's engagement in this practice process varies. For example, Joanna and Angela were readily able to take responsibility in the sessions for completing diary sheets and making written summaries of their learning. However, this was much more difficult for Raymond, who experienced automatic thoughts about making a mistake and having this witnessed by the therapist. This negative thought was easily turned into an advantage, as the therapist used Raymond's automatic thought about practicing this skill as the vehicle for teaching him how to identify and modify automatic thoughts. Use of the therapy process actually afforded an opportunity to demonstrate the relevance of the agreed homework assignment designed to monitor the influence of automatic thoughts and emotions on his behavior in day-to-day situations.

Examples of Typical Homework Assignments

The standard cognitive therapy treatment protocol for depression readily suggests a range of homework assignments that are helpful in ameliorating depressive symptoms (Beck et al., 1979; Moore & Garland, 2003). These include activity scheduling and graded task assignment, identifying and modifying automatic thoughts and behavioral experiments, identifying and modifying conditional and unconditional beliefs using a variety of methods, including behavioral experiments, pie charts, positive data logs, surveys, and the like. The real skill in using cognitive therapy is how these standard interventions are used within an individual treatment plan that takes into account the idiosyncratic nature of each client's presentation and formulation of his or her problems. Thus, while it is often possible to identify a common thread of psychological themes that lead individuals to become vulnerable to depression (e.g., high standards, the need for approval, a sense of failure or worthlessness), the impact and consequences of these for each client are often very different. Taking an individualized approach to treatment is a central aspect of constructing meaningful homework assignments in cognitive therapy.

For example, Raymond and Joanna both held the conditional belief "If I can't do something properly, there is no point in doing it at all." However, how this manifests itself in behavioral terms and how this shaped their view of themselves was very different. As a consequence, different homework assignments needed to be developed in order to tackle the demand they placed on themselves to do things properly. For Raymond, who fundamentally saw himself as "insignificant" and a "failure," others as judgmental and rejecting, and the world as a hostile place, being able to do things properly was a measure of personal effectiveness (success) and acceptance from others. Raymond's chief coping strategy for ensuring that none of these perceptions were activated was avoidance. In the early stages of therapy, this was his general coping strategy for managing homework assignments. When it came to homework, Raymond often did not even attempt the negotiated task, as he became anxious that he would not be able to complete it to a high enough standard. However, as is often the case, his belief system kept him in a no-win position because noncompletion gave rise not only concerns that the therapist would reject him but to self-depreciating automatic thoughts, both of which gave rise to feelings of guilt and depression. Thus, in the early stages of treatment, when homework assignments aimed to help Raymond increase his overall activity levels, it quickly became apparent that asking Raymond to complete an activity schedule in a standard way (Beck et al. 1979) was going to be an overwhelming source of distress and needed to be modified in a way that enabled him to engage in treatment. As well as utilizing behavioral avoidance strategies, Raymond also used emotional and cognitive avoidance tactics in order to manage his mood. Thus, his avoidance of focusing on his thoughts and feelings meant that he was unable to explain to himself his reasons for not engaging in homework assignments, and this led him to be silent in session—an experience that accessed feelings of shame and humiliation. As a result Raymond and his therapist negotiated two goals for the focus of early treatment: (a) to help Raymond reengage in activities he had given up and (b) to develop a shared understanding of what was maintaining his avoidance.

As a result it was agreed that early homework assignments would focus on reengaging with some avoided activities. An example of this was woodwork. A whole session was devoted to drawing up a plan of reengaging with a small, half-completed project—namely, polishing a carving based on the principles of using graded task assignments (Fennell, 1990). Raymond knew exactly what he needed to do and did not feel the task was too difficult. His main stumbling block was his sense of pointlessness to the activity, his automatic thought being "So what, this won't change my life." Rather than entering into the task of trying to modify this thought, we agreed to treat it as an experiment, with the hypothesis, "Let's try this and see what happens." Given Raymond's tendency to leave the session and banish all thoughts of therapy from his mind, we agreed that he would try and complete the task as soon as he got home from the session. Raymond also had an audiotape of the session that he was asked to listen to prior to tackling the activity. Overall, it took three sessions before Raymond engaged in the task. The sessions where Raymond had experienced difficulty in completing the task were used to identify what processes were at work that interfered with homework completion. This enabled therapist and client to further develop the formulation outlined above. This approach was used repeatedly throughout treatment and it took many repetitions of testing out predictions and summaries of learning from activities in order to help him modify to some extent his view that doing anything was pointless. Work with Raymond was challenging because several of his beliefs were often active simultaneously. It was therefore necessary to carry out behavioral experiments to target not only his need to do things properly but also his sense that other ... ular ...

... day functioning.

... held the same belief, its function served a very different purpose for her. Namely, enabled her to maintain the high standards that, she believed, would enable her to elicit the approval and love that, to her, represented a measure of her worth. She was especially susceptible to perceived or actual criticism and experienced others as potentially critical and rejecting and the world as judgmental should she not maintain her high standards. As is illustrated by Joanna's conscientious approach to therapy, she was very successful at winning praise from others. However, as might be anticipated, this often became a source of stress to her, because once a particular standard had been set, at the very least she had to keep it and ideally had to improve on it. When standards are maintained in this way, it provides a potentially rich resource for behavioral experiments which, when planned with care, often yield profitable results. Indeed, Joanna accepted this idea readily, and early in therapy began carrying out behavioral experiments aimed at doing things less than properly. This included taking a graded approach to housework. Since becoming depressed, Joanna had experienced difficulty in completing her household chores within the demands of her rule about doing things properly. Thus, her ideal was to clean her home from top to bottom all in one day. Since becoming depressed, she had not had the resources to do this and so had largely given up on housework, a typical black-and-white position taken by depressed individuals. Joanna responded well to the idea of graded task assignment and appeared to lower her standards with little difficulty. Like Raymond, Joanna also used avoidant coping. However, her tactics were much more subtle, and she was very skilled at presenting what she anticipated the therapist wanted to hear and avoiding more challenging situations, where she had an opportunity to engage in behavioral experiments aimed at lowering her standards. Joanna had much more difficulty lowering her standards in situations where she felt she was overtly courting the disapproval of others. An example of this was her avoidance of inviting friends to her home for meals, something that prior to becoming depressed she had enjoyed. Exploration of this revealed that to invite friends over for a meal and do things properly meant, in her view, preparing three courses and making every dish from fresh ingredients. On the basis of this, behavioral experiments were devised that involved inviting friends to visit and ordering a take-out meal or providing preprepared food. These experiments involved much preparatory work both in session and as homework assignments, including identifying and modifying interfering automatic thoughts, developing a formulation of the origins of the belief and its relationship to her sense of worth, surveys to collect data on how others approached the task of providing food for visitors, and so on. Over time, after a series of behavioral experiments, Joanna began to collate evidence that not completing tasks following her own exacting standards did not result in the disapproval and rejection she anticipated.

In contrast to Raymond and Joanna, Angela readily accepted the cognitive therapy treatment rationale and quickly generalized its principles to tackle her problems. Early in treatment, Angela attended a session where she was very upset about a situation at work in which she saw herself as being treated unfairly. As a result, she had become very angry and had an argument with a colleague. During the session, the therapist worked with Angela to identify her automatic thoughts and relate these to the critical incident that had led to the onset of her depression. This was related to her place of work, where someone with less experience but who was related to the company's owner had been promoted above Angela. Aspects of Angela's upbringing echoed the same themes of unfairness. Helping Angela to make these connections enabled her to stand back from the situation at work. With minimal help from the therapist, Angela generated a behavioral experiment to test out her automatic thoughts by taking what she termed "a reality check" and not acting on her "first assumption" that she was being treated unfairly. This involved returning to work and talking through the situation with her colleague and trying to view the situation from a range of perspectives. This experiment proved so helpful to Angela that by the time she returned to the next session, she had carried out several behavioral experiments across a range of situations and had gained some valuable insight on the utility of "not acting on my first assumption." She quickly internalized this insight, and became useful in devising further behavioral experiments.

Client Reasons for Noncompletion of Homework

As discussed above, a homework assignment needs to be constructed in a way that maximizes the chances of completion and presents the individual with a "no lose" scenario. However, noncompletion is very common, and the therapist needs to develop a series of questions to identify in a nonjudgmental way the likely reasons (Padesky, 1993). From our clinical experience, some of the most common reasons for noncompletion of homework are as follows:

The client has not understood the homework. ... why they are to undertake a task, it is hardly surprising that they will be unlikely to complete it. It is essential to allocate sufficient therapy time to discuss the negotiated homework with the client, to explain the unique benefits to that individual in undertaking the task, to elicit any specific concerns the client may have regarding completion of the assignment, and to jointly anticipate any practical obstacles to its completion, ideally resolving such roadblocks before the task is attempted.

The client did not see the assignment as useful and relevant. This problem frequently arises when the therapist has prescribed the homework rather than negotiated it jointly with the client. Ideally, the therapist uses a questioning format (Padesky, 1993) with the client to identify and plan homework that is in line with the goals of therapy and forms part of the specific treatment plan for that individual. Ideally, the task should be so important to clinical progress that the client's investment in its completion matches or exceeds that of the therapist.

The client experienced a range of automatic thoughts that interfered with completion of the assignment. It is useful, from an early stage of therapy, to work with the client to identify and modify automatic negative thoughts that interfere with the completion of homework. It may be that these automatic thoughts are associated with the meaning the client attaches to the notion of "homework" or other negative thoughts associated with the fear of being judged. Clearly, these need to be considered and, where necessary, modified to enable the routine use of homework during the course of therapy.

What Is the Role of the Therapist in the Homework Process?

Some guiding principles on how to construct homework assignments are built into the cognitive therapy treatment rationale. However, there are some potential pitfalls to be avoided. First, homework assignments are an exercise in collaboration, so the therapist needs to avoid being prescriptive, as this would critically undermine the philosophy of working together (Padesky, 1993). However, skills central to gathering evidence that allows the goals of therapy to be achieved need to be introduced as early as possible. Thus, the therapist needs to be vigilant, so that the rationale for completing activity schedules and daily thought records can be introduced at the first reasonable opportunity. Second, it is recommended that the therapist avoid collecting and keeping clients' homework diary sheets (e.g., completed activity schedules, automatic thought diaries, positive data logs, and the like) in the case notes. This carries an implicit message of a pupil handing homework in to a teacher. For clients like Raymond and Joanna, this would reinforce unhelpful perceptions about themselves and how others view them. In keeping with the spirit of working as a team, the results of homework assignments are examined by the client and therapist together and then handed back to the client. The clients can then use these notes as a prompt and/or a template to enable them to undertake similar homework tasks in the future and to overcome similar problems during or after the course of therapy. However, it is important that the therapist not only record in the clients' case notes that homework has been completed but also note the outcome and any specific learning that has occurred as a result. It is also helpful for both therapist and client to make a written note of what new homework assignment has been agreed to, so that the homework review at the next session can be managed effectively with a shared responsibility for remembering the task and its purpose.

Cognitive therapists need to understand the rationale for the use of homework in order to overcome any frustration they may experience if a client does not complete assignments as agreed. It is easy, particularly for the novice therapist, to jump to a range of conclusions regarding the client on the basis of noncompletion of homework assignments. Examples of such automatic thoughts include the following: "The client is not committed to therapy," "The client is not psychologically minded," "The client isn't trying," "The client is resistant," "The client doesn't want to get better," "The client doesn't listen in session," or "The client is not suitable for therapy." When the therapist recognizes that she is experiencing these commonly occurring automatic thoughts, it is helpful to consider how her own beliefs and values may be influencing their expectations of the client and of the therapy. It is useful for the therapist to share any such concerns with her supervisor and explore her own negative automatic thoughts. There is emerging research data to support this method as a means for developing cognitive therapy skills (Bennett-Levy et al., 2003). In this way, therapists can clearly identify whether their own standards and value judgments are acting on the client's ability to engage with the homework. Such a review may reveal that the actual issue is the inelegant use of a specific technique, as when the therapist and client fail to agree on clear goals for a specific homework or do not negotiate the tasks in a collaborative and timely manner.

The novice therapist may have difficulty matching interventi

pace at which th

overload th

level of d

is con

clie

e

...........complete a mood and thought record or a diary

activities? This exercise often helps therapists learn at an experie   level the myriad of factors that influence completion of homework. The therapist quickly recognizes that procrastination and poor planning are not confined to individuals with depression. The reasons clients cite for noncompletion of homework (my child was unwell all week; I had a terrible time at work; unexpected visitors arrived the day I planned to do the task) also occur in the lives of therapists. It is a salutary lesson that even the most highly motivated individual with a considerable knowledge of cognitive therapy and an absolute commitment to the rationale for engaging in homework can be diverted from achieving his own goals despite good intentions! Thus, rather than acting on the first negative automatic thought about the client and her commitment to change, it is more productive to develop a position of compassion with the client and a shared curiosity about the barriers to homework completion. This, combined with effective problem solving, may be a more helpful approach to tackling a lack of concordance.

Conclusion

Homework plays a central role as a mechanism of change in cognitive therapy. There is some evidence from outcome trials that clients who complete homework assignments make a better or faster recovery from their depressive illness than clients who do not complete homework (Hollon, Shelton, & Davies, 1993; Kazantzis et al., 2000; Persons, Burns & Peloff, 1988). It is also thought that homework is an effective way of generalizing learning from the therapy session into the client's everyday life. Furthermore, if the client undertakes a homework exercise in a problematic situation, this appears to promote learning at an experiential level. This level of learning is more closely associated with effective emotional processing, which indicates a change in perspective at both a cognitive and emotional level. When this type of learning takes place, problematic behaviors are more likely to recede. Homework also enables clients to develop specific skills to tackle their problems, such as identifying and testing out automatic thoughts. Thus, inherently, cognitive therapy is a self-help model. In this respect homework assignments provide the testing ground for the independent practice of skill outside of the therapy session. This is more likely to increase clients' belief that they themselves can solve problems rather than relying on the therapist to do this for them. Acquiring this sense of self-efficacy is crucial if gains from treatment are to be maintained once contracted sessions are completed.

References

Beck, A. (1967). *Depression: Clinical, experimental and theoretical aspects.* New York: Harper & Row.

Beck, A., Rush, A., Shaw, B., & Emery, G. (1979). *Cognitive therapy of depression.* New York: Guilford Press.

Beck, A. T., Ward, C.H., Mendelson, M., & Erbaugh, J. K. (1961). An inventory for measuring depression. *Archives of General Psychiatry, 4,* 561–571.

Bennett-Levy, J., Lee, N., Travers, K., Pohlman, S., & Hamernik, E. (2003). Cognitive therapy from the inside: Enhancing therapist skills through practicing what we preach. *Behavioral and Cognitive Psychotherapy, 31,* 143–158.

Burns, D., & Spangler, D. L. (2000). Does psychotherapy homework lead to improvement in depression in cognitive-behavioral therapy or does improvement lead to increased homework compliance? *Journal of Consulting and Clinical Psychology, 68,* 46–56.

Cox, D. J., Tisdelle, D. A., & Culbert, J. P. (1988). Increasing adherence to behavioral homework assignments. *Journal of Behavioral Medicine, 11,* 519–522.

Detweiler, J. B., & Wishman, M. A. (1999). The role of homework assignments in cognitive therapy for depression: Potential methods for enhancing adherence. *Clinical Psychology: Science and Practice, 6,* 267–282.

Fennell, M. J. V. (1990). Depression. In K. Hawton, P. M. Salkovskis, J. Kirk, & D. M. Clark (Eds.), *Cognitive Behavior Therapy for Psychiatric Problems: A Practical Guide.* Oxford, UK: Oxford Medical Publications.

Garland, A., Harrington, J., House, R., & Scott, J. (2000). A pilot study of the relationship between problem-solving and outcome in major depressive disorders. *British Journal of Medical Psychology, 73,* 303–309.

Hollon, S., Shelton, R., & Davies, D. (1993). Cognitive therapy for depression: conceptual issues and clinical efficacy. *Journal of Consulting and Clinical Psychology, 61,* 270–275.

Kazantzis, N., Deane, F. P., & Ronan, K. R. (2000). Homework assignments in cognitive and behavioral therapy: A meta-analysis. *Clinical Psychology: Science and Practice, 2,* 189–202.

Moore, R., & Garland, A. (2003). *Cognitive therapy for chronic and persistent depression.* Chichester, UK: Wiley.

Padesky, C. A. (1993). Socratic questioning: Changing minds or guided discovery? Keynote Address given at the European Congress of Behavioral and Cognitive Psychotherapies, London.

Paykel, E. S., Scott, J., Teasdale, J. D., Johnson, A. L., Garland, A., Moore, R., Jenaway, A., Cornwall, P. L., Hayhurst, H., Abott, R., & Pope, M. (1999). Prevention of relapse in residual depression by cognitive therapy, *Archives of General Psychiatry, 56,* 829–835.

Persons, J., Burns, D., & Perloff, J. M. (1988). Predictors of drop out and outcome in cognitive therapy for depression in a private practice setting. *Cognitive Therapy and Research, 12,* 557–575.

Scott, J. (1996). Review: Cognitive therapy and affective disorders. *Journal of Affective Disorder, 1,* 1–11.

Scott, J. (2000). New evidence in the treatment of chronic depression. *New England Journal of Medicine, 342,* 1518–1520.

Scott, J., House, R., Harrington, J., & Ferrier, N. I. (1996). A preliminary study of the relationship between personality, cognitive vulnerability, symptom profile and outcome in major depressive disorder. *Journal of Nervous and Mental Diseases, 18,* 503–505.

Williams, J. M. G., Fraser, N. F., MacLeod, C., & Mathews, A. (1997). *Cognitive psychology and emotional disorders.* New York: Wiley.

CHAPTER 13

Substance Abuse

LISA M. NAJAVITS

What saves a man is to take a step. Then another step.
It is always the same step, but he has to take it.
Antoine de Saint-Exupery (1900–1944)

The nature of substance use disorders (SUD) is lack of control, impulsivity, deterioration, and disorganization. Homework in therapy is the opposite: carefully planned, paced, and building strength. Cognitive behavioral therapy (CBT), uniquely among psychotherapies, created the innovation of homework as a way to improve patients' progress. Homework has been a mainstay of CBT since its early history in the 1970s (Beck, 1979). Its application to SUD began primarily in the 1990s with a variety of manual-based treatments that have undergone empirical testing over the past decade (Najavits, Liese, & Harned, in press).

In this Chapter, a variety of SUD therapies will be used to illustrate how homework in CBT can increase the power of the treatment. Four sections are provided: common barriers, types of homework, strategies for effective homework, and case examples. SUD here refers to both substance abuse and dependence, milder and more severe forms of the disorder, respectively (American Psychiatric Association, 1994).

Common Barriers to Homework Assignments

SUD patients are widely viewed as hard to treat (Najavits & Weiss, 1994). In addition to substance problems, co-occurring psychiatric disorders are the norm rather than the exception (Kessler et al., 1997; Regier et al., 1990). A variety of life problems may be directly caused by SUD or strongly associated with its lifestyle, including poverty, homelessness, medical conditions such as AIDS and cirrhosis, domestic violence, legal problems (e.g., drug-dealing charges), parenting problems, poor self-esteem, accidents, trauma, and long-standing family histories of addiction and mental illness. Indeed, part of the definition of SUD is that the addicted person continues to use a substance despite the significant harm it is causing in multiple life areas (American Psychiatric Association, 1994). Such areas are commonly identified as legal, family/social, psychological, medical, employment, and financial (McLellan et al., 1992; Miller, Zweben, DiClemente, & Rychtarik, 1995).

In therapy, the SUD patient may present numerous challenges that affect homework compliance as well as the entire treatment experience. The disorder often involves lying, denial, or minimization of substance use, notoriously high dropout rates, unstable alliances with treaters (ranging from distrust to excessive dependency), and intense transference (such as power struggles, anger, passivity, and entitlement) (Imhof, 1991; Miller et al., 1995). Homework may become a pivotal domain in which such difficult treatment dynamics play out. Homework may be misinterpreted by patients as an attempt to overcontrol their lives, may evoke shameful feelings of personal weakness or failure when assignments cannot be completed, or may simply be refused by patients with low motivation. Some patients may genuinely want to complete homework but repeatedly forget or are often too inebriated or disorganized to remember. The "split self" is also common in substance use, marked by ambivalence or dissociated sides of the self (Najavits, 2002). As patients describe it, their state of mind in the session is committed to recovery. However, after leaving the session, a different state of mind may take over and they relapse, as if a different self were now present. Therapists too may have strong feelings when patients do not complete homework, knowing that SUD can be a life-or-death issue and feeling helpless when patients keep using substances or are unable to take essential action to move forward in life, as by getting a job or leaving a partner who is abusive.

Types of Homework

The range of CBT homework for SUD is as varied as the numerous treatments available. Some examples from empirically supported therapies are provided in Table 13.1, with emphasis on assignments that directly relate to substance use. In addition, homework may include other standard CBT assignments not solely related to substance use, such as mood monitoring or behavioral activation (Beck, 1979).

Strategies for Effective Homework

In this section, key strategies for effective homework in CBT for SUD are explored. Many strategies are effective for CBT in general, while others might be relied on more heavily for SUD treatment (e.g., case management, involvement of family members).

Provide Good Reasons

A strong rationale can help motivate patients to complete homework. Typical reasons might include the following: homework can help you progress faster; it can help you resist substances; it can build psychological strength, just as working out builds muscles; it can help you learn about yourself; it can improve your ability to cope. Also, the specific homework assignment should have a rationale (e.g., mood monitoring can clarify whether certain feelings are triggering your substance use). The homework should involve some benefit to the patient and not be assigned simply because the therapist wants the patient to do homework.

Focus on Urgent Problems

Often in SUD treatment, both the patient and therapist may be overwhelmed by the many tasks in front of them. Help patients learn to prioritize the most urgent issues first. Usually this will be the substance use itself (a commitment to eliminating or decreasing use), but it may also include other self-destructive behavior (e.g., not showing up for work). Maslow's (1970) famous hierarchy provides the useful principle that physical survival needs should be addressed prior to more psychological needs. Case management, which involves referring patients to necessary services such as sober housing, job counseling, and child care, may be unfamiliar or unappealing to the clinician who prefers higher-level insight work. Also, the task should be appropriate to the patient. One therapist, for example, insensitively suggested that a SUD patient engage a personal trainer for exercise when in fact the patient was impoverished, had SUD, and had many more serious and immediate needs.

Believe in the Importance of Homework

As Carroll observes, "patients who do homework tend to have therapists who value homework, spend a lot of time talking about homework, and expect their patients to actually do the homework" (1998, p. 23). If the therapist is half-hearted or unconvinced about the need for homework, patients are likely to perceive this. In Najavits (2002), therapists are encouraged to try the treatment's coping skills in their own lives so as to be better able to persuade patients to use them.

Call It Something Other Than "Homework"

Many SUD patients did not do well in school and therefore the term *homework* evokes negative associations. Also, homework implies a power dynamic in which patients are completing it for the therapist rather than for themselves. Other terms include *practice exercise* (Kadden et al., 1995) and *commitment* (Najavits, 2002).

Create Success Experiences

The best homework is that which patients are able to accomplish. Selecting homework is a balancing act between an assignment that is difficult enough to provide growth and measurable change yet not so difficult that the patient cannot do it. Choose tasks that are realistic and make sure the patient "buys into" them. Concepts such as "do something, anything" and "a good plan today is better than a perfect one tomorrow" can guide the choice. For example, the patient early in treatment can be advised to do a task for just 10 minutes and gradually build up to longer time periods (e.g., cleaning the house or making essential phone calls). Sometimes the therapist may need to counsel the patient not to take on too much. Usually one task per session is standard.

Consider Providing Choices

Some CBT therapies for SUD require one particular homework assignment based on the session topic (e.g., Carroll, 1998; Kadden et al., 1995). Others provide a menu of options from which patients can choose, or they can make up their own (e.g., Najavits, 2002). Similarly, in some CBT therapies, homework is always written while others offer nonwritten options as well (e.g., "Try calling a hotline once this week"). Creativity also helps, as SUD patients may become bored easily. See Table 13.1 and Case Study 1 below for a range of assignments.

Write it Down, With a Copy for Both Patient and Therapist

Keep track of patient assignments. This may seem basic, but many therapists do not (the "Do as I say and not as I do" approach). Unless therapists model accountable behavior, their patients are unlikely to take homework seriously. One simple suggestion is to routinely take a piece of paper at the end of the session, tear it in half, and write the homework on both halves,

TABLE 13.1 Examples of Homework in CBT for SUD

Record episodes of substance cravings, and how you handled them.

Write out the pros and cons of using substances.

Rehearse refusing substances, practicing in front of a mirror, with a partner, or in writing.

Find role models (e.g., ask people who have attained abstinence how they did it).

Fill out a work sheet, such as on problem-solving, coping with crises, cognitive restructuring, self-monitoring of substance use and cravings, reducing HIV risk, pursuing job leads, or functional analysis of behavior (i.e., the relation between events and associated thoughts, feelings, and behavior).

Complete case-management tasks, such as attending Alcoholics Anonymous or a doctor's appointment.

Read a self-help book about substance abuse, information sheets, or other therapy-relevant material.

Take medication (e.g., disulfiram to promote abstinence from alcohol).

Have your partner praise abstinent behavior once per day.

Obtain an HIV test.

Note. Examples of homework assignments are drawn from Beck, Wright, Newman, & Liese (1993); Carroll (1998); Galanter (1993); Kadden et al. (1995); Marlatt & Gordon (1985); Miller et al. (1995); Najavits (2002); O'Farrell & Cutter (1984).

giving one to the patient and retaining the other. Another suggestion is to use a carbon-copy paper pad, so that the therapist can keep a copy of the assigned homework activity (Shelton & Ackerman, 1974). Indeed, there is some empirical support for the utility of providing a written copy of the homework assignment for patients (Cox, Tisdelle, & Culbert, 1988).

Create Meaning

While homework is typically quite concrete, even mundane, its meanings are much richer. One can help inspire patients to complete homework if such higher-order meanings are discussed. For example, the task might be to schedule a dental appointment, but the higher meaning may be is that one is taking care of one's body, showing respect for one's future, or learning how to face fear. Also, it is notable that SUD is the only disorder in which spirituality is openly advised as a method of recovery (e.g., Alcoholics Anonymous). For patients who reject spirituality, this needs to be respected, but for those who ally with it, this too can provide higher-level meanings that reinforce homework (e.g., "How this task, fit into the work you're doing on developing your higher power?").

Identify Obstacles

Help patients notice what gets in the way of completing homework. This might occur before they attempt it, such as while establishing the assignment, or may occur if they show up to the next session having failed to complete it. Solutions can include using a tape recorder if the patient resists written assignments (Carroll, 1998), identifying exactly where to keep the homework list so as not forget it (e.g., "Put it in your wallet next to your money, on your car dashboard, or refrigerator"), or completing the homework just after the session so it will always occur at the same time. A "walk-through" for some assignments can also be useful (Najavits, 2002). For example, if the patient agrees to see a doctor to obtain psychiatric medication, the therapist might ask the patient questions to make sure it will actually happen: "Do you have the name of a doctor? Do you have transportation to get there? Do you have insurance or money to pay for it? Do you have any concerns about the appointment? Do you have child care (if needed)?" Role plays may also be useful.

Teach Patients How to Respond to Feelings

Many SUD patients live by emotions. Substances are used to create positive feelings (e.g., a high) or to escape negative feelings (e.g., depression). Also, SUD patients may have grown up in families where they did not learn basic behavioral principles, such as following through on commitments. They may say, "I meant to do the homework when I left your office last week, but then I just didn't feel like it later." The patient may need instruction in how to notice their feelings but complete the task anyway. A humorous quotation can be helpful, such as that of Strauss (2002): "It's a little like wrestling a gorilla. You don't quit when you're tired, you quit when the gorilla is tired." That is, keep going until the task is done.

Involve People in the Patient's Life

SUD impacts a network of people in addition to patients themselves. Involving key people in the network is a way to strengthen treatment goals. One SUD therapy titled "network therapy" (Galanter, 1993) focuses primarily on this principle. In other SUD therapies, involving significant people is part of the treatment (Carroll, 1998; Kadden et al., 1995; Najavits, 2002; O'Farrell & Cutter, 1984). Select people who are not currently abusing substances and who are willing to help support the patient. This may include a partner, other family, friends, or even an AA sponsor. Sometimes there is just one person, other times there are several people. Their role may include helping to monitor substance use, providing praise when the patient is abstinent, contacting others in the patient's social or treatment network during crises, providing physical help such as transportation, or following through on previously agreed contingencies. For example, this could include engaging in a positive activity together if the patient has remained abstinent from substances that week. Such tasks are a form of homework in that they occur outside of sessions as part of the treatment. Typically, the people involved are invited into at least one session to choose and discuss the assignment. However, some SUD patients may have no one to bring in. Thus the therapy and related homework would focus on how to engage in new relationships.

Provide Reinforcement

Reviewing the patient's homework at the next therapy session is a key method of reinforcement, providing direct praise from the therapist as well as attention to the patient's experiences. In some SUD therapies, only such verbal and social reinforcement is used (Kadden et al., 1995). In other SUD treatments (Anker & Crowley, 1982; Higgins et al., 1994), formal positive and negative contingencies are a central component of the treatment. For example, vouchers for gifts are used in the therapy by Higgins et al. (1994) to reward patients for "clean" urinalyses verifying that the patient remained abstinent from substances. A progression of increasingly higher dollar amounts can be used to make the system even more reinforcing over time. An example of negative reinforcement is the contingency contracting method of Anker and Crowley (1982). For example, one might send a letter to the patient's employer reporting substance use (if this was previously established as the agreed-on contingency). In all of these examples, the homework is staying abstinent from substances, although other homework may also be used.

Use Technology

Technology can support the homework process. Asking the patient to "check in" via voice mail or e-mail about the homework can help the patient stay motivated to complete it.[1] Other uses of technology include having the patient complete CBT modules designed for computer-based homework or having the patient search the Internet for information related to SUD or CBT.

---

[1]One must inform the patient ahead of time, however, that such communications are one-way only; that is, the therapist will not respond unless otherwise agreed. Also such communications should be separated from actual emergency communication in a clear fashion so that the patient knows how to obtain a response from the therapist if that is part of their working arrangement, such as by pager or after-hours coverage.

Explore Countertransference

The therapist may have a variety of countertransference responses to homework. It is important to honestly "own" these and find ways to manage them or use them as part of the treatment. For example, the therapist may believe the patient cannot really improve and thus does not encourage homework enough ("This patient has relapsed so often that it feels hopeless"). Or, the therapist may dislike conflict and repeatedly fail to hold the patient accountable for the homework, ignoring the fact that the patient keeps forgetting to do it. Or the therapist may assign too much homework, exceeding the patient's capacity to complete it, perhaps due to the therapist's frustration with slow progress. It can be useful to understand countertransference as representing both the therapist's own unresolved emotional issues as well as an enactment of the patient's pathology that can inform the therapy. An example of the latter is when the patient's disavowed emotions, such as hopelessness, get expressed by the therapist more than the patient.

Be a Role Model by Completing "Homework" Yourself

At times the therapist may need to complete specific tasks between sessions, such as locating a case-management referral, calling another treater on behalf of the patient, or copying therapy-related materials. Following through provides important role modeling (similar to the point made earlier in this section about the need to remember what the patient's homework is). In one interesting study (McLellan, Woody, Luborsky, & Goehl, 1988), SUD clinicians who appeared the most organized and thorough in their professional record keeping, enforcement of clinic rules, and use of treatment resources were found to have the best outcomes with opiate-dependent patients.

Take Into Account Stages of Change

A major breakthrough in the treatment of SUD has been the recognition that patients may be at different levels of motivation. One widely used model hypothesizes five stages of change (Prochaska, DiClemente, & Norcross, 1992): precontemplation (the patient continues to use substances, denying it is a problem), contemplation (the patient continues to use but admits it is a problem), preparation (the patient is still using but is willing to make a plan in the near future to stop), action (the patient is willing to engage in treatment to stop using), and maintenance (the patient has achieved at least 6 months of abstinence from substance use). Homework for SUD patients can also be understood within this framework. Early in treatment, some patients are unwilling to do homework. It may be more helpful to accept this fact than to struggle with it. Homework can gradually be reintroduced later. Similarly, many patients initially do not feel motivated to work toward their own recovery but are in treatment only because of some external pressure (e.g., being mandated by a court, fear of job loss) or other influence (e.g., doing it for their children or spouse). Here too, accepting such external motivations, rather than expecting or requiring internal motivation, is more likely to succeed. Thus, homework can be tied to how it will help the patient with such external goals. For example, "If you went to Alcoholics Anonymous, how might that help you to keep your job?"

Explore Resistance From a Schema Perspective

If a patient repeatedly agrees to homework but fails to complete it, the usual steps are to help deal with whatever is getting in the way and to create more realistic assignments. However, if such efforts still do not work, the therapist needs to move to explore underlying schemas (which may be unconscious for the patient). Homework schemas might include beliefs such as "I shouldn't have to work in therapy," or "I don't really believe in therapy"; or they may be associated with Axis II disorders (Young, 1999). A collaborative exploration with the patient may be useful: e.g., "I can keep suggesting homework, but I notice you keep losing the paper each week—what do you think might be going on?"

Case Studies

In this section, two cases are provided to help elucidate the principles described above. In the first, the emphasis is on the range of homework within treatment of one long-term patient; in the second, actual dialogue is provided on a single homework assignment session.

Case Study 1: Homework in a Long-Term CBT Therapy

Jim is a 42-year-old with a long-standing history of both posttraumatic stress disorder (PTSD) and multiple substance dependencies (cocaine, marijuana, and alcohol). His PTSD originated in childhood physical and sexual abuse by his mother and an uncle, and later included being assaulted in violent incidents when buying drugs in dangerous neighborhoods. He works as a production assistant for a local film company, though he wants to return to school to obtain a degree in medical technology. He lives alone and only recently began establishing friendships, though he has a history of multiple romantic relationships that have lasted from a few months to a year. He has been in numerous treatments since a first serious suicide attempt at age 15 (followed by eight other attempts over the next 20 years). He has been in his current individual CBT therapy for 3 years, which began during an inpatient stay after a suicide attempt and then continued in weekly outpatient therapy. He attends therapy regularly except during substance relapses, when he sometimes disappears for up to a month at a time. During the past 3 years, he had four detoxification inpatient admissions, two day-treatment episodes, and intermittent attendance at AA and outpatient group therapy. He is on a variety of psychiatric medications. His treatment is funded by public assistance programs.

Homework in the CBT therapy has appeared to be helpful for Jim. He was willing to engage in it from the start of the therapy and felt that the therapist's focus on homework showed that she cared about his progress. They would write down the assignments and review them at each session. They established a rule that if he could not complete one, he would leave her a voice mail in advance of the session to let her know he had not done it (thus demonstrating that he remembered it, even if he could not always accomplish it). Developmentally, he was quite young and appeared to want to please the therapist, with homework being one demonstration of this. She praised his homework efforts, and they worked collaboratively to create the assignments. After the first year of therapy, his homework compliance began to diminish, but the therapist's persistence and hopefulness about his ability to keep doing it seemed to serve an important function during this phase of the work. The patient was aware of viewing the therapist as a parent ("the type of parent I wish I had growing up"), and her ability to work with him to resolve his homework problems rather than giving up or blaming him was a new experience for him. Sometimes he would ask the therapist how she herself accomplished tasks, and she shared some of her strategies (in a limited way that was not revealing of details of her life). The therapy was the longest one he had ever remained in.

The types of homework assignments they developed varied greatly. Case management was the focus early on and after periods of relapse. They took the approach that as long as he was willing to try additional treatments, he could later choose whether to continue them; this eased his fear of being forced to attend treatments he did not like. As part of some of his prior treatment experiences, he was required, for example, to stay with therapists he did not like or to attend AA even when he felt he was getting nothing out of it. Other homework focused on daily life tasks that he found overwhelming at times, such as eating a healthy diet, getting enough sleep, taking care of his apartment, and applying for a job (when needed). Therapy-related homework included doing a "trial run" of paging the therapist to rehearse how they might talk in case of emergency, in case he became suicidal again. He also agreed to tasks such as reading self-help books, filling out therapy-related work sheets (see, for example, Figure 13.1), and trying to experience real-life examples of what was being addressed in the therapy (e.g., "Try being honest with your girlfriend about your substance use" or "Try speaking up at an AA meeting"). To prevent substance relapse, he was willing to make efforts such as throwing away his dealer's phone number, rearranging his finances so that he would have limited access to cash (which was a trigger for drugs), and writing out a dialogue of how he could say "no" to offers of substances. For a while, he developed an Internet addiction, particularly to games, but was willing to cancel his Internet account to stop this. Other miscellaneous assignments included going to a public library to learn how to search for career-planning information, writing a list of coping skills, taking up a hobby to use as distraction when he became anxious or depressed (e.g., working on car repair), writing a dialogue to respond to his frequent negative views of himself (e.g., "I'm a bad person..."), and reading information about PTSD.

Example of an Action Plan

B E F O R E	**I promise to ...** Throw out my marijuana and rolling paper. I am promising this to myself, to my therapist, and to my sponsor.
	By when? 8:00 tonight.
	I will use the following strategies to accomplish my commitment: Call my sponsor and write myself a "letter" about why I need to do this.
	To overcome my emotional blocks, I will ... Talk to my therapist and focus on the good that can come of this.
	It is important for me to complete this commitment because ... My future depends on it; my health will improve; I'll honor my word.
	If I complete it, I will reward myself with ... A safe "treat" (a new video, book, CD, or go out to dinner).
	Signed:
A F T E R	*Result: Describe how it went.* I hated doing it, but I did it. I miss the marijuana, but I feel stronger. I bought myself a nice dinner afterward.
	Anything you'll do differently next time? No, it went okay.

Fig. 13.1 Example of a homework sheet in CBT for SUD. Reprinted with permission from Najavits (2002).

Homework for Jim was not always easy, nor was it always a simple part of the therapy. At times when Jim would not do assignments, the therapist became worried that she was doing something wrong. They sought to read such episodes at a deeper level and sometimes they explored his anger at her absences (e.g., during vacations) or his own hopelessness after struggling so long with substances and PTSD. Sometimes they erred in creating assignments that were too difficult, which had the unwanted effect of increasing his depressive and anxious symptoms. At other times, he was unwilling to agree to tasks that the therapist thought might truly benefit him, such as attending AA more regularly. Nonetheless, throughout the therapy, the overall result of the homework was a sense of increased self-confidence for Jim and a variety of lessons from which he benefited. In addition to gaining from the tasks themselves, he learned that he was able to be more consistently responsible than earlier in his life (and in contrast to members of his family, who had repeatedly broken promises to him). He also learned that progress required a multitude of tasks and that he needed to keep making the effort—as in the well-known saying that "recovery is a process, not an event."

Although Jim may continue to need therapy for a while to come, particularly in light of his difficulty sustaining abstinence at times, he has made significant gains since starting. These gains include his longest periods of abstinence, his ability to work at a job (where previously he had been fired or quit after a few months), his willingness to attend therapy, a substantial reduction in PTSD symptoms and suicidal impulses, and his greater use of coping skills. As he says, "I used to think life was supposed to be easy. I see now that it's much harder. I have to keep making efforts over and over. It's like a road where I'm paving each step of the way with my own hands. But I also have more hope now and see myself as someone who can live a decent life. That's a long way from where I was."

Case Study 2: Example of Dialogue From Session

Anita is a 50-year-old waitress who abused alcohol for 10 years, but she has now been sober for 2 years. However, her quality of life remains very poor, as she focuses only on trying to help her 27-year-old son, Jackson, who has had severe polysubstance drug dependency since adolescence. He has been admitted to over 20 treatment programs of all types all over the country (e.g., inpatient, day programs, residential, outpatient) but lasts only a few months before being caught using. Anita's partner of 15 years recently moved out, saying that Anita was unable to forge any life other than constantly attending to the crises with Jackson. Her partner also complained that their house was always a mess, with enormous clutter and lack of maintenance, and that Anita seemed unable to follow through on her repeated plans to fix these problems. He was unwilling to attend couples therapy. She has no friends and no leisure activities.

Anita sought out a therapist 6 months earlier to obtain consultation on how to help her son. The therapist engaged her in trying to focus on building her own life in addition to continually helping him and referred her to Al-Anon meetings (designed for family members of alcoholics). She was also referred to a psychiatrist and began antidepressant medication. Anita attends therapy every 2 weeks (she chose this because of her schedule). Both Anita and her son have attention deficit hyperactivity disorder (ADHD), and she has great difficulty getting anything done. For years she has wanted to leave her job but cannot seem to organize herself to do so. She has many regrets and sadness over how she has lived her life, including blaming herself for her son's problems and wishing she had had more than one child. Her style in sessions is anxious, with repeated ruminations about how to find yet another program for Jackson. The therapist gives her these issues and provides referrals treatment for him. However, she tries to steer Anita to also focus her own life as well (which she largely resists). Many people, including the therapist, have advised her to detach more from her son as a way to help both of them, with the idea that he will not progress until she stops rescuing him from the consequences of his addiction. But she worries that he will overdose and she will forever blame herself for his death. Attempts by the therapist to have her face deeper-level sadness over these various issues do not go far, as she is unable to stay with such feelings and instead returns to anxious rumination.

At this point, the therapist has decided to take a largely behavioral approach to helping Anita with some basic tasks. However, homework in the therapy thus far has been difficult. Anita agrees to assignments but usually shows up without having done them. The therapist is tries to work with her on a very concrete level to help her become more organized and to have some small success experiences. The dialogue below illustrates the therapist's attempt to engage Anita in homework. This part of the dialogue is about 20 minutes into their 50-minute session, as the therapist wants to allow a lot of time to focus on the task. The prior 20 minutes were spent listening to Anita's updates and giving her time to talk about some issues that were important to her. At this point, the therapist feels she has enough material to delve into some homework preparation. Unlike other patients, who sometimes need just a few minutes at the end of the session to establish homework, Anita needs a lot of time, as her difficulty in accomplishing tasks outside of sessions goes to the heart of her most fundamental problems. The therapist's thoughts are given in italics.

Anita: My house is a mess and I can't find anything. I'm worried about paying bills that are overdue. My partner left me because I kept promising to get my life together. I was never able to follow through. Also, I can't invite people over because of this.

Therapist: I can hear how damaging it's been not to be able to follow through on things. Could we take one specific thing to work on and see if we can make headway on that? If so, what would it be?

[Up until now in the session, I've been listening for a mention of something that would make a good homework assignment. When she talks about the house being a mess, I think this might be good area, but I must be sure to find out if this is something she wants to address; that is, the focus shouldn't just come from me.]

Anita: I guess getting my papers organized. They're in different boxes all over, and I can't get to anything. Every time I try to, I pick up a piece of paper and get caught up with that, and an hour goes by and I still have all those boxes.

Therapist: Do you have any system for your papers, like files, to-do lists, and such?

[I need more detail to intervene effectively. Often homework and other interventions fail because therapists make assumptions based on their prior experience rather than on directly hearing the details from the patient.]

Anita: Yes, I have many different systems, but that's the problem. I never stick to one system, and nothing gets done, and I can't remember what the system is, so I start new ones too often.

Therapist: Would you be willing to work with me on coming up with one system, and agreeing to just stick to it as part of our therapy? That would mean you wouldn't change the system without talking with me first.

[I'm trying to get some basic foundation of work going for this problem. Most patients would not need this level of detail, but she does. I want to set it up as success experience, so I make sure to arrange that she and I will work together on it, as she hasn't been able to solve it on

her own thus far. And, again, I ask for her collaboration
and permission at each step.]

Anita: Yes, I can do that.

Therapist: Okay, well it sounds like the goal is just getting some
of the papers organized. What do you think would be
the first step?
[I'm most likely to succeed if we start with where she's
at. Also, my question conveys that I believe she can
come up with ways to solve problems.]

Anita: Getting them out of boxes. I can't find anything and I
can't get to my file cabinets because the boxes are in
front of them.

Therapist: Good. Could we just plan on one step this week—just
getting the boxes unloaded without organizing the
papers? You would just take the papers out and put
them in the available file cabinets. Later we can work
on getting them sorted.
[I'm trying to break the task down into very small
steps.]

Anita: I don't have enough file cabinets.

Therapist: Okay. Can you buy some more file cabinets, or some
large bins from the store that can be stacked, and use
those too?
[I'm helping her brainstorm some solutions.]

Anita: Yes, that sounds good, and that will look better than
the boxes. I can stack the bins against a wall.

Therapist: Excellent. Can you write that down on your list?
[Every time we come up with some decision or task, I
have her write it down to help build this as a habit.]

Anita: Sure.

Therapist: What section would it go in?
[She still needs help keeping track of assignments, par-
ticularly given her ADHD. I'm watching for nonverbal
cues to make sure she doesn't feel patronized by this
level of detail, but she seems fine with it and engaged in
the process.]

Anita: I guess under the section in my notebook "Do immediately."

Therapist: Nice plan. And how will you remember to look at
your list?

[I use praise a lot as she seems to be very responsive to it. I also keep getting her to concretize the task.]

Anita: I don't know.

Therapist: Could you buy the bins on the way home from our session today and call me once you get home, to let me know you did it?

[My key goal at this point is just getting her to follow through. She's more likely to remember if she does the task sooner rather than later. Also, I ask her to leave me a voice mail to let me know she did it, as a form of reinforcement.]

Anita: Okay, then at least it would really happen.

Therapist: Exactly. And, what do you notice about this process of how we're working on solving this problem of getting your papers organized?

[I'm guiding her to notice not just the concrete task but also the larger process, to build generalization of the behavior. I want to help her see what it takes to make something happen. I start with her impressions first to find out what she's actually understanding.]

Anita: Well, it's very step-by-step. And I feel better about it because we're working on it together. I don't feel so alone with it.

Therapist: I'm very glad to hear that, and happy to keep working on it with you over time until we get it fully solved.

[She conveyed that social support in our therapy relationship is important to her, so I reinforce that in a positive way, as well as trying to build in an expectation of success.]

Anita: That sounds good.

Therapist: Also, how do you think it'll feel if we truly make this happen? If you picture yourself at home, and your papers are organized, and you can invite people over?

Anita: That would feel really good.

Therapist: Do you think also it might help your son in some way if he could see you succeed at getting the house together?

[I want to build higher-order meaning from the task. I take something she cares about most, which in this case is her son. She does not yet tend to build in these higher-order meanings, so I try to suggest one.]

Anita: Yeah, I guess all through his growing up I wanted to be better about getting my life organized because he has ADHD too and we both were just chaotic, and not able to get things done.

Therapist: So even though you can't redo the past, you can still show him now that people can change, that you can do this now?

[Often it's helpful to pull in something about the past, especially for patients with her level of profound and long-standing life problems. Even though our work is present-focused, she has had decades of difficulty with these issues, and I need to try to help her make peace with the past, learn from it, and move beyond it.]

Anita: That would be positive. It won't take away my guilt about how I failed him as a parent, but it would be something, I guess.

Therapist: Could you write that down too in your notebook, so you'll remember that accomplishing this task has higher-level meanings too? How might you word it?

[I make a mental note that at some point that we'll need to come back to the issue of guilt about her son, but I don't want to go to that now as it would take us away from finishing this task.]

Anita: I can write "Getting my papers organized will help Jackson, because he can see that it's never too late to get one's life together."

Therapist: Good! Anything else that we should discuss at this point before we end?

Anita: No, I think I'm set for now.

Therapist: Excellent. Can you just review with me what you're going to do before we meet next?

[I always take a few moments at the end of the session for her to review the homework, to make sure we're in agreement.]

Anita: I'm going to get my papers organized.

Therapist: Can you pull out the notebook you've been writing in, and read it to me from that? I just want to make sure you have all the elements we discussed.

[I try to reinforce her for using the list. She needs this to become a habit, and it isn't yet. I phrase it in a way that gives her control by asking it as a question.]

Anita: Okay. It says, "Get bins on way home now, and call you once I get home to say I did it." Then put all my papers into there. I don't have to organize them yet, just get them out of the middle of the room. Also it says, "Getting my papers organized will help Jackson, because he can see that it's never too late to get one's life together."

Therapist: That's it; you've got it! How likely do you think you are to accomplish this task?
[I ask her to predict as a way to help her learn over time how her predictions compare with the reality, a cognitive strategy.]

Anita: Maybe 70%. I want to and I know it's here in my notebook, but I also know things derail me sometimes.

Therapist: I understand. Well, hopefully it really will happen. I'd be delighted to hear that you did it.
[Social reinforcement and alliance building.]

Anita: Thanks.

The session ends.

Conclusion

Homework in CBT for SUD is widely considered a helpful strategy (Beck, Liese, & Najavits, in press; Carroll, 1998; Kadden et al., 1995; Najavits et al., 2004; O'Farrell & Cutter, 1984). This Chapter reviewed background about why homework can be potentially so useful, yet given the nature of SUD, may be quite difficult for patients to accomplish. Strategies for enhancing the likelihood of successful homework experiences were provided, with emphasis on both practical details of the homework process (e.g., "Provide good reasons," "Create meaning," "Identify obstacles"), yet also the importance of the therapists themselves (e.g., "Explore countertransference," "Be a role model"). Two case studies were offered. One elaborated the types of homework that might occur over a long-term CBT case (as many SUD patients will indeed be in long-term treatment), while the second case provided the opportunity to explore dialogue within a session.

The quotation from Saint-Exupery at the beginning of this Chapter summarizes the essence of homework: "It is always the same step." That is, while homework is highly diverse and changes with each patient and session, the fundamental process is the same: if the patient can keep taking steps forward, recovery from SUD and its associated problems becomes possible.

References

American Psychiatric Association. (1994). *Diagnostic and Statistical Manual of Mental Disorders IV.* Washington, DC: American Psychiatric Association.

Anker, A., & Crowley, T. (1982). *Use of contingency contracts in specialty clinics for cocaine abuse.* NIDA Research Monograph, 41, 452–459.

Beck, A. T. (1979). *Cognitive Therapy of Depression.* New York: Guilford Press.

Beck, A. T., Wright, F. D., Newman, C. F., & Liese, B. S. (1993). *Cognitive Therapy of Substance Abuse.* New York, NY: Guilford Press.

Beck, J., Liese, B., & Najavits, L. (in press). Cognitive therapy. In R. J. Frances & S. I. Miller & Mack (Eds.), *Clinical Textbook of Addictive Disorders* (3rd ed.). New York: Guilford Press.

Breslin, F. C., Sobell, M. B., Sobell, L. C., Sdao-Jarvie, K., & Sagorsky, L. (1996). Relationship between posttreatment drinking and alternative responses to high-risk situations proposed during treatment by problem drinkers. *Journal of Substance Abuse, 8,* 479–486.

Carroll, K. (1998). *A cognitive-behavioral approach: Treating cocaine addiction.* NIH Publication 98–4308. Rockville, MD: National Institute on Drug Abuse.

Cox, D. J., Tisdelle, D. A., & Culbert, J. P. (1988). Increasing adherence to behavioral homework assignments. *Journal of Behavioral Medicine, 11,* 519–522.

de Saint-Exupery, A. (2001, August 21). Quotation downloaded from www.cybernation.com.

Galanter, M. (1993). *Network Therapy for Alcohol and Drug Abuse: A New Approach in Practice.* New York: Basic Books.

Higgins, S. T., Budney, A. J., Bickel, W. K., Foerg, F. E., Donham, R., & Badger, G. J. (1994). Incentives improve outcome in outpatient behavioral treatment of cocaine dependence. *Archives of General Psychiatry, 51,* 568–576.

Imhof, J. (1991). Countertransference issues in alcoholism and drug addiction. *Psychiatric Annals, 21,* 292–306.

Ingram, J. A., & Salzberg, H. C. (1990). Effects of in vivo behavioral rehearsal on the learning of assertive behaviors with a substance abusing population. *Addictive Behaviors,* 15, 189–194.

Kadden, R., Carroll, K., Donovan, D., Cooney, N., Monti, P., Abrams, D., Litt, M., & Hester, R. (1995). *Cognitive-behavioral coping skills therapy manual: A clinical research guide for therapists treating individuals with alcohol abuse and dependence* (Vol. 3). Rockville, MD: U. S. Department of Health and Human Services.

Kessler, R. C., Crum, R. C., Warner, L. A., Nelson, C. B., Schulenberg, J., & Anthony, J. C. (1997). Lifetime co-occurence of DSM-III-R alcohol abuse and dependence with other psychiatric disorders in the National Comorbidity Survey. *Archives of General Psychiatry, 54,* 313–321.

Marlatt, G., & Gordon, J. (1985). *Relapse prevention: Maintenance strategies in the treatment of addictive behaviors.* New York: Guilford Press.

Maslow, A. (1970). *Motivation and personality* (2nd ed.). New York: Harper & Row.

McCrady, B. S., Noel, N. E., Abrams, D. B., Stout, R. L., Nelson, H. F., & Hay, W. M. (1986). Comparative effectiveness of three types of spouse involvement in outpatient behavioral alcoholism treatment. *Journal of Studies on Alcohol, 47,* 459–467.

McLellan, A. T., Kushner, H., Metzger, D., Peters, R., Smith, I., Grissom, G., Pettinati, H., & Argeriou, M. (1992). The fifth edition of the Addiction Severity Index. *Journal of Substance Abuse Treatment, 9,* 199–213.

McLellan, A. T., Woody, G. E., Luborsky, L., & Goehl, L. (1988). Is the counselor an "active ingredient" in substance abuse rehabilitation? An examination of treatment success among four counselors. *Journal of Nervous and Mental Disease, 176,* 423–430.

Miller, W. R., Zweben, A., DiClemente, C. C., & Rychtarik, R. G. (Eds.). (1995). *Motivational Enhancement Therapy Manual* (Vol. 2). Rockville, MD: U.S. Department of Health and Human Services.

Najavits, L. M. (2002). *Seeking Safety: A treatment manual for PTSD and substance abuse.* New York, NY: Guilford Press.

Najavits, L. M., Liese, B. S., & Harned, M. (2004). Cognitive-behavioral therapy. In J. H. Lowinson, P. Ruiz, R. B. Millman & J. G. Langrod (Eds.), *Substance Abuse: A Comprehensive Textbook* (4th ed.). Baltimore: Williams & Wilkins.

Najavits, L. M., & Weiss, R. D. (1994). The role of psychotherapy in the treatment of substance use disorders. *Harvard Review of Psychiatry, 2,* 84–96.

O'Farrell, T. J., & Cutter, H. S. (1984). Behavioral marital therapy couples groups for male alcoholics and their wives. *Journal of Substance Abuse Treatment, 1*, 191–204.

Prochaska, J. O., DiClemente, C. C., & Norcross, J. C. (1992). In search of how people change: Applications to addictive behaviors. *American Psychologist, 47*, 1102–1114.

Regier, D. A., Farmer, M. E., Rae, D. S., Locke, B. Z., Keith, S. J., Judd, L. L., & Goodwin, F. K. (1990). Co-morbidity of mental disorders with alcohol and other drug abuse: Results from the Epidemiologic Catchment Area (ECA) study. *Journal of the American Medical Association, 264*, 2511–2518.

Shelton, J. L., & Ackerman, J. M. (1974). *Homework in counseling and psychotherapy: Examples of systematic assignments for therapeutic use by mental health professionals.* Springfield, IL: Charles C Thomas.

Strauss, R. (2002, December 27). Quotation downloaded from www.cybernation.com.

Young, J. E. (1999). *Cognitive therapy for personality disorders: A schema-focused approach* (3rd ed.). Sarasota, FL: Professional Resource Press.

CHAPTER 14

Delusions and Hallucinations

HAMISH J. MCLEOD AND HAZEL E. NELSON

The main manuals on cognitive behavioral therapy (CBT) for psychosis all make reference to the benefit of using homework assignments (Kingdon & Turkington, 1994; Fowler, Garety, & Kuipers, 1995; Chadwick, Birchwood, & Trower, 1996; Haddock & Slade, 1996; Nelson, 1997; Morrison, 2002). In common with CBT for other disorders, the rationale for using homework assignments as an integral part of treatment is fourfold: (a) it helps to ensure that the work done within the therapy session is relevant to the patient's problems and experiences in their life outside the session; (b) it allows strategies devised within therapy sessions to be tested in and adapted to daily living situations; (c) it substantially increases the amount of time per week that the patient is actively engaged in therapy; and (d) it helps to develop the patient to be her own therapist, who can respond flexibly and adaptively to new situations as they arise.

Common Barriers to the Use of Homework Assignments

Unlike CBT for nonpsychotic disorders, where detailed homework assignments are an important core component of the treatment program from the start, it is common for people with psychosis to be able to do little or no set homework between sessions, especially in the early stages of therapy. As a general rule, the more complicated the homework task and the more paperwork involved in recording the results, the less likely it is to be

283

agreed on or completed. There are three broad reasons why homework adherence and completion are problematic, and they are rooted in the psychotic disorder itself. These are a lack of insight, concomitant cognitive impairments, and concomitant negative symptoms.

Lack of Insight[1]

As a general rule, people engage in therapy because they hope that it will help in some way with the problems they are experiencing. If they do not believe that medical or psychological factors play a part in their problems, then it is unsurprising if they think that psychological treatment will not be helpful or worth pursuing. Homework that may appear important from the therapist's viewpoint may seem irrelevant, inappropriate, or even frankly undesirable from the patient's perspective. To take an extreme example, someone with a strongly held persecutory delusion about being vulnerable to attack by gunmen waiting outside his house is likely to view any well-meaning suggestion to visit the local social center as foolhardy at best or, at worst, as demonstrating the therapist's complete misunderstanding or disregard for the danger. Even an apparently neutral monitoring task may seem irrelevant and not worth attempting if there is lack of insight. For example, what would be the point of making the effort to keep a record of your thoughts and feelings prior to the onset of the abusive voices from next door when you know full well that they have nothing whatsoever to do with you. It is your neighbor's thoughts and feelings that need to be exposed, not yours.

The principal way of overcoming the effects of low insight on homework engagement is to find a rationale for the task that makes sense from the patient's point of view. In some cases, this may entail using the patient's conceptualization and terminology to describe the homework task rather than the therapist's. This is consistent with the recommended approach of working from within the patient's belief system (Nelson, 1997). For example, one patient recorded how often the Archangel spoke to her rather than how often she hallucinated. Another patient monitored the effectiveness of his medication for the brain damage he had suffered when younger rather than its effectiveness at treating his psychosis. Although the patient and therapist may not have a shared understanding about the *causes* of the symptoms, they can have a shared understanding about the *effects* they have, such as the distress they evoke and/or the

---

[1]The term "lack of insight" is used here as it is used in the standard literature, namely to denote that the patient's beliefs about the nature and origin of his symptoms are not the same as those held by the therapist, which is not necessarily "insight" in the true sense.

negative consequences of responding to them in particular ways. So it may be possible to use these aspects to develop a shared rationale for setting and completing the homework task. For example, it may make sense to the patient to refrain from retaliating against his abusive neighbors on the grounds that this leads to involvement with the police, whereas it may not make sense on the grounds that the neighbors were not being abusive.

Another factor that can influence willingness to undertake suggested homework tasks is that of trust and respect for the therapist. If there is a strong therapeutic relationship, then the patient may be willing to do the homework because the therapist thinks it could be useful, either to help the patient directly or to help the therapist gain understanding and thereby help the patient. Also, if some of the therapist's suggestions have been helpful in the past (e.g., suggestions for coping strategies), then the patient may be more prepared to try something else that the therapist thinks might be helpful.

If the patient does not have a good reason for doing the homework, then it is important to keep the effort required as low as possible. Practicing the techniques or tasks within the session may help to build the patient's confidence, and *any* attempt to complete the tasks outside of the session should be reinforced with praise and encouragement. However, even when the patient does have a solid rationale, it is common for homework not to be completed or even attempted because of concomitant cognitive impairments and/or negative symptoms.

Concomitant Cognitive Impairments

The occurrence of cognitive impairments in people with psychosis, particularly in the domains of memory and executive functioning, is well established (Aleman, Hijman, de Hahn, & Khan, 1999; Green, 1996; Green, Kern, Braff, & Mintz, 2000; Pantelis, Barber, Barnes, Nelson, Owen, & Robbins, 1999). In particular, there is evidence that difficulties with episodic encoding and retrieval may lead to overly general recollections of past events (Riutort, Cuervo, Danion, Peretti, & Salame, 2003; McLeod, 2003). Hence, it can be difficult for the patient to retrieve specific event-related information during therapy sessions. This would suggest that diary homework to record the details of thoughts, emotions, and behaviors as they occur would be helpful. However, this should not be too complicated or time-consuming.

If patients forget what the homework task is, then the usual way to try to overcome this is for therapist to write it down (having checked that the patient can read the therapist's writing). Specific instructions on what should be done, when, in what context, and for how long are likely to be easier for the patient to adhere to than general statements (e.g., "Try to ignore the voices"). It is also likely to be helpful if the homework is not altered too often, so that the patient can build up a regular habit with the task. Forgetting to do the homework may be overcome by providing reminder cues. For example, a patient might stick a Post-it note on her Walkman to remind her to note down which tape she was using and how effective it was in reducing the troublesome voices. Alternatively, patients may wish to involve a caring friend or relative to remind her about her homework and when to do it.

Even when patients remember their homework, their ability to complete it adequately may be adversely affected by impairments in their concentration and a short attention span. To try to overcome this, the homework task should be kept short and simple. The complexity of the task and its monitoring may be increased over time. A programme of cognitive remediation may help to improve concentration and task performance (Wykes, Reeder, Comer, Williams, & Everitt, 1999), but this treatment is not widely available at present.

The presence of severe thought disorder may substantially reduce the possibility of using even informal homework assignments. Even if the patient understands what the homework assignment is and why he are doing it, his chaotic and disordered thinking makes it particularly likely that he will be unable to recall or execute the task when the need arises. In these circumstances, the best chance of getting any homework completed is to involve another caring person to remind and guide him through it.

Needless to say, it is the therapist's responsibility to make sure that the patient understands exactly what she is supposed to be doing. The task should be clearly and succinctly explained, and feedback should be obtained as to what the patient understands the task to be. The task requirements may need to be repeated or restated a number of times in order to counteract cognitive impairments. Therapists should also bear in mind that while diaries, charts, and diagrams come as second nature to them, members of the general public may be less familiar with these and may be unpracticed or uncomfortable with writing things down.

Concomitant Negative Symptoms

It is common for people with delusions and hallucinations to manifest some of the negative symptoms of schizophrenia. As far as completing homework assignments is concerned, lack of motivation and lack of energy are particularly pernicious. Establishing a shared understanding of the rationale for the homework and gradually increasing the difficulty of the task, so that the patient experiences some success from the beginning, may help to surmount this problem. Obtaining subjective ratings of the patient's confidence that she will be able to complete the task (e.g., from 0, or not at all confident, to 100, or completely confident) may be used to calibrate difficulty to a level that increases the likelihood of success (e.g., by only prescribing tasks that the patient is more than 70% confident that he or she will be able to complete)(Glaser, Kazantzis, Deane, & Oades, 2000). Similar ratings may be used retrospectively to determine how difficult the patient found the task that had been set at the previous session (Tarrier, Beckett, Harwood, Baker, Yusupoff, & Ugarteburu, 1993).

Negative symptoms are sometimes misinterpreted as a simple lack of motivation. However, such deficits are due in part to a basic failure of the brain to formulate the possibility of action and bring it to conscious awareness. Thus, unlike the case in depression, where the person is aware of the possibility of action but is too depressed to carry it out, in psychosis the person may not take action because she fails to reliably generate or recall action plans (Frith, 1992). Providing external reminders of action plans may reduce the impact of this problem.

Understanding the nature of the requested homework task does not necessarily translate into motivation to complete the exercise, possibly because of additional factors such as depression and hopelessness (Dunn, Morrison, & Bentall, 2002). As far as possible, the therapist should attempt to modify the patient's negative beliefs about the future, which underlie the hopelessness and depression.

With a robust therapeutic relationship, the therapist is in a good position to be a potent reinforcer for the patient in completing homework tasks. However, for some people with psychosis, social contact is not rewarding, so the person will be less rewarded by any social reinforcement that the therapist may give. In these circumstances and where considered appropriate, other forms of reinforcement may be negotiated (e.g., an escorted visit to a distant relative). Following the behavioral principle that immediate reinforcement is more effective than delayed reinforcement, attempts should be made to arrange for an immediate reward for homework engagement (e.g., from a caring other rather than waiting to discuss it at the next therapy session).

Patients generally think more clearly when they are less symptomatic and on medication than when they are psychotic and not on medication (King & Green, 1996). Nevertheless some antipsychotic medication can cause patients to feel tired and sleepy, such that they lack the energy to undertake homework tasks. If it is possible to alter the medication regimen without adversely affecting the antipsychotic benefits, this may be worth trying.

Types of Homework Assignments

Homework assignments take place in the context of a planned treatment program and are not used until an initial assessment has been made. The greatest risk of jumping in too quickly with a homework assignment is that the task or the rationale given for its use may inadvertently challenge the patient's delusional beliefs or may imply that he is mentally ill *before* it is known whether this would be a helpful target. Therefore, a key aspect of the initial assessment is to evaluate patients' "insight" and understanding about of their experiences. Particularly important in this respect is to determine (a) whether or not they attribute their experiences to an illness (and if so, what they understand this illness and its effects to be) and (b) whether they would feel positive or negative about such a suggestion.

As a general rule, homework tasks are not employed as part of the CBT programme until the goals for belief modification have been rigorously set and, if appropriate, any preliminary preparatory work has been done (see Nelson, 1997 for a discussion of total and partial goals and how to "prepare" the goal to render it acceptable and functional for the patient). The major exceptions to this are that some coping strategies are safe to use from the earliest contact with the patient and some information-gathering tasks may be given in order to inform the process of goal setting.

Information Gathering

In the initial stages of therapy, diary assignments may be used to gather assessment information that will serve to facilitate case formulation and goal setting and to provide the basis for discussions within therapy sessions. At this stage, care should be taken to construct monitoring tasks using the patient's own beliefs, concepts, and verbal descriptions so that they are relevant and meaningful for the patient and they do not inadvertently challenge her delusional beliefs too soon. For these reasons, early diary tasks often focus on the negative functional consequences of symptoms (such as distress and socially stigmatizing or dangerous behavior) rather than the symptoms per se. Also, this approach to information gathering increases the chances of identifying interventions that will be relevant and meaningful from the patient's perspective. Table 14.1 gives an example of a monitoring sheet for a 34-year-old woman who experienced persistent problems with intrusive auditory hallucinations that she believed were coming from former school friends..

Several points can be made about the rationale and aims of this monitoring exercise. First, the task was calibrated to a level that maximized the chances that the patient would be able to complete it with some "success." Second, even though only two entries were made, they provided material

TABLE 14.1 Sample Recording of Auditory Hallucination Content and Affective and Behavioral Response

Date & time	Who?	What did they say?	What did you do and how did you feel?	How distressing was it? 0—not at all 10—extremely distressing
Feb. 28, 2003, 5:34 p.m.	Colin and Angela	"You owe me—I'm going to psych you out and punish you if you don't obey me" (she's going to burn me if I don't do what she says).	I shouted at Angela and called her a whore and slammed the door and cried because of the frustration of being incapable of stopping it.	7
March 1, 2003, 3:40 p.m.	Colin	"Don't do your washing or have a shower—we are all watching you and can see you naked."	I shouted, "Get lost you f--- ing bastard" and got angry with him.	8

for discussion in the therapy sessions and allowed for the identification of potential problem areas, namely the emotional distress and disturbed shouting behavior. Third, the task was structured so as not to impose the therapist's beliefs about the origin of the voices. At this early stage of engagement and rapport building, the aim was to shape an inquisitive and open attitude to discussions of her symptoms and not to challenge her delusional beliefs directly.

Other types of homework tasks that may be used at the initial assessment and formulation stage include frequency counts of high-rate events (such as intrusive auditory hallucinations or ideas of reference) and antecedents-consequences-consequences (ABC) charts, which are designed to identify eliciting stimuli and situational factors associated with the onset of problematic symptoms (Chadwick et al., 1996).

Even if every precaution has been taken to make the information-gathering exercise a neutral one with respect to challenging the patient's delusional beliefs, the therapist should be aware of the possible implications to the patient of the particular task set—implications that may not be helpful in the early stages. For example, (a) the very fact that patients have been asked to focus on a particular class of voices, thoughts, feelings, or events (etc.) may imply that the therapist views these as different or "abnormal" in some way; (b) focusing on a symptom and writing about it may change its frequency and intensity (e.g., focusing on auditory hallucinations may actually decrease their occurrence (see Slade and Bentall, 1988); (c) recording the frequency of a symptom that the patient has been trying to minimize may force the him to recognize that it occurs more frequently or with more adverse effects than previously acknowledged; (d) some information gathering may trigger a "natural" CBT effect by focusing and clarifying the evidence. For example, gathering information about the antecedents of paranoid thoughts may prematurely reveal that there is no hard evidence to justify the sense of threat. Reaching this conclusion before the patient has developed an alternative to her delusional belief may provoke a defensive reaction and possibly lead her to withdraw from therapy.

As treatment progresses, information gathering may be used to develop specific, targeted CBT strategies. For example, having gained the understanding that his voices came from within his own brain, one patient kept a diary of when he heard the voices and how he knew that they were "voices" rather than coming from an actual person outside of himself. Certain themes emerged around the content of what was said and the quality and tone of the voice. A checklist was then developed to help him decide about the origin of the voices, when he was not sure, or when the experiences were more intense and it was more difficult for him to label them as hallucinations.

Coping Strategies

It has been reported that even simple behavioral coping strategies can be effective in reducing symptom occurrence and associated distress (Fowler et al., 1995). Distress-reducing coping strategies can be used as homework even before the goals for delusional belief change have been formally set *provided* that the strategy used is not perceived by the patient as contradicting or challenging her belief system. Coping strategy enhancement is developed throughout therapy as strategies are tried, assessed, and refined.

Many patients with psychosis have learned their own ways of coping (Falloon & Talbot, 1981), but some use their strategies haphazardly and unreliably. In these cases, the therapist can help the patient to use them in a more targeted and systematic way (Tarrier et al., 1993; Yusupoff & Tarrier, 1996; Haddock, Slade, Bentall, Reid, & Faragher, 1998). This may be done by discussion, to make the patient more aware of the strategy and how she could use it in everyday situations and/or to identify and develop cues to trigger the use of the strategy when needed.

Some strategies that patients develop themselves to cope with the intrusion of symptoms may have negative consequences as well as positive ones. For example, drinking alcohol or smoking cannabis to alleviate the anxiety associated with a paranoid belief may help in the short term but may worsen the problem over time. Similarly, shouting back at intrusive voices may provide temporary relief, but the increased arousal may increase the likelihood of their recurrence. Shouting is also likely to be socially stigmatizing and may provoke a punishing response from others. In these cases, the therapist should try to find an alternative coping strategy that incorporates the positive but avoids the negative aspects of the original one. For example, other anxiety-management techniques could be used to replace the alcohol and cannabis use, suggestions made about socially "safe" places to go to do the shouting, or information could be given about the use of subvocal speech. However, it is not always possible to find an alternative that is effective or that the patient is willing or able to use. Here, the therapist's role is to gently discuss the disadvantages as well as the advantages of the behavior so that patients can make an informed decisions about whether the advantages outweigh the disadvantages.

Another potential problem may occur if the patient's coping strategy is a safety behavior that protects him from a feared event and thereby reduces the probability that he will confront evidence that is inconsistent with his delusional belief. For example, a paranoid patient may incorrectly conclude that carrying a mobile phone with the emergency services number programmed into it is the reason that he has not been attacked by gangsters. In a study of factors that maintain persecutory delusions, Freeman, Garety, and Kuipers (2001) found that all the patients exhibited one or more safety behaviors in the month prior to assessment. Therefore the therapist should check the patient's interpretation of the successful use of his behavioral coping strategies and attempt to modify any dysfunctional conclusions.

In many cases, the therapist may want to suggest that the patient try a coping strategy that has not been tried before. Usually behavioral coping strategies are safe to use, but if there is any chance that the strategy may inadvertently "challenge" the delusional belief before it has been determined whether or not this would be functional, then the therapist should check with the patient to determine how he or she would interpret a "successful" outcome before setting the task as homework. For example, if something as simple as earplugs were effective in stopping "the voice of God," then the hearer might conclude that the voice did not come from God after all, which might or might not be helpful at this stage of therapy.

Of course, later on in therapy, the very fact that a simple coping strategy can reduce the unwanted experience may be used as evidence to substantiate a desired belief modification: for example that the symptoms are not uncontrollable, the voice is not powerful, or that there is an illness-based explanation for the symptoms (Tarrier, et al., 1993; Chadwick et al., 1996; Nelson, 1997).

Altering the Environment

These can be some of the simplest but most effective coping strategies. Changes can be made to either the physical and/or social (i.e., involving other people) environments. Some examples from the authors' clinical experiences include sleeping with a night light to counter the fear of voices heard in the dark, switching on a light to dispel visual hallucinations, moving to a different room to avoid misinterpreting partially heard voices from the street, requesting a parent not to ask detailed personal questions, and not getting into discussions about a contentious issue. Analysis of situations in which delusional thinking and hallucinations occur and of the factors that exacerbate the distress caused by them can suggest some beneficial changes that could be made. The information required may be obtained by discussing the situations in depth with the patient and/or by using more formal information-gathering homework tasks (e.g., keeping a diary documenting situational and environmental factors associated with the onset of specific noxious psychotic experiences).

Counterstimulation

The rationale for counterstimulation strategies is that sensory input and/ or self-generated mental activity competes for mental resources and thereby blocks noxious auditory hallucinations or delusional ideas. Given the limited capacity of human working memory (Baddeley, 1990), the aim is for the patient to engage in situations or activities that provide a competing stimulus to the psychotic experience. Research studies have focused on the use of counterstimulation strategies for auditory hallucinations. Therapists may be able to use the underlying principles to devise similar strategies for visual and tactile hallucinations, depending on how these are experienced by the patient (e.g., using a visual computer game to block visual hallucinations).

The most commonly used and effective counterstimulation strategy for auditory hallucinations is the use of a Walkman to listen to music.

Although some types of music may be more effective in blocking hallucinations than others, in practice people typically listen to what they most enjoy. However, if hallucinations are triggered by the patient's choice of music, the therapist should intervene and suggest that other music should be tried instead (e.g., nonvocal). Wax or foam earplugs may also be effective in blocking or reducing the voices, but some people find they are too uncomfortable to use even if effective. It is recommended that one earplug be used in either ear (the patient should experiment to see if there is an ear preference). Some people prefer to plug both ears. The key advantage of the Walkman and earplug strategies is that they require no active involvement of the patient and can be used for long periods of time. Other counterstimulation strategies such as subvocal counting and singing, naming objects as rapidly as possible, and mental arithmetic tasks may be useful to stop the voices but can become onerous if carried out for extended periods. However, they can be useful as a means of interrupting continuous voices or as a temporary control method for particularly sensitive situations. For example, one patient was particularly vulnerable to critical voices when she was queuing at the supermarket checkout counter. She found it helpful to name the items of food to herself as they were carried along the conveyor belt.

Cognitive Distraction

Cognitive distraction strategies work by a combination of distraction and counterstimulation. Examples include computer games, radio and TV, reading, crossword puzzles, and puzzle games. Generally speaking, these coping strategies only work for the time that they are being employed, so it is important that the distraction task is something that the patient enjoys doing. If not, it is unlikely that he or she will spend time using it even if it were found to be effective.

Increasing Social Contact and Activity

Social isolation has been identified as one of the factors that may contribute to the maintenance of positive psychotic symptoms (Garety, Kuipers, Fowler, Freeman, & Bebbington, 2001). Increasing social contacts and activities are some of the most commonly used coping strategies for delusions and hallucinations. They may be effective for a number of reasons. First, they provide a distraction from the delusional thoughts and hallucinations. Second, they give patients a chance to use the language areas of their brains in conversation, thereby providing a source of counterstimulation. Third, the other people engaged in the social contact may say or do things that help to counter a delusional belief. For example, someone saying "It's good to see you again" or just smiling as a cup of tea is passed may help to counter a paranoid belief about one's social acceptability. Fourth, because we are social beings, just being in the company of other people may have beneficial effects on arousal and our sense of safety and confidence (Gilbert, 1989). Individuals with a self-focused and ruminative presentation may particularly benefit from increased social interaction.

As with all aspects of homework assignments, increasing social contact and activity should be carefully planned and graded by the therapist and patient together to ensure that the social contacts made at each stage of the program are rewarding and reinforcing. For example, one young man who was socially isolated at home, spending most of his time in his own room, started by visiting the library with his therapist, then visiting the library with his brother, then visiting the pub with just his brother, and then with his brother and friends. All of this was done before attempting one of his main goals, to attend his local day-center, where he was able to meet other young people and received vocational training.

Decreasing Social Activity

Although the majority of patients benefit from social interactions, in some cases higher levels of social stimulation may exacerbate symptoms such as paranoia, ideas of reference, and auditory hallucinations. Thus, withdrawing to a less stimulating environment may at times be recommended. The caveat is that care should be taken to avoid inadvertently reinforcing maladaptive social withdrawal. To minimize this risk, the therapist should determine with the patient how long it takes for his symptom experiences to return to a tolerable level (e.g., 20 minutes spent alone in his bedroom). The patient should be encouraged to reengage with his normal social activities after this time.

Increasing Physical Activity

Increasing physical activity may improve the patient's mood through the general beneficial physiological effects associated with exercise and activity. Higher activity levels may be particularly effective when the onset of the target symptom is associated with noxious arousal, agitation, or physical tension. In these circumstances, taking exercise or going for a walk may help to discharge arousal that develops in response to the symptoms. Increasing physical activity is also likely to involve a change of environment. As such, it may also help by serving as a distraction.

Despite the potential benefits of physical activity, the combination of illness and/or medication effects may make even apparently simple physical exercises too demanding and difficult for many patients. If the exercise has some additional purpose, such as walking the dog or meeting a friend, this may make it more acceptable and likely to occur.

Relaxation Training

High arousal can exacerbate hallucinations and delusions, especially those with a paranoid or anxious theme. Any strategy that reduces arousal may be helpful in these cases (e.g., relaxation training). Progressive muscular relaxation, diaphragmatic breathing, and autogenic relaxation have all been recommended as part of the CBT treatment approach (e.g., Tarrier, et al., 1993). Regular relaxation practice may be helpful in two ways: (a) by generally lowering arousal levels and (b) by giving the patient a means of keeping her arousal down when she is in stressful situations. For example, one patient burned a lavender candle during her relaxation practice sessions and then carried with her a handkerchief impregnated with a drop of lavender oil, which she sniffed when she went into stressful situations to help her relax. Another patient repeated the words "calm and relaxed" during his regular relaxation practice. Repeating these words in stressful situations helped to block the voices by counterstimulation and also reduced the anxiety that tended to make his symptoms worse.

An additional advantage of learning relaxation skills is that they can be combined with graded exposure to the cues that provoke anxiety, including the voices themselves (Haddock et al., 1998). Unfortunately, it is our experience that many patients will not engage in formal relaxation training. Such resistance might be overcome by practicing relaxation strategies within therapy sessions and then drawing attention to subjective reductions in tension and arousal experienced by the patient (e.g., using an arousal rating scale of 0 to 100 before and after the relaxation exercise). A successful reduction in arousal may then be used to justify the possible benefits of practicing the relaxation exercises as homework. When the reluctance appears to be due to motivational problems or simply forgetting to complete the task, some patients might benefit from prompting by another caring person or relative between sessions.

Developing and Evaluating Coping Strategy Homework

In collaboration with the patient, the therapist should draw up clear plans for the use of each coping strategy and put these into writing. Where possible, the strategy should be practiced first in the therapy session. If the patient finds it helpful, then the therapist should also make specific suggestions about when, where, and how it is to be tried out of session. For example, if the plan is to try to increase social activity as a way of reducing time spent ruminating on a delusional belief, the patient and therapist should construct a list of possible social activities, putting them in order of preference or convenience, and ensure that all the practicalities of putting them into effect have been worked out in advance.

Ideally, the patient will keep a detailed record of what was tried, where and when it was tried, and the outcome. The effectiveness of each strategy attempted can then be evaluated and refinements made. Where detailed record keeping is likely to be too onerous for the patient, the charts or records should be simplified. But if the patient is able to give a only verbal report of what happened in the next session, it is still much better to have had the strategy tried but not formally recorded than for it not to have been tried at all.

Belief-Modification Strategies

It is safer to test belief-modification strategies in a treatment session than in homework assignments. No matter how careful therapists are to construct a thorough case formulation, it is always possible that there are additional factors not known to them that may cause problems when the strategy is tried. This is particularly salient when the therapist is from a different cultural background than the patient; a cautious approach should be taken in these circumstances until the relevance of any subcultural beliefs or practices has been determined. Also, it may be much harder for patients to adopt a CBT approach to their experiences when they are on their own away from the safety of the therapy session. Therefore trying out new strategies out of sessions carries a greater risk of distressing the patient or even making the symptoms worse, particularly if they tax the patient's resources. However, CBT strategies initiated during treatment sessions can be greatly enhanced by the use of homework assignments to test, refine, and practice new strategies.

Evidence Evaluation and Logical Reasoning

Once patients conclude that there could be an alternative explanation for their experiences other than the delusional one, a very useful homework assignment is for them to evaluate the evidence or experience, using logical reasoning, whenever the target symptom occurs. Commonly this involves using arguments and testing questions developed and practiced during the therapy sessions to see whether the evidence really does support the delusional belief and whether the other explanations and alternative belief(s) that have been discussed would apply. For example, a patient who tended to interpret anyone who walked behind him as following him learned to consider and evaluate other possible reasons why that person might be traveling the same route. Another patient checked for other people's reactions when she heard foul language being shouted aloud to test the alternative explanation that these were inner voices.

Reality Testing

Reality testing is a key component of belief modification and may involve testing the evidence supporting the delusional belief or directly testing the delusional belief itself. Some reality testing may be possible within the therapy session, but most reality testing, by its very nature, has to take place outside sessions in the situations in which the symptoms occur. In keeping with standard practice in CBT, reality tests should be developed in collaboration with the patient and be specified clearly and precisely (Nelson, 1997). It is also important that the implications of the test be fully discussed with the patient before it is set as homework. In particular, the therapist should check how the patient would interpret all the possible outcomes of the test, and there should be agreement as to what will constitute supporting versus nonsupporting evidence.

Reality tests are tailor-made for the particular beliefs and circumstances of the individual concerned, but an example of a commonly used reality test is that used to test the belief "other people can read my mind." In this test the patient thinks, "If within the next five minutes you come to me and say 'I claim the £5 note that you have in your inner pocket,' then I will give it to you." The details of this test can be varied according to the person's particular circumstances, the key requirement being that the patient consider the incentive sufficient to ensure that, if anyone *could* read his mind, then he *would* respond to what they read there. The test details must be clearly specified to ensure that everyday occurrences could not be interpreted as a response to receiving the message (e.g., someone asking to borrow some money a couple of days later). Similarly, it would not be a good idea to use cigarettes as the incentive being offered if the person lived in a community where people commonly asked one another for cigarettes.

Cue Cards

Belief modification will typically involve the identification and rehearsal of counterevidence to delusional ideas and/or the content of hallucinations as well as the development of coping statements and behaviors for the patient to use outside of the therapy session. However, patients may forget what the strategies are or they may forget to use them when they need to do so. Therefore it is important to use cues that will trigger homework use. Giving the patient an audiotape of the session to listen to between sessions may help with the retention of relevant information (Glaser et al., 2000). More commonly, written cue cards are developed collaboratively by the patient and therapist to summarize the key points from the therapy sessions to date (Fowler et al., 1995). The content of cue cards will be unique to the specific problem(s) that any given patient may experience, but typically they will be designed either to remind the patient to do something (e.g., "When my anxiety about being harmed by the people around me reaches more than 6 out of 10, I should go to my room for 15 minutes and practice my breathing exercises until the anxiety goes back down below 5 out of 10") and/or contain information that the patient may have trouble remembering when in a distressed state (e.g., "Even though I feel frightened when the voices tell me they will cut off my arms, I know they are lying because they have lied to me before, such as telling me that I was Jack the Ripper, and I know that if I ignore them by listening to my Walkman, they will go away"). In order to keep cue cards short and simple, it is usual to have a cue card for each relevant aspect of treatment (e.g., for "When the voice calls me stupid," " Why I know the voice has no power," "When my mother tells me what to do"). Patients usually collect a number of cue cards as therapy progresses.

Of course, putting the required information onto the cue cards does not guarantee that it will be available for use when required. In some cases, the homework task will need to address the issue of helping the patient to remember to *use* the card when appropriate. Use of the card is likely to be increased if the patient carries it with her or displays it in a prominent position in her home (provided that this does not have any negative social consequences). Or she may be advised to read it regularly, whether she needs it or not (e.g., when she wakes up or at mealtimes) to increase her chances of recalling the material when needed. Alternatively, with the patient's agreement, other caring persons may be asked to remind the patient to read the cards, or they may have copies of the cards so that they can reinforce the key points when required.

Developing and Generalizing CBT Strategies

Diary exercises may be given to help to generalize useful CBT strategies to a wide range of situations. In effect, this is training the patient to be his own CBT therapist for the future. These exercises are similar in type to those used to record and counter the negative thoughts of depression. As with their use in depression, the benefits of this type of homework include (a) writing down the counterarguments and evidence helps to clarify them and fix them in memory for future use and (b) any incident that cannot be countered by the patient at the time may either be countered by him later, when the intensity of the experience is less. Alternatively, it can be brought to therapy for discussion with the therapist and reconsidered there, thereby increasing the patient's repertoire of cognitive responses. For example, one patient reached the stage in therapy when he understood that perceiving routine events as highly significant was actually a symptom of his illness. As homework, he recorded every incident when this occurred and then either immediately or later, if he was unable to do so immediately, worked out and wrote down why the situation was unlikely to have any special significance. This was based on the rational reasoning he had developed in sessions. Having the task as a formal, written homework assignment helped him to focus on and think about the experiences when they occurred rather than just accepting or avoiding them. Subsequent discussions during therapy sessions about the arguments he had used at the time helped him to further develop and refine his reasoning skills for future occasions.

Secondary Symptoms

Homework assignments may also include work on psychological problems that develop in response to the effects that the delusional thinking and hallucinations have on the person's life. These include anxiety, phobias, depression, hopelessness about the future, loss of self-esteem and social withdrawal. Treatment and homework tasks follow the standard practice for these disorders (see Chapters 5 and 6) and usually take place together with, and integrated into, the CBT treatment for the delusions and hallucinations.

Case Study

The patient was a male in his late twenties who had been on holiday in Turkey at the time when England beat Turkey at football in an acrimonious game. He was not a football fan and so wore his England rugby shirt in the hotel restaurant the next day without thinking. He reported being aware of some hostile looks from Turkish residents at other tables and was worried that he had caused offence. Thereafter, he became increasingly anxious and paranoid as a number of threatening incidents occurred and he developed the belief that there was a conspiracy to harm or even kill him because of what had happened. From his descriptions, the incidents appeared to be the result of a mixture of auditory hallucinations and misinterpretation of events during the onset of an acute psychotic episode.

When he came to therapy, his paranoid belief was being maintained by a combination of auditory hallucinations, misinterpretations of partially heard speech, and misinterpretations of events. By this time, he had developed a phobic response to people of Turkish or Mediterranean appearance. The resultant fear he experienced helped to maintain his belief that these people were a threat to him.

The optimal goal of therapy was for the patient to understand that the anxiety and threat that he had felt both in Turkey and at home in England were aspects of an illness and therefore that there was not and never had been a conspiracy to harm him in any way. However, the most important part of that goal was for him to understand that whatever might have happened in Turkey, there was definitely no conspiracy to get him in England. This belief modification would both reassure him about his safety and enable him to function normally again in his everyday life. An alternative explanation for the "threatening incidents" was determined by gently testing options with the patient. This was that his fear could cause his brain to become oversensitized and overvigilant, so that it misinterpreted neutral events and "misheard" what it feared but also expected to hear. He only partially accepted the notion of "mental illness," and for him this was not a persuasive alternative explanation for his experiences. Homework assignments were used from an early stage of therapy to extend and develop the CBT work undertaken in the sessions.

Social Withdrawal

Patients may withdraw or become isolated from social contacts for a number of reasons. The withdrawal may be a direct consequence of the delusions and hallucinations: for example, when it protects a paranoid patient from the dangers presented by other people, or it may occur as a result of concomitant negative symptoms (e.g., low energy, low motivation, and anhedonia). Added to this, the experience of having been ill may mean the loss of a valued job, with implications for socializing, earning money and self-esteem. A lengthy illness may also mean that the person loses touch with normal social contacts; low self-esteem and the stigmatization of mental illness may make it difficult for such an individual to reenter his or her old social scene.

Homework assignments to reverse social withdrawal are likely to include some form of simple activity scheduling, so as to gradually reintroduce the patient into rewarding social situations. Setting specific goals for the patient to report back on in the next therapy session may function to provide extra cueing and motivation, thus helping to restart the socializing behavior. As with all homework tasks, the aim is to select achievable goals from the outset and to increase task demands only at a rate that secures continued task engagement and success.

In the early stages of social reintegration, a primary source of reinforcement for task completion is likely to be the therapist. But in order for the socialization to continue, the social activities themselves will need to provide the necessary reinforcement. Where the social isolation is due to severe negative symptoms, it is likely to be necessary to set very simple social goals. If social skills training is indicated (e.g., Marder, Wirshing, Mintz, & McKenzie, 1996), then this aspect of treatment will also generate appropriate homework tasks.

Some people may recover from the acute stage of their illness but feel frustrated that they are unable to return to full-time employment. Although paid work may be the preferred option for clinical improvement (Bell & Lysaker, 1997), where this is not possible, some form of voluntary work may be helpful. Voluntary work can provide some of the social contacts and status, pleasurable activity, and regular routine that would be provided by paid employment but without the pressures of a regular commitment to an employer. Homework assignments for this aspect of treatment may include reintroduction into voluntary and/or paid employment following a graded program. The advantage of having continued contact with a therapist at this stage is that it may allow problems to be identified and dealt with before or as soon as they occur.

Relapse Prevention

The long-term aim of CBT with psychosis is to enable the person to cope with their symptoms so that they do not cause distress or disruption to their lives and to prevent relapse by recognizing when the illness is becoming active and taking appropriate steps to limit its effects (Birchwood, 1992). Therefore an important aspect of the CBT treatment program is for the patient and therapist to identify signs of relapse. This is normally done when the illness is in remission, using the patient's and other people's recollections of what happened in earlier relapses. The signs are listed in order of their appearance as the illness worsened and then, for each sign or group of signs, there is an agreed plan of action to be taken. If the patient wishes it, caring others and health professionals may also be involved in the relapse prevention plans. The list of relapse signs that others have is likely to be different in some respects from that of the patient, since their perception of the effects of the illness will be different. However, the patient should be fully involved in and retain full control over the actions he or she would like to see taken if signs of illness should reemerge.

Putting the relapse prevention cards into effect is a very important, ongoing homework assignment. Typically, not all the actions initially identified as being suitable will be put into effect when the psychosis is active. For example, once insight is lost, a paranoid patient may not follow the coping strategy "Phone my friend and ask him if he can see any gunmen outside my door: if he says no, then I will know it is safe to go outside." He may also not react well to being told by a family member that he is becoming ill again and needs to see the doctor, even though when well he had identified these as appropriate actions to take when the time came. Therefore an important aspect of relapse prevention is to review the usefulness of the action plan after it has been tried and tested and to make alterations

TABLE 14.2 Homework Assignmnets in a Patient With a Paranoid Delusion

Assignment	Purpose
1. Record the ongoing incidents involving the conspiracy.	To provide detailed information about the "evidence" confirming the delusion To enable reevaluation of this evidence during therapy using logical reasoning and alternative explanations
2. Relaxation practice: 15 minutes a day (This was continued throughout therapy and recommended as a permanent practice when formal therapy ended.)	To reduce arousal levels To increase ability to relax in stressful situations. For use in the desensitization program
3. Record ongoing incidents involving the conspiracy and counter arguments of why these interpretations could be mistaken.	To remove evidence supporting the delusion by re-evaluating it as it occurred To strengthen the alternative explanations for these experiences
(This was gradually tailed off towards the end of therapy as the patient became more adept at mentally challenging the incidents.)	To enable new lines of reasoning to be explored during therapy sessions and then tried out in practice
4. Write down all the conspiracy related incidents he could recall from his time in Turkey.	To enable the evidence of past events, relating to Turkey, to be reevaluated during sessions in order to weaken the belief about the conspiracy in Turkey (This line of work was only partially successful and was discontinued when there appeared to be a risk of strengthening his belief in some of his interpretations as he sought to recall the details of the incidents.)
5. Graded exposure to people of Turkish/Mediterranean appearance. For example: Look at magazine pictures. Watch video of travel program. Travel on London train. Eat in Turkish restaurant.	To transfer the imaginal desensitization undertaken in sessions to real life situations To provide opportunities to practice and refine the logical reasoning and coping strategies developed for these situations

(continued)

TABLE 14.2 Homework Assignmnets in a Patient With a Paranoid Delusion *(continued)*

Assignment	Purpose
6a. Record "threats" overheard, then, move to 6b.	To provide detailed information so that logical reasoning and alternative explanations could be developed during therapy sessions to counter the perceived content of the voices and also the belief about their origin/nature
6b. Record threats overheard and counterarguments as to why these could have been "misperceptions of my brain." (These incidents grew fewer and fewer as the patient came to understand what they were, and as his belief in the conspiracy in England faded away.)	To re-evaluate and remove any evidence supporting the conspiracy as it occurred, using the cognitive strategies developed in the therapy sessions To strengthen the alternative explanation for the hallucinations and misperceptions

in the light of this experience. Several cycles of relapse may be necessary in order to develop optimal plans for best possible self-care.

Conclusions

As with any CBT treatment program, the use of homework assignments in CBT for psychosis is recommended to enhance the value of therapy undertaken in individual sessions. However, in clinical practice, *engaging* the patient in homework can be difficult because of features of the illness, such as lack of insight, disturbed thinking, and low motivation and energy. In the authors' experience, many CBT interventions for delusions and hallucinations have to proceed with few or no formally set homework assignments being possible, at least in the initial stages. Fortunately, some successful treatment outcomes can still be achieved when the therapist addresses the crucial task of collaborating with the patient to develop a set of strategies that can be used to reduce distress and improve daily functioning. The homework tasks described in this Chapter provide a starting point for tailoring a comprehensive and individualized treatment package. The chances of enhancing engagement in homework may be increased by adhering to the following principles:

Find a rationale for the homework that makes sense to the patient.
Make sure that the task has been satisfactorily explained and understood.
Suggest only tasks that are within the patient's present capabilities.

Ensure that the patient experiences some task "success"; start with easy tasks and increase the difficulty only within this requirement. Reinforce whatever homework comes back. Make sure there are no negative consequences for the patient for failing to attempt or complete a given task.

Adapt the homework task to what is possible in fact (which might be extremely limited), not to what might be desirable in an ideal therapeutic world.

References

Aleman, A., Hijman, R., de Hahn, E. H. F., & Khan, R. S. (1999). Memory impairment in schizophrenia: A meta-analysis. *American Journal of Psychiatry. 156*, 1358–1366.

Baddeley, A. D. (1990). *Human memory theory and practice.* Hove, UK: Erlbaum.

Bell, M. D., & Lysaker, P. H. (1997). Clinical benefits of paperwork activity in schizophrenia: One-year follow-up. *Schizophrenia Bulletin. 23*, 317–328.

Birchwood, M. (1992). Early intervention in schizophrenia: theoretical background and clinical strategies. British Journal of Clinical Psychology, 31, 257–278.

Chadwick, P., Birchwood, M., & Trower, P. (1996). *Cognitive therapy for delusions, voices and paranoia.* Chichester, UK: Wiley.

Dunn, H., Morrison, A. P., & Bentall, R. P. (2002). Patients' experiences of homework tasks in cognitive behavioral therapy for psychosis: A qualitative analysis. *Clinical Psychology and Psychotherapy, 9*, 361–369.

Falloon, I. R. H., & Talbot, R. E. (1981). Persistent auditory hallucinations: Coping mechanisms and implications for management. *Psychological Medicine, 11*, 329–339.

Firth, C. D. (1992). *The Cognitive Neuropsychology of Schizophernia.* Hove: Lawrence Erlbaum.

Fowler, D., Garety, P. A., & Kuipers, E. (1995). *Cognitive behavior therapy for psychosis.* Chichester: Wiley.

Freeman, D., Garety, P. A., & Kuipers, E. (2001). Persecutory delusions: Developing the understanding of belief maintenance and emotional distress. *Psychological Medicine, 31*, 1293–1306.

Garety, P. A., Kuipers, E., Fowler, D., Freeman, D., & Bebbington, P. E. (2001). A cognitive model of the positive symptoms of psychosis. *Psychological Medicine, 31*, 189–195.

Gilbert, P. (1989). *Human nature and suffering.* Hove, UK: Erlbaum.

Glaser, N. M., Kazantzis, N., Deane, F. P., & Oades, L. G. (2000). Critical issues in using homework assignments with cognitive-behavioral therapy for schizophrenia. *Journal of Rational-Emotive and Cognitive-Behavior Therapy, 18*, 247–261.

Green, M. F. (1996). What are the functional consequences of neurocognitive deficits in schizophrenia? *American Journal of Psychiatry, 153*, 321–330.

Green, M. F., Kern, R. F., Braff, D. L., & Mintz, J. (2000). Neurocognitive deficits and functional outcome in schizophrenia: Are we measuring the "right stuff"? *Schizophrenia Bulletin, 26*, 119–136.

Haddock, G., & Slade, P. D. (1996). *Cognitive-Behavioral Interventions with Psychotic Disorders.* London: Routledge.

Haddock, G., Slade, P. D., Bentall, R. P., Reid, D., Faragher, E. B. (1998). A comparison of the long-term effectiveness of distraction and focusing in the treatment of auditory hallucinations. *British Journal of Medical Psychology, 71*, 339–349.

King, D. J., & Green, J. F. (1996). Medication and cognitive functioning in schizophrenia. In C. Pantelis, H. E. Nelson, & T. R. E. Barnes (Eds.), *Schizophrenia: A neuropsychological perspective.* Chichester, UK: Wiley.

Kingdon, D. G., & Turkington, D. (1994). *Cognitive-behavioral therapy of schizophrenia.* Hove, UK: Erlbaum.

Marder, S. R., Wirshing, W. C, Mintz, J., & McKenzie, J. (1996). Two-year outcome of social skills training and group psychotherapy for outpatients with schizophrenia. *American Journal of Psychiatry, 153,* 1585–1592.

McLeod, H. J. (2003). *Autobiographical memory retrieval impairments and delusional ideation.* Ph.D. thesis, University of London.

Morrison, A. P. (2002). *A case book of cognitive therapy for psychosis.* Brighton, UK: Psychology Press.

Nelson, H. E. (1997). *Cognitive behavioral therapy with schizophrenia. A practice manual.* Cheltenham, UK: Stanley Thornes.

Pantelis, C, Barber, F. Z., Barnes, T. R. E., Nelson, H. E., Owen, A. M., & Robins, T. W. (1999). Comparison of set-shifting ability in patients with chronic schizophrenia and frontal lobe damage. *Schizophrenia Research, 37,* 251–270.

Riutort, M., Cuervo, C., Danion, J., Perretti, C. S., Salamé, P. (2003). Reduced levels of specific autobiographical memories in schizophrenia. *Psychiatry Research, 117,* 35–45.

Tarrier, N., Beckett, R., Harwood, S., Baker, A., Yusupoff, L., Ugarteburu, I. (1993). A trial of two cognitive-behavioral methods of treating drug-resistant residual psychotic symptoms in schizophrenic patients: I. Outcome. *British Journal of Psychiatry. 162,* 524–532.

Wykes, T., Reeder, C., Corner, J., Williams, C., & Everitt, B. (1999). The effects of neurocognitive remediation on executive processing in patients with schizophrenia. *Schizophrenia Bulletin, 25,* 291–307.

Yusupoff, L., & Tarrier, N. (1996). Coping strategy enhancement for persistent hallucinations and delusions. In G. Haddock & P. D. Slade (Eds), *Cognitive-behavioral interventions with psychotic disorders.* London: Routledge.

CHAPTER 15

Sexual Problems

NANCY A. PACHANA and KATE SOFRONOFF

Four main classes of sexual problems are commonly encountered in clinical practice—sexual dysfunctions (the most common), sexual drive problems, gender problems, and sexual variations and deviations. In a recent British study, approximately 10% of patients attending general practice clinics reported some type of current sexual or relationship difficulty (Watson & Teifion, 1997). Similar figures are reported in psychological practices, although prevalence rates for specific disorders differ by such variables as age group, country or culture studied, and type of study (Dunn, Jordan, Croft, & Assendelft, 2002). The challenge for psychologists working in the area of sexual disorders includes the fact that while the number of sexually naïve and inexperienced individuals referred for therapy declines, numbers of complex or chronic cases involving a wider age range and physical or psychiatric comorbidities have increased (Schover & Leiblum, 1994). The dysfunctions or problems that are the focus of this Chapter include those sexual dysfunctions that affect heterosexual or gay relationships, namely disorders of sexual desire, arousal, orgasm, or sexual pain. An overview of the use of homework in cognitive and behavioral therapy for such sexual problems, including the applications of specific types of homework activities for particular sexual difficulties, as well as practical guidelines for the successful clinical application of homework techniques are described.

The sexual desire disorders include hypoactive sexual desire disorder, which is described as "persistently or recurrently deficient or absent sexual fantasies and desire for sexual activity" (APA, DSM-IV, 1994). The diagnosis of this disorder is based on the clinical judgment of a clinician, taking into account factors such as age, sex, and the context of the individual's life. There are various manifestations of this disorder, but a referral is most likely when there is an imbalance in the levels of desire experienced by partners or changed sexual interest on the part of one partner. A lack of sexual desire is a very common presenting problem (Weeks, 2002).

Disorders of arousal involve both male and female sexual problems. Impaired sexual arousal includes male erectile disorder, described as "persistent or recurrent partial or complete inability in a male to attain or maintain erection until completion of sexual activity or persistent or recurrent lack of a subjective sense of sexual excitement and pleasure in a male during sexual activity" (APA, DSM-IV, 1994). Segraves and Althof (2002), in a review of the literature, suggested that male erectile disorder is the most common complaint for males who present to sex therapy clinics.

Impaired sexual arousal is also seen in females and can be paired with sexual disorders involving pain during intercourse. Vaginismus in women involves painful spasms of the vaginal muscles, which prohibits intercourse. Dyspareunia is defined as "recurrent and persistent genital pain in either a male or female before, during, and after sexual intercourse" (APA, DSM-IV, 1994). The disorders of orgasm include inhibited female orgasm, inhibited male orgasm, and premature ejaculation. Sexual aversions and phobias may also develop in both genders.

Therapists using interventions for the amelioration of sexual and/or relationship problems often work within a cognitive behavioral therapy (CBT) framework. Clients may include individuals, although work with the dyad or couple is much preferred. This work can encompass secondary prevention, that is, helping people for whom such problems are already present, as well as primary prevention of sexual dysfunction, as when psychoeducation and work on the relationship itself is offered. Techniques applied to sexual problems encompass both behavioral approaches, such as modeling, reinforcement of target behaviors, and graded exposure to feared situations, as well as cognitive approaches, such as increasing positive self-statements and restructuring irrational attitudes and beliefs (Dattilio, 2002; Spence, 1991). In order to best decide how to proceed in treatment, therapists should begin with a thorough assessment of the couple's sexual functioning, including the range of sexual behaviors engaged in, attitudes held about sex, and levels of sexual satisfaction. A structured inventory, such as the Derogatis Sexual Functioning Inventory (Derogatis,

1975), assists with both the formulation and planning of useful homework suitable for the individual needs of a given couple.

Sexual problems present in various ways. Patients can be greatly embarrassed by speaking about sexual matters and are often hesitant to discuss their sexual problems openly. They fear using the wrong words to describe their difficulties or giving offense by being too explicit. Often they have no way of conceptualizing what it is that is wrong; frequently, somatic complaints or vague references to dysphoric mood act as proxies for sexual problems. Therapeutic rapport as well as a common language needs to be established early in therapy.

The importance and sequelae of a sexual problem for the patient and his or her partner(s) need to be understood before the most appropriate course of management can be offered. Initial assessment sessions are aimed at determining a formulation for the sexual problem and identifying underlying emotional issues. Past history of sexual functioning must also be clarified, as this can greatly inform the clinician about the nature of the current problems. History taking is therefore the paramount skill underpinning decisions about management, along with forming a positive alliance with the patient. Any course of action should be jointly discussed between all parties so as to maximize understanding and cooperation. Without that, the best treatment in the world may be of little practical value.

For example, patients may have difficulty talking about the broad spectrum of sexual function, shying away from giving details about their likes and dislikes, their experience of sex, and so on. Other patients may appear superficially to be at ease in discussing sexual matters yet fail to disclose critical thoughts or behaviors concerning sexual functioning. In both cases the intake process, formulation of the case, and design and implementation of a therapeutic strategy, including homework, may be jeopardized. Again, reinforcing the therapeutic alliance, and breaking down myths and stereotypes that may be preventing better communication between therapist and client is essential.

Increasing attention has been paid to the cognitive underpinnings of sexual behavior and sexual dysfunction. A cognitive approach emphasizes that thoughts arising before, during, and after attempts at intercourse may be maintaining the problem. For example, a man with erectile dysfunction may have difficulty attending to erotic stimuli, especially when an erection develops, tending instead to think about the quality of his erection or whether he will be able to maintain it. This preoccupation with sexual adequacy coupled with intrusive thoughts can lead to a dysfunctional cycle in which progression to arousal is repeatedly impeded. The integration of cognitive and behavioral approaches involves pairing recognition of distorted thought processes with carefully structured behavioral assignments aimed at modifying dysfunctional behaviors.

It is likely, however, that therapists are currently seeing clients who are vastly different from those initially treated very successfully by therapists trained in the techniques pioneered by Masters and Johnson. The clients of today have most likely read several of the readily available books about sexual dysfunction and may have accessed information via the Internet. There is also an array of surgical and medical alternatives to therapy that may seem both quicker and more effective than an intervention with a therapist. The result of this increased awareness and increased choice is that the clients who do present with sexual problems are likely to pose more complex cases than those seen in the 1970s.

Having said this, it is still the case that within whatever paradigm a therapist works, strategies that originated with Masters and Johnson are very likely to be included. Because we do now work in a much more complex arena, the notion of a set of strategies suitable for all sexual problems is more than ever a misconception. The recommendation of using a scientist-as-practitioner approach to all cases is well founded. Hypoactive sexual desire disorder can serve as a case in point. An extensive list of individual and relationship causes is correlated with low sexual desire (LoPiccolo & Friedman, 1988). These include strict religious upbringing, depressive symptomatology, obsessive-compulsive disorder or personality, gender identity issues, sexuality issues (heterosexual, homosexual, bisexual), sexual phobias, fear of loss of control over sexual urges, fear of sexually transmitted diseases, fear of pregnancy, sexual trauma (rape or child sexual abuse), marital discord and infidelity, age-related concerns, hormone deficiency, medical issues, and medication issues. This is not an exhaustive list, but it gives an indication of the possible complexity of an individual case.

Types of Homework

The scientist-as-practitioner approach is based on the belief that each case is unique and that treatment should be founded on a thorough assessment of the individual involved. Interventions are based on hypotheses generated from the assessment. These hypotheses lead us to formulate the individual case and to form an opinion regarding cause and maintenance of the problems experienced by the client. It may be the case that a client will benefit from an intervention that targets depressive symptoms in conjunction with one that targets sexual problems. A couple may need to address current sexual problems in the context of other marital issues. A couple with problems caused by a medical disorder or medication may need to look at alternative methods of achieving intimacy and sexual fulfillment.

The therapist often begins treatment by giving the couple accurate information about sexual matters appropriate to their particular circumstances. Various books and videos are available that couples may find helpful (Kingsberg, Althof, & Leiblum, 2002). For example, the series of videotapes entitled *The Lovers' Guide* Parts 1 to 3 (Stanway, 1991, 1992, 1993) provides explicit and useful advice on sexual development for couples. It can be important to stress that therapy for sexual problems is to be viewed as "education rather than healing, as growth rather than treatment" (Lazarus, 1985, p. 82).

Information about changes in sexual functioning with age is often greatly appreciated. The myth that a decline in sexual functioning is a normal part of aging should be addressed directly with information about how psychosocial changes (e.g., loss of one's partner) and physiological factors (such as disease states or medication side effects) can directly contribute to sexual problems later in life. In one review of sexual activity survey data, all studies supported the fact that close to 70% of men and women in their seventies who were free of disease and not taking medications with sexual side effects had sex about once a week (Kaplan, 1991).

Receiving information about aging changes related to sexual functioning may also have direct positive effects on an older client's mood. Distress over sexual dysfunction, coupled with myths about the aging process and the meaning of age-related physiological changes, can directly contribute to elevated levels of depression and anxiety. Often patients or couples have not been given simple factual information about age-related sexual functioning, a situation which at times reflects more the anxiety and lack of knowledge of the health practitioner. Older adults are often reluctant to seek additional information or a second opinion; in such cases the damage from misinformation or lack of information can have significant negative effects on their relationships, their self-esteem, and their identity. Receiving such information sets the stage for more positive therapeutic engagement.

Through therapy sessions and homework assignments, couples can learn new sexual behavioral patterns and improve their relationship skills. The contribution of homework, as in all CBT approaches, is crucial, and the therapists must be skilled to guide often reluctant patients through these homework sessions. This reluctance may stem from a number of sources, including embarrassment, ambivalence, or relationship issues, including a belief that one's partner is unwilling or incapable of change (Weeks & Treat, 2001). Homework tasks should be aimed at facilitating and maintaining positive changes, enabling the couple to work toward resolving their difficulties in the privacy of their own home and at times to suit their lifestyle.

Provision of a safe environment in which to discuss and resolve emotional and sexual conflicts is paramount to ensuring successful treatment. Therapy can uncover and help resolve hidden conflicts long denied. Issues about relationships may be explored in this context, and communication between partners, often difficult in the presence of sexual problems, can be facilitated. Family influences and cultural and gender issues may also be seen as important. An environment of emotional support and understanding can help patients work out their own solutions, with the establishment of realistic goals and support for any changes in lifestyle. However, within such an environment, therapists need to avoid negative interpretations of behaviors, including patients' inability or unwillingness to complete homework assignments; such judgments will only increase the couple's own tendency to be self-critical or accusatory.

In working with clients presenting with a sexual problem, the focus is generally on a cooperative approach involving both partners, in which the issues are reframed so as to be seen as problems to be shared rather than foci of blame. It is also the case that much of the intervention will be carried out by the couple as home-based tasks, because of the private nature of sexual behavior. Therefore compliance with home-based tasks is essential to successful outcome.

The CBT approach to intervention has possibly the most stringent empirical evidence base of all approaches across a wide range of disorders, including sexual dysfunction. One of the core components of CBT is homework completed by the client. Many studies across multiple disorders attest to the fact that a major prognostic indicator is compliance with homework tasks. This is very much the case in work with sexual problems (Hawton & Catalan, 1986; Halford, 2001; Spence, 1991; Weeks & Treat, 2001; Whitehead & Matthews, 1986).

Research into the effectiveness of the various components of CBT with sexual problems is a relatively new area. The vast majority of approaches incorporate multiple techniques, and it is almost impossible to determine which are exerting an active therapeutic effect. The techniques used include an education component designed to increase sexual knowledge, training in sexual skills, graduated exposure to a range of sexual situations, relaxation training, creating nondemand situations, sexual communication skills exercises, marital therapy, exposure to erotic materials, Kegel exercises, cognitive restructuring, and so on. Part of the difficulty in evaluating the effective components is the overlap between those components.

This is especially the case when we look at skills training and gradual exposure exercises such as sensate focus or the squeeze technique for premature ejaculation.

What seems to be the case is that tailoring components to individual problems will have the best outcome for clients. In cases where education is relevant, such as Case Study 1, the effect will be powerful. When cognitive issues are intruding, these will need to be dealt with, or a skills-based approach may seem mechanistic to the client. A combination of appropriate strategies negotiated with the client is most likely to result in compliance with home-based tasks and a more successful outcome.

Behavioral Approaches to Specific Sexual Problems

Disorders of Desire

Sensate focus involves a series of tasks, first described by Masters and Johnson in 1970, which couples can undertake in the privacy of their own homes. Often used with problems involving sexual desire, the goal is a ban on sexual intercourse or any genital contact until anxiety about performance has subsided and trust between the couple has been reestablished. This prohibition of genital touching ensures that physical intimacy can develop without the goal being the sexual act. Homework involves the couple setting aside time to explore each other's bodies in turn by touching, stroking, caressing, and massaging. Sensual touching progresses through to erotic and then sexual touch gradually over time.

Such sensate focus exercises may raise compliance issues in one or both members of a couple; keeping separate journal records of their experiences during the exercises may help reinforce positives and uncover negatives within the exercises. These issues can be explored in greater detail in session, with each couple able to refer to their journals rather than having to rely on memory.

Premature Ejaculation

The "pause-squeeze technique" (St. Lawrence & Madakasira, 1992) is commonly used on men with premature ejaculation difficulties and involves a series of graded masturbatory exercises by which the patient may learn to delay his ejaculation. The aim of the exercises is to enable the patient to recognize the feelings in his penis at different levels of arousal and, by modifying the stimulation, learn to slow his response (Ramage, 1998).

However, although good response to this technique is reported, part of the therapeutic gains may be less enduring than desired, as latency to ejaculation is greatly increased by frequent ejaculation (LoPiccolo & Friedman, 1988). In such cases, using the technique as part of a maintenance program, which includes use of the technique on a less frequent basis, guards against possible relapse.

Erectile Dysfunction

Erectile dysfunction is a common sexual complaint that becomes more common later in life (Bortz, Wallace, & Wiley, 1999). Erectile dysfunction often has both a physiological (e.g., diabetes, medication side effects) and psychological (e.g., performance anxiety) etiology. Sensate focus exercises are often used in men with erectile dysfunction, sometimes in conjunction with cognitive exercises and relaxation techniques. Pharmacological and other physiological interventions are also commonly used.

When sensate focus exercises are used as homework in the treatment of psychogenic erectile dysfunction, often men will begin experiencing erections during either nongenital or genital sensate focus stages. The therapist should specifically encourage focus on pleasurable sensations and discourage negative thoughts about performance. Thought-stopping techniques have been successfully used to stop obsessions over performance and partners' orgasms (Kaplan, 1974). Anxiety reduction and an increase in positive communication can ensure that completion of the exercises progresses well.

Vaginismus

Vaginismus has been linked to chronic low levels of sexual functioning and less positive sexual self-schema (Reissing, Binik, Khalife, Cohen, & Amsel, 2003) as well as contextual issues such as obesity (Jagstaidt, Golay, & Pasini, 2001). Both behavioral and cognitive behavioral approaches for vaginismus have been discussed in the literature and may include direct techniques to improve sexual functioning (such as Kegel exercises) as well as CBT approaches to increase self-esteem, improve communication skills, and ameliorate mood disturbance.

Although the empirical literature on specific treatments for sexual disorders is expanding, controlled studies using rigorous research requirements are limited. In the next decade, there is a pressing need for the development of therapies of proven efficacy, particularly for female sexual disorders, as well as a more precise definition of the indications for biological therapy alone, psychotherapy alone, and combined therapy approaches (Segraves & Althof, 2002).

Strategies for Effective Homework

Although, in practice, homework should ideally be tailored to suit the individual needs of the couple as much as possible, several authors have identified common elements in homework. Structural elements such as negotiating the scheduling of homework, its frequency and duration, where it will take place, and who will be an initiator are common elements that are important both to ensure clarity of the assignment as well as increase compliance (Weeks, 2002). The criteria for successful completion of the homework as well as the goals of the homework assignment should also be made clear (McCarthy, 1985).

Homework should not only reflect a continuation of work begun in the session but may, initially, need to be deliberately nonthreatening in order for a couple locked in conflict to feel safe enough to use the exercise. Depending on the nature of the presenting problems, the degree of distress in the relationship, and the couple's own comfort level, homework may be seen as another situation to be avoided or during which to assign blame or simply as another issue to quarrel over. For example, a hostile couple presenting with a sexual problem may need to start with simple communication tasks and only move on to touching and sensate focus work when they are able to communicate more effectively and are beginning to negotiate reciprocity.

Homework should also encourage the couple in boundary keeping and finding time to play and have fun in addition to making time to talk to each other. For some couples, issues of giving the other person time to themselves, or finding moments to share issues encountered during the day, may be important for improving relationship skills. Initial homework exercises aimed at improving and strengthening relationship skills will help provide the basic communication skills necessary to move through later exercises with a better chance of success. Such exercises also get the couple used to carrying out such exercises in less threatening circumstances, in which their chances of success are high. Such experiences can give the couple a vital boost in confidence, again paving the way for successful completion of later exercises.

Making time for assignments and communication requires a commitment that should be negotiated early on to prevent difficulties in later sessions. Although commitment to homework needs to be discussed and agreed on by the couple, it is necessary to point out that the difficulties involved in completing homework can and should be discussed in session. Couples should be encouraged to discuss, in session, topics of disagreement and resentment without anger and in a constructive manner, including difficulties in negotiating homework exercises.

Homework as a component of sexual therapy has broadened in scope to encompass a range of exercises beyond those traditionally associated with sexual therapy (such as sensate focus). Increasingly, therapists are opting to work simultaneously on core relationship issues, and when this approach is adopted within a CBT framework, homework becomes a vital aspect of the therapeutic process.

Common Barriers to Homework Assignments

Seeking treatment for a sexual problem is not an easy decision, and there are several widely recognized barriers to compliance with home-based tasks. The therapist should carefully consider the terminology used to describe assignments to be completed outside of the therapy session. Several authors (e.g., Dattilio, 2001) have suggested that clients may respond negatively to being asked to complete "homework," as this may evoke unpleasant memories of school days and compulsory tasks, or may decrease self-esteem by making patients feel as though they did not know what they were doing. Such feelings may be more pronounced with older couples or those for whom power struggles are already an issue within the relationship. The term *home-based task* has been suggested as being more neutral; such small changes in terminology and presentation may help increase compliance with the tasks (Dattilio, 2001; Spence, 1991).

Analogous to any other task that clients are asked to complete outside a therapy session, the task needs to be clearly explained so that the clients knows precisely what is expected of them. If a task seems confusing, it is easier not to complete it than to get it wrong. Second, clients must be given a clear and cogent rationale for completing additional tasks outside sessions as well as a rationale for each specific exercise they are asked to do. Furthermore, if a task does not seem intuitively appropriate or relevant to a couple, this can cause noncompliance and even client dropout.

It is extremely important that the difficulty of an apparently straightforward task not be underestimated. Often what seems to be a simple task, such as "sensate focus 1" (nongenital pleasuring), can be extremely difficult for some clients. Spence (1991) suggests that there may be a range of negative thoughts that interfere with a client undertaking such a task, for example: "I shouldn't have to do this…this is stupid…everyone ought to know what to do in sex…," and so on. It is important that any negative thinking associated with engaging in tasks be dealt with inside the sessions, otherwise progress with tasks outside the sessions is unlikely to occur.

Patients may not directly express their concerns over homework and may instead develop avoidance patterns or undertake the homework only in a superficial manner. It is important that the homework assignments be discussed in sufficient depth to ascertain both successful strategies as well as problematic areas for individual clients. Specific issues that may warrant addressing in individual cases include homework specificity, parameters of time and place, agreement by partners about the nature of the homework task, and external events that may changing the feasibility or timing of homework completion.

Enquiring about anticipated difficulties in completing homework tasks is extremely important in order to minimize noncompliance, as such unhelpful learning experiences may be frustrating and disheartening for patients. A useful strategy for ensuring that the homework assignment is not too taxing involves asking clients for a confidence rating of their perceived ability to complete the task. This is of greatest utility when all components of the task have been thoroughly discussed. Using a metric from "not at all confident" (0%) to "completely confident" (100%), confidence can be rated; a 70% or less confidence rating suggests that the task should be reexamined and renegotiated (Kazantzis & Deane, 1999). It is prudent for therapists to be cautious about patients whose ratings always come quickly, endorsing either end of the scale (e.g. "Of course, that is no problem—I am 100% sure I can do this.")

It may be the case that one or both partners are unwilling to suggest engaging in the home-based tasks. There can be the thought that "I will wait until the therapist suggests that we do the task." It may also be the case that one partner believes that the other has the problem and that it is therefore the other partner's responsibility to negotiate doing the tasks. It is likely that for many couples there will be a level of embarrassment surrounding doing the tasks, and it will be easier for many to avoid them completely rather than look or feel silly. In some cases, there is likely to be significant anxiety about engaging in activities of a sexual nature at all. The therapist must recognize this so that the clients are not rushed into tasks with which they are not comfortable. Thus, for the therapy to advance and for homework assignments to be completed successfully, a sense of mutual responsibility for the problem as well as its solution must be fostered.

Attitudinal change may need to be addressed if therapy fails to progress. Negative attitudes brought into the current relationship from the family of origin, sensitivity to stereotyped beliefs in what is "proper" or "allowed" in sexual relationships, and past traumatic sexual experiences may act as impediments in the therapeutic process. Thus, explanations for the fact that therapy may not be progressing may lie in the individual, in the dyad, or in the family of origin of one or both partners (Weeks, 1989). It is vital that such issues be explored as early in the therapeutic relationship as possible, so that homework assignments will be designed with such issues in mind and at a pace appropriate to the individual or couple. However, realistically, it can take some time for a patient to become comfortable and develop sufficient trust to disclose such information. Thus, the therapist must remain alert to indications that issues lying below the surface of therapy may be contributing to noncompletion or only partial completion of homework assignments.

At times the therapist must intervene more directly in the context surrounding the completion of homework assignments. For example, in a couple for whom sex assumes the lowest priority at all times, being permissible only when all tasks are completed or only under "ideal" or "special" circumstances, the therapist may prescribe dates, request that babysitters be engaged on certain days, or that the couple reinforce within the family their own private time, during which interruptions are not generally permissible. Such a change in the environment can contribute to intimacy being viewed in a more positive light, and can greatly increase homework compliance.

In the face of repeated avoidance of either homework assignments in general or specific aspects of home-based practice exercises, the therapist can suggest a range of possible explanations and then explore this list in detail with the couple to gain insight into the issues which may be causing the impasse (Hawton, 1985). In this manner dysfunctional thoughts and attitudes, environmental barriers to successful completion of the work, or faulty expectations of the process or the behaviors and feelings of the partners themselves may be addressed.

However, not all noncompliance with homework assignments should be conceptualized as unhelpful, either to the client or to the therapist. There may in fact be positive outcomes to the noncompletion of home-based tasks. For example, often it is productive to negotiate a timetable for sex as part of treatment. Generally sex is agreed via negotiation to occur on specific days of the week, with the agreement being that sex will not occur on the other days of the week. The couple may agree in session to the schedule but then fail to adhere to it. It may be that the negotiation was not in good faith (e.g., an acquiescence only to please the therapist), and this comes to light only as a result of the inability of the schedule to be workable in practice. In other instances, use of such a schedule may decrease the number of arguments around the frequency and timing of sex, thereby uncovering other unspoken issues that are then aired. The exposure of such issues may thwart the completion of the assignment but may also allow the couple to work on material that was previously not discussed or acknowledged in therapy.

Case Study 1

Nigel, a 65-year-old man, was originally from the United Kingdom but had recently moved to a small seaside retirement community with Emily, his wife of nearly 40 years. Nigel came to therapy originally for treatment of "dysphoria and lack of energy" on the recommendation of his physician. Nigel had been treated for type II diabetes for 10 years, and over the past 5 years, he has noticed changes in his sexual functioning. For example, during sex with Emily, he noticed that it took longer to become aroused and that his erection was less "robust" than it had been in his earlier days. Although Emily appeared satisfied, both with the totality of their relationship as well as its sexual components, Nigel felt he was "letting the side down" in terms of his sexual performance. In fact, nearly a year ago he had experienced an episode of impotence and was so shaken by this event that he had avoided intimacy with his wife ever since. Their relationship was becoming strained, and Emily's attempts to try to ascertain what the difficulties were did not meet with dialogue but rather strained silences or abrupt changes in topic. This had led Nigel over time to feel sad and "empty," as well as guilty over his "bad treatment of the missus." He was spending longer periods of time away from their home, and no longer took part in the gardening, which had been a mutual and much-loved activity for many years. This time away was mainly spent in solitary walks on the beach; recently, even this activity had deteriorated into long stints of sitting in his car and feeling miserable. His new physician, an energetic younger woman, had queried his recent weight loss and lack of energy and had recommended a visit to a psychologist, even though Nigel had not confided to her the source of his discomfort.

The therapy moved through a series of phases and was largely based on CBT approaches. First, once the source of Nigel's change in mood was revealed, several sessions were devoted to education about the changes in sexual functioning that accompany increasing age, as well as what changes could be expected in light of his diabetes. Normal changes in sexual functioning for males were explained, including lengthened time to full arousal, reduced firmness in erection, and decreased strength of ejaculation (Zeiss, Delmonico, Zeiss, & Dornbrand, 1991). However, even with such changes, penetration remains possible, even when paired with the decrease in lubrication common in older women. This is particularly true if external lubricants are used and manual guidance of the penis for intromission is practiced. With increasing age, erectile function becomes more vulnerable to the physiological sequelae of emotional stress and anxiety (*Kellett*, 1991). However, climax and the experience of sexual pleasure remain largely unaffected by aging, although for males the refractory period may be lengthened, sometimes substantially. However, worry about such changes, particularly concern over a single instance of impotence, can greatly increase performance anxiety and thereby contribute to loss of normal sexual functioning. Such rumination about performance was particularly salient in Nigel's case, where one experience of impotence led to complete avoidance of the sexual act.

Diabetes, and the peripheral vascular disease changes that accompany the disorder, can have an impact on sexual functioning in both sexes. For males, the estimated prevalence rate of sexual dysfunction among older diabetics in one study was significantly higher (89.2%) than in a hypertensive group of similar age (43.6%) (el-Rufaie, Bener, Abuzeid, & Ali, 1997). The most common presentations of sexual dysfunction among diabetic men include impaired morning and spontaneous erections, erectile weakness, and ejaculatory disturbances, while reduced sexual interest and complete erectile dysfunction are generally less common. Depression can itself be associated with diabetes (Leedom, Meehan, Procci, & Zeidler, 1991); it is also associated with reduced sexual functioning and can contribute to poorer control of diabetes (Lustman, Griffith, Freedland, & Clouse, 1997). This information about the potential psychosocial and sexual effects of diabetes was received with great interest by Nigel, who had assumed that since his diabetes was well controlled, it could have no further impact on his day-to-day life.

The difficulty of sharing this new-found information with Emily was the topic of a session where discussion of gender-based stereotypes of behaviors predominated. While Nigel did feel strongly that sexual matters were not an appropriate discussion topic with his wife, their intimate connection with his medical condition and overall health offered a less threatening avenue to begin such a dialogue. Nigel reported a great sense of liberation upon sharing his worry about his sexual functioning with his wife, and they had spent several days "catching up," sharing mutual concerns about health, aging, and their relationship. Emily had responded with great relief that Nigel was not angry or ill, both thoughts that had begun to preoccupy her over the past months. However, Emily's assurances that his difficulties with sex did not worry her, and that she "did not care if they could not have sex" had served to alarm Nigel. These assurances brought back fears that his sexual functioning was "all behind him" and that he might not be able to resume a full sexual partnership with his wife.

At this point, several sessions of couples therapy were negotiated and sensate focus exercises and homework assignments introduced. Since the couple's communication skills and relationship satisfaction were already quite good, emphasis was placed on the gradual introduction of physical intimacy into their lives. Nigel was also encouraged to keep track of dysfunctional thoughts and to focus more on pleasurable thoughts and sensations. A major barrier to completion of homework emerged when Emily became quick to reassure Nigel that it was "OK if you want to stop." This message was interpreted by Nigel as a wish on Emily's part not to be intimate. Emily confessed that she had been so shaken by Nigel's withdrawal from their relationship that she was frightened that he could "leave" again at any moment. After a session where these fears were discussed more fully, and reassurances offered, the therapy moved forward. Nigel and Emily were told to focus more thought and energy on enjoying the process of being intimate rather than being "goal-centered." They also began to plan weekly "dates," where they would spend a relaxing evening away from home having dinner; this spontaneously progressed on one occasion to their renting a room at a hotel at which they had enjoyed such a dinner date. This event proved a turning point in the therapy, with Nigel able to perform without anxiety on this occasion, which greatly boosted his self-esteem. Nigel and Emily were able to resume their former level of intimacy, with an enhanced appreciation for communicating their concerns and desires, including sexual concerns and desires, within their relationship.

Case Study 2

Amanda was 35 years old when she first presented for therapy for a sexual dysfunction. Amanda had been married for 10 years to James, age 37, and they had two children, 7 and 9 years of age. Amanda described the marriage as happy; she loved her husband and her children and enjoyed being a wife and mother. Amanda also worked as an accountant and said that she was always very busy and found herself to be tired at the end of a day. The problem that Amanda described was a complete lack of interest in sex with James. She said that increasingly she was avoiding situations where she would expect that James might initiate sexual contact. In the evenings she would either go to bed early to be asleep when James joined her or would stay up later to avoid the possibility of sexual contact. When James did try to initiate a sexual encounter, Amanda said that she would make excuses or she would participate to please her husband but later felt resentful that she had done so.

Amanda described her family of origin as strict and religious. Her father was a lay preacher and her mother was also very religious. She said that as she was growing up she was aware of her parents' disapproval of young people who hugged or kissed in public, and she knew that her parents believed that sex before marriage was a sin. Amanda said that she also came to espouse many of her parents' beliefs, and for this reason had insisted on remaining a virgin until she was married. She described the early stages of her sexual relationship with James as difficult and further said that he had been very patient with her. On becoming pregnant with her first child, Amanda said that she felt she did not want to engage in sexual intercourse because she feared it might harm the baby. Following the birth of her child, she also said that it took her a long time to feel comfortable about having sex, and by the time she did, she found she that was pregnant again. Following the birth of her second child, she said that she did not really have any sexual feelings at all. Amanda wanted to know whether there was something wrong with her, whether there was anything she could do about her problem; she was concerned that she might lose her husband. She reported that disagreements over seemingly trivial matters were becoming more frequent. She also believed that James was fed up with her continued disinterest in sex.

It was apparent that Amanda had many negative thoughts about sex. On further probing she admitted that she thought sex was really only meaningful for procreation, and she believed that sex for fun was quite superficial. A session was spent examining some of Amanda's thoughts about sex, examining some of the negative opinions she held, and raising the suggestion of sex as an expression of intimacy and closeness as well as purely for procreation. Amanda conceded that there was a feeling of increasing distance between her and James and said that she would like to be able to regain intimacy. It was decided to ask James to attend the next session in order to gain his perspective before deciding how to proceed. During the next session James talked about his own feelings of inadequacy in relation to his being unable to "turn his wife on". He said that at times he felt like "a failure" as a man and thought that he must be doing something wrong. James's willingness to disclose his own feelings opened the way for some constructive communication between the couple about their feelings for each other, about their sexual relationship, and about their need to maintain closeness in their relationship. James had not previously realized his wife's views on sex and was able to understand her thoughts and feelings even though he did not agree with them himself.

Amanda said that she was committed to working to improve the sexual relationship but wanted to avoid the feeling that she had to deliver sex on demand. The therapist outlined the sensate focus exercise that asks the couple to engage in nonsexual touching. This task, which can seem simplistic to some couples, was appealing to Amanda. She said that she would think of it as a sensual massage that was a positive experience just for her and required no delivery of sex at the end of it. The proscription on continuing to intercourse was included in this task to avoid the possibility of any performance anxiety or expectation from either party. Within-session a time for the sensate focus to occur was negotiated for each partner.

The couple were asked to perform the task as often as they wanted to but at least twice each week for the next 2 weeks.

The couple returned together for the next session and reported that they had completed the sensate focus task and that each of them had enjoyed the experience on each occasion. Amanda said that it was wonderful to feel so pampered and also to feel close to James without any pressure to proceed to sexual intercourse. James said that he had found that they were talking more together, smiling at one another, and arranging to do more activities together as a couple. Amanda said that she had felt very self-conscious on the first occasion and had found it very difficult to think that this was just for her and that she did not need to reciprocate in any way. She also said that she had found James's tolerance for her difficulties very touching and that she believed this experience was bringing them closer together. Some time was spent in this session revisiting Amanda's earlier thoughts about sex being only for procreation. She said that she was now able to challenge this belief and could see that a good marriage also included a physical component to give closeness and intimacy.

Together James and Amanda decided to proceed to the second sensate focus task, genital pleasuring without full intercourse. The therapist suggested that in this task genital stimulation might lead to arousal, and that if the couple chose to proceed to orgasm, that would be okay. Amanda expressed some reservations about this but said that she had so much enjoyed the renewed contact with James in the previous 2 weeks that she was prepared to see where the exercise went. Once again the couple had clear instructions about the task and had negotiated times to do the task.

The couple returned after 2 weeks and reported that they had completed the task and that they had both enjoyed the experience. On the first occasion they had not proceeded to orgasm and Amanda said that this made her relax more on the second occasion, because she knew there was no expectation of her. On subsequent occasions the couple had achieved orgasm both via oral sex and full intercourse. Amanda said that she had enjoyed it each time. She went on to say that she was starting to think about sex quite differently now and was beginning to realize that not every encounter needed to end with sex and orgasm. Maintaining closeness in the relationship was very important to her, and relaxing and communicating with her husband was an integral part of the relationship.

This turned out to be a fairly straightforward case. In essence the success of the case rested with the cognitive shift that occurred for Amanda, coupled with James's supportive patience and their willingness to proceed with the homework tasks. There was a chance that Amanda would not be prepared to go ahead with the second sensate focus task, but by this stage she had begun to think very differently. She now saw her physical involvement as contributing to the closeness and intimacy of the relationship, rather than seeing it as a duty that she would rather not do. The facilitation of communication between the couple was also an important component. Each partner was able to see the perspective of the other in a nonthreatening way, and in this case each was then willing to accommodate the other as much as possible. Once the hidden fears were brought to light and resolved—for example, that James would leave for someone else or that Amanda found James inept as a lover—the couple began to talk much more openly about their thoughts and feelings. Completion of the home-based assignments and the initiation of increasingly open dialogue between the couple progressed the therapy to the point where sexual issues became less prominent and the therapy shifted to focus more on lingering relationship issues. Trust had been the key to allowing the homework assignments to proceed, which in turn resulted in dramatic improvements.

Process Issues

An important issue to consider is whether a particular homework assignment itself becomes a barrier in the larger treatment picture. Again using the example of a schedule for sex, it can become apparent that one partner may be invested in the indefinite use of such a schedule because it affords an opportunity to discuss issues of sex in the relationship in a more open and possibly confronting manner. In this situation, the partner, who may wish to experiment with a more flexible arrangement for intimacy, may feel that his or her wishes are marginalized. If the couple has previously used the technique successfully, the dilemma for the therapist becomes how to renegotiate the use of a helpful therapeutic intervention without undoing the positive progress in the relationship to date. It may be helpful to state early on that such schedules and exercises need to be reviewed periodically to prevent them from going "stale." This foreshadows the possible future need to tinker with any structures put in place in the relationship (e.g., "date nights," schedules for sex). Alternatively, the therapist may suggest a planned "vacation" from the schedule, with an invitation for the couple to be playful and enjoy this "time off" from their routines.

Cultural considerations also need to figure into planning successful homework assignments. For example, some religious systems put restrictions on premarital sex or on marital sex according to the phases of the moon, the menstrual cycle, or religious festivals (Crowe, Ridley, & Skynner, 2000). Sensitivity to such issues will both strengthen therapeutic rapport and increase acceptance and compliance with home-based assignments.

The "culture" of the therapy itself, as created and maintained by the therapist, can have a direct effect on a couple's progress in resolving intimacy issues. Inexperienced therapists may devote too little time to the adequate exploration of positive and negative experiences encountered by the couple in the course of home-based practice sessions. Inadequately addressing such issues during homework review will decrease the efficacy of home-based activities as an intervention and may lead the couple to believe that since it is not of importance to the therapist, such homework is optional or of less importance than in-session work. Overeager therapists may display disappointment with noncompleted homework (or perhaps even with homework not completed in the manner in which the therapist envisioned), thereby introducing added pressures and anxiety into the couple's relationship. Such difficulties should be anticipated by the therapist and actively utilized as a means to gain insight into problems that have yet to surface within the relationship. Similarly, if a couple is rushed into the next phase of therapy without adequate preparation or skills, therapeutic progress may be undone (Hawton, 1985).

An indication of the therapist's skill in managing the therapy is his or her ability to predict what may happen between sessions, including responses to homework assignments (Hawton, 1985). This can be a useful private exercise for the therapist to gain further insight into a couple's difficulties by comparing predicted with actual responses to home-based assignments. If shared judiciously with clients, such predictions may help to defuse anxiety (as in "Sometimes people feel awkward in writing out their fantasies, but this may allow you to be less vague about your own desires. This may make things easier to share with your husband, as you've both said conversations about such matters are either avoided or vague.").

Finally, the therapist's own comfort level may be a factor in successful movement in therapy, including homework efficacy. If therapists have failed to explore their own issues around sexuality, therapy outcome may suffer (Schnarch, 1992). Personal insight and self-awareness achieved while working with couples is a valuable (but too infrequently discussed) addition to a therapist's growth process as a professional and as a person. Therapist maturity expands with the ability both to allow for and manage emotional intensity (Shaw, 2001).

Conclusions

Sexual problems, whether they present as a primary focus of treatment or take on significance in the course of addressing relationship difficulties, remain a challenging area of therapeutic work. CBT approaches to the treatment of both focused functional issues as well as broader intimacy and relationship issues has been the focus of much research. Information and education play key roles in addressing sexual concerns, particularly with regards to the dispelling of myths surrounding sexual functioning with increasing age. Homework or home-based tasks can play an important role in the efficacy of the treatment of sexual problems. Barriers such as noncompliance may require added resourcefulness on the part of the therapist and at times may even offer added insight and a chance for further processing of critical material. Above all, therapists must remain attuned to the sensitivities of their patients and reflective of their own growth and maturation if their interventions are to be of therapeutic effect.

References

American Psychiatric Association. (1994). *Diagnostic and Statistical Manual, 4th ed.* Washington DC: American Psychiatric Association.

Bortz, W. M., Wallace, D. H., & Wiley, D. (1999). Sexual function in 1,202 aging males: Differentiating aspects. *Journals of Gerontology: Biological Sciences and Medical Sciences, 54A,* M237–M241.

Crowe, M., & Ridley, J. (2000). *Therapy with Couples: A systems-systems approach to marital and sexual problems.* London: Blackwell.

Dattilio, F. M. (2002). Homework assignments in couple and family therapy, *Journal of Clinical Psychology, 58,* 535–547.

Derogatis, L. R. (1975). *Derogatis sexual functioning inventory.* Baltimore: Clinical Psychometrics Research.

Dunn, K. M., Jordan, K., Croft, P. R., & Assendelft, W. J. J. (2002). Systematic review of sexual problems: Epidemiology and methodology. *Journal of Sex and Marital Therapy, 28,* 399–422.

el-Rufaie, O. E., Bener, A., Abuzeid, M. S., & Ali, T. A. (1997). Sexual dysfunction among type II diabetic men: A controlled study. *Journal of Psychosomatic Research, 43,* 605–612.

Halford, W. K. (2001). *Brief therapy for couples: Helping partners help themselves.* New York: Guilford Press.

Hawton, K. (1985). *Sex therapy: A practical guide.* Oxford, UK: Oxford University Press.

Hawton, K. (1992). Sex therapy research: Has it withered on the vine? *Annual Review of Sex Research, 3,* 49–72.

Hawton, K., & Catalan, J. (1986). Prognostic factors in sex therapy. *Behavior Research and Therapy, 24,* 377–385.

Hawton, K., Catalan, J., & Fagg, J. (1991). Low sexual desire: Sex therapy results and prognostic factors. *Behavior Research and Therapy, 29,* 217–224.

Jagstaidt, V., Golay, A., & Pasini, W. (2001). Relationship between sexuality and eating disorders in obese women. *New Trends in Experimental and Clinical Psychiatry, 17,* 69–77.

Kaplan, H. S. (1974). *The new sex therapy.* New York: Brunner/Mazel.

Kaplan, H. S. (1991). Sex therapy with older patients. In W. A. Myers (Ed.), *New techniques in the psychotherapy of older patients.* Washington DC: American Psychiatric Association.

Kazantzis, N., & Deane, F. P. (1999). Psychologists' use of homework assignments in clinical practice. *Professional Psychology: Research and Practice, 30,* 581–585.

Kellett, J. M. (1991). Sexuality of the elderly. *Sexual and Marital Therapy, 6(2),* 147–155.

Kingsberg, S., Althof, S. E., & Leiblum, S. (2002). Books helpful to patients with sexual and marital problems. *Journal of Sex and Marital Therapy, 28,* 219–228.

Lazarus, A. A. (1985). Adjusting the carburetor: Pivotal clinical interventions in marital and sex therapy. In R. C. Rosen & S. R. Leiblum (Eds.), *Case Studies in Sex Therapy* (pp. 81–95). New York: Guilford Press.

Leedom, L., Meehan, W. P., Procci, W., & Zeidler, A. (1991). Symptoms of depression in patients with type II diabetes mellitus. *Psychosomatics, 32,* 280–286.

LoPiccolo, J., & Friedman, J. (1988). Broad-spectrum treatment of low sexual desire: Integration of cognitive, behavioral, and systemic therapy. In S. R. Lieblum & R. C. Rosen (Eds.), *Sexual Desire Disorders* (pp. 107–144). New York: Guilford Press.

Lustman, P. J., Griffith, L. S., Freedland, K. E., & Clouse, R. E. (1997). The course of major depression in diabetics. *General Hospital Psychiatry, 19,* 138–143.

Masters, W. H., & Johnson, V. E. (1970). *Human sexual inadequacy.* Boston: Little, Brown.

McCarthy, B. W. (1985). Use and misuse of behavioral homework exercises in sex therapy. *Journal of Sex and Marital Therapy, 11,* 185–191.

Ramage, M. (1998). ABC of sexual health: Management of sexual problems. *British Medical Journal, 317,* 1509–1512.

Reissing, E. D., Binik, Y. M., Khalife, S., Cohen, D., & Amsel, R. (2003). Etiological correlates of vaginismus: Sexual and physical abuse, sexual knowledge sexual self-schema and relationship adjustment. *Journal of Sex and Marital Therapy, 29,* 47–59.

Schnarch, D. M. (1992). The person of the therapist: Inside the sexual crucible. *VOICES: The Art and Science of Psychotherapy, 28,* 20–27.

Schover, L. R., & Leiblum, S. R. (1994). The stagnation of sex therapy. *Journal of Psychology and Human Sexuality, 6,* 5–30.

Segraves, T., & Althof, S. (2002). Psychotherapy and pharmacotherapy for sexual dysfunctions. In P. E. Nathan & J. M. Gorman (Eds.), *A guide to treatments that work* (2nd ed., pp. 497–524). London: Oxford University Press.

Shaw, J. (2001). Approaching sexual potential in relationship: A reward of age and maturity. In P.J. Kleinplatz (Ed.), *New directions in sex therapy* (pp. 185–209). Philadelphia: Taylor & Francis.

Spence, S. H. (1991). *Psychosexual therapy: A cognitive-behavioral approach.* London: Chapman & Hall.

St. Lawrence, J. S. & Madakasira, S. (1992). Evaluation and treatment of premature ejaculation: A critical review. *International Journal of Psychiatry in Medicine, 22,* 77–97.

Stanway, A. (1991). *The lovers guide: How to enhance your loving and sexual relationship.* London: Lifetime Vision.

Stanway, A. (1992). *The lovers guide 2.* London: Lifetime Vision.

Stanway, A. (1993). *The lovers guide 3.* London: Lifetime Vision.

Watson, J. P. & Teifion, Davies. (1997). ABC of mental health: Psychosexual problems. *British Medical Journal, 315,* 239–242.

Weeks, G. R. (1989). An intersystem approach to treatment. In G. Weeks (Ed.), *Treating couples: The intersystem model of the Marriage Council of Philadephia* (pp. 317–340). New York: Brunner/Mazel.

Weeks, G. R. (2002). *Hypoactive sexual desire: Integrating sex and couple therapy.* New York: Norton.

Weeks, G. R., & Treat, S. R. (2001). *Couples in treatment: Techniques and approaches for effective practice.* Philadelphia: Brunner/Routledge.

Whitehead, A., & Matthews, A. (1986). Factors related to successful outcome in the treatment of sexually unresponsive women. *Psychological Medicine, 16,* 373–378.

Zeiss, R.A., Delmonico, R.L., Zeiss, A. M., & Dornbrand. L. (1991). Psychological disorder and sexual dysfunction in elders. *Clinics in Geriatric Medicine, 7,* 133–151.

CHAPTER 16

Borderline Traits

ARTHUR FREEMAN and GINA M. FUSCO

A therapist comes into her office in the morning and sits down at her desk with her morning coffee to review the day's patient schedule. As she reviews the names and lists the case files to be pulled, she stops mid-sip. At noon that day she is seeing Alice. Alice, age 34, had been seen for almost a year at that point in therapy. She has met eight of nine criteria for borderline personality disorder (BPD). Her inner life, interpersonal relationships, family interactions, and stormy marriage each moved quickly to the top of her list of life crises throughout her therapy.

The therapist has developed both countertransference stress[1] and a countertransference structure[2] related to Alice, who has been demanding of the therapist's time, effort, energy, good will, and patience. The therapist is having great difficulty maintaining unconditional positive regard for Alice, who would likely have vexed Carl Rogers. The sessions have been difficult, at times stormy. Alice has demanded reparenting therapy, touch therapy, and intensive psychoanalysis. She went into crisis when the therapist's vacation time came around, when snow emergencies closed the clinic, or when car problems kept her from coming to a session.

---

[1] *Countertransference stress* refers to the session-by-session reactions of the therapist to the patient. They are brief and fleeting.

[2] *Countertransference structure* refers to a more stable reaction that goes beyond the session and becomes a more common way in which the patient is perceived by the therapist.

If anything in the description of Alice sounds familiar, it is because Alice is a common type of patient for most therapists, regardless of theoretical orientation. She may be the most difficult and troubling patient in a therapist's caseload.

The treatment of BPD has been discussed at length by many clinicians practicing cognitive behavioral therapy (CBT) as well as by psychodynamic clinicians who endorse a CBT approach to treatment (Linehan, 1993; Beck, Freeman, & Associates, 1990; Beck, Freeman, Davis, & Associates, 2004; Freeman & Fusco, 2004; Freeman, Pretzer, Fleming, & Simon, 2004; Fusco & Freeman, 2004; Layden, Newman, Freeman, & Morse, 1993; Livesley, 2003; Millon, Davis, Millon, Escovar, & Meagher, 2000; Millon & Davis, 1996; Stone, 1980, 1986, 1993). Coming from a range of theoretical orientations from psychoanalytic to CBT, the treatment of BPD engenders points of disagreement as well as becoming a meeting point, inasmuch as several commonalties emerge. These include the need for a stable and highly structured approach to therapy, maintaining control of the session, the need to be aware of countertransference, the need to make self-injurious behaviors unrewarding, the goal of helping patients to modulate their behavior, and the use of homework as both a central component and an essential part of the therapy.

The element of homework is the focus of this Chapter, which is structured to offer discussion of (a) the CBT conceptualization of BPD, (b) the importance of homework in CBT, (c) specific homework interventions, and (d) the extent to which homework is used in the session. The Chapter ends with a detailed case example illustrating the use of homework.

General Treatment Conceptualization

Few diagnostic categories elicit as negative a reaction as does that of BPD. In point of fact, BPD has become more than a diagnostic category, it has become a ubiquitous label for difficult patients, an insult when the staff dislikes a patient, a rationale for treatment resistance, and an excuse for treatment failures. BPD may well represent the most difficult, misunderstood, and poorly conceptualized diagnosis applied to any patient in the clinician's caseload. Part of the difficulty stems from the multiple meanings that the diagnosis has acquired over the years. From its earliest meaning descriptive of the patient's position on the "border" between neurosis and psychosis, it has come to have meaning as a syndrome, as a description of a level of functioning, as a dynamic constellation, as a prognostic statement, and as an accusation. It has become, in many cases, less a diagnosis and more of a trash-can category than a way of specifying psychological disorder for treatment.

According to Campbell (1996), the term has been used to refer to preschizophrenic or latent schizophrenic patients (p. 528). Hoch and Polatin (1949) used the term *pseudoneurotic schizophrenia* to describe the patient who was on that border between neurosis and psychosis. In their view, borderline patients appeared "healthier" or more "normal" than they really were, and under the stress of psychoanalysis, decompensated to a schizophrenic state. This originally thin line between normal and abnormal has now enlarged to become an area that appears to have continually widened over successive years. The decision to diagnose a patient as neurotic or psychotic was often difficult for clinicians in the past, when these two major designations made up the few choices available.

Stern (1938, 1945, 1948) is considered to be the first to explicitly use the term *borderline*. From these modest beginnings, the notion of the patient existing on this border has grown until it now occupies a section in DSM-IV-TR as "borderline personality disorder." The essential features are described as "a pervasive pattern of instability of interpersonal relationships, self-image, and affects, and marked impulsivity that begins by early adulthood and is present in a variety of contexts" (APA, 2000, p. 706). Should this trend continue to expand, we might expect this condition to be still further enlarged by observing its manifestations even earlier and see this disorder identified in adolescence and childhood (Freeman & Rigby, 2003). There may even be other areas in which to expand and enlarge this diagnosis.

The diagnostic category has evolved over time from DSM-I (1952) through to the present iteration. The interaction between the multiple factors related to the borderline disorder (genetic, physiological, social, interpersonal, intrapersonal, global functioning) and the patient factors of emotional, dynamic, and family history combine to create a complex and usually chronic situation. Add to this the therapist factors of therapeutic skill, previous training, and ability to deal with powerful countertransference, and the therapeutic picture becomes even more convoluted.

Borderline personality disorders are apparently common, with the prevalence estimated to be about 2% of the general population, about 10% among individuals in outpatient mental health clinics, and about 20% among psychiatric inpatients. Finally, estimates range from 30% to 60% among populations with personality disorders (American Psychiatric Association, 2000, p. 708). Despite its "popularity" as a diagnosis, it is a diagnostic category with which many clinicians have limited familiarity and which has received limited attention from authors presenting CBT approaches to psychotherapy.

Cognitive Behavioral Conceptualization

The patient with BPD is conceptualized as an individual who is hyperreactive to both internal and external stimuli. These patients seem to lack the ability to modulate their responses. Stone (1993) offers the conceptual framework shown in Figure 16.1 for explaining the patient's hyperreactivity. Stone's hypothesis is that patients with BPD have a lowered threshold and a more reactive central nervous system. This would account for their high levels of arousal. The patient with BPD sometimes seems unable to withstand even the mildest stimuli. As an exaggeration, such a patient may complain about the molecules of air constantly bombarding his exposed skin, thereby making him exquisitely sore. The difficulty in being so exquisitely sensitive and hyperreactive can be illustrated for the patient in a graphic metaphor. Freeman (1992) uses graphic representations to share with the patient his view of the problem of BPD (Figure 16.2).

The suggestion of the metaphor is that the patient with BPD is tenuously balanced at the apex of a mountain, vulnerable to every slight breath of air. The mildest breeze will quite quickly cause such an individual to

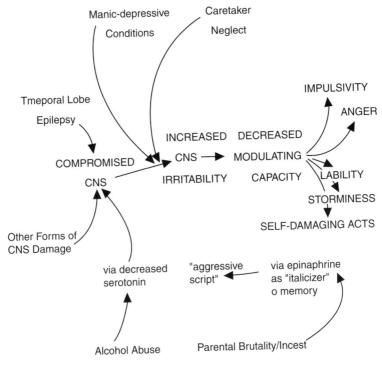

Fig. 16.1 Conceptualization of the etiology of borderline personality disorder.

Fig. 16.2 Patient with borderline personality disorder balanced "on the brink."

lose her balance. Therefore she must fight to maintain her balance and avoid being blown over, falling from the mountain, and being severely injured or killed. Following the graphic metaphor, the goal of therapy is to work to help the patient establish a "stable base" that will allow her to be more flexible in the world. She would no longer be subject to the slight or mild stressors that previously rocked her to her very core (Figure 16.3).

Building the stable base is the basis of therapeutic work with the patient with BPD. It requires, in large part, a strong working alliance and is integrally related to the therapeutic relationship.

It is within the stable base that the second part of the therapeutic process occurs. This involves explicating the patient's schema. An essential element of CBT is understanding and making explicit the person's underlying schemas. This is the essential dynamic level of CBT. Beck and associates have suggested that schemas generate the various cognitive distortions seen in patients (Beck, 1967, 1976; Beck, Freeman, Davis, & Associates, 2004; Freeman et al., 1990, 2004). These schemas or basic rules of life begin to be established as a force in cognition and behavior from the earliest moments in life, and they are well fixed by the middle childhood years.

Fig. 16.3   Patient with borderline personality disorder with a "stable base."

They are the accumulation of the individual's learning and experience within a family group, the religious or ethnic group, the gender category, regional subgroups, and the broader society.

The schemas are very rarely isolated and separate, but like the distortions, they occur in complex combinations and permutations. The schemas become, in effect, how one defines oneself, both individually and as part of a group. Schemas can be active or dormant, with the more active schemas being the rules that govern day-to-day behavior. The dormant schemas are called into play to control behavior in times of stress. The schemas may be either compelling or noncompelling. The more compelling the particular schema, the more likely it is that the individual or family will respond to the schema. The particular extent of a schema's effect on an individual's life depends on several factors: (a) How strongly held is the schema? (b) How essential does the individual perceive that schema to be for personal safety, well-being, or existence? (c) Does the individual engage in any disputation of the particular schema when it is activated? (d) What was learned previously regarding the importance and essential nature of a particular schema? (e) How early was a particular schema internalized? (f) How powerfully, and by whom, was the schema reinforced? Schemas are in a constant state of change and evolution. From the child's earliest years, there is a need to alter old schemas and develop new schemas to meet the different and increasingly complex demands of the world.

A particular schema may engender a great deal of emotion and be emotionally bound by the individual's past experience, by the sheer weight of the time in which that schema has been held, or by the relative importance and meaning of the individuals from or with whom the schema were acquired. A cognitive element of the schema pervades the individual's thoughts and images. The schemas are cognitive in that we can often, with the proper training, describe schemas in great detail. We can also infer schema from behavior and from automatic thoughts. Finally, a behavioral component of each schema involves the way the belief system governs the individual's responses to a particular stimulus or set of stimuli. In seeking to alter a particular schema that has endured for a long period of time, it would be necessary to help the individual to deal with the belief from as many different perspectives as possible. A purely cognitive strategy would leave the behavioral and affective perspectives untouched. The purely affective strategy is similarly limited, as is the strictly behavioral approach. In many cases, an individual's particular schemas are consensually validated. Significant others not only help to form the schemas, but also help to maintain the particular schemas, be they negative or positive. McGoldrick and Giordano (1996) emphasize that families view the world through their own cultural filters, so that the particular belief systems may be familial or more broadly cultural. An example of a family schema based on the culture in which the family is immersed might be basic rules regarding sexual behavior; reaction to other racial, ethnic, or religious groups; or particular religious beliefs.

Patients often describe themselves as having displayed particular characteristics "as far back as I can remember." Objective observation may support such a patient's views in this regard. What, then, differentiates the child who develops a schema that is held with moderate strength and is amenable to change later on and the individual who develops a core belief that is powerful and apparently immutable? Several possibilities exist: (a) In addition to the core belief, the individual maintains a powerful associated belief that cannot be changed; (b) the individual's belief system is powerfully reinforced by parents or significant others; (c) while the dysfunctional belief system may not be especially reinforced, any attempt to believe the contrary may not be reinforced or may even be punished (e.g., a child might or might not be told "You're no good," but any attempt on the part of the child to assert her worth would be ignored); (d) the parents or significant others may offer direct instruction that undermines the child's development of a positive image (e.g., "It's not nice to brag" or "It's not nice to toot your own horn, because people will think less of you").

Strategies for Effective Homework

CBT is characterized as being active, directive, time-limited, proactive, structured, psychoeducational, problem-oriented, solution-focused, collaborative, and dynamic. Nowhere are these aspects as focused as in the use of homework as an essential technique in CBT (Freeman & Rosenfield, 2002). Often, the therapist is at a loss as to determine what homework assignments might be most useful, productive, and fruitful for a particular patient. By identifying the issues to be addressed, the therapist can choose among a number of potential self-help homework assignments.

CBT can be distinguished by its approach to transfer and generalization through the use of intersession "homework." Systematic extension of the work of therapy to nontherapy hours results in faster, more comprehensive improvement (Burns & Auerbach, 1992; Meichenbaum, 1987; Neimeyer & Feixas, 1990; Freeman & Rosenfield, 2003; Kazantzis, Deane, & Ronan, 2000). Although this empirical support is growing, there are no specific data on the effects of homework assignments in CBT for borderline traits.

Skills, new cognitions, and new behaviors must be applied *in vivo*. Learning and changes relative to one situation must be actively generalized to other, similar situations. In this way, new learnings become natural and automatic aspects of the person's behavioral and cognitive repertoire. As noted earlier, homework can be cognitive, affective, situational, or behavioral. Most often, it comprises some combination of all these elements. Homework early in therapy focuses on helping the person to interrupt automatic routines, and to observe the connections between thought, behavior and mood. Thus, early homework tasks may include observing automatic thoughts through the use of the dysfunctional thought record (DTR), activity scheduling, incident logs to record experiences, collecting evidence for and against one's attributions and expectancies, and mastery and pleasure ratings. In the middle of therapy, homework includes trying out new behaviors through graded task assignments; acting differently in order to gather information about alternative hypotheses; noticing, catching, interrupting and responding to negative thoughts and behaviors; and enacting a plan designed to lead to a specific goal.

Homework may be an unfortunate term to use in describing the things people do between sessions to extend the therapy into their lives. It carries connotations that, for some, may sound authoritarian, suggesting that homework is "assigned." Patients' adherence to recommendations that they act between sessions to further their therapy is affected by the way the "homework" is conceived, the follow-up that occurs, and the complexity of the tasks themselves. A number of suggestions to increase adherence have been given by Meichenbaum and Turk (1987).

1. Homework should be collaboratively developed. The therapist can "lead" the discussion in such a way that clients themselves develop ideas for the work that is needed. The therapist lays the groundwork by asking questions, reflecting on what is already known or the skills the person has, and what is missing, and "going public" with her rationale or theories.

2. Tasks should be simple. For tasks that are beyond the person's skill level, the smaller the task and the greater the likelihood of success, the better. For a more skilled client, more challenging tasks are better. Regardless, it must be possible for the person to perform the task with a reasonable expenditure of time and effort.

3. Provide the client with a choice. If more than one method exists to monitor behaviors or thoughts, using the one the person prefers increases the likelihood of follow-through. Choice, or the perception of choice, enhances a person's sense of control and self-efficacy.

4. Specify what will be done, when, and how. Moderately specific plans result in better adherence than overly specific ones, particularly with longer-term goals. Moderately specific plans give the person choices and engage him or her in decision making.

5. Engage significant others in the task, in reinforcing the person for completing or engaging in the task, and in determining the task whenever possible.

6. Directly, and in a stepwise fashion, teach monitoring skills, including recording, interpreting, and using the results.

7. Specify contingencies that follow adherence or nonadherence. Specify the results the person can expect from the task or the purpose of the task. "Go public" with the rationale for the task. Better yet, have the person identify the rationale as part of collaboratively designing the task.

8. Offer mild counterarguments about completion of the task. For example, anticipate difficulties, drawbacks, and obstacles the person is likely to face in attempting the task. Help the person to plan cognitive and behavioral responses to obstacles and to identify partial success or partial completion as useful.

9. Provide the person with feedback on adherence and on the accuracy of his performance of the task. Defocus from the product and focus on the attempt: effort and new information are more important than specific results.

10. Record positive behaviors rather than negative ones. Assign "do" tasks rather than "don't do" tasks. Particularly when the task involves interrupting an old routine, plan a substitute behavior or cognition. In the absence of a better plan, the person will fall back on old behaviors and cognitions. The therapist can use the homework to help the person to internally attribute success and improvements that result from treatment adherence. Depressed persons tend to self-attribute blame and to see good events or results as being due to uncontrollable external forces. Internal attribution of success enhances self-efficacy. Shelton and Levy (1981) suggested that a homework assignment should specify what the person is to do, how often or how many times, how they are to record their efforts, what they are to bring to the next appointment (e.g., the record), and consequences or contingencies attendant on either adherence or nonadherence.

Client, Therapist, and Therapy Factors in Effective Homework

Activity

One of the first requirements for CBT is activity. By activity we mean that for therapy to be successful, the patient must be an active participant in the therapy. This is true for CBT whether the treatment is directed toward problems of depression, anxiety, substance misuse, or the more complex problem of BPD.

Willingness

While this seems obvious, not every patient with BPD is willing and/or able to participate in the therapeutic endeavor. Given that therapeutic activity involves the patient's willingness and ability to establish a working alliance, the patient with BPD is at a distinct disadvantage. This is often the very source of such a patient's difficulty. The conundrum is that building a working alliance is important, and the patient with BPD often avoids alliances of any sort. The willingness or ability to change is related to several factors, including ambivalence over changing and being different, fear of changing and being different, the issue of whether change is really necessary, and the notion that the environment and system should also change accordingly (a circumstance not easily part of the therapeutic work).

The patient with BPD may not come to therapy willingly but may have been referred by another person or agency. These individuals may not want to be in therapy and are angry that they are being forced to go somewhere, to do something in a particular manner. In addition to this background, patients may be resistant, have a low level of insight into their thoughts and actions, and may not be terribly articulate. The patient's willingness to try to change may mean that she will show up for most of the sessions, do some of the homework, and talk most of the time, or that she will generally take her medication. Though limited, this may be enough of a commitment for therapy to begin. Given that therapy cannot be fully accomplished within the consulting room, the use of activities and experiences in addition to the face-to-face work is necessary. This out-of-session work, or homework, gives the patient an opportunity to experiment with thoughts, feelings, and actions. The homework must be related to the session material, be agreed to by the patient, and have a clear and specific goal. The patient must be well prepared to attempt the homework before leaving the session so that the chances of success are increased.

Difficulty

The activity required by homework must be carefully metered. If too much homework is used, the patient may be overwhelmed and concomitantly believe that the purpose of the homework is for the therapist to avoid doing therapy. The therapist must be clear that the homework is part of the therapy, and by going over the homework in the following session, the therapist illustrates his caring and attention.

Directiveness

A second element of the CBT model is that it must be directive. The directive nature of the therapy is the parallel and equivalent of the activity for the patient. It is essential that when the therapist and patient are in the consulting room, one of them should have an idea, focus, and direction for the therapy. A directive approach may take many different forms and may involve a number of strategies and interventions; these can include offering information and serving as a resource, providing the patient with a venue for developing more effective coping techniques, and helping the patient to acquire basic skills. The directive nature of the therapy is not in any way meant to exclude the collaborative empiricism discussed by Beck (Beck, et al., 1979).

The directiveness of the therapist would be dictated by the patient's problems, personal style, and the goals of the therapy. The goal is not to take over a patient's life but to direct the therapy in terms of focus, speed, goals, and purpose. For example, a highly motivated patient coming to therapy with specific goals and purposes would require less direction than the patient without direction or focus. Probably the prime example of direction occurs in dealing with a patient with BPD who is self-injurious or threatens suicide. In these cases the therapist should actively and directly question or even challenge the patient's powerful idea that suicide is a reasonable action and that death is the only solution to life's travail.

It is the therapist who must guide the patient, via Socratic dialogue, to choose the best possible homework that will produce the maximum return for the time and energy spent. Essentially, the therapist must be responsible for guiding the therapeutic endeavor.

Proactive

Therapy must be proactive, not just reactive. The patient with BPD is, by nature and inclination, highly impulsive and reactive. This is all the more reason for the therapist to model a treatment strategy that views planning, thoughtfulness, and problem solving as key issues and of the utmost importance. The reactive model leads patients to enter therapy with the expectation that they will start the therapeutic flow and that the therapist will just "goes with the flow." This model involves the expectation that the therapist's role is to respond, restate, reframe, reflect, and interpret the material produced spontaneously (or with some small amount of urging) by the patient.

A proactive stance involves multilevel treatment planning, which would include a central plan and direction for therapy with several alternate plans. Each part of the plan must include elements that require the patient to do some work independently. If the patient never acquires a "homework thought set," therapy will ultimately fail, for once therapy has ended, the patient's life will be all homework.

The first part of the treatment would require having the patient complete a list of therapy goals as a homework assignment. This can be followed by in-session work to then prioritize the goals. This helps the patient to plan for change. By developing a treatment plan with the patient, the therapist can assess and account for the patient's motivation, abilities and goals along with the therapist's own abilities and motivation. It is essential for the therapist to plan for the session and to have on hand several alternate homework plans.

Time-Limited

Can a patient with BPD be treated in 10 or 12 sessions? Often, the too rapid response is "No." However, "No" is the response to the question "Can a patient with BPD be cured in 10 or 12 sessions?" Using a time-limited approach to therapy helps to keep the therapy on track and the therapist and the patient focused on the treatment goals.

We would recommend working in no more than five-session modules. This allows for planning proximal goals for both in-session and homework experiences. We can now combine the directive approach with a time-limited focus. The proactive, time-limited, and directive nature of the model means that we are going to have to plan what we can do in the time available. This would involve setting treatment goals for every module. This session number is arbitrary and might be anywhere from 5 to 10. This encourages setting short-term, workable goals for the session module.

The scheduling of sessions is also important. Sessions do not have to be held on a weekly basis. The therapist may decide to have a session a month, given that the patient would be willing to do homework between sessions. We may decide to have two sessions in week one, skip a week and arrange to have the total number of 10 sessions over 15 weeks or almost 4 months. The key ingredient is the homework that the patient will do between sessions. Depending on the patient, the therapist must think about flexibility of scheduling. If the patient says, for example, "I don't want to do any homework or work in therapy," it may not matter if she is seen weekly, triweekly or daily.

Collaborative

Therapeutic collaboration is not necessarily 50:50. We cannot demand that the patient do half or more of the therapy work. With some patients collaboration may, by necessity, be 90:10. The patient with BPD might be at a stage of anticontemplation (Freeman & Dolan, 2001) and willing or able to offer only 10% of the collaboration. The therapist may then need to do 90% of the work. (This is also what makes working with BPD patients so wearing and difficult for the therapist.) Over the course of therapy, the relative weight of the collaboration may shift. We cannot expect every patient to be an equal and willing contributor to the therapy. That, in fact, may be impossible, because of these patients' skill deficits.

A caveat is for the therapist to carefully assess what the patient is able to bring to therapy and then to expect that portion of the collaboration. The danger is that the therapist may become overwhelmed and/or overinvolved with the patient and believe that he must continuously provide 100% of the work, even when this is counterproductive and antitherapeutic. When the homework is set collaboratively, the patient has an opportunity to contribute to what is being planned and to identify the roadblocks that may interfere with the successful completion of the work.

Problem-Oriented

When patients seek therapy, they often come with complaints rather than with problems. This is often a difficult issue to resolve at the outset of therapy for both therapist and patient. The confusion between complaints and problems will serve to negatively impact on the therapy and can potentially lead to treatment failure. Based on the assessment, the therapist must focus on those factors that are central to the diagnosis and the complaint. When the problem is BPD, one simple focus is to use the Freeman Diagnostic Profiling System (Freeman, 2004) (Figure 16.4).

By assessing each of the nine criteria for BPD, the therapist can focus the treatment and design homework for those areas that are the most troubling, least maladaptive, or most amenable to change in the time available. The complaints then are the shorthand labels that are used to encapsulate the problem. The therapist must expand and set out the component pieces and definitions of the problem. Once again, setting out vague goals will lead to vague therapy and thereby vague results. It is not sufficient to identify problems without moving the patient to the next therapeutic step, that of solving them.

Solution-Focused

It would be wonderful if therapy ran as smoothly and quickly as it does on TV and in the movies. In the movies, a simple interpretation would immediately lead to insight and to "cure." The therapy must take the focus of helping the patient to build problem-solving strategies. This may take the form of having the patient with BPD acquire a solution that can then be generalized to other life situations. Or, more likely, the therapist will help the patient to develop a problem-solving approach to problems in general. The elements of this approach are data collection, evaluating the data, developing hypotheses, and being willing to test out the hypotheses, often using a homework experience as a way of collecting data. For some problems, the necessary solutions are more cognitive and require the patient to learn how to challenge some ideas and accept others. For other problems, the need is for more directed behavioral solutions and skill building. For yet other problems, affect regulation may be necessary. Finally, environmental manipulation to alter life circumstances may be needed.

Structured

CBT is structured in two main ways. At the beginning of therapy, we must first identify (with the patient) the goals of therapy in very specific terms. This involves setting out a specific, proximal, and mutually agreeable problem list. The list is then prioritized and examined in terms of several factors:

Your therapist will help you complete this worksheet.

FREEMAN DIAGNOSTIC PROFILING SYSTEM
(© FREEMAN, 2003) REVISED EDITION

Date of Assessment: _____

Session#: _____ Evaluator: _____

Patient Name: _____ Patient#: _____ Location: _____

Birthdate: _____ Age: _____ Race: _____ Gender: _____ Birthorder: _____ Marital/Children: _____

Employment: _____ Education: _____ Disability: _____ Medication: _____

Physician: _____ Referral Question: _____

Instructions: Record the diagnosis including the code number. Briefly identify the criteria for the selected diagnosis. Working with the patient either directly as as part of the data gathering of the clinical interview, SCALE the SEVERITY of EACH CRITERION for the patient at the PRESENT TIME. Indicate the level of severity on the grid.

DIAGNOSIS (DSM/ICD) with Code:

Axis I: _____

Axis II: _____

Axis III: _____

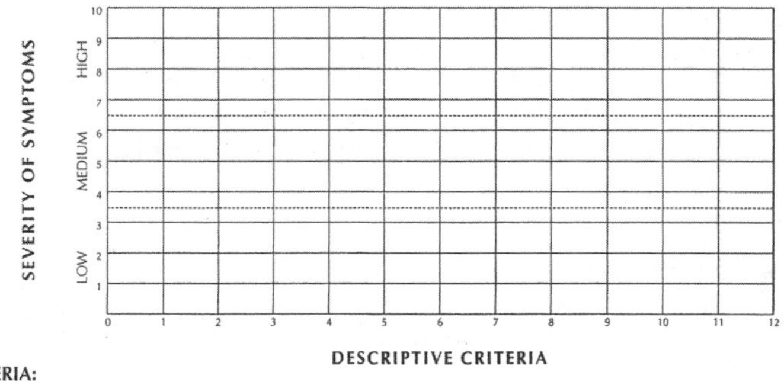

CRITERIA:

DESCRIPTIVE CRITERIA

1 _____   7 _____

2 _____   8 _____

3 _____   9 _____

4 _____   10 _____

5 _____   11 _____

6 _____   12 _____

Do you believe that the above noted criteria are a reasonably accurate sample of the patient's behavior? **YES** or **NO**

If **NO**, please indicate why: _____

Are there any reasons to believe that this individual is an imminent danger to himself/herself or others? **YES** or **NO**

If **YES**, please indicate the danger: _____

Fig. 16.4 Freeman Diagnostic Profiling System.

1. Patient's interest and motivation
2. Patient's repertoire of skills
3. Therapist's repertoire of skills
4. Time needed
5. Chronicity and likelihood of change

This structuring offers the parameters for the therapy. If the patient moves away from the problem list, the therapist can inquire as to what brings the new focus and whether there are key themes that can be addressed. It is within the structure of the therapy that homework is introduced. Using graded homework experiences, the patient learns from the first session that the homework is not in addition to the therapy but that it is structured to provide the connecting points between therapy sessions.

A second structuring must take place within the session. The therapist practicing CBT can best use the available time by using agenda setting. Having the patient collaboratively set an agenda at the beginning of each session offers definition and format to the session. The agenda must be seen as a guide and not as having been graven in stone and therefore unyielding and unchangeable. In all cases, it is empowering to the patient to invite them to decide how to deal with a digression or shift. The agenda must include the review of the previous session's homework as well as the homework to be attempted for the succeeding session. Of course, this agenda must then be monitored and paced by the therapist.

Dynamic

The dynamic cognitive approach to therapy promotes self-disclosure of individual cognitions in order to increase the patient's understanding of his or her thoughts, beliefs, and attitudes. One way of conceptualizing the change process is to use the Piagetian idea of adaptation, with its two interrelated processes of assimilation and accommodation (Rosen, 1985, 1989). The therapist can help patients to see that their self-schemas may be self-selective, as they are filtered through the template of the schema. Individuals may even ignore environmental stimuli that they were not able to integrate or synthesize. The assimilative and accommodative processes are interactive and stand in opposition to one another. Assimilation is an active and evolutionary process through which existing perceptions and cognitive structures are applied to new functions, whereas accommodation requires that new cognitive structures be developed in order to serve old functions in new situations. Some individuals may persist in using old structures (assimilation) without fitting them to the new circumstances (accommodation) in which they are involved; instead, they use the old structures in toto, without measuring fit or appropriateness. They may further fail to accommodate or build new structures for other situations. This is pointed out to the patient throughout the therapy. The goal would be for the patient to use old rules more adaptively and to create new structures when needed.

Psychoeducational

For many patients, the problems that bring them into therapy derive from skill deficits. A prime example for the patient with BPD are the limited skills of problem solving, being aggressive rather than assertive, impulse control difficulties, or social skills deficits. While they may have *adequate* skills to cope with many of the exigencies of life, it is often the case that they are skill-deficient. It may be as simple as the patient having limited strategies for pleasure seeking, which contributes to their depression. For another patient, deficit in self-calming may lead to or exacerbate a panic problem.

Types of Homework

The range of homework assignments is as varied and numerous as the clients presenting with BPD diagnoses (Freeman, 2002). Examples of the types of homework assignments are provided in practitioner and client texts specifically written for the CBT treatment of BPD (i.e., Freeman & Fusco, 2004; Fusco & Freeman, 2004). For example, "incident charts" allow the patient to identify physiological responses, cognitions, emotions, and behaviors prior to, during, and subsequent to a targeted "incident." The homework described on the incident charts can then be explicated and can include an assessment of the situational triggers, physical triggers, emotional triggers, cognitive triggers, and behavioral triggers. The more traditional DTR and an assessment of relevant schema are also used to help the patient (and the therapist) to develop a clearer idea of the patient's functioning. A treatment goals work sheet is also assigned to patients to complete (Figure 16.5). This allows them to literally "take control" by establishing treatment goals in a prioritized manner from highest to lowest. This is then used by the therapist as a life-learning lesson. The notion of prioritizing rather than seeing everything as needing the same level of care or concern is the idea here.

Case Study

Alice, 34 years old, was referred by a psychiatrist because of her ongoing depression. Pharmacotherapy had been ineffective, as had a year of insight-oriented therapy. Alice had been married to Gerry, an accountant, for 15 years. She had completed a master's degree in education and had worked as a teacher for 6 years early in their marriage. At the point of entering therapy she had not worked in 9 years. She stayed at home, "too depressed to do anything."

Given the referral for depression, Alice was asked, as a first homework assignment, to make a list of her negative thoughts. She began her list with

Treatment Goals

This worksheet asks you to identify your treatment goals, the sypmtoms that prevent you from obtaining your goals, the schemas that are associated with those goals, and the change for which you are hoping. Are you able to imagine yourself completing the goals? Complete this chart with the help of your therapist and prioritize the importance of each of these goals.

	Symptoms that prevent you from obtaining goal	Schema associated with goal	Hoped-for change	Realisitic or unrealistic?	How outcome looks if goal is reached
Goal 1: Highest priority					
Goal 2: High priority					
Goal 3: Moderate priority					
Goal 4: Low priority					

Fig. 16.5 Treatment goals work sheet.

"I was bad before I was born, I was a bad fetus." When she was asked to explicate this idea, she told how her mother had regaled her for years with how bad she (Alice) had been *in utero*. Her mother had a difficult first trimester of pregnancy, with a great deal of nausea; she could not sleep because of chronic lower back pain in the second trimester and was bed-ridden for the last 4 months of her pregnancy. Her mother explained that this was all because Alice was bad even before she was born.

Alice had few friends throughout her childhood and adolescence. Her mother attempted to inoculate Alice against the "viciousness" of the world by slapping Alice across the face almost daily. If Alice cried, her mother kept hitting her, to teach her to resist the pain of the world. Finally, Alice could accept the slaps without crying. At that point, Alice's mother would hit her so Alice would be more emotionally responsive.

When Alice graduated from high school and discussed going to college, her mother became distraught. Her mother told Alice, "I can't stand the thought of you going away. I'll die without you here. You are all I have to live for. Can't you forget college and get a job in town? Please don't leave me." Alice chose a college relatively close to home for the first 2 years and commuted 1½ hours each way to school daily. Her second 2 years were spent on a campus some distance from her home. Alice reported that this caused her mother to become so depressed that she took to her bed and barely ate for the next several years.

The homework at this point focused on Alice examining the evidence for and against her being the sole cause of her mother's depression (or apparently psychotic withdrawal). This homework was largely unsuccessful in that while Alice could articulate the issues her mother dealt with, she maintained the belief that she was the cause, above and beyond all other factors.

Therapy proceeded for 13 months before Alice felt she could begin to trust the therapist. Throughout this time, therapy was a stormy road. After a 2-foot snowfall that closed down the city on a day Alice had a therapy appointment, the therapist called her to rearrange the time. Alice's husband said that she had left some 2 hours earlier. The therapist left for the office and arrived about a half hour late for the appointment. Alice was sitting on the floor in the corridor crying. Her tears quickly turned to anger once inside the office. "If I can be here, even after a 2½-hour trip, why couldn't you? You knew that there was to be snow. You could have planned to leave earlier."

When the therapist told Alice about an impending vacation 3 months hence, she withdrew from therapy. "What is the use of being in therapy when you are leaving?" she said in response to the therapist's inquiries. When told that the therapist did intend to return, Alice questioned, "How do I know that?" Alice saw any separation as irrevocable. Alice saw the therapist's return as anticlimactic. Here again, homework that focused on examining evidence (the therapist's being available, being on time, never missing an appointment, even in the snow, having phone sessions when Alice was ill) were also of little value. She responded with the tone of "Yes, but."

She feared the coming year and the impending separation of next summer's vacation. Alice had few ideas as to how her mistrust and fear of separation (and abandonment) came to be. The journal writing and schema identification became useful forms homework. Alice could begin to pair her emotions with specific feelings and thoughts. These thoughts and beliefs could then be examined in the session.

After the second year of therapy, Alice told the therapist about an incident that had occurred when she was 7 years old. Her father was in the U.S. Navy, stationed in Japan. Her mother had Alice spend a week at the beginning of the summer with Alice's paternal grandmother. Alice was told that during that time, Alice's father would return home and her mother and father would come to get her. Alice's grandmother worked as a matron at a state orphanage. For the first week, Alice lived in her grandmother's room. When her mother and father did not call or come to get her, Alice was moved into the girls' dormitory. She stayed in the dormitory for the balance of the summer. Her grandmother made plans for Alice to attend school at the orphanage. Three days before school was to begin, she was brought to her grandmother's room, where her parents greeted her. Her mother's only comment was, "Your father was delayed." When questioned as to why she had never mentioned that experience, Alice replied, "I didn't think that it was all that important."

Using the abandonment as a clue, the therapist inquired as to whether there were other incidents of being left, abandoned, separated, or taken from her parents. Alice developed an extensive list as another homework assignment. Within the session, Alice went on to describe several other instances of being emotionally abandoned (her mother would get angry at her and not speak to her for weeks at a time) or physically abandoned (being left sitting on a bench for hours in a shopping mall or store and told not to move until mother returned, hours later). Given these early experiences, Alice's schema about being abandoned were powerfully in place. When asked about her relationship with her husband, she said that she did not trust that he would stay with her for very long.

The goals of the therapy were, first, to carefully try to challenge the idea that she would always be abandoned. Alice was unwilling at first to take the risk that the therapist would leave and return or that the therapist would leave, return, and still be willing to work with her. Her distortion in this regard was that the therapist would forget about her while she was away.

A second goal of therapy was to work with Alice and her husband to try to improve the marital relationship. Couples sessions were instituted to help her husband better understand Alice and her problems and for Alice to risk telling her husband of her dissatisfaction with many aspects of the relationship.

In the third year of weekly therapy, Alice was less depressed and less anxious than she had been initially. At this point, it was questionable whether Alice would be able to maintain paid employment. The therapeutic relationship, being the microcosm of her relationships with the world, continued to be the arena in which Alice would seek to understand her fear of abandonment and to frame experiments to test this early schema as part of homework.

With the major focus being Alice's fear of abandonment, Alice's assessment of the severity of the issue was stated (Figure 16.6). The schema work sheets were of great value in helping Alice identify her schema. She could identify the source of her ideas and their meaning for her, but she found the schemas difficult to modify in that she believed them so powerfully. Finally, the "dichotomous thinking chart" (Figure 16.7) was valuable in helping Alice to move away from her black-and-white construction of the world.

Summary and Conclusion

By coordinating the patient's workbook possibilities with the guidance of the therapist's manual, we can offer the high degree of structure required in therapy. Further, the focus on those specific elements move the therapist away from the broad, vague, global, and amorphous issues that are part of treating BPD as a unitary phenomenon. The initial and important issue for the therapy is to help these patients to understand the nature of BPD. They need to understand what it is and what it is not. A corollary is to help the patient to accept the impact and the severity of BPD.

The homework must be designed to help the patient develop the skills to cope more effectively with BPD. Given that these patients have been trying for a good portion of their lives to adapt and survive, their motivation might suffer. The therapy (and ultimately the homework) must be designed to build the motivation to cope with BPD. Key to the treatment will be to work against the inevitable frustration of having a BPD. The patient will ask, "Why me?" Sometimes that question can be answered by pointing to early family-of-origin conflict. More often, the sources of the disorder are not entirely clear.

It is often essential for the patient to develop a support network for the difficult days when things are not going well or when the patient may be having situational, emotional, cognitive, or behavioral conflicts, with the net result being that the patient is upset and in a high state of negative arousal. These support persons can be homework supporters, homework

Schemas

What are your rules or schemas related to relationships? Take a moment to write them down.

_____

_____

_____

_____

_____

_____

_____

Choose any of these specific rules and fill in each of the columns. Indicate what the rule is, where (or whom) it comes from, what meaning it has for you, and how likely or easy it would be for you to change that rule. Once you have identified your particular schemas, how strong they are, and whether or not they can be changed, you can begin to create treatment goals.

Schema	Where it comes from	Meaning to me	Easy to change?

Fig. 16.6 Schema work sheet.

assistants, or homework encouragers. The homework can also serve, in this regard, to help maintain patients' willingness to engage in the therapeutic collaboration. This help-seeking also needs to be carefully monitored so that it does not replicate other high-demand behaviors that have not helped the individual but rather have been hurtful because they tend to push people away.

The Dichotomous Thinking Chart

Black

He's terrible

Gray(s)

He's not always so bad

White

He's perfect

I have a hard time mixing grays related to

Fig. 16.7 Dichotomous thinking chart.

The homework can focus on building the ability to self-monitor and to reasonably monitor others. The homework can help these patients to build an optimistic view of the world that is also realistic. It will help them to control negative arousal, take a problem-solving approach, establish and maintain boundaries, maintain a structure for treatment, and finally, develop the skill to see trouble on the horizon and to deal with it effectively.

References

American Psychiatric Association. (1952). *Diagnostic and statistical manual of mental disorders*, Washington, DC: American Psychiatric Press.

American Psychiatric Association. (2001). *Diagnostic and statistical manual of mental disorders* (4th ed., text revision). Washington DC: American Psychiatric Press.

Beck, A. T. (1967). *Depression: Clinical, experimental, and theoretical aspects*. New York: Harper & Row.

Beck, A. T. (1976). *Cognitive therapy and the emotional disorders*. New York: International Universities Press.

Beck, A. T., Freeman, A., & Associates. (1990). *Cognitive therapy of personality disorders*. New York: Guilford Press.

Beck, A. T., Freeman, A., Davis, D. D, & Associates. (2004). *Cognitive therapy of personality disorders*. (2nd ed.). New York: Guilford Press.

Beck, A. T., Rush, A. J., Shaw, B.F., & Emery, G. (1979). *Cognitive therapy of depression*. New York: Guilford Press

Campbell, R. J. (1996). *Psychiatric dictionary*. New York: Oxford University Press.

Freeman, A., & Fusco, G. M. (2004). *Borderline personality disorder: A therapist's guide to taking control*. New York: Norton.

Freeman, A., Pretzer, J., Fleming, B., & Simon, K. M. (1990). *Clinical applications of cognitive therapy*. New York: Plenum Publishers.

Freeman, A., Pretzer, J., Fleming, B., & Simon, K. M. (2004). *Clinical applications of cognitive therapy* (2nd ed.). New York: Kluwer.

Freeman, A., & Rigby, A. (2003). Personality disorders in childhood. In M. A. Reinecke, F. M. Dattilio, & A. Freeman (Eds.), *Cognitive therapy with children and adolescents* (2nd ed.). New York: Guilford Press.

Fusco, G. M., & Freeman, A. (2004). *Borderline personality disorder: A patient's guide to taking control*. New York: Norton.

Hoch, P., & Polatin, P. (1949). Pseudoneurotic forms of schizophrenia. *Psychiatric Quarterly, 23*, 248–276.

Kazantzis, N., Deane, F. P., & Ronan, K. R. (2000). Homework assignments in cognitive and behavioral therapy: A meta-analysis. *Clinical Psychology: Science and Practice, 7*, 189–202.

Layden, M. A., Newman, C. F., Freeman, A., & Morse, S. B. (1993). *Cognitive therapy of borderline personality disorder*. Needham Heights, MA: Allyn & Bacon.

Linehan, M. M. (1993). *Cognitive behavioral treatment of borderline personality disorder*. New York: Guilford Press.

Livesley, W. J. (2003). *Practical management of personality disorder*. New York: Guilford Press.

McGoldrick, M., Giordano, J., & Pearce, J. K. (Eds.). (1996). *Ethnicity and family therapy* (2nd ed.). New York: Guilford Press.

Meichenbaum, D., & Turk, D. (1987). *Facilitating treatment adherence: A practitioner's handbook*. New York: Plenum Publishers.

Millon, T., & Davis, R. D. (1996). *Disorders of personality: DSM-IV and beyond*. New York: Wiley.

Millon, T., Davis, R. D., Millon, C., Escovar, L., & Meagher, S. (2000). *Personality disorders in modern life*. New York: Wiley.

Shelton, J. L., & Levy, R. L. (1981). *Behavioral assignments and treatment compliance: A handbook of clinical strategies*. Champaign, IL: Research Press.

Stern, A. (1938). Borderline group of neuroses. *Psychoanalytic Quarterly, 7,* 467–489.

Stern, A. (1945). Psychoanalytic therapy in the borderline neuroses. *Psychoanalytic Quarterly, 14,* 190–198.

Stern, A. (1948). Transference in borderline neuroses. *Psychoanalytic Quarterly, 17,* 527–528.

Stone, M. H. (1980). *The borderline syndromes: Constitution, personality and adaptation.* New York: McGraw-Hill.

Stone, M. H. (Ed.). (1986). *Essential papers on borderline disorders: One hundred years at the border.* New York: New York University Press

Stone, M. H. (1993). *Abnormalities of personality.* New York: Norton.

PART IV

Model for Practice and Conclusions

CHAPTER 17

A Guiding Model for Practice

NIKOLAOS KAZANTZIS, JAMIE MACEWAN, and
FRANK M. DATTILIO

Anything that we have to learn to do we learn by the actual doing
of it.

Aristotle, Nicomachean Ethics, Book II, p. 91

In this Chapter, our aim is to provide a comprehensive account of the
process of using homework assignments within the scope of cognitive
behavioral therapy (CBT). We draw on the theoretical and empirical foundations in Part I of the book and the clinical recommendations offered in
Parts II and III, and discuss specific recommendations for the practicing
clinician. In particular, we address the question: *How can homework
assignments be more effectively integrated into the treatment of clients?*

As outlined in Parts II and III of this book, the content and specific
strategies for the effective use of homework differ across different clinical
problems. We do not attempt to provide a detailed summary or list of all
clinical recommendations in this model. Instead, we seek to synthesize the
common features of the process that are generally applicable as a guiding
model for practice. The material in this section will build on the original
description of integrating homework assignments into Beck's cognitive
theory and therapy (A. T. Beck, 1964, 1976; A. T. Beck, Rush, Shaw, &
Emery, 1979) and traditional behavioral therapy (Wolpe, 1958, 1973).

Homework is a logical extension of previous models (i.e., Shelton & Levy, 1981), and this Chapter is designed to enhance the therapist's skill in integrating specific assignments into therapy by making the process more explicit.

This Chapter is divided into two main sections; the first half of the Chapter is devoted to discussing the importance of the therapeutic relationship and the role of therapists' assumptions about using homework assignments. In the second half, specific therapist behaviors are discussed. This section describes in detail how to employ each step of our practice model and includes specific clinical examples. This Chapter represents the third step of our *Cognitive Behavior Therapy Homework Project*, forming the basis of a manualized protocol for future prospective process outcome research (see Chapter 1).

The advances over previous models for practice are threefold: (a) increased focus on facilitative qualities of the therapeutic relationship, the facilitative qualities of the therapist, and therapist beliefs; (b) expanded incorporation of cognitive theory and behavioral foundations in recommending strategies for enhancing homework completion; and (c) better grounding in the specific recommendations for using homework with various clinical presentations, discussed in Parts II and III of this book. In providing this guiding model, we wish to delineate the conditions under which client learning through the completion of homework can be maximized. We begin with a brief overview and critique of current recommendations for clinical practice.

Existing Recommendations for Practice

Recommendations for the use of homework assignments are not new to the professional literature. A number of early psychotherapy practitioner-theoreticians recommended the use of therapeutic work between sessions (e.g., Dunlap, 1932). Reflecting the predominant therapeutic approach of the first part of the twentieth century, several writers advocated for clients to record their dreams, engage in and record "free association activities," or deliberately expose themselves to fearful situations for later discussion with the therapist in session (Freud, 1952; Herzberg, 1941; Karpman, 1949). George Kelly's fixed role therapy involved clients taking on roles that were opposite to their own self-image in order to experience the benefits of social reinforcement for different possibilities (Kelly, 1955).

The 1960s and 1970s witnessed the development of psychotherapy formulations that transferred the responsibility for change to the client. Several therapies advocated for a view of homework assignments as *the* central focus of therapy around which other interventions and other in session processes were based (e.g., Kanfer & Phillips, 1966). In particular, carefully structured homework was central to couples sex therapy (i.e., Masters & Johnson, 1970; LoPiccolo & LoPiccolo, 1978). Building on the conceptual basis of Kanfer and Phillips' behavioral formulation, Shelton and Ackerman (1974) devised a clinician's guide with a list of 150 homework assignments that could be used to treat behavioral problems. Shelton and Ackerman also provided examples and guidance on how to integrate homework assignments into the therapeutic process.

In the early 1980s, a specific "model for practice" that outlined recommendations for the integration of homework into behavioral therapy was proposed (Shelton & Levy, 1981). The model was consistent with recommendations that had been emphasized in A. T. Beck et al.'s (1979) *Cognitive Therapy of Depression,* emphasizing that each session should begin and end with the discussion of homework and that therapists should work to attain a degree of behavioral specificity in assigning homework (see also Shelton & Ackerman, 1974). These early recommendations featured the following elements:

1. Homework is an interpersonal process that requires a strong therapeutic relationship.
2. Homework should be relevant to the client's problems and goals for treatment.
3. Homework should be within the client's ability.
4. Homework should be practiced in session.
5. Homework compliance should be discussed, with successes praised, and problems considered.
6. Private and public statements of commitments to homework are required.
7. Homework should be assigned with a clear description of task variables: where, when, how often, and how long.
8. A written copy of the homework should be provided.

The Shelton and Levy (1981) model for practice also operated on the assumption that *clients should be motivated to comply with assignments* and suggested that noncompliance with homework was due to a lack of client skill, cognitions that interfere with completion, or environmental barriers (see also Table 17.1). The Shelton and Levy model was based on empirical work aimed at improving medication compliance. For example, the third proposition, that compliance should be reinforced, was based on the data that positive reinforcement had been demonstrated to improve compliance in various treatments (i.e., Agras, Barlow, Chapin, Abel, & Leitenberg, 1974; Haynes et al., 1976; Mahoney, Moura, & Wade, 1973; Reiss, Piotrowski,

TABLE 17.1 Propositions for the Improvement of Homework Compliance

---

1. The therapist should be sure that assignments contain specific detail regarding response and stimulus elements relevant to the desired behavior.

2. The therapist should give direct skill training when necessary.

3. Compliance should be reinforced.

4. The therapist should begin with small homework requests and gradually increase assignments.

5. The therapist should use cueing.

6. The therapist should have the client make a public commitment to comply.

7. The therapist should help the client develop a private commitment to comply.

8. The therapist should use cognitive rehearsal strategies to improve success with assignments.

9. The therapist should try to anticipate and reduce the negative effects of compliance.

10. The therapist should closely monitor compliance with as many sources as possible.

11. The therapist should use paradoxical strategies when necessary.

Note. Adapted from *Behavioral Assignments and Treatment Compliance: A handbook of Clinical Strategies* by J. L. Shelton and R. L. Levy (1981).

& Bailey, 1976). However, we suggest that many clients are likely to require more than a public or private statement of commitment or paradoxical strategies to address their cognitions about the homework assignment.

As part of our *Cognitive Behavior Therapy Homework Project*, we conducted a series of practitioner surveys to examine whether practitioners use homework in a manner consistent with the Shelton and Levy (1981) model. Data from two of our surveys (i.e., Kazantzis & Deane, 1999; Kazantzis, Busch, Merrick, & Ronan, 2005) found that only a small minority of cognitive behavioral therapists routinely followed Shelton and Levy's (1981) model in assigning homework (see Chapter 3). One interpretation of this finding is that therapists are departing from clinical theory and recommendations for practice. Another interpretation is that the model does not accurately capture the process of using homework. For example, it is often not possible to specify exactly when or where a particular homework activity will be carried out. This is usually the case when clients are to apply a particular intervention in response to a naturally occurring cognitive, emotional, physiological, or behavioral trigger. Thus, a major concern with the Shelton and Levy model and with other early models is the extent to which they are sufficiently flexible to accommodate the range of homework assignments in CBT.

Another concern with these models is that they do not adequately address the role of the collaborative therapeutic relationship in determining homework completion. Though the therapeutic relationship has been mentioned as an important condition, there has been little attention to what specific relationship qualities and therapist qualities may facilitate or hinder homework completion. There has also been limited consideration of the therapists' own beliefs and how these may influence behavior in discussing homework. As two of our practice surveys have linked therapist beliefs and use of homework assignments (i.e., Fehm & Kazantzis, 2004; Kazantzis, Lampropoulos, & Deane, in press), it would seem that greater consideration of "therapist factors" is warranted.

Still another drawback of the Shelton and Levy (1981) model and other early recommendations is that they do not adequately address the role of client cognition in explaining homework completion. As outlined in Chapter 2, there are a host of cognitive theory foundations that suggest clients have beliefs that determine whether a particular homework assignment will be attempted. Clients also form beliefs based on their experience of having completed homework, which, in turn, influences future behavior. It is not surprising that several authors have illustrated the role of the client's cognitive conceptualization in explaining noncompliance with homework assignments in cognitive therapy for depression (i.e., J. Beck, 1995; Persons, 1989; Persons, Davidson, & Tompkins, 2001). Commonly observed psychological barriers to homework compliance in depression include perfectionism/unrelenting standards, fear of failure/procrastination, forgetting, and desire for social acceptance. Again, the role of client beliefs in relation to homework completion is not fully addressed by the early models. Absent in the current literature is a generic model for practice that takes into account theoretical foundations that determine homework completion.

The Collaborative Therapeutic Relationship

A frequent misconception about the CBT approach is that the therapeutic relationship is not important and that, as a result, there is an exclusive focus on structure and technique. This misconception may be in part based on the fact that some cognitive behavioral practitioner texts focus on the teaching of techniques and intervention and only briefly summarize the tenets of collaborative empiricism. However, the evolution of CBT carries with it an increased emphasis on the therapy relationship in research and practice (see discussion in Blackburn & Twaddle, 1996), something that is represented in this model as well as elsewhere (Dattilio, Freeman, & Blue, 1998).

Assuming that the therapist and client have developed a strong therapeutic relationship that is collaborative, the process of working through homework assignments can further their work as a team. However, because homework is assigned from the very first therapy session, the assignments present an immediate challenge for the therapeutic relationship. In an effort to underscore the position that homework assignments can be used effectively only with strong collaboration, we integrate some discussion on therapeutic relationship issues throughout this model. First we present a discussion of the relationship and therapist qualities that are *requisite* for the effective use of homework.

Relationship Qualities

Providing CBT for people in distress can be a highly effective and rewarding service. It can also be difficult and frustrating, especially if the therapist has been working with the client for some time and has not seen much client benefit. Although therapists strive to maintain positions of positive regard, neutrality, and objectivity, persistent difficulties with homework completion have the potential to activate the therapist's own beliefs and emotions (Stevens, Muran, & Safran, 2003), which may be less than supportive. If a client exhibits a marked demanding, avoidant, and/or suspicious interpersonal style, there may be a greater risk of therapist reactivity (or countertransference). Therefore care and sensitivity are required in discussing homework (see Chapter 16 for context on borderline personality traits). Occasionally, the actual presenting problems of the clients may elicit negative thoughts, emotions, and behaviors in therapists (see Chapters 13 for substance abuse and Chapter 15 for sexual problems). Although clients present for therapy with various learned interpersonal styles, it remains the therapist's responsibility to create an environment in which the client can be an active collaborator in discussing homework. Chapters 6 and 7 provide further useful examples of the role of therapeutic collaboration when working with adolescents and older adults, respectively.

The collaborative emphasis in CBT is the basis for meeting the needs, problems, and abilities of each individual client through homework. Active client involvement is required to achieve these aims (A. T. Beck et al., 1979). This level of involvement can be difficult to achieve if the client has been socialized into a relationship as a compliant student or passive recipient of structured assignments. Common barriers to collaboration include distrust of the therapist, unrealistic expectations, personal shame, externalized blame, depreciation of self or others, and fear of rejection and failure (A. T. Beck, Freeman, Davis, & Associates, 2004). In fact, novice therapists' efforts to adhere to structure and interventions in CBT often lead to rigid and insufficiently individualized and collaborative therapy (see Gibbons, Crits-Christoph, Levinson, & Barber, 2003). Persistent noncompletion of homework is often an indicator of a rupture in the alliance or difficulty in communication within the collaborative therapeutic relationship. In our view, an awareness and willingness to foster an individualized therapy that is collaborative is necessary for the effective use of homework assignments.

Consistent with the tenets of collaboration, we encourage therapists to only assign homework activities that they would be prepared to carry out themselves. We also encourage therapists to complete common homework assignments themselves from time to time. This is usually helpful in enabling the therapist to fully appreciate what is involved in a given assignment as well as to experience the array of practical obstacles that the client may run into while attempting it.

Therapist Qualities

According to Young and A. T. Beck (1982), there is a series of therapist qualities that can serve to encourage collaboration/engagement and trust. The authors recommend that therapists be able to communicate genuineness, transparency, sincerity, and openness. The goal is to foster an impression of the therapist as being forthcoming with information, expressive of his or her ideas, and direct in responding to questions. Another set of recommended therapist qualities includes warmth, concern, empathy, and curiosity. A therapist's empathy is conveyed both in what is said and what is expressed through tone, body language, and eye contact. Warmth can also be conveyed through the supportive use of humor (see Basco & Rush, 1996; A. T. Beck, Wright, Newman, & Liese, 1993; Young & A. T. Beck, 1982). Further, by showing curiosity, the therapist subtly sends the message that clients will provide the majority of the information that determines the outcome and guides the design of new homework (Tompkins, 2002).

Professionalism and consistency are also essential attributes for therapists. With regard to the first, the goal is to strike a balance between a professional demeanor (courteous, conscientious, and businesslike) and a relaxed therapeutic style. In the present context, professionalism can be observed when a therapist expresses encouragement about the client's progress with learning through homework completion and when the therapist provides positive feedback about its completion (see Chapter 2).

Consistency on the part of the therapist is an attribute that sends the message that homework is important throughout therapy (Tompkins, 2003). If homework is not reviewed or planned as described by various authors in Parts II and III, then a host of negative interpretations may be made by the client. The client may assume that the therapist did not feel that the homework was important or perhaps that he or she did not believe that the client was capable of doing it. Such assumptions are likely to influence clients' level of collaboration and efforts to complete future homework assignments.

With therapist qualities and the therapeutic collaboration as the foundation, there are further therapist factors that can promote or prevent the client from engaging in opportunities for learning. We now turn our attention to therapists' own assumptions and beliefs that guide their behavior in using homework.

Unhelpful Therapist Beliefs and Behaviors

Some therapists assume that a structured therapy format will cause important information or therapeutic maneuvers to be missed, or that it will lead the client to feel overcontrolled or underacknowledged (J. Beck, 1995, and Chapter 6). Other therapists believe that assigning homework to a client who is already distressed will be unproductive, or that it will cause the client to feel coerced and controlled. Homework assignments are a core component of the therapy process, and we now have sufficient data to show that therapists' assumptions relate to the way in which homework assignments are delivered in practice (Kazantzis et al., in press). Indeed, therapists' attention to their own interpersonal process is a cornerstone of effective therapy relationships (Padesky, 1999).

When we train practitioners in using homework, we encourage them to test out their own beliefs about its role in CBT. Common indications that therapists may have unhelpful cognitions regarding its use include the following:

1. Often allows the client to leave session without discussing any issues regarding homework
2. Does not discuss new/revised homework when client is highly distressed
3. Rushes through any discussion of homework
4. Discusses homework but provides no rationale for its utility
5. Is directive in discussing homework
6. Lets client leave without encouraging practice during the session
7. Reaches only a vague agreement about how homework will be completed
8. Forgets to review homework
9. Provides excessive praise for homework completion
10. Often feels frustrated/irritated about homework noncompletion

When therapists exhibit these behaviors and emotions, it can be helpful for them to identify their own automatic thoughts for later discussion in supervision, so that they can ascertain whether or not their own beliefs or attitudes are influencing clients' learning. Another useful way to facilitate increased monitoring of therapists' interpersonal processes is to have them complete their own thought records, identifying thoughts about the client, themselves, and the session or treatment plan that has been devised (see example in Table 17.2). This content should not necessarily be revealed to the client. The next section discusses a series of adaptive therapist beliefs that we have found helpful when training practitioners (see Table 17.3).

Adaptive Therapist Beliefs Regarding Homework

Homework Is Therapy

We have witnessed many therapists discuss homework as an auxiliary or complementary component to CBT. Any therapeutic activity assigned for clients to complete between sessions represents a 'homework" assignment, but often therapists will talk about assignments involving activity schedules, exposure activities, reading information, behavioral experiments, thought records, and so forth as if they were different from homework. Others see homework as a specific intervention or technique (i.e., Goisman, 1985), whereas it was originally conceptualized as a *therapeutic process* or "vehicle" by which skills are transferred out of the therapy session (A. T. Beck et al., 1979). Indeed, some authors argue that unless the therapist designs, assigns, and reviews homework assignments as a routine part of every therapy session, therapy cannot be considered cognitive or cognitive behavioral (Thase & Callan, in press).

We encourage therapists to reframe *in-session work* and *homework* as not being distinct entities but rather as reflecting a continual process of learning. The application of adaptive skills begins at the first session, continues between sessions, and extends long after the end of therapy. The goal is for clients to take skills learned through homework and integrate them into their lives on an ongoing basis. Implicit in this reframe is the idea that *homework is therapy* (see also discussion in Chapter 7, on older adults).

It is certainly the case that clients spend more time engaged in homework than in any other therapeutic activity. Figure 17.1 shows hypothetical data for a client involved in 25 therapy sessions, follow-up sessions, and assessment and formal psychometric testing procedures. Even with the addition of fairly substantial timeframes for assessment, a client engaged in homework (for an estimated average of 3 hours per week) is still likely to spend far more time involved in homework than in any other activity.

Homework Assignments Require Substantial In-Session Time

The process of designing, assigning, and reviewing homework requires a significant portion of therapy time. Adequate time should be allocated to

TABLE 17.2 A Therapist's Dysfunctional Thought Record for Homework Noncompletion

Situation	Automatic Thoughts	Emotions	Distortion	Rational Response	Outcome
Describe: 1. Actual event leading to unpleasant emotion, or 2. Stream of thoughts, day dreams, or recollection, leading to an unpleasant emotion, or 3. Distressing physical sensations.	1. Write automatic thought(s) that preceded emotion(s). 2. Rate belief in automatic thought(s) 0–100%	Describe: 1. Specify sad, anxious/angry, etc. 2. Rate degree of emotion 0–100%	1. All or nothing thinking. 2. Over generalization 3. Mental filter 4. Disqualifying the positive 5. Jumping to conclusions 6. Magnification or minimization 7. Emotional reasoning 8. Should statements 9. Labeling and mislabeling 10. Personalization	1. Write rational response to automatic thought(s). 2. Rate belief in alternative response 0–100%	1. Re-rate belief in automatic thought(s) 0–100%. 2. Specify and rate subsequent emotions 0–100%
Client does not complete their homework assignment, explains that they have forgotten to complete it, even though time was allocated to problem solving "difficulty remembering" at the end of last session	This client will never do their homework - they will never improve! - they're not motivated! (65% each) We are not making any progress with this treatment plan, I don't know what to do next. (75%)	frustration (55%) disappointed (10%) uncertain (30%)	2, 5	Frustration on my part will not be helpful here (90%). I could stop making negative predictions and talk with the client some more about the practical obstacles that might have happened over the past week (90%) I could also explore their beliefs about the task, and see how it fits with their current coping stategies (85%) Its possible they had good reason for not engaging in the homework (99%) I know that homework will likely provide helpful conceptual information (85%) It would be helpful to focus on that and emphasize this as progress (99%)	35% each thought 10% frustration 0–2% disappointment 5% uncertain

TABLE 17.3 Adaptive Therapist Beliefs Regarding Homework

Homework is therapy.

Homework assignments require substantial in-session time.

Homework should be relevant to the clients' goals.

Homework should be aligned with the clients' existing coping strategies.

Homework compliance is a necessary, but not sufficient condition for
  improvement.

Homework noncompletion is a common occurrence.

Homework noncompletion is part of the learning process.

Homework noncompletion should be conceptualized.

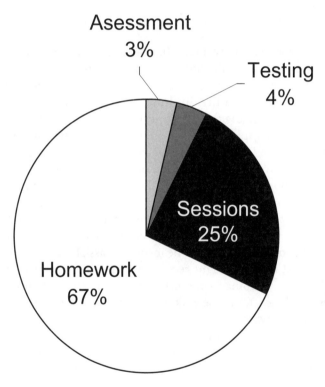

Fig. 17.1 Proportion of client time involved in therapy activities.

new skills so that emerging ideas or strategies are not rushed and there is
an opportunity for practice during the session (see Chapter 6).

As has been discussed elsewhere (Kazantzis & Lampropoulos, 2002),
we find it helpful to view the integration of homework into therapy as a

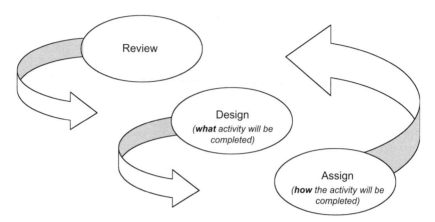

Fig. 17.2 Integrating homework into therapy using the guiding model.

three-step process. Figure 17.2 illustrates that each session involves moving from discussing the homework task(s) from the previous week (*homework review*), to what new or revised task(s) will be carried out (*homework design*), and then to how they will be practically implemented (*homework assign*). Though this structure may be very clearly defined in the therapist's mind, we recommend a smooth transition between each step. In our view, regularly adhering to this broad structure facilitates a systematic integration of homework into therapy.

The proportion of time allocated to the review, design, and assign is not consistent during the course of therapy. We find that all aspects of this process initially benefit from careful attention and discussion in the therapy session. As therapy progresses and clients take the lead in designing and deciding how homework will be instituted, assigning homework takes less time. That is, the thought record may require little or no time for "design" and for reaching a consensus as to when, where, how often, and how long it will take for homework to be completed ("assigned"). Reviewing the extent to which the homework was completed and dealing with practical obstacles also takes less time later in therapy than at the outset. Figure 17.3 illustrates hypothetical data on "session time" required for the design, assign, and review of homework for sequential homework assignments.

Homework Should Be Relevant to Clients' Goals

The therapist should first ask the client to describe his views about the presenting problems and the current strategies for managing his distress before assigning homework. In most mood disorders, for instance, clients are likely to be withdrawing from activity and interpersonal interaction in

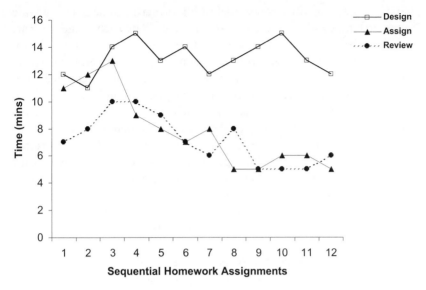

Fig. 17.3 Time involved in reviewing, assigning, and designing homework.

an effort to avoid triggering negative views and emotions about themselves, other people, the world, and their future (A. T. Beck, 1976). In most anxiety presentations, clients engage in a degree of subtle or overt avoidance in an attempt to lessen their experience of apprehension or fear about their ability to cope in specific situations. Identification of the client's particular strategies forms the basis of an individualized cognitive conceptualization, which, in turn, facilitates therapist and client understanding of the array of presenting problems (J. Beck, 1995; Needleman, 1999). Consequently, the individualized cognitive conceptualization guides the goals and direction of therapy, and homework assignments should be tailored for the client based on that conceptualization (Burns & Auerbach, 1992; Johnson & Kazantzis, 2004). A failure to link the content of the homework assignment to a collaborative conceptualization and treatment goals for the client is likely to render the assignment irrelevant or unhelpful to the client. Relating homework content to client goals was emphasized for the use of homework with adolescents (Chapter 6) and older adults (Chapter 7) as well as in working with mood and substance abuse problems (Chapters 12 and 13, respectively).

Homework Should Be Aligned With the Clients' Existing Coping Strategies

Clients' coping strategies are directly related to their views about the causes and function of their disorders and their problems. Whether the therapist uses a cognitive conceptualization primarily designed to provide an understanding of a specific situation for the client, such as the five-part model (Padesky & Mooney, 1990), or a more comprehensive formulation of the client's historical background, presenting problems, and underlying cognitive structures (e.g., J. Beck, 1995; Persons, 1989), clients' views of their presenting problems and coping strategies should be incorporated into the conceptualization (Kazantzis, Pachana, & Secker, 2003). Clients present for therapy with strong evidence to suggest that their current coping strategies are in some way useful in providing relief from emotional distress. The education and conceptualization process is a means of helping clients to evaluate to what extent their strategies are helpful or are serving to maintain their presenting problems. Chapter 10 provides a poignant discussion of the view of alcohol in coping with anxiety, and Chapter 14 skillfully illustrates the role of insight in understanding delusions and hallucinations.

Unfortunately, some therapists incorrectly assume that clients are unable to contribute to their treatment plans, so they do not encourage their clients to contribute—or, worse still, they dismiss their clients' efforts. Setting treatment goals and selecting homework assignments should in some way incorporate, or at least be aligned with, clients' own views about their presenting problems and current coping strategies (Tryon & Winograd, 2001). Even where the purpose of the assignment is to provide an opportunity to test out a client's view of her presenting problems, it is the content of the belief and the client's own strategy that forms the basis of the behavioral experiment.

Homework Compliance Is a Necessary, but Not Sufficient Condition for Improvement

As outlined in Chapter 3, there is strong empirical support for the association between homework completion and treatment outcome in CBT. There is also emerging evidence to suggest that the quality of the client's homework, or degree of learning, is a strong predictor of treatment outcome (see Chapter 4). Taken together, this means that therapists can regard the degree of learning through the completion of homework as a key indicator of treatment outcome.

It is unfortunate that psychotherapy research has mainly focused on "compliance," rather than the degree of learning from the homework assignment. Concentrating on whether a client has fully or partially completed the homework or not completed it at all provides only limited information about the client's learning or degree of skill acquisition. For example, compliance provides an indication of whether or not a client took an opportunity to carry out a behavioral experiment, but it does not tell us whether that experiment was useful in uncovering evidence to support or counter the client's beliefs. Unlike the context of a pharmacological intervention, where adequate completion with a medication protocol ensures that the client has received treatment, successful CBT requires much more than simple compliance with homework assignments. Instead, the emphasis is on the degree of skill acquisition and cognitive change. Thus we conclude that homework compliance is a necessary but not sufficient condition for improvement. We have discussed these issues in some depth in Chapter 4 and have proposed an alternative, more comprehensive means of assessing the completion of homework assignments.

Homework Noncompletion Is a Common Occurrence

Homework noncompletion is a relatively widespread phenomenon. We are not suggesting that most clients do not engage in homework at all, but rather that most clients do not complete *all* of their homework assignments.

As discussed in Chapter 3, empirical research has confirmed the link between client completion of homework assignments and treatment outcome in CBT. However, for homework compliance to be correlated with outcome requires a degree of variability in both compliance and outcome. This means that those studies that link homework compliance with outcome must have measured a degree of variability in client compliance; that is, some clients did not complete some of their homework. Given the high degree of consistency between studies linking homework compliance and treatment outcome, it logically follows that homework noncompletion has been a frequent occurrence in research studies.

Further evidence for the proposition that clients may not complete their homework is apparent from the results of practitioner surveys. Data from two early studies indicate that therapists consider poor client homework compliance to be problematic for their clinical practice (i.e., Hansen & Warner, 1994; Kemmler, Borgart, & Gärke, 1992). A third survey of a randomly selected sample of North American therapists found that therapists provided a range of estimations for client homework completion (i.e., Kazantzis et al., in press). Specifically, the Kazantzis et al. study found that therapist estimations of compliance generally ranged from "low" (20%) to "moderate" (73%), with only a small proportion reporting a "high" (7%) rate of compliance. Moreover, a survey of cognitive behavioral therapists in Germany ($N = 77$) added further weight to the idea that practitioners regularly experience homework noncompletion in their practice (Helbig & Fehm, 2004). Thus we conclude that homework noncompletion is a common occurrence and should be expected by practitioners.

Homework Noncompletion Is Part of the Learning Process

It is often emphasized that just as much can be learned from the client not completing or engaging in the homework assignment as from its completion (e.g., J. Beck, 1995). A therapist's emphasis on obtaining useful data from homework as an "experiment" or a "no-lose" situation often determines whether a client will openly and candidly discuss noncompletion. For example, Dattilio (2002) illustrates that couples who avoid completing homework assignments may provide the therapist with important information about their difficulties with communication or current motivation to change.

Discussion of homework noncompletion may also reveal client beliefs about the assignment, including that it was misunderstood, seen as irrelevant, or considered ineffective. At other times, homework can reveal that therapy is off track, prompting the therapist and client to adjust treatment goals and the conceptualization (i.e., a process that provides assessment data). There is case study support for this suggestion, which highlights that noncompletion of homework reflects the conflict between two quite different views of the predicted outcome of the assignment (Dunn, Morrison, & Bentall, 2003; March, 1997). Thus, although we advocate for the position that homework completion represents a key indicator of therapeutic progress, we suggest that noncompletion is also useful for therapy. Furthermore, homework noncompletion is a necessary or expected part of learning for some clients.

John, a 57-year-old account manager, began cognitive therapy for panic disorder and agoraphobia following the experience of a severe panic attack while driving to work. After engaging in the process of guided discovery about the meaning of his bodily sensations during a panic attack, the general purpose and function of anxiety was discussed during a session. John then participated in a hyperventilation exercise during the session and agreed to do the exercise outside the session on one occasion during the upcoming week. However, John did not practice the hyperventilation exposure for homework. After two hyperventilation exercises during sessions, John explained that he "knew" his anxiety was excessive and unrealistic and that he could not see the benefits of additional exposure. It was only after further behavioral experiments that John decided there was some benefit to testing out his specific interpretations of the induced symptoms through repeated practice in different situations. In realizing that benefit, he also observed how difficult it was to progress with in vivo exposure homework assignments at shopping malls and cinemas without having repeatedly evaluated his interpretations through additional symptom exposure. Deciding not to complete homework was clearly part of the learning process for this client.

Homework Noncompletion Should Be Conceptualized

When noncompletion is discussed with a client, the discussion usually reveals negative automatic thoughts that contribute to the development of the individualized conceptualization. In so doing, the discussion may reveal schemas, intermediate beliefs, and compensatory strategies that had not previously been identified. Thus, therapists should consider both noncompletion and completion of homework assignments within the context of the individualized cognitive conceptualization.

It is rare that clients do no homework or, on the other hand, that they complete every single assignment. There are many reasons for noncompletion of homework assignments other than the client "not making an effort" or "being unmotivated." But no matter the reasons, it is important that the therapist conceptualize the behavior. When clients outright refuse to complete homework assignments or consistently do not engage in homework, we find that it is *essential* to consider these responses in the context of the conceptualization. Chapters 9 (couples) and 11 (obsessions and compulsions) provide helpful clinical examples of outright refusal of homework.

Noncompletion of homework may trigger clients' more fundamental beliefs about themselves or their problems; if these are not addressed, therapists may inadvertently support homework noncompletion. Several Chapters exemplify how homework noncompletion can be conceptualized in therapy for couples (Chapter 9), depression (Chapter 12), and substance abuse (Chapter 13).

As prior resources on using homework assignments in CBT have not generally emphasized the role of the conceptualization in understanding homework noncompletion, we continue this section with three clinical examples. Each example is presented with a case conceptualization diagram (J. Beck, 1995) in which the discussion of homework is used as the basis for each specific situation.

Juan was a 34-year-old Mexican who was receiving CBT for social phobia and a comorbid major depressive disorder. Married for 6 years and the father of an 18-month-old son, Juan presented for treatment after a series of distressing events had led to a worsening of his anxiety and depression. Figure 17.4 portrays a cognitive conceptualization diagram for Juan, illustrating early criticism and physical abuse from family members and a core belief of "I am not good enough," which is linked to a high degree of approval seeking and placing other people's needs ahead of his own. Early in therapy, Juan was involved and worked collaboratively to design homework assignments. After two sessions of not engaging in homework, it was helpful to work with Juan to gain more

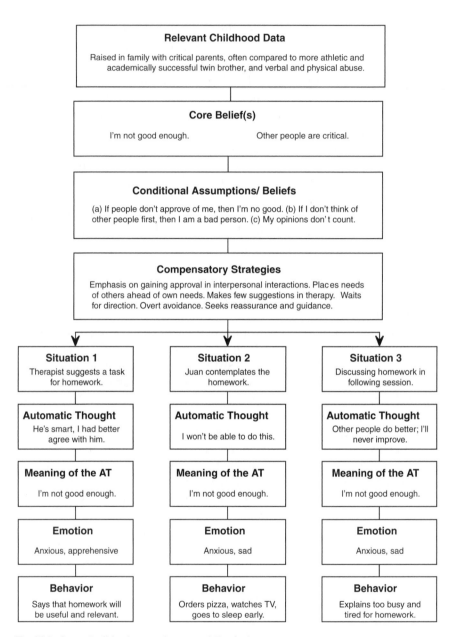

Fig. 17.4 Conceptualizing homework noncompletion for Juan.

information about his experience in contemplating the homework assignment and build his response into the evolving conceptualization. A discussion of the role of homework as a learning opportunity was helpful, as was a description of the rationale. However, the key in Juan's case was to use guided discovery, beginning with informational questions about the many ways in which people have the opportunity to form initial impressions of others (i.e., interaction with staff working in shops, banks, noticing pedestrians on the street, and so on). Juan was more prepared to engage in the initial social skills training experiment of asking people at his local library for assistance in finding a book after concluding that it can "sometimes" be reasonable to make requests of others. Throughout the course of therapy, it was essential to give Juan the primary responsibility of designing and determining the rate at which he would progress with his exposure hierarchy as a homework assignment. Discussing the homework facilitated Juan's evaluations of his underlying assumptions and core beliefs, which later formed the focus of therapy. Juan's responsibility for homework translated into a clear sense that he was also responsible for the improvements he experienced during treatment. To further aid the progression toward treatment goals, his homework completion was later used as the basis for in-session exposure to criticism and the practice of assertiveness.

Bob, a 27-year-old marketing executive, presented for CBT for panic disorder following dissatisfaction with the moderate symptom relief provided by his psychotropic medication. Bob explained that he had become impatient with his psychiatrist's efforts, which prompted him to seek assistance from a cognitive behavioral therapist. Figure 17.5 displays the therapist's cognitive conceptualization based on two sessions with Bob. After initially expressing interest and being engaged in completing a situational conceptualization in the first session (Padesky & Mooney, 1990), Bob became angry when it was suggested that he complete his first homework assignment. Bob terminated his second therapy session when the therapist asked him to put the review of homework on the agenda. Engaging Bob in a productive therapeutic relationship was crucial. However, Bob continued to balk at even the mere suggestion of brief and relatively straightforward homework assignments throughout the course of therapy, though the subsequent suggestions were met with less hostility than in the first session. After 27 sessions, Bob noted that he had been making use of some of the ideas in therapy, explaining, "They are things that I used to do, or are extensions of things I am already doing." Toward the end of therapy, Bob summarized the things he thought would be useful for future reference. Although much of the cognitive conceptualization outlined in Figure 17.5 was discussed in session, Bob had achieved his goal of reducing anxiety and panic attacks. Unfortunately, therapy did not proceed to evaluating his core beliefs, but

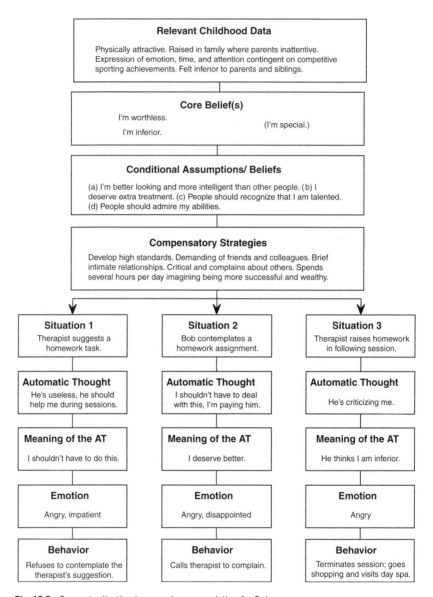

Relevant Childhood Data

Physically attractive. Raised in family where parents inattentive. Expression of emotion, time, and attention contingent on competitive sporting achievements. Felt inferior to parents and siblings.

Core Belief(s)

I'm worthless.

I'm inferior.

(I'm special.)

Conditional Assumptions/ Beliefs

(a) I'm better looking and more intelligent than other people. (b) I deserve extra treatment. (c) People should recognize that I am talented. (d) People should admire my abilities.

Compensatory Strategies

Develop high standards. Demanding of friends and colleagues. Brief intimate relationships. Critical and complains about others. Spends several hours per day imagining being more successful and wealthy.

Situation 1	**Situation 2**	**Situation 3**
Therapist suggests a homework task.	Bob contemplates a homework assignment.	Therapist raises homework in following session.
Automatic Thought	**Automatic Thought**	**Automatic Thought**
He's useless, he should help me during sessions.	I shouldn't have to deal with this, I'm paying him.	He's criticizing me.
Meaning of the AT	**Meaning of the AT**	**Meaning of the AT**
I shouldn't have to do this.	I deserve better.	He thinks I am inferior.
Emotion	**Emotion**	**Emotion**
Angry, impatient	Angry, disappointed	Angry
Behavior	**Behavior**	**Behavior**
Refuses to contemplate the therapist's suggestion.	Calls therapist to complain.	Terminates session; goes shopping and visits day spa.

Fig. 17.5 Conceptualization homework noncompletion for Bob.

it was later uncovered that Bob's early resistance to the homework assignments had a lot to do with his need to maintain control, which is a common factor in individuals suffering from anxiety.

Michelle, a 28-year-old accountant, presented for CBT as an adjunct to psychotropic medication prescribed by her family doctor for low mood and suicidal ideation. Michelle had high expectations of her work and herself as a professional, and it was helpful to conceptualize her homework noncompletion in the context of her presenting problems. Despite describing herself as a "perfectionist," Michelle was unable to engage in her homework for the first few sessions. She described a list of unexpected last-minute events that prevented her from finding time for homework. Situational conceptualizations with Michelle regarding her experience in contemplating her homework were helpful in understanding the function of her noncompletion (see Figure 17.6). Guided discovery enabled Michelle to consider the idea that *although something is not done perfectly, it still has value*, which grew out of her experience of enjoying her 5-year-old son's art work. Michelle also found guided imagery helpful as a way of covertly rehearsing the completion of thought records at a time when she was feeling sad. Later in therapy, the focus shifted to encouraging Michelle to set clear limits on the amount of time and effort that she spent doing the homework, as she had begun to produce detailed, professionally formatted pieces of work. It was also useful to encourage Michelle to take on more challenging tasks rather than lingering with skills she had already mastered. It was important not to challenge Michelle's personal value of *doing things well* but to design behavioral experiments and data logs that would enable her to determine when things were *good enough*. The process of homework administration itself was used as an opportunity for Michelle to evaluate her own performance in a more balanced way, without excessively personalizing the feedback and activating her core beliefs.

Our position in presenting this model for practice is that both the content and the process of integrating homework into therapy should be guided by the individualized conceptualization for the client. Further, with regard to the examples in this section, therapists may elect to provide less direction in the design of homework with perfectionistic clients (Chapter 11, on obsessions and compulsions) or with entitled or aggressive clients (Chapter 13, on substance abuse).

In summary, we have outlined eight key adaptive beliefs and assumptions that are useful for therapists to consider in contemplating their use of homework during the course of therapy. Given the survey data linking therapist beliefs and use of homework (Fehm & Kazantzis, 2004; Kazantzis et al., in press), we find it helpful to encourage therapists to determine their extent of belief in each one of these assumptions and to conduct their own behavioral experiments to evaluate them. We have also outlined a series of indicators that can signal the need for therapist supervision in the process of integrating homework into therapy. What follows is a comprehensive discussion of specific therapist behaviors in using homework.

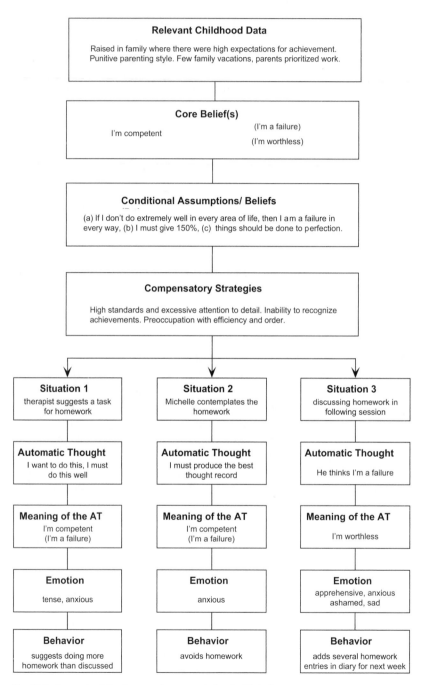

Fig. 17.6 Conceptualizing homework noncompletion for Michelle.

Specific Therapist Behaviors in Using Homework

We begin this section by discussing the process of socializing the client to homework and the use of terminology in that process. We then cover the specific therapist behaviors in designing, assigning, and reviewing homework. Clinical examples illustrate the role of client beliefs in determining homework completion and show how guided imagery may be used in designing homework. Little has been published on these aspects of the process. Throughout this section, readers are provided with a series of concept checks and diagrams to help them assimilate the recommendations outlined.

Socialization to Homework

In order to facilitate collaboration, it is essential that clients gain a clear rationale for the use of homework assignments at the very first therapy session (J. Beck, 1995). It should be explained that therapy is usually limited to 50 or 60 minutes per week, so the majority of therapeutic work needs to be carried out between sessions. The therapist can also point out that therapy consisting entirely of in-session work has been demonstrated to be less effective than that supported by out-of-session work (Kazantzis, Deane, & Ronan, 2000); therefore it is unlikely to be sufficient for overcoming long-term problems (A. T. Beck, Emery, & Greenberg, 1985). Many clients present for therapy with the expectation that they will be the passive recipients of treatment, and they may be surprised to learn that considerable time and effort is required on their part. However, other clients have read about different therapy approaches and come to CBT with the expectation that their active participation is required. This socialization process does not usually take very long. Clients often understand the value of between-session work, particularly when they consider that their everyday lives differ greatly from what occurs in therapy sessions.

The strong empirical support for the positive effects of homework assignments in CBT should be shared with clients. They are usually interested and reassured to hear that this therapeutic process has been empirically tested. Just as patients contemplating a medical operation want to know about success rates, the possibility of relapse, and so forth, psychotherapy clients are interested in the correlation between homework completion and the effectiveness of therapy. Chapters 10 (PANIC AND GENERALIZED ANXIETY) and 13 (SUBSTANCE ABUSE) highlighted the role of homework in preventing relapse as part of the rationale for homework.

It is helpful to use Socratic questioning to encourage clients to link some aspect of their prior experiences to the process of learning skills with which to help themselves. The majority of clients can identify having previously engaged in academic, athletic, artistic, or other activity that involved a degree of learning and skill acquisition and maintenance. As this socialization to the role of homework in CBT usually occurs in the first session, the client should be asked to recall an experience for use as a metaphor to be used throughout the therapy and beyond. For example, clients might liken learning through homework to refining their golfing technique, to using different tools in the garden, to employing new strategies for refinishing furniture, or to finding new ways to do repairs on their homes or their cars. Through drawing on the client's prior experience and changing the terminology for therapy based on that experience, the therapist can facilitate a process for using homework that is rooted in the client's world view. Chapter 11 provides an example of the use of metaphor in socializing clients to the use of homework in therapy.

Terminology

We suggest abandoning the term *homework compliance* in clinical practice. The term *compliance* is counterproductive in this context, as it implies that the client will be merely complying with a recommendation.

There are also negative associations with the term *homework,* as it often reminds clients of unpleasant academic experiences. Several authors have observed that clients hold negative associations with the term and may covertly draw inferences from therapists' behavior in assigning tasks (Coon & Gallagher-Thompson, 2002; Dattilio, 2002; Hudson & Kendall, 2002; Kazantzis et al., 2003). These negative associations are considered within various contexts in earlier Chapters in this book in regard to working with children (Chapter 5), adolescents (Chapter 6), and older adults (Chapter 7). Three other Chapters note that the term *homework* can prove counterproductive in couples therapy (Chapter 9 and 15) and in treating substance use disorders (Chapter 13).

One of our practitioner surveys found that this negative association is also held by practitioners (i.e., Fehm & Kazantzis, 2004). Of course, there are clients who are also comfortable with the idea of "work to be done at home, or homework," without any prompting from the therapist. We suggest picking up whatever term the client uses when the rationale for homework is being linked to some prior learning experience.

Homework Design

Several taxonomies have been proposed for the choice of homework assignments based on the theoretical (i.e., Brown-Standridge, 1989; De Shazer, 1988; Hay & Kinnier, 1998) and empirical literature (i.e., Mahrer, Nordin, & Miller, 1995; Scheel, Seaman, Roach, Mullin, & Mahoney, 1999). Although these classification frameworks have the potential to be useful in some contexts, we suggest that therapists first consult the relevant cognitive model for the particular presenting problem. For example, CBT is an empirically supported treatment for depression, and there is a clear list of learning objectives, skills, and corresponding assignments for the therapy. Thus, our broad recommendation for designing homework is that the tasks should be drawn from the relevant "generic" cognitive model(s).

Choosing Homework Based on the Individualized Conceptualization

The choice of interventions should be further guided by the individualized conceptualization. One client may begin homework by engaging in behavioral activation through activity schedules, whereas another may focus on greater interpersonal interaction to achieve the same aim of increasing pleasure and mastery. Thus we caution against the use of "practice planners" that present lists of predetermined homework assignments (e.g., Schultheis, 1998), as these do not encourage practitioners to individualize homework for clients. A homework assignment that is not obviously tailored to the client's specific problems can result in a reduced sense of ownership and relevance for the client and thus a reduced sense of responsibility for carrying the homework out (Moore & Garland, 2003). Contributors writing on the use of homework with adolescents (Chapter 6) and sexual problems (Chapter 15) have clarified the importance of using homework based on the conceptualization.

In discussing a new homework assignment, whatever the specific content, therapists should make a clear attempt to solicit the client's opinions or attitudes toward the task. The underlying principle is an ethical one: clients have a right to be informed in order to consent to the treatment interventions that they will receive.[1] With the exception of clients who are acutely distressed or at some safety risk, there are usually several types (or formats) of homework assignments available.

CBT is aimed at helping clients to help themselves beyond the end of treatment sessions. Thus, the therapist's goal should be to create a therapeutic environment in which clients design their own homework assignments. This means that the choice of homework early in therapy is guided by the client's goals and priorities (Young & Beck, 1982). Thus, homework should be relevant to the client's goals and aligned closely with the client's coping strategies.

Quick Reference

Guided discovery to identify coping strategies and beliefs
Use disorder-specific cognitive model and individualized conceptualization

---

[1]Chapter 18 provides further discussion on the issue of obtaining informed consent for a psychotherapy that incorporates homework.

Areas of Difficulty

As outlined in Chapter 2, the process of learning involves evaluating or synthesizing the consequences or outcomes of having engaged in a particular behavior. The implication is that therapists should be careful not to suggest homework assignments that are too difficult, too tedious, or possibly too overwhelming for the client. It is good general practice to focus on smaller, more specific tasks at the outset of therapy. The more successful a client can be with his or her initial homework tasks, the better. A. T. Beck et al. (1979) emphasize the importance of ensuring that clients experience early success through the completion of homework assignments, which will in turn predispose them to engage in subsequent homework assignments. This point was consistently emphasized by the contributors describing the use of homework with various clinical populations in Parts II and III of this book.

Every client brings to treatment different abilities and coping strategies to deal with his or her presenting problems. Consequently there can be no universal ranking for the difficulty of homework assignments (Johnson & Kazantzis, 2004; Kazantzis et al., 2003). Some clients experience a great deal of difficulty in identifying and rating their emotions; others find the beginning steps of a thought record to be relatively straightforward. Since the level of difficulty of an assignment depends on the client's subjective experience, the therapist should consider his or her writing, reading, and concentration ability as well as the level of skill acquisition (e.g., ability to identify automatic thoughts, identify and rate intensity of emotions, and clearly specify relevant aspects of problematic situations before beginning to complete a thought record). As a rule, we suggest that homework assignments be challenging but not overwhelming.

If the client feels uncomfortable with the notion of bringing written accounts of his or her experience to a therapy session, it may be helpful to explain that the focus will be on the content of what is written rather than on how it is written. To further emphasize this point, the therapist can tell the client to keep the original copies of any written homework assignment, so that they can be used for future reference.

Client Beliefs About the Task—Its Rationale and Difficulty

Client beliefs about the homework relate to the relevance of its specific content, its perceived utility, and its difficulty. In Chapter 2, when we considered the cognitive theory foundations for the use of homework assignments, it was explained that clients have a series of task-related beliefs that serve to determine whether or not a homework assignment is carried out. For example, many clients describe the process of recording their thoughts to be rather unusual at first, both because of the task involved and the thoughts that may be revealed (Blackburn & Davidson,

1990). Other clients may think that recording their thoughts will increase their intensity or exacerbate their discomfort (Leahy, 2002).

Some clients are simply not used to writing, allocating a number (or percentage) to describe the intensity of their emotions, and some feel shy about their handwriting, grammar, and spelling. Other clients view writing down aspects of their cognitive or emotional experience as inconsistent with their cultural views. This may require respectful discussion of the rationale for the homework or, in many cases, consideration of an alternative format for achieving the same learning goals. A written record can also reify one's thoughts by making them more concrete or exacerbating the associated emotion, which may be another reason to avoid it. Chapter 10 (Panic and Generalized Anxiety) provided a useful illustration of how clients can view some homework assignments as worsening their clinical condition, and it showed how one client's view of the homework conflicted with the view of his "deep-seated" presenting problem. Chapter 11 (Obsessions and Compulsions) discussed how clients can have unhelpful beliefs about the consequences of exposure homework, and Chapter 15 (Sexual Problems) described instances when clients' views of assignments conflicted with their sense of what constitutes "proper" behavior.

In sum, homework noncompletion may indicate that the client does not believe that the homework assignment will contribute to the goals of treatment. That is, the homework assignment may seem irrelevant or require too much time and effort in return for too little gain (see Dunn et al., 2002). The following case study illustrates the role of clients' beliefs in homework noncompletion.

Jane, 37 years of age, was receiving CBT for major depressive disorder and a comorbid panic disorder without agoraphobia. Jane had completed six sessions of therapy and was quickly able to complete the thought record assignment. Although Jane was able to effectively complete a thought record after an event, she had difficulty making use of the skill in situations in which she experienced emotional distress. This was frustrating for Jane, who presented at her seventh session tearfully stating, "The techniques aren't working. I am never going to be able to learn this."

Jane had been raised in a family where she learned to suppress her spontaneous emotional experience. She explained that the family was characterized by rigid rules about academic performance, and her parents had employed a rather punitive parenting style. Jane said that she was often shouted at for making mistakes in her schoolwork, and that her mother also physically reprimanded her on a repeated basis. In discussing her family history, Jane remembered a series of events surrounding her father's extramarital affair, which occurred when she was a child. She described that her mother had become very suspicious, angry, and negative following the affair, and though these feelings were initially directed at her father, her suspicion gradually spilled over to the children, other family members, and neighbors. Eventually, the mother's state deteriorated into widespread paranoia and delusions, causing her to be hospitalized and medicated. Jane came away from these early life experiences believing that *experiencing emotion was a bad thing*, and, "If I experience emotion, then I am out of control." Guided discovery was helpful for Jane because it enabled her to identify these rules. In particular, Jane observed that she had a series of automatic thoughts whenever she experienced emotion, including, "I must stop this feeling," "I can't let myself feel this way." It was helpful to engage in Socratic dialogue and guided discovery within the session about the experience, as well as the suppression and acceptance of emotions, and then to extend it as the next homework assignment. In later sessions, the rationale for cognitive restructuring using thought records was discussed as a means for Jane to deal with negative emotions and being aligned with her own coping strategies.

There is also some empirical support for the importance of client beliefs regarding homework. One interesting study in the counseling literature found a surprisingly low 41% concordance rate between therapist and client perceptions of the assigned homework (Scheel, Hoggan, Willie, McDonald, & Tonin, 1998). This study underscores the value of making written notes of homework for clients to take with them, but it also highlights the point that therapists and clients have different views and beliefs about homework. Further, there has been considerable inconsistency between therapist and client ratings of homework compliance in empirical research (Kazantzis, Deane, & Ronan, 2004).

A second study examined the predictors of acceptability of homework assignments to clients; it identified three key predictors: (a) the link between treatment goals and the content of the assignment, (b) the assignment's level of difficulty, and (c) the extent to which the homework was designed to build on client strengths (Conoley, Padula, Payton, & Daniels, 1994). Thus, there are preliminary data to support the assertion that clients' and therapists' beliefs about homework differ and that client beliefs have the potential to determine completion.

Some of the most common oversights in designing homework are (a) not linking homework to the treatment goals and individualized conceptualization, (b) selecting an assignment that does not address the client's primary presenting problem, and (c) assigning too many homework activities. The novice therapist may try to proceed too fast and recommend assignments that are beyond the client's level of skill, or he or she may unintentionally overload the client with too many assignments. Some therapists may underestimate the demands of the particular homework activity or expect clients to work on their homework at a rate that is unrealistic. We encourage therapists to discuss with clients the "perceived importance" of the homework and the client's "readiness to engage in the assignment," both of which can often be determined by using a range of 0 (not important/not ready) to 100 (extremely important/completely ready) (see Miller & Rollnick, 2002). These ratings provide a check that the client has accepted the rationale for the homework and sees it as serving a useful purpose (see Glaser, Kazantzis, Deane, & Oades, 2000; Kazantzis & Lampropoulos, 2002).

Clients' level of understanding of their readiness and responsibility for change is a key issue in assigning homework to those who present with personality disorders (Freeman & Rosenfield, 2002). In this text, Chapters 10 (Panic and Generalized Anxiety) and 13 (Substance Abuse) also provide examples of how readiness to change influences homework success.

Quick Reference

Collaboratively select tasks.
Present a rationale that aligns with the client's treatment goals.
Ask about the client's ability and perceived task difficulty.

Guided Imagery

There is evidence to suggest that learning occurs in different ways. Although clients may be able to rationalize about their existing coping strategies being unhelpful, it is markedly different to actually experience the benefits of an alternative strategy. Teasdale, Segal, and Williams (1995) suggested that cognitive therapy for depression provides clients with the opportunity to adopt an alternative view and then to put this more helpful perspective into practice (see also Fennell, 2004; Salkovskis, 1996). The idea is to encourage clients to generate alternative ways for understanding their difficulties and then to allow them to experiment as part of homework practice to determine what works. These opportunities can sometimes occur through in-session discussion with the therapist using Socratic questioning and guided discovery, but they occur mainly through direct personal experience outside the therapy room. This distinction between cognitive and experiential learning is prominent in working with clients who have anxiety disorders. In many instances, these clients present for their initial assessment with some degree of insight, realizing at an intellectual level that their anxiety is excessive yet plagued by a high degree of apprehension, fear, and distress in actual situations.

A key practice step is to bridge the gap between rational and experiential learning by ensuring that clients have some in-session experience of the activity being recommended for homework. One way to do this is through therapist modeling and/or actual engaging in the task within the session (see Chapter 12, on depression). Consistent with this recommendation, we encourage the use of guided imagery whenever the client decides to take on a new assignment (J. Beck, 1995). Guided imagery provides the opportunity for the client to rehearse engaging in the homework assignments in response to environmental cues or triggers, and it greatly aids in the identification of obstacles. Anticipating predictable and unpredictable outcomes is good behavioral practice for assuring that behaviors are generalized from one situation to another (Stokes & Baer, 1977). Following is a clinical example of the use of guided imagery in designing homework.

Chris, a 51-year-old single woman, presented for therapy for a major depressive disorder. Chris had been married three times, but none of the marriages had lasted more than 6 months. Although she was a successful graphic designer, her career had been marked by interpersonal difficulties in the workplace. She explained that she became frustrated by the incompetence of her coworkers and resented it when they asked her to help them with their work. Chris also said that she avoided talking to the senior partners of the firm about her work on projects, explaining that their comments were often rude and unappreciative of her efforts. Her relationships with coworkers had worsened over the previous year, culminating in her being fired from the position of senior designer.

Early in therapy, Chris was asked to complete an activity schedule. Following some in-session discussion and practice at identifying and rating moods and after some Socratic questioning and guided discovery about her current situation, Chris remembered that she used to keep a daily diary during adolescence and concluded that it would be helpful to know some more about her day-to-day mood changes.

The activity schedule was introduced as one means of gaining useful information about how depression "works" for her unique situation. Chris liked the idea of the activity schedule as "saving time" and making therapy "more efficient." As part of in-session practice, Chris completed the activity for the previous day, during which it was collaboratively decided that a rating of sadness and activity would be sufficient. Chris gave some consideration to the number of times per day that she would need to complete the thought record to be "efficient" and concluded that completing it at mealtimes would work. After this discussion, the therapist guided Chris through imagery for her first completion of the assignment later in the evening. Chris was able to identify feeling "interested" and "apprehensive" and some associated autonomic arousal in beginning to complete the activity schedule. After talking with Chris about what was going through her mind in the situation, she identified that she was apprehensive about having to write down how she had been feeling, and that "she might not complete the schedule correctly" and that "it was strange writing down how she was feeling."

During imagery, the therapist asked Chris to think back to her conclusion that the activity was similar to her diary. This discussion was helpful in associating the activity with a strategy that Chris had used in the past. The therapist also asked Chris to remember what it had been like to complete some of the activity schedule during the session, at which point Chris suggested that she could look over what she had completed already as a future guide for how to do it.

After guided imagery, the therapist took some time to talk about the assignment as an experiment, and about how, as with previous assignments, the emphasis was on learning. The therapist noted that it is difficult to predict exactly what information will be obtained on an activity schedule and that any information gathered would be useful in understanding Chris' situation more fully (i.e., a no-lose scenario). The therapist also negotiated with Chris to have the activity schedule completed only once during the course of therapy.

Chris realized that the discussion with the therapist had prompted her to think about resuming the use of her diary. The therapist asked Chris whether there was anything from the thought record that she could use in her own personal diary, such as the labeling of moods and rating of intensity. As a result of this homework assignment, Chris continued to keep a mood rating in her diary when making entries.

When used in conjunction with a situational conceptualization, such as the "five-part model" (Padesky & Mooney, 1990), guided imagery facilitates the design of homework in the following ways: (a) identification of situationally bound emotional, physiological, and cognitive triggers that indicate that the particular homework activity should be attempted; (b) identification of cognitive (beliefs about the homework task, beliefs that apply across different activities) and practical obstacles to engagement in the task; (c) indication of whether or not the activity challenges but does not overextend the client's existing skills; and (d) signs that this process gives the client an experience of the consequences of engaging in the activity. During imagery, the therapist should ask the client for continual feedback about his or her attitudes toward homework, its rationale, and the client's comprehension of what is involved in the activity as well as his or her view of its perceived difficulty. Figure 17.7 summarizes the process of designing homework within the guiding model for using homework.

Quick Reference

In-session practice of task
Guided imagery to begin experiential learning

Assigning Homework

As with other aspects of the therapeutic process, the progression from deciding on what homework will be carried out (designed) to how it will be practically implemented (assigned) should be a seamless one. If the therapy session has been spent on in-session practice of an activity that will be assigned for homework, then it may be appropriate to move directly to assigning homework. In other instances, the identification of a particular assignment may happen earlier in the session (i.e., homework design), but discussion of how it will be practically integrated may occur toward the end of the session. It is helpful to consider the pragmatics of everything that is being assigned for homework when the client is completing more than one assignment. For instance, a client receiving treatment for depression may have thought records as the only homework assignment for several sessions. As the client achieves a sense of mastery and experiences emotional relief from maintaining the thought record, he or she can begin to take on additional tasks.

Specificity

There are significant pitfalls in assigning vague homework (McCarthy, 1985). When homework assignments have not been clearly discussed in terms of content, clients often present at the following session saying that they were unsure about the assignment. As therapy progresses and clients become involved in several different assignments, it is important to be specific about what is and what is not being asked to be completed between sessions. A statement such as, "This is a thought record, I'd like you to record your automatic thoughts, emotions, and cognitive distortions between now and next session," is vague and may overwhelm the client. This type of communication can lead to a host of misconceptions about what is being requested. For instance, a client may interpret such a directive to mean that a comprehensive list of thoughts, emotions, and distortions is expected. The client should leave the therapy session with a clear and concise description of what has been discussed for homework. Several Chapters emphasize the importance of specificity in assigning homework with adolescents (Chapter 6), couples (Chapter 9), older adults (Chapter 7),

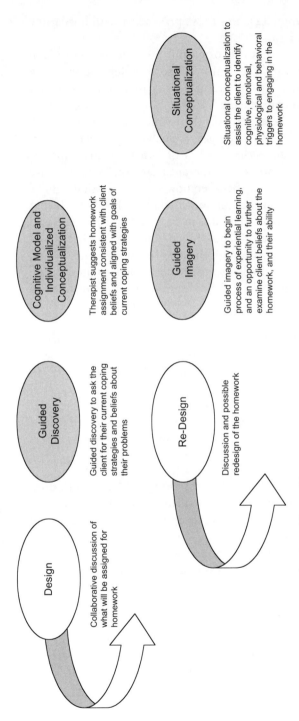

Fig. 17.7 Designing homework using the guiding model.

depressed patients (Chapter 12), and those presenting with borderline personality traits (Chapter 16).

Although we appreciate that it is often not possible to clearly plan where, how often, or how long it might take to complete a homework activity, we do recommend that therapists work to attain a degree of behavioral specificity in considering how the homework will be conducted. Since clients are the experts on their time commitments, they should be encouraged to lead this discussion. Such an approach encourages collaboration and enhances clients' sense of ownership and responsibility for designing the homework. The therapist can ask, "Since we have decided on what you will be doing between now and next session, I'd like us to consider some of the specifics on how it will be carried out. Is that OK? When do you think you would be able to carry out the activity? Based on your experience in today's session, how much time do you think should be set aside for the activity?" Although the discussion on when, where, how often, and how long is initially detailed and perhaps taxing, clients quickly become socialized to making these decisions in a fluid manner. In fact, most clients say that they enjoy the process when giving session feedback.

Depending on the nature of the assignment, exactly where it is carried out and the amount of time it takes for it to be completed may not be of clinical importance, and these things may be left to the client to decide. In other instances the "when" will be in response to some internal cognitive, emotional, physiological, or behavioral trigger. However, under such circumstances it should be clearly noted that the client can make decisions regarding the completion of homework as appropriate.

Specificity Does Not Equal Difficulty

Attaining a high degree of specificity in assigning the homework does not necessarily mean that homework will be difficult. A relatively straightforward assignment, such as reading *Coping with Depression* prior to the second session, can still be specified in terms of when, where, and how often it should be done as well as how long it should take. Figure 17.8 summarizes the process of assigning homework within the guiding model.

Quick Reference

Ask client to summarize rationale in relation to therapy goals.

Collaborate to specify how the task will be practically possible (i.e., when, where, how often, and how long it will take).

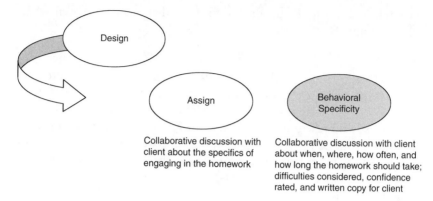

Fig. 17.8 Assigning homework using the guiding model.

Practical Obstacles

Consistent with early recommendations for the use of homework in therapy, the clinical Chapters presented in Parts II and III illustrated the importance of considering practical obstacles to the homework. Some assignments are confined to specific times and locations that may present unexpected practical obstacles. For example, clients may have a very clear mental picture about the context in which they are to engage in their exposure homework after guided imagery, but some aspect of the real-life situation may be different or prevent the homework from being undertaken. A client may not accurately anticipate how busy the theater will be for a particular film, or how crowded a mall may be during lunch hour, thereby creating the impression for the client that he or she is moving up the exposure hierarchy too quickly. Some clients will report that they were not in a situation when they could practice thought record completion, when actually they had not understood that the thought record would be useful for negative emotions. Thus, the therapist should work with clients to ensure they understand what is involved in the homework, what might present obstacles, and the various contexts in which assignments are appropriate.

Practical obstacles are to be distinguished from factors such as clients' beliefs about the homework task or its benefits. Although beliefs are relevant, we encourage therapists to think about these separately. Practical obstacles are often revealed in reviewing homework and in considering when, where, and how often it should be done as well as how long it will take. When clients respond quickly and state that there are absolutely no obstacles, we express curiosity about their certainty, and we emphasize that most clients have difficulty with at least some homework assignments. This type of discussion normalizes the experience of obstacles and often encourages clients to discuss those difficulties that might have been otherwise discounted.

Homework as an "Experiment"

The emphasis on homework as a process designed to facilitate learning can be conveyed by presenting the assignment as an "experiment" (A. T. Beck et al., 1979). Consistent with the scientist-as-practitioner paradigm, the therapist should take time to note that any given assignment will produce clinically useful information, much in the same way as collecting data in a research study provides helpful information that can be used to evaluate hypotheses. Chapters 7 (older adults) and 12 (depression) describe this as a "no-lose" scenario.

Quick Reference

Consider potential difficulties (i.e., obstacles identified during review). Emphasize learning "experiment" focus.

Therapy Notes

We encourage our clients to make notes about the same learning points or conclusions that are discussed in the therapy session. This strengthens the collaborative relationship and the view that the therapist and client are working as a team. Clients usually respond positively to the idea of taking their own notes, as they can find it difficult to remember everything that goes on in a session. Clients also report that it is helpful to read over their session notes as part of their homework and as part of maintaining their skills after the end of therapy. When clients respond positively to the idea of keeping notes, it can be helpful for them to have a book or folder in which they can also place their completed homework assignments and therapy handouts.

Written Copy

There is empirical support for ensuring that clients have a written copy of the homework assignment. One study randomly assigned clients to one of two therapy conditions that varied in the method of homework administration (i.e., Cox, Tisdell, & Culbert, 1988). Clients who received written copies of their assignments showed significantly greater homework compliance. Given that an important consideration in designing homework is tailoring the degree of difficulty to the individual client, a written account also ensures that a clear limit is set regarding how much is expected. Setting such parameters is particularly useful for clients with high standards and for those who do more of the homework than was assigned. Written homework also serves as a memory prompt, which is especially helpful for those experiencing memory difficulties as part of their presenting problems (Dunn et al., 2002; Glaser et al., 2000) or as a result of the aging process (Kazantzis et al., 2003). Written reminders can also be beneficial if the homework assignment involves several components, such as a behavioral experiment to be carried out in more than one situation, or when reading information for therapy, scheduling activities, and sleep hygiene are assigned in one session. Writing the homework assignment down also makes public a statement of commitment to engage in the activity. The role of written homework was specifically underlined in working with children (Chapter 5), adolescents (Chapter 6), couples (Chapter 9), depression (Chapter 12), and substance abuse (Chapter 13).

The Homework Assignment Form

Once there has been a collaborative discussion of how the homework assignment will be integrated into the client's daily life, we find it constructive to summarize the information on the Homework Assignment Form. As shown in Figure 17.9, the form provides space for a brief description of the assignment, its learning goal, as well as the specifics of when, where, and how often the homework should be done as well as how long it should take. The form can also help to prompt collaborative discussion on these specifics with the client. The form includes a space for a subjective rating of confidence about the ability to execute the assignment from 0 *(not at all confident)* to 100 *(totally confident).*

Interestingly, even when clients have discussed the specifics of when, where, how often, and how long, they often rate themselves less confident than the therapist might guess. As a rule, we take the opportunity to renegotiate the homework assignment with the client if the rating is less than 70% on the confidence scale, asking the client, "What would it take to raise your confidence? Are there any other barriers to the task that we have not considered yet?" We are also careful to more fully explore the question when clients rate themselves as 100% confident immediately. Nothing should be written on the form until the client has made his or her confidence rating, as this enables renegotiation of the homework assignment more readily.

Our clients usually, although not always, end up completing the Homework Assignment Forms themselves, which further enlarges their role in therapy and bolsters the impression that they are becoming their own therapists. We have this form printed on duplicate carbon-copy paper so that it can be completed once, and the original can go to the client and the copy to the file (Shelton & Ackerman, 1974).

Homework Assignment Form*

Today's Date: _____ Next Appointment Date: _____

Session Number:

Homework Description:

Learning Goal   (e.g., test idea/practice skill   ):

When (e.g., 11:45 am before lunch   ):

Where (e.g., in the bedroom / at work   ):

How often   (e.g., times per day/hour/week   ):

How long   (e.g., hours/minutes   ):

Confidence Rating   (circle one):

0   10   20   30   40   50   60   70   80   90   100
Not at all   Moderately   Totally
confident   confident   confident

Homework Description:

Learning Goal   (e.g., test idea/practice skill   ):

When (e.g., 11:45 am before lunch   ):

Where (e.g., in the bedroom / at work   ):

How often   (e.g., times per day/hour/week   ):

How long   (e.g., hours/minutes   ):

Confidence Rating   (circle one):

0   10   20   30   40   50   60   70   80   90   100
Not at all   Moderately   Totally
confident   confident   confident

Homework Description:

Learning Goal   (e.g., test idea/practice skill   ):

When (e.g., 11:45 am before lunch   ):

Where (e.g., in the bedroom / at work   ):

How often   (e.g., times per day/hour/week   ):

How long   (e.g., hours/minutes   ):

Confidence Rating   (circle one):

0   10   20   30   40   50   60   70   80   90   100
Not at all   Moderately   Totally
confident   confident   confident

Fig. 17.9 Homework assignment form.

Quick Reference

Ask client to summarize task and obtain rating of readiness, importance, and confidence (renegotiate if <70%).

Make a written note of the homework for the client (or use homework form).

Reviewing Homework

There is empirical support for the utility of reviewing homework assignments in CBT. One study found that the therapist's review of homework from the previous session achieved a significant correlation with client compliance, $r = .39$ (Bryant, Simons, & Thase, 1999). The authors of this study did point out, however, that therapists were not particularly vigilant about the reviews, resulting in a very small data set. Similar support for the value in reviewing homework was found by Worthington (1986), with therapist review of homework being the strongest predictor of the factors examined. A study by Startup and Edmonds (1994) did not find significant evidence that therapist adherence to systematic administration principles affected compliance, but, as noted earlier, the low numbers used in the analysis make the results somewhat unreliable.

Timing

It is useful, and respectful, to review homework assignments early in each therapy session. Clients spend a lot of time and energy on their homework activities, and it simply shows respect to talk with them about their experiences and learning. Reviewing homework at the outset of therapy also coveys the message that homework assignments are important, as well as creating opportunities to deal with practical barriers to homework completion and discuss what was learned from its completion. If homework assignments are not reviewed near the beginning of the session, the client is likely to notice this and may draw the conclusion that homework is not important. Furthermore, clients may assume that there is something wrong with the relationship or, worse yet, decide that they have not completed the assignment correctly (Moore & Garland, 2003).

Praise

In reviewing a homework assignment, the therapist should praise the client for any aspect of it that has been completed. Congratulating clients for homework completion is an effective strategy in reviewing homework (A. T. Beck et al., 1979). The implication is that praise is not provided when the client has not engaged in the homework activity. Thus, signs of praise and encouragement make up one component of the *contingencies* for homework completion. As outlined in Chapter 2, the naturally occurring internal contingencies for engaging in the homework—namely, reduced emotional distress, increased sense of pleasure, or a sense of mastery— are often powerful. Therefore when clients have experienced a benefit from engaging in the homework, they usually present for therapy appearing optimistic and enthusiastic. Completed homework should be met with sincere enthusiasm, encouragement, and praise from the therapist.

Several Chapters in this text discuss the role of specific reinforcement for homework completion. External reinforcers were recommended as part of the use of homework in working with children (Chapter 5) and in treating substance use (Chapter 13), delusions and hallucinations (Chapter 14), and borderline personality traits (Chapter 16).

As discussed at the outset of this Chapter, homework noncompletion is a common phenomenon in therapy. This means that it should be anticipated by the therapist even when a homework assignment has been carefully designed and assigned during the previous session. The therapist will use the homework review to determine what was and was not completed and then discuss with the client either the experience in completing part of it or the decision not to do it at all.

The critical issue in the review is to create a therapeutic atmosphere in which the client does not feel judged and is able to talk honestly and openly about the assigned homework activities and patterns of completion. Discussion of the client's cognitions about homework and doubts about it, as well as opportunities to explore practical and psychological barriers to completion, are essential to the success of homework. This process involves continual feedback about the homework itself and the completion process.

Although some practitioners choose to keep copies of completed homework in their clinical files, this practice is generally not recommended. Some clients can benefit from keeping their completed activity schedules and thought records, but others may react to their assignments being "submitted for marking" much in the same way they did with schoolwork (Garland & Scott, 2000).

Focus on Quality, not Quantity of Completion

Few practitioners would say that they are primarily interested in whether or not the client completed the homework without a consideration of how well it was carried out. Despite this, Chapters 3 and 4 of this book illustrate that research on homework assignments has focused almost exclusively on "compliance" (i.e., quantity of completion). Those studies that have examined *quality* of homework completion, otherwise known as the degree of learning through skill acquisition, have illustrated that quality predicts treatment outcome better than quantity (e.g., Neimeyer & Feixas, 1990; Schmidt & Woolaway-Bickel, 2000). The practical implication is that therapists should attend not only to whether or not the homework was completed but also to how well it was carried out. It is conceivable that a client could carry out a thought record every day but not attain any clinical benefit.

Quick Reference

Discuss noncompletion and *quantity and quality* of completion.
Provide verbal reinforcement for *any* portion carried out.

Client Beliefs about the Homework Activity, Its Utility, and the Synthesis of Learning

Current behavioral and cognitive conceptualizations of the use of homework in therapy rely heavily on the assumption that clients will be honest in their feedback and disclosure of their attitudes and beliefs about the task (see Persons, 1989). Clients' hesitancy to report openly about the process of therapy, or the homework discussed with therapist, often reflects a deficit in the relationship (Hill, Thompson, Cogar, & Denman, 1993). Clients may wish to present themselves in a socially desirable light and may not wish to reveal confusion, disagreement, lack of commitment, or a negative prediction about the task. A therapeutic relationship that does not allow for the expression of ambivalent views also does not allow for the exploration of differences in beliefs about the activity. The therapist may not have described the rationale for the homework activity clearly, or the client may have been hesitant to ask for more information.

As part of reviewing the extent to which the homework assignment was completed and what was learned, therapists should work to obtain a conceptualization of a specific situation in which the homework was completed (e.g., Padesky & Mooney, 1990). In addition to providing data on the cues to homework completion for the client (i.e., physiological, emotional, cognitive, behavioral), this is the primary means for gathering information on clients' beliefs about the activity. Clients hold beliefs about the homework's relevance for their particular set of presenting problems, and that can form a range of conclusions in reflecting or synthesizing their experiences. Clients may find that engaging in the homework assignment is reinforcing because it decreases the experience of a negative emotion or set of cognitions. Other clients may find that the homework gives them a degree of control over their problems by reducing emotional distress or bolstering the sense that progress is being made in therapy. As outlined in Chapter 2, clients form beliefs based on their experiences regarding the *benefits* and *costs* involved in engaging in the assignment.

In addition to considering specific beliefs about the homework, it is usually worthwhile to consider the context of the clients' individualized conceptualization. Some clients do not remember to do homework, are unable to find time for homework, or consider almost any homework task to be overwhelming. Other clients present for therapy demanding that the therapist address in session everything that is to be assigned for homework, whereas others are suspicious of the value and motives behind the assignment. Still other clients complete more than what has been assigned for homework, and some report instantaneous and rather exaggerated benefits from having engaged in the homework. In every one of these instances, it is important for the therapist to make sense of the client's response in the context of the beliefs identified in the cognitive conceptualization. The three cases described at the outset of this Chapter illustrate the links between homework noncompletion and the cognitive conceptualization.

Quick Reference

Situational conceptualization to identify beliefs about the consequences of homework (i.e., synthesis of learning).

Use individualized conceptualization to make sense of noncompletion.

Sometimes Practical Difficulties Are Just Practical Difficulties

There may also be a range of practical obstacles that prevent the client from being able to carry out the homework assignment. In considering the range of environmental influences, Freeman and McCloskey (2003) note that psychosocial stressors (e.g., financial strain, ongoing family tension, limited support networks), family pathology, family or cultural mores about seeking help, and demands by family and significant others can all serve as impediments to effective therapy.

Clients are busy people with busy lives. Allocating time to learn a new set of skills can be challenging to an already hectic schedule and even more challenging when acquiring those skills involves exposure to a degree of emotional distress. As much as therapists and clients plan for homework during sessions, not every practical obstacle can be anticipated for every client, and there are some things that simply cannot be predicted. For this reason, several authors recommended involving other people to assist with homework assigned to children (Chapters 5 and 11), adolescents (Chapter 6), and when substance use is a part of the equation (Chapter 13). Figure 17.10 summarizes the process of reviewing and designing homework within the guiding model.

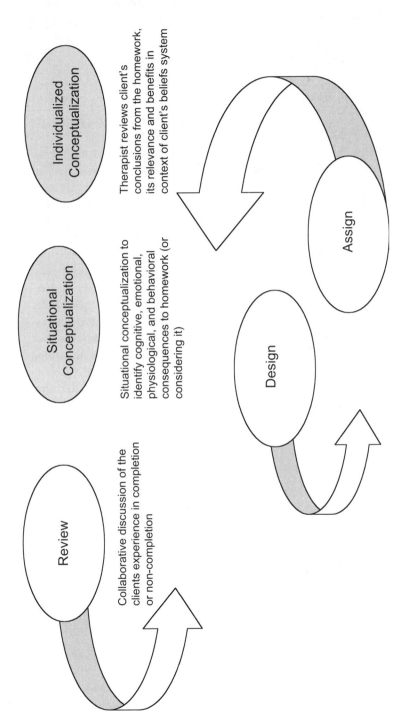

Individualized Conceptualization

Therapist reviews client's conclusions from the homework, its relevance and benefits in context of client's beliefs system

Situational Conceptualization

Situational conceptualization to identify cognitive, emotional, physiological, and behavioral consequences to homework (or considering it)

Review

Collaborative discussion of the clients experience in completion or non-completion

Design

Assign

Fig. 17.10 Reviewing, designing, and assigning homework using the guiding model.

Quick Reference

Problem-solve obstacles.

Record homework completion in session notes.

Summary and Future Directions

This Chapter was written to provide the reader with a comprehensive account of the process of using homework assignments in CBT. The aim was to draw on the theoretical and empirical foundations in Part I of the book as well as the clinical recommendations offered in Parts II and III and to discuss specific recommendations for the practicing clinician within a guiding model for practice. We sought to build upon the original description of integrating homework assignments into Beck's cognitive theory and therapy (A. T. Beck, 1976, A. T. Beck et al.,1979) and to extend previous models (i.e., Shelton & Levy, 1981).

In the first half of the Chapter, we covered the role of the therapeutic collaboration, the role of therapists' assumptions, and some adaptive therapist assumptions about using homework. We consider the therapeutic relationship and the emphasis on collaboration as essential to the successful use of homework. We also encouraged therapists to identify their own beliefs about the role of homework assignments in therapy and illustrated how their cognitions, emotions, and resultant behaviors can emerge during the interpersonal interaction with the client. We recommended that therapists complete their own thought records as a means of understanding clients' responses to therapy and to increase their interpersonal awareness, key for a strong therapeutic collaboration.

In the second half of the Chapter we discussed specific therapist behaviors for the integration of homework in therapy. We emphasized the role of the individualized cognitive conceptualization at each stage of the homework administration process and provided case examples of how both the content and discussion of homework can be tailored for the individual client. We recommended that basic CBT skills such as Socratic questioning and guided imagery be folded into the process of integrating homework into therapy. In line with the intention to facilitate therapist skill and mastery in integrating homework into therapy by making the process more explicit, we summarized the specific behaviors of the therapist in the "Quick Reference" sections. An overall summary of these guidelines is included in the Appendix.

The material in this Chapter will form the basis of a manualized protocol for future prospective process outcome research within our *Cognitive Behavior Therapy Homework Project.* We are currently in the process of designing a therapist adherence and competence measure that will be subject to psychometric evaluation and research. Once combined with our evaluation of the HRS II measure of client homework completion (Chapter 4), we will be in a position to evaluate the specific mechanism by which homework produces its effects. Ultimately, our goal is to conduct controlled outcome studies to determine the specific role of this model in enhancing homework efficacy in CBT.

References

Agras, W. S., Barlow, D. H., Chapin, H. N., Abel, G. C., & Leitenberg, H. (1974). Behavior modification of anorexia nervosa. *Archives of General Psychiatry, 30,* 279–286.

Aristotle. (1976). *The Nicomachean Ethics.* London: Penguin.

Basco, M. R., & Rush, A. J. (1996). *Cognitive-behavioral therapy for bipolar disorders.* New York: Guilford Press.

Beck, A. T. (1964). Thinking and depression: Theory and therapy. *Archives of General Psychiatry, 10,* 561–571.

Beck, A.T. (1976). *Cognitive therapy and the emotional disorders.* New York: International Universities Press.

Beck, A. T., Davis, D. D., Freeman, A., & Associates. (2004) *Cognitive therapy of personality disorders* (2nd ed.). New York: Guilford Press.

Beck, A. T., Emery, G., & Greenberg, R. L. (1985). *Anxiety disorders and phobias: A cognitive perspective.* New York: Basic Books.

Beck, A. T., Rush, J. A., Shaw, B. F., & Emery, G. (1979). *Cognitive therapy of depression.* New York: Guilford Press.

Beck, A. T., Wright, F. D., Newman, C. F., & Liese, B. S. (1993). *Cognitive therapy of substance abuse.* New York: Guilford Press.

Beck, J. (1995). *Cognitive therapy: Basics and beyond.* New York: Guilford Press.

Blackburn, I., & Davidson, K. M. (1990). *Cognitive therapy for depression and anxiety: A practitioner's guide.* London: Blackwell Science.

Blackburn, I., & Twaddle, V. (1996). *Cognitive therapy in action.* London: Souvenir Press.

Brown-Stanridge, M. D. (1989). A paradigm for constructing of family therapy tasks. *Family Process, 28,* 471–489.

Bryant, M. J., Simons, A. D., & Thase, M. E. (1999). Therapist skill and patient variables in homework compliance: Controlling a uncontrolled variable in cognitive therapy outcome research. *Cognitive Therapy and Research, 23,* 381–399.

Burns, D. D., & Auerbach, A. H. (1992). Does homework compliance enhance recovery from depression? *Psychiatric Annals, 22,* 464–469.

Conoley, C. W., Padula, M. A., Payton, D. S., & Daniels, J. A. (1994). Predictors of client implementation of counselor recommendations: Match with problem, difficulty level, and building on client strengths. *Journal of Counseling Psychology, 41,* 3–7.

Coon, D. W., & Gallagher-Thompson, D. (2002). Encouraging homework completion among older adults in therapy. *Journal of Clinical Psychology, 58,* 549–563.

Cox, D. J., Tisdelle, D. A., & Culbert, J. P. (1988). Increasing adherence to behavioral homework assignments. *Journal of Behavioral Medicine, 11,* 519–522.

Dattilio, F. M. (2002). Homework assignments in couple and family therapy. *Journal of Clinical Psychology, 58,* 535–549.

Dattilio, F. M., Freeman, A., & Blue, J. (1998). The therapeutic relationship. In A. S. Bellack & M. Hersen (Eds.), *Comprehensive Clinical Psychology* (229–249). Oxford, UK: Elsevier Science, Ltd.

De Shazer, S. (1998). *Clues: Investigating solutions in brief therapy.* New York: Norton.

Dunlap, K. (1932). *Habits, their making and unmaking.* New York: Liveright.

Dunn, H., Morrison, A. P., & Bentall, R. P. (2002). Patients' experiences of homework tasks in cognitive behavioral therapy for psychosis: A qualitative analysis. *Clinical Psychology and Psychotherapy, 9,* 361–369.

Fehm, L., & Kazantzis, N. (2004). Attitudes and use of homework assignments in therapy: A survey of German psychotherapists. *Clinical Psychology & Psychotherapy, 11,* 332–343.

Fennell, M. J. V. (2004). Depression, low self-esteem and mindfulness. *Behaviour Research and Therapy, 42,* 1053–1067.

Freeman, A., & McCloskey, R. D. (2003). Impediments to effective psychotherapy. In R. L. Leahy (Ed.). *Roadblocks in cognitive behavior therapy: Transforming challenges into opportunities for change* (pp. 24–49). New York: Guilford Press.

Freeman, A., & Rosenfield, B. (2002). Modifying therapeutic homework for patients with personality disorders. Journal of Clinical Psychology, 58, 513–524.

Freud, S. (1952). Inhibitions, symptoms, and anxiety. In R. M. Hutchins (Ed.), *Great books of the Western world* (Alix Strachey, Trans., pp. 718–734). Chicago: Encyclopedia Britannica. (Original work published 1926.)

Garland, A., & Scott, J. (2000). Using homework in therapy for depression. *Journal of Clinical Psychology, 58,* 489–498.

Gibbons, M. B. C., Crits-Christoph, P., Levinson, J., & Barber, J. (2003). Flexibility in manual-based psychotherapies: Predictors of therapist interventions in interpersonal and cognitive-behavioral therapy. *Psychotherapy Research, 13,* 169–185.

Glaser, N. M., Kazantzis, N., Deane, F. P., & Oades, L. G. (2000). Critical issues in using homework assignments within cognitive-behavioral therapy for schizophrenia. *Journal of Rational-Emotive and Cognitive-Behavior Therapy, 18,* 247–261.

Goisman, R. M. (1985). The psychodynamics of prescribing in behavior therapy. *American Journal of Psychiatry, 142,* 675–679.

Hansen, D. J., & Warner, J. E. (1994). Treatment adherence of maltreating families: A survey of professionals regarding prevalence and enhancement strategies. *Journal of Family Violence, 9,* 1–19.

Hay, C. E., & Kinnier, R. T. (1998). Homework in counseling. *Journal of Mental Health Counseling, 20,* 122.

Haynes, R. B., Sackett, D. L., Gibson, E. S., Taylor, D. W., Hackett, B. C., Roberts, R. S., & Johnson, A. L. (1976). Improvement of medication compliance in uncontrolled hypertension. *Lancet, 1,* 1265–1268.

Helbig, S., & Fehm, L. (2004). Problems with homework in CBT: Rare exception or rather frequent? *Behavioural and Cognitive Psychotherapy, 32,* 291–301.

Herzberg, A. (1941). Short-term treatment of neurosis by graduate tasks. *British Journal of Medical Psychology, 29,* 36–51.

Hill, C. E., Thompson, B. J., Cogar, M., & Denman, D. W. (1993). Beneath the surface of long-term therapy: Therapist and client report of their own and each other's covert processes. *Journal of Counseling Psychology, 40,* 278–287.

Hudson, J. L., & Kendall, P. C. (2002). Showing you can do it: Homework in therapy for children and adolescents with anxiety disorders. *Journal of Clinical Psychology, 58,* 525–534.

Johnson, M., & Kazantzis, N. (2004). Cognitive behavioral therapy for chronic pain: Strategies for the successful use of homework assignments. *Journal of Rational-Emotive and Cognitive Behavioral Therapy, 22,* 189–218.

Kanfer, F., & Phillips, J. (1966). A survey of current behavior and a proposal for classification. *Archives of General Psychiatry, 15,* 114–128.

Karpman, B. (1949). Objective psychotherapy. *Journal of Clinical Psychology, 5,* 140–148.

Kazantzis, N., Busch, R., Ronan, K. R., & Merrick, P. L. (2005). Mental health practitioners' use and perceived importance of homework assignments in psychotherapy. Manuscript submitted for publication.

Kazantzis, N., & Deane, F. P. (1999). Psychologists' use of homework assignments in clinical practice. *Professional Psychology: Research and Practice, 30,* 581–585.

Kazantzis, N., Deane, F. P., & Ronan, K. R. (2000). Homework assignments in cognitive and behavioral therapy: A meta-analysis. *Clinical Psychology: Science and Practice, 7,* 189–202.

Kazantzis, N., Deane, F. P., Ronan, K. R. (2004). Assessing compliance with homework assignments: Review and recommendations for clinical practice. *Journal of Clinical Psychology, 60,* 627–641.

Kazantzis, N., & Lampropoulos, G. L. (2002). Reflecting on homework in psychotherapy: What can we conclude from research and experience? *Journal of Clinical Psychology, 58,* 577–585.

Kazantzis, N., Lampropoulos, G. L., & Deane, F. P. (in press). A national survey of psychologists' attitudes towards homework assignments. *Journal of Consulting and Clinical Psychology.*

Kazantzis, N., Pachana, N. A., & Secker, D. L. (2003). Cognitive-behavioral therapy for older adults: Practical guidelines for the use of homework assignments. *Cognitive and Behavioral Practice, 10,* 325–333.

Kelly, G. A. (1955). *The psychology of personal constructs.* New York: Norton.

Kemmler, L., Borgart, E.-J., & Gärke, R. (1992). Der Einsatz von Hausaufgaben in der Psychotherapie. Eine Praktikerbefragung. *Report Psychologie, 8,* 9–18.

Kornblith, S. J., Rehm, L. P., O'Hara, M. W., & Lamparski, D. M. (1983). The contribution of self-reinforcement training and behavioral assignments to the efficacy of self-control therapy for depression. *Cognitive Therapy and Research, 7,* 499–528.

Leahy, R. L. (2002). Improving homework compliance in the treatment of generalized anxiety disorder. *Journal of Clinical Psychology, 58,* 499–511.

LoPiccolo, J., & LoPiccolo, L. (Eds.). (1978). *Handbook of sex therapy.* New York: Plenum Press.

Mahoney, M. J., Moura, N. G., & Wade, T. C. (1973). Relative efficacy of self-reward, self-punishment, and self-monitoring techniques for weight loss. *Journal of Consulting and Clinical Psychology, 40,* 404–407.

Mahrer, A. R., Nordin, S., & Miller, L. S. (1995). If a client has this kind of problem, prescribe that kind of post-session behavior. *Psychotherapy, 32,* 194–203.

March, P. (1997). In two minds about cognitive-behavioural therapy: Talking to patients about why they do not do their homework. *British Journal of Psychotherapy, 13,* 461–472.

Masters, W. H., & Johnson, V. E. (1970). *Human sexual inadequacy.* Boston: Little Brown.

McCarthy, B. W. (1985). Use and misuse of behavioral homework exercises in sex therapy. *Journal of Sex & Marital Therapy, 11,* 185–191.

Miller, W. R., & Rollnick, S. (2002). *Motivational interviewing: Preparing people for change* (2nd ed.). New York: Guilford Press.

Moore, R. G., & Garland, A. (2003). *Cognitive therapy for chronic and persistent depression.* Chichester, UK: Wiley.

Needleman, L. D. (1999). *Cognitive case conceptualization: A guidebook for practitioners.* Mahwah, NJ: Erlbaum.

Neimeyer, R. A., & Feixas, G. (1990). The role of homework and skill acquisition in the outcome of group cognitive therapy for depression. *Behavior Therapy, 21,* 281–292.

Padesky, C. A. (1999). *Therapist beliefs: Protocols, personalities, and guided exercises* (Cassette Recording No. TB1). Huntington Beach, CA: Center for Cognitive Therapy.

Padesky, C. A., & Mooney, K. A. (1990). Presenting the cognitive model to clients. *International Cognitive Therapy Newsletter, 6,* 13–14.

Persons, J. B. (1989). *Cognitive therapy in practice: A case formulation approach.* New York: Norton.

Persons, J. B., Davidson, J., & Tompkins, M. A. (2001). *Essential components of cognitive-behavior therapy for depression.* Washington, DC: American Psychological Association.

Reiss, W., Piotrowski, W., & Bailey, J. S. (1976). Behavioral community psychology: Encouraging low-income parents to seek dental care for their children. *Journal of Applied Behavior Analysis, 9,* 387–397.

Salkovskis, P. M. (1996). The cognitive approach to anxiety: Threat beliefs, safety-seeking behaviour, and the special case of health anxiety and obsessions. In P. M. Salkovskis (Ed.), *Frontiers of cognitive therapy* (pp. 48–74). New York: Guilford.

Scheel, M. J., Hoggan, K., Willie, D., McDonald, K., & Tonin, S. (1998). *Client understanding of homework determined through therapist delivery.* Poster presented at the 106th Annual Convention of the American Psychological Association, San Francisco.

Scheel, M. J., Seaman, S., Roach, K., Mullin, T., & Mahoney, K. B. (1999). Client implementation of therapist recommendations predicted by client perception of fit, difficulty of implementation, and therapist influence. *Journal of Counseling Psychology, 46,* 308–316.

Schmidt, N. B., & Woolaway-Bickel, K. (2000). The effects of treatment compliance on outcome in cognitive-behavioral therapy for panic disorder: Quality versus quantity. *Journal of Consulting and Clinical Psychology, 68,* 13–18.

Schultheis, G. M. (1998). *Brief therapy homework planner.* New York: Wiley.

Shelton, J. L., & Ackerman, J. M. (1974). *Homework in counseling and psychotherapy: Examples of systematic assignments for therapeutic use by mental health professionals.* Springfield, IL: Charles C Thomas.

Shelton, J. L., & Levy, R. L. (1981). *Behavioral assignments and treatment compliance: A handbook of clinical strategies.* Champaign, IL: Research Press.

Startup, M., & Edmonds, J. (1994). Compliance with homework assignments in cognitive-behavioral psychotherapy for depression: Relation to outcome and methods of enhancement. *Cognitive Therapy and Research, 18,* 567–579.

Stevens, C. L., Muran, J. C., & Safran, J. D. (2003). Obstacles or opportunities? A relational approach to negotiating alliance ruptures. In R. L. Leahy (Ed.), *Roadblocks in cognitive behavior therapy: Transforming challenges into opportunities for change* (pp. 274–294). New York: Guilford Press.

Stokes, T. F., & Baer, D. M. (1977). An implicit technology of generalization. *Journal of Applied Behavior Analysis, 10,* 349–367.

Teasdale, J. D., Segal, Z. V., & Williams, J. M. G. (1995). How does cognitive therapy prevent relapse, and why should attentional control (mindfulness) training help? *Behaviour Research and Therapy, 33,* 225–239.

Thase, M. E., & Callan, J. A. (in press). The role of homework in cognitive behavior therapy of depression. *Journal of Psychotherapy Integration.*

Tompkins, M. A. (2002). Guidelines for enhancing homework compliance. *Journal of Clinical Psychology, 58,* 565–576.

Tompkins, M. A. (2003). Effective homework. In R. L. Leahy (Ed.), *Roadblocks in cognitive behavior therapy: Transforming challenges into opportunities for change* (pp. 49–69). New York: Guilford Press.

Tryon, S. G., & Winograd, G. (2001). Goal consensus and collaboration. *Psychotherapy, 38,* 385–389.

Worthington, E. L., Jr. (1986). Client compliance with homework directives during counseling. *Journal of Counseling Psychology, 33,* 124–130.

Wdpe, J. (1958). *Psychotherapy by recipical inhibition.* Oxford, England: Stanford University Press.

Wdpe, J. (1973). *The Practice of behavior therapy.* (2nd ed.). Oxford, England: Pergamon.

Young, J. E., & Beck, A. T. (1982). Cognitive therapy: Clinical applications. In A. J. Rush (Ed.), *Short-term psychotherapies for depression: Behavioral, interpersonal, cognitive, and psychodynamic approaches* (pp. 182–214). New York: Guilford Press.

CHAPTER 18

Summary and Conclusion

NIKOLAOS KAZANTZIS, FRANK P. DEANE, KEVIN R. RONAN,
and LUCIANO L'ABATE

The aim of this book has been to present focused teaching on the use of homework assignments in cognitive behavioral therapy. We assumed that the reader had knowledge and practical experience of A. T. Beck's (1976) cognitive theory and system of psychotherapy for depression (A. T. Beck, Rush, Shaw, & Emery, 1979). As the behavioral and cognitive theory foundations for the use of homework had not been previously discussed in the literature, we presented a comprehensive account as a preface to clinical discussions (Part I). The main section of this book comprises a series of clinically focused Chapters illustrating the use of homework assignments in cognitive behavioral therapy (CBT) for a range of clinical populations (Part II) and presenting problems (Part III). In Part IV, we synthesized the clinical recommendations from earlier Chapters in order to present a guiding "model for practice."

This final Chapter provides a concise summary and discusses avenues for future work. Specifically, we summarize key points from the theoretical and empirical foundations for homework as well as the innovations for clinical practice presented in this book. We then suggest some future directions for empirical research.

Theoretical and Empirical Foundations

Theoretical foundations for using homework were presented in Chapter 2. Drawing on classical and operant conditioning principles, we explained

405

that homework is linked with both antecedents and consequences that serve to create the conditions under which the homework is increased or decreased. Drawing on cognitive theory, we illustrated that beliefs based on prior homework experiences and the perceived benefit of the specific homework task, as well as the degree of encouragement from the therapist, also serve to determine homework completion. We also discussed the role of practical obstacles and noted the relevance of shaping and the frequency of benefits (and other contingencies) in determining the extent to which a homework activity is generalized and maintained in the client's everyday life. We described how clients form conclusions about the homework assignment based on their synthesis of events, which in turn serves as evidence on the basis of which the benefits of the current and future homework can be evaluated.

Empirical foundations for the use of homework were presented in Chapter 3. It was noted that there are now sufficient data to show that homework assignments produce increased effects on CBT outcomes. A separate line of research enquiry has shown that client completion of homework is correlated with positive treatment outcome. There are also emerging data in support of client beliefs as predictors of homework completion, but we have noted that surprisingly few data exists on the specific mechanism by which homework produces its effects.

After reviewing the research linking homework to outcome, we provided a review of the practitioner survey research. The data showed that homework is frequently used among practitioners in the field, but CBT practitioners are significantly more systematic in their use of homework.

We also reviewed the contemporary literature in support of the use of homework assignments in the treatment of the range of specific population and clinical disorders covered in this book. Specifically, we critiqued the available research examining the role of homework assignments for children, adolescents, older adults, couples, and families (Part II). We then critiqued the available research examining homework for panic and agoraphobia, generalized anxiety, obsessions and compulsions, depression, substance abuse, delusions and hallucinations, sexual problems, and borderline personality disorder (Part III). In several instances, we noted that there is an absence of empirical data to support specific homework effects for some clinical populations.

Innovations for Clinical Practice

A number of innovations for clinical practice were provided in this book. Building on the theoretical and empirical foundations in early Chapters, we then presented a review of existing operational definitions and methods of assessing homework (Chapter 4), and the main section comprised detailed clinical Chapters illustrating the use of homework (Chapters 5 to 16). We also provided a model for practice that synthesized general clinical recommendations from earlier Chapters (Chapter 17).

Assessing Homework Completion

It was noted that the range of terms used in the literature have led to a blurring of the operational definition of the term *homework*. After proposing a definition based on the founding literature of CBT, we presented a revision of our Homework Rating Scale (HRS) to assist in the assessment of homework completion. We described how HRS content has been based on behavioral and cognitive theory foundation of homework completion and noted that it is designed to measure a range of determinants of homework completion. The HRS obtains self-report data on the client's experience in completing homework. The revision of the HRS presented in this book has been designed to take account of the social desirability bias known to influence adherence ratings; we have observed this in our own use of the original measure with clients. We have research studies under way to examine the psychometric properties for the revised HRS, but the absence of existing psychometric data means that currently we recommend its use only as a tool to inform clinical practice.

Homework for Different Clinical Populations and Problems

The main parts of this book presented clinically focused teaching on the use of homework assignments for different client groups by expert CBT clinician-researchers. Each Chapter provided a discussion of common barriers to homework, strategies for the effective use of homework, a brief outline of different types of homework assignments within the appropriate CBT model, and detailed case studies of CBT practice. We have sequenced the Chapters on children, adolescents, older adults, couples, and families to appear earlier so that their implications can be considered in reading the problem-focused Chapters.

Emphasis on Therapeutic Collaboration

This book reflects the increasing potential for homework to be useful within CBT as a means of enhancing therapeutic collaboration, tailoring therapy to address the client's goals, and ensuring that the benefits for the individual client are maintained in the long term. Homework is a process that is contingent upon the active involvement of the client and requires a degree of explicitness from the therapist. Thus a collaborative therapeutic relationship of equality and partnership provides the opportunity for clients to benefit from homework (A. T. Beck et al., 1979; Blackburn &

Davidson, 1995). As described in this book, homework assignments can present challenges for therapeutic collaboration in encouraging clients to engage in therapeutic activities between sessions. Our guiding model for practice emphasizes the utility of therapists attending to their own emotions and cognitions in the interests of facilitating client learning. Several Chapters illustrate a useful therapist position of curiosity, interest, and empathy as facilitating the process of client and therapist working together as a team. Other Chapters illustrate the role of therapist beliefs in integrating homework into therapy.

Emphasis on Conceptualization

This book also strongly underscores the importance of guiding therapy based on the cognitive conceptualization (J. Beck, 1995). With regard to homework, the cognitive conceptualization should determine both the choice of homework task *and* the way in which it is discussed. More specifically, this book provides a detailed illustration of the extent to which (a) idiosyncratic beliefs that maintain client problems, (b) client beliefs about the presenting problems, and (c) client beliefs about coping strategies should all influence the way in which the therapist integrates homework into therapy. Each Chapter in Parts II and III offer detailed case examples that model how therapists can adapt and guide the process of integrating homework into therapy based on the individual cognitive conceptualization. Challenges to the use of homework assignments should also be conceptualized, and this is a focus of the "model for practice" presented in Part IV.

Cultural Considerations

An important consideration regarding the conceptualization concerns the extent to which client thoughts and beliefs are culturally determined and culturally appropriate. Some clients view their therapist as authorities or wise people and may begin to question their competence or lose respect if treatment is not targeted on presented problems or gains are slow. Culture can also determine their views of their presenting problems or the meaning and significance of their coping strategies. In New Zealand, it is considered culturally appropriate for Maori (indigenous people) to hear the voices of their ancestors communicate with them, an experience that would be considered unusual for Pakeha (New Zealanders of non-Maori background). Furthermore, Maori hold a more holistic view of health, incorporating spirituality, family and social relationships, physical growth and development, and thoughts and feelings (Durie, 1977, 1994). These components require a conceptualization of presenting problems and targeted homework assignments that are culturally appropriate. For example, spirituality can play a key role in the choice of homework assignments, which may be based on prayer, meditation, consultation with elders, immediate or broader family.

Therapists need to be aware of the barriers to homework facing some clients from other cultures. For example, impoverished clients may not have access to transportation, child care, or access to public services. Clients who are refugees may face language problems and discrimination. A suggestion to draw on help from individuals help outside their families may be inappropriate for some clients. Attempting new strategies for coping in a way that incorporates the family's needs may also prove challenging for clients from some cultures.

Several of the Chapters in Parts II and III provided useful discussion and case examples of the consideration of client culture in using homework. The important issue is that therapists are responsive to client culture when integrating homework assignments. Therapists need to be aware of such cultural considerations, ask clients about potential obstacles and barriers, and be sensitive to different individual needs. Without such consideration, clients may feel disrespected and may devalue the therapeutic process.

Informed Consent

Throughout this book, there has been an assumption that clients are informed about the treatment options that are available to them. There has also been an assumption that clients agree and consent to treatment and the procedures that therapy involves. This has been assumed because CBT is a collaborative approach that incorporates ethical principles of informed consent. Some ethical guidelines for professional practice advocate the use of consent forms to formalize this informed consent process. Therapists should explicitly mention the role of homework assignments wherever formal documentation is required. Whatever the regional regulations for ethical clinical practice, we encourage therapists to inform clients about the role of between-session activities from the outset of the therapeutic interaction and obtain their consent to be involved in these assignments.

Future Empirical Directions

This text has illustrated the scientific basis for homework within a CBT framework. In this section, we discuss some potentially fruitful avenues for extending the field's understanding of this core process of therapeutic change. We suggest that advancement to our understanding is likely to occur through research on specific populations, investigation of the theoretical foundations to homework, comprehensive measurement of homework completion, and measurement of therapist adherence and competence in using homework. In particular, we believe that the field would benefit from a prospective examination of homework's effects that incorporates assessment of therapist competence in administering homework within CBT over the course of therapy (Kazantzis, Ronan, & Deane, 2001).

Specific Populations

Existing research has advanced our understanding to the extent that engagement with homework can be taken as an indicator of treatment outcome for some populations. However, an important future direction for homework in CBT is the gathering of further empirical evidence to support its use for the range of clinical populations and problems in which CBT is applied. In Chapter 3, we noted that there is no existing empirical support for the specific effects of homework assignments with child and adolescent populations, or clients with personality disorders. Since homework assignments are clearly part of the application of CBT to a range of clinical presentations (c.f., Glaser, Kazantzis, Deane, & Oades, 2000; Johnson & Kazantzis, 2004; Kazantzis, Pachana, & Secker, 2003), it is important that empirical work be carried out to support these clinical observations.

As part of our *Cognitive Behavior Therapy Homework Project*, we are participating in a collaborative effort to evaluate the role of homework completion in CBT *group* therapy for depression. We are also beginning a preliminary investigation of the role of homework in therapy for borderline personality disorder.

Theoretical Foundations

As noted, there has been relatively little previous discussion on the specific theoretical foundations for the use of homework assignments in CBT. Given this situation, it is not surprising that much of the existing research has progressed without a clear theoretical basis. Previous studies of the role of homework in therapy have either examined the administration of homework compared to no-homework conditions (e.g., Kazdin & Mascitelli, 1982; Neimeyer & Feixas, 1990), or conducted a correlational investigation relating homework compliance to outcome (e.g., Addis & Jacobson, 2000; Bryant, Simons, & Thase, 1999; Edelman & Chambless, 1993, 1995). These two methodologies examine two distinct research questions, the first being an examination of the unique effects of homework assignments in therapy and the second being an investigation of the relationship between homework compliance and therapy outcome. Neither of these lines of research explain *how* homework assignments produce their effects, or how homework assignments should be incorporated into practice in order to maximize the opportunity for client learning through homework completion.

The mechanism by which homework produces its effects has only begun to be explored. For instance, the links between outcome and the acceptance of therapy rationale (Addis & Jacobson, 2000), or initial client coping skills (Burns & Nolen-Hoeksema, 1991) have only been examined in selected studies. As discussed in Chapter 3, there has been a handful of psychotherapy process studies conducted to evaluate the factors that are associated with client compliance with homework assignments. The studies have been largely exploratory, conducted within a particular approach to psychotherapy, or have yet to be replicated with larger samples. The study by Burns and Spangler (2000) is an excellent example of the research we are advocating, even though we respectfully disagreed with the causal conclusions from cross-sectional data that does not capture all the relevant theoretical foundations. (i.e., Kazantzis et al., 2001). As a first step towards clarifying the mechanism for homework effects, we believe that the field would benefit from a reliable and valid measure that captures homework completion.

Focus on "Quality," not Quantity of Completion

Researchers have given very little attention to the assessment of the *quality* of homework completion, and have focused on the *quantity*. As discussed throughout this book, homework noncompletion usually provides useful clinical information and often is part of the natural learning process for clients (see Chapter 17). Indeed, emerging evidence suggests that that the quality or degree of learning through homework completion is a better predictor of treatment outcome than the degree of client *compliance*. Our HRS measure obtains ratings on the quantity, quality, difficulty, obstacles, comprehension, rationale, collaboration, specificity, match with therapy goals, pleasure, mastery, and sense of progress achieved through homework completion.

As part of our *Cognitive Behavior Therapy Homework* Project we are conducting preliminary studies of the internal consistency, factor structure, and criterion related validity of the HRS. A further study is under way to evaluate the extent to which ratings on the HRS predict treatment outcome in CBT for depression.

Therapist Behaviors

There has been only limited work on the extent to which therapist behaviors in the process of designing, assigning, and reviewing homework influence client homework compliance and treatment outcome (Bryant et al., 1999; Shaw et al., 1999). This is not particularly surprising, as the role of the therapist has only relatively recently become the focus in the wider context of psychotherapy research (Dobson & Kazantzis, 2003).

Drawing on theoretical foundations, this book has suggested a greater focus on the therapeutic collaboration and basing homework administration on the conceptualization. The "model for practice" also provided an extensive list of therapist facilitative behaviors theorized to encourage homework completion. Clearly, the next step is to conduct empirical research to evaluate these recommendations. Such specific data would be helpful for clinical training, practice, and supervision. In other words, advancement in our understanding of the mechanism by which homework produces its effects is likely to occur through the assessment of the interaction between therapist competence, client homework completion, and other theoretically relevant factors.

As part of our *Cognitive Behavior Therapy Homework Project* we are evaluating a new measure designed to assess *therapist* adherence and competence in the use of homework assignments. Following pilot testing, the measure will undergo psychometric evaluation and be examined for its ability to predict outcomes in CBT for depression.

Types of Homework Assignments

Our "model for practice" has taken a generalist approach, focusing on the process of reviewing, designing, and assigning homework. However, the fact remains that there are specific "types" of homework assignments for different clinical populations and problems. The contributors in Parts II and III have provided numerous examples of the types of homework used for different clients. Consistent with the progression away from listing "empirically supported therapies," future research would be usefully aimed toward the identification of empirically supported interventions and empirically supported homework assignments for different problems (see recent discussions in *Clinical Psychology: Science and Practice*, volume 12, number 4).

Maintenance and Prevention

The goal of therapy is to enable clients to manage and overcome their difficulties to live more fulfilling lives. This statement carries the idea that effective therapy should be able to be maintained and prevent the relapse of symptoms and perhaps provide a foundation for continuing growth and enhancement of functioning. CBT shows considerable promise as a psychotherapy that can lead to long-term benefits for clients.

A reasonable hypothesis is that greater homework completion during the course of therapy leads to a higher degree of maintenance and relapse prevention. However, research has not consistently demonstrated a link between homework compliance and the maintenance of gains *after* the end of treatment. Some studies have demonstrated that client completion of homework assignments is associated with improvement at posttreatment and 2-year follow-up (e.g., Park et al., 2001), but others have been unsuccessful in linking compliance with maintenance of treatment gains at 6-month follow-up (i.e., Elderman & Chambless, 1995, see also Neimeyer & Feixas, 1990). There are also data to suggest that some clients who complete homework assignments can experience rapid early response in CBT (i.e., Fennel & Teasdale, 1987), which is not easily explained in terms of a mechanism of targeted cognitive change (Ilardi & Craighead, 1994). Given the inconsistency in the available data, we encourage researchers to investigate the extent to which homework completion facilitates generalization and maintenance of therapeutic gains.

The Cognitive Behavior Therapy Homework Project

As noted in the introduction, this book project has resulted from our team's collaboration in the *Cognitive Behavior Therapy Homework Project*. Our efforts have resulted in a variety of theoretical, empirical, and writing projects that were intended to contribute to the field's knowledge and understanding of homework's role in therapy. In this Chapter we have described our current empirical projects designed to evaluate our measures of homework completion and therapist adherence and competence. With these projects under way, we are now turning our attention toward prospective treatment outcome research to evaluate the utility of the guiding "model for practice." We look forward to continuing in these efforts and contributing to the knowledge on this aspect of CBT.

Conclusion

It was intended that readers of this text would gain a broad perspective on the current knowledge for the theory, empirical, and practical use of homework assignments in CBT. It was further intended that practitioners who follow recommendations outlined for each problem focus and the generic model of practice will be able to maximize the potential for homework assignments in their own practices.

Homework assignments represent the core change process in CBT. Homework connects the therapeutic collaboration and individualized conceptualization together with analytic and experiential learning for the client. Individually tailored in their content, homework assignments serve as a main vehicle by which clients generalize their skills to their everyday lives. With such a crucial and integrated role, it is not surprising that homework assignments are incorporated into CBT for so many problems and clinical populations. As the theory, research, and practice of CBT continue to evolve, homework assignments are likely to remain central to this evolution.

References

Addis, M. E., & Jacobson, N. S. (2000). A closer look at the treatment rationale and homework compliance in cognitive behavioral therapy for depression. *Cognitive Therapy and Research, 24,* 313–326.

Beck, A. T. (1976). *Cognitive therapy and the emotional disorders.* New York: International Universities Press.

Beck, A. T., Rush, J. A., Shaw, B. F., & Emery, G. (1979). *Cognitive therapy of depression.* New York: Guilford Press.

Beck, J. (1995). *Cognitive therapy: Basics and beyond.* New York: Guilford Press.

Blackburn, I. M., & Davidson, K. M. (1995). *Cognitive therapy for depression and anxiety: A practitioner's guide.* London: Blackwell.

Bryant, M. J., Simons, A. D., & Thase, M. E. (1999). Therapist skill and patient variables in homework compliance: Controlling a uncontrolled variable in cognitive therapy outcome research. *Cognitive Therapy and Research, 23,* 381–399.

Burns, D. D., & Nolen-Hoeksema, S. (1991). Coping styles, homework compliance, and the effectiveness of cognitive behavioral therapy. *Journal of Consulting and Clinical Psychology, 59,* 305–311.

Burns, D. D., & Spangler, D. (2000). Does psychotherapy homework lead to changes in depression in cognitive behavioral therapy? Or does clinical improvement lead to homework compliance? *Journal of Consulting and Clinical Psychology, 68,* 46–56.

Dobson, K., & Kazantzis, N. (2003). The therapist in cognitive-behavioral therapy: Introduction to a special section. *Psychotherapy Research, 13,* 131–134.

Durie, M. (1977). Maori attitudes to sickness, doctors and hospitals. *New Zealand Medical Journal, 86,* 483–485.

Durie, M. H. (1994, March). *Kaupapa hauora Maori. Policies for Maori health.* Address at the proceedings of Te Ara Ahu Whakamua. Proceedings of the Maori Health Decade Hui, Te Puni Kokiri, Wellington, New Zealand.

Edelman, R. E., & Chambless, D. L. (1993). Compliance during sessions and homework in exposure-based treatment of agoraphobia. *Behaviour Research and Therapy, 31,* 767–773.

Edelman, R. E., & Chambless, D. L. (1995). Adherence during sessions and homework in cognitive-behavioral group treatment of social phobia. *Behaviour Research and Therapy, 33,* 573–577.

Fennell, M. J. V., & Teasdale, J. D. (1987). Cognitive therapy for depression: Individual differences and the process of change. *Cognitive Therapy and Research, 11,* 253–271.

Glaser, N. M., Kazantzis, N., Deane, F. P., & Oades, L. G. (2000). Critical issues in using homework assignments within cognitive-behavioral therapy for schizophrenia. *Journal of Rational-Emotive and Cognitive-Behavior Therapy, 18,* 247–261.

Ilardi, S. S., & Craighead, W. E. (1994). The role of nonspecific factors in cognitive-behavior therapy for depression. *Clinical Psychology: Science and Practice, 1,* 138–156.

Johnson, M., & Kazantzis, N. (2004). Cognitive behavioral therapy for chronic pain: Strategies for the successful use of homework assignments. *Journal of Rational-Emotive and Cognitive Behavioral Therapy, 22,* 189–218.

Kazdin, A. E., & Mascitelli, S. (1982). Covert and overt rehearsal and homework practice in developing assertiveness. *Journal of Consulting and Clinical Psychology, 50,* 250–258.

Kazantzis, N., Pachana, N. A., & Secker, D. L. (2003). Cognitive-behavioral therapy for older adults: Practical guidelines for the use of homework assignments. *Cognitive and Behavioral Practice, 10,* 325–333.

Kazantzis, N., Ronan, K. R., & Deane, F. P. (2001). Concluding causation from correlation: Comment on Burns and Spangler (2000). *Journal of Consulting and Clinical Psychology, 69,* 1079–1083.

Neimeyer, R. A., & Feixas, G. (1990). The role of homework and skill acquisition in the outcome of group cognitive therapy for depression. *Behavior Therapy, 21,* 281–292.

Park, J. M., Mataix-Cols, D., Marks, I. M., Ngamthipwatthana, T., Marks, M., Araya, R., Al-Kubaisy, T. (2001). Two-year follow-up after a randomized controlled trial of self- and clinician-accompanied exposure for phobia/panic disorders. *British Journal of Psychiatry, 178,* 543–548.

Shaw, B. F., Elkin, I., Yamaguchi, J., Olmsted, M., Vallis, T. M., Dobson, K. S., Lowery, A., Sotsky, S. M., Watkins, J. T., Imber, S. D. (1999). Therapist competence ratings in relation to clinical outcome in cognitive therapy of depression. *Journal of Consulting and Clinical Psychology, 67,* 837–846.

Appendix – Clinician Resources

This Appendix includes a number of resources to assist the practitioner in using homework assignments in cognitive behavior therapy. Guidance for the use of these resources is contained in specific chapters. Please note these resources extend the teaching conveyed in this book and are not designed as stand-alone clinical tools. For help in using the Homework Rating Scale – Revised (*HRS II*) and its variants, please refer to Chapter 4 of this book. For help in using the "*Homework Assignment Form*" and "*Therapists' Quick Reference*", please refer to Chapter 17 of this book. Practitioners who purchase this book are permitted to copy these forms for their own clinical practice. Individuals interested in using these forms for research purposes are asked to contact Nikolaos Kazantzis, Ph.D. at the address below:

Nikolaos Kazantzis, Ph.D.
School of Psychology
Massey University
Private Bag 102904, NSMC
Albany, Auckland
New Zealand
N.Kazantzis@massey.ac.nz

Instructions: Many people find ways to engage in activities between therapy sessions in a way that suits them. This may differ from the way in which the activity was discussed with their therapist. This questionnaire asks about your activities from last session. Below are some ways in which people have said that they have engaged and learned from their activities. Please read each question carefully, and for each of the statements, circle the **one response** that best applies to you.

1. Quantity
I was able to do the activity

- 0   not at all
- 1   a little
- 2   some
- 3   a lot
- 4   completely

2. Quality
I was able to do the activity well

- 0   not at all
- 1   somewhat
- 2   moderately
- 3   very
- 4   extremely

3. Difficulty
The activity was difficult for me

- 0   not at all
- 1   somewhat
- 2   moderately
- 3   very
- 4   extremely

4. Obstacles
I experienced obstacles in doing the activity

- 0   not at all
- 1   a little
- 2   some
- 3   a lot
- 4   extensive

5. Comprehension
I understood what to do for the activity

- 0   not at all
- 1   a little
- 2   somewhat
- 3   a lot
- 4   completely

6. Rationale
The reason for doing the activity was clear to me

- 0   not at all
- 1   somewhat
- 2   moderately
- 3   very
- 4   completely

7. Collaboration
I had an active role in planning the activity

- 0   not at all
- 1   a little
- 2   some
- 3   a lot
- 4   extensive

8. Specificity
The guidelines for how to carry out the activity were specific

- 0   not at all
- 1   somewhat
- 2   moderately
- 3   very
- 4   extremely

9. Match with Therapy Goals
The activity matched with my goals for therapy

- 0   not at all
- 1   a little
- 2   somewhat
- 3   a lot
- 4   completely

10. Pleasure
I enjoyed the activity

- 0   not at all
- 1   a little
- 2   somewhat
- 3   a lot
- 4   extremely

11. Mastery
I gained a sense of control over my problems

- 0   not at all
- 1   a little
- 2   somewhat
- 3   a lot
- 4   extensively

12. Progress
The activity helped with my progress in therapy

- 0   not at all
- 1   a little
- 2   somewhat
- 3   a lot
- 4   extremely

Homework Rating Scale II – Client Version © Copyright 2005 by Nikolaos Kazantzis, Frank Deane, and Kevin Ronan. From the book "*Using Homework Assignments in Cognitive Behavior Therapy*", by N. Kazantzis, F. P. Deane, K. R. Ronan, & L. L'Abate (2005). New York: Routledge.

Instructions: This questionnaire consists of 12 questions regarding your client's homework completion from last session. Please read each question carefully, and circle the number of the **one response** that best describes your impression of the client's experience. If several statements apply equally well, circle the lowest number for that group. Be sure not to choose more than one response for any question.

1. Quantity
The client was able to do the activity

0   not at all
1   a little
2   some
3   a lot
4   completely

2. Quality
The client was able to do the activity well

0   not at all
1   somewhat
2   moderately
3   very
4   extremely

3. Difficulty
The activity was difficult for the client

0   not at all
1   somewhat
2   moderately
3   very
4   extremely

4. Obstacles
The client experienced obstacles in doing the activity

0   not at all
1   a little
2   some
3   a lot
4   extensive

5. Comprehension
The client understood what to do for the activity

0   not at all
1   a little
2   somewhat
3   a lot
4   completely

6. Rationale
The reason for doing the activity was clear to the client

0   not at all
1   somewhat
2   moderately
3   very
4   completely

7. Collaboration
The client had an active role in planning the activity

0   not at all
1   a little
2   some
3   a lot
4   extensive

8. Specificity
The guidelines for how to carry out the activity were specific

0   not at all
1   somewhat
2   moderately
3   very
4   extremely

9. Match with Therapy Goals
The activity matched with the client's goals for therapy

0   not at all
1   a little
2   somewhat
3   a lot
4   completely

10. Pleasure
The client enjoyed the activity

0   not at all
1   a little
2   somewhat
3   a lot
4   extremely

11. Mastery
The client gained a sense of control over their problems

0   not at all
1   a little
2   somewhat
3   a lot
4   extensively

12. Progress
The activity helped with the client's progress in therapy

0   not at all
1   a little
2   somewhat
3   a lot
4   extremely

HRS ID

How much did you practice? Tick the box that describes how much you practiced the task (activity) from your last session. This form will be kept private from other people. Please answer all three questions. Thank you.

---

1. How **much** did you practice the task?

| None | A little | Quite a lot | A lot | All the time |

---

2. How **well** did you practice the task?

| Not at all | Somewhat | Quite well | Very well | Extremely well |

---

3. How **hard** was the task?

| Not at all | Somewhat | Quite hard | Very hard | Extremely hard |

Homework Assignment Form*

Today's Date: _____ **Next Appointment Date:** _____

Session Number:

Homework Description:

Learning Goal (e.g., test idea/ practice skill):

When (e.g., 11:45 am before lunch):

Where (e.g., in the bedroom / at work):

How often (e.g., times per day/ hour/ week):

How long (e.g., hours/ minutes):

Confidence Rating (circle one):

0	10	20	30	40	50	60	70	80	90	100
Not at all confident					Moderately confident					Totally confident

---

Homework Description:

Learning Goal (e.g., test idea/ practice skill):

When (e.g., 11:45 am before lunch):

Where (e.g., in the bedroom / at work):

How often (e.g., times per day/ hour/ week):

How long (e.g., hours/ minutes):

Confidence Rating (circle one):

0	10	20	30	40	50	60	70	80	90	100
Not at all confident					Moderately confident					Totally confident

---

Homework Description:

Learning Goal (e.g., test idea/ practice skill):

When (e.g., 11:45 am before lunch):

Where (e.g., in the bedroom / at work):

How often (e.g., times per day/ hour/ week):

How long (e.g., hours/ minutes):

Confidence Rating (circle one):

0	10	20	30	40	50	60	70	80	90	100
Not at all confident					Moderately confident					Totally confident

For next time

Today's Date is : _____

My activity is...

How Often?

When?

How long should it take me..?

.. and where should i do it?

I am this sure that I can do this Stuff..

0   1   2   3   4   5   6   7   8   9   10 !!!

Not
Sure
at All
              Only a Little
Bit Sure
              Really
Sure

Therapists' Quick Reference*

1. HOMEWORK REVIEW	2. HOMEWORK DESIGN	3. HOMEWORK ASSIGN
◆ Discuss Non-Completion and Quantity and Quality of Completion	◆ Guided Discovery to Identify Coping Strategies and Beliefs	◆ Ask Client to Summarize Rationale in Relation to Therapy Goals
◆ Provide Verbal Reinforcement for any Portion Carried-Out	◆ Use Disorder Specific Cognitive Model and Individualized Conceptualization	◆ Collaborate to Specify How the Task Will be Practically Possible (i.e., when, where, how often, and how long it will take)
◆ Situational Conceptualization to Identify Beliefs about the Consequences to Homework (i.e., synthesis of learning)	◆ Collaboratively Select Tasks	◆ Consider Potential Difficulties (i.e., link to obstacles identified during review)
◆ Use Individualized Conceptualization to Make Sense of Non-Completion	◆ Present a Rationale that Aligns with the Clients' Treatment Goals	◆ Emphasize Learning 'Experiment' Focus
◆ Problem-Solve Obstacles	◆ Ask about Client's Ability and Perceived Task Difficulty	◆ Ask Client to Summarize Task and Obtain Rating of Readiness, Importance, and Confidence (renegotiate if < 70%)
◆ Record Homework Completion in Session Notes	◆ In-Session Practice of Task	◆ Make a Written Note of the Homework for the Client (or use Homework Form)
	◆ Guided Imagery to Begin Experiential Learning	
	◆ Situational Conceptualization to Identify Beliefs and Situational Triggers	

Therapists' Quick Reference © Copyright 2005 by Nikolaos Kazantzis, Frank Deane, and Kevin Ronan. From the book "*Using Homework Assignments in Cognitive Behavior Therapy*", by N. Kazantzis, F. P. Deane, K. R. Ronan, & L. L'Abate (2005). New York: Routledge.

Index

425